# The Era of
# BAJI RAO

An Account of the Empire of the Deccan

Uday S. Kulkarni

Mula Mutha Publishers
Pune, India

## Mula Mutha Publishers

Office 5, Ideal Chambers, Paud Road,
Pune 411 038.
Tel.: 020–25424599 / 25442311
Email: mulamuthapublishers@gmail.com

The maps drawn in this book are as relevant to the period that the book deals with. Present national boundaries have not been incorporated in the maps.

Publishing History :

First Edition : 08 January 2017

ISBN :  978-81-921080-32

Non Fiction : History

Designing and Printing :
Mudra
383 Narayan Peth,
Pune 411 030.
Email: mudraoffset@gmail.com

Cover design : Uday S. Kulkarni

Picture front cover : Shrimant Baji rao Peshwa.

Courtesy - Chhatrapati Shivaji Maharaj Vastu Sangrahalay, Mumbai.

Picture back cover : 'Hilt of the Peshwa's Sword'.

Courtesy - Yale Centre for British Art.

Dedicated to

## Dr Snehalata Sadashiv Kulkarni
(1931-2016)

My mother, to whom I owe most of everything.

The place of Baji rao I in India's history comes home to us with unmistakeable force and vividness when we compare the political situation of this country in 1740 with that in 1720. These twenty years of his active career witnessed a complete revolution in the character of the Maratha national state and an entire redistribution of political power throughout India. No historian can deny the fact that both these changes were the work, conscious or unconscious, of Baji rao.

- Jadunath Sarkar.

Chhatrapati Shahu

Shrimant Baji rao Peshwa I

'तुरंगमावरी मूर्ति शोभे, एका रिकिबीत पाय
दुजा आडवा घोड्यावरती, घोडा ठुमकत जाय
     मानेवरती ठेऊनि दिधली, अनीन घोड्याची ती
     स्कंधी भाला हसत मुखावरी शोभे अनुपम कांती
मंदिल मस्तकी रुभरि, आंगी अंगरखा तो साजे
पचंग कटीला वस्त्र नेसले, ब्राह्मणघाटीचे जें
     स्वत:च हाती कणसे चोलुनी दाणे टाकी वदनी
     लाल ठेविल्या मिरच्या, त्यातुनी खाई मधुनी मधुनी.'


'Atop a horse, with one foot in the stirrup,
and the second across, the horse trots along...
The reins thrown over the neck,
a spear on his shoulder, a smile beatifies a face of indescribable lustre;
A *zari* turban on his head, a befitting robe on the body,
the garment around the waist tied in Brahminical style,
He rubs the ear of corn with his own hands,
and throws the grain in his mouth,
And the red chillies he carries, he chews - now and then.'

# Contents

# Book Three – The Rising Sun

# Book Four – High Noon

## Book Five – The Eclipse

ॐकॐकॐ

# A Note

The book uses the 'Old Style' for dates that was prevalent in England until 1752. Portuguese dates are of the 'New Style' until this year and were eleven days ahead in the eighteenth century. The dates after 1752 are of the present Common Era.

The names of some places have changed since the eighteenth century. So, Madras is now Chennai, Bombay is Mumbai, Bassein is Vasai, and so on. The old names have been retained in the letters of the times used in the book.

# Illustrations

# Maps

# Principal Characters

(in Alphabetical Order)

- Abdullah Khan *Qutb-ul-mulk-* The elder of the Sayyid brothers, brought Farrukh Siyar to the Mughal throne, only to regret it at leisure.

- Abhay Singh – the ambitious raja of Jodhpur.

- Aivaz Khan – a loyal chief of the Nizam-ul-mulk, also related to him.

- Ajit Singh – Chief of Jodhpur, reluctant father-in-law of Farrukh Siyar.. murdered by his own son.

- Alam Ali – a twenty year old nephew of the Sayyid brothers who took on the wizened Nizam-ul-mulk …and met his fate.

- Ambaji *pant* Purandare – *mutalik* at Shahu's court, represented the Peshwa.

- Anand rao Sumant – Chhatrapati Shahu's envoy; only, he began liking the Nizam's court.

- Andre Reberro Coutinho – a Portuguese officer in Vasai.

- Asad Khan – Aurangzeb's *Wazir*. Was doing alright till he miscalculated at the fag end of his life.

- Aurangzeb – Mughal Emperor. Set on the conquest of the Deccan. His ambition and fanaticism ruined his Empire.

- Avaji Kavade – Baji rao's chief, and trouble-shooter.

- Ayamal – Sawai Jaisingh's minister at Jaipur.

- Azam Shah – The ambitious Mughal prince who lost the war of succession on Aurangzeb's death.

- Azim-us-shan – Could have been Emperor and changed the course of Mughal history; but he had antagonised the powerful Zulfiquar Khan.

- Babu rao Malhar – Baji rao's brother-in-law and envoy in Delhi.

- Babuji Naik Joshi – the money lender from Baramati whose brother was married to Baji rao's sister Bhiu bai. He aimed high and wanted to be Peshwa someday.

- Bahadur Shah – son of Aurangzeb who won the succession stakes and became Emperor after him.

- Bahiro *pant* Pingle –The Peshwa from Moro *pant* Pingle's family. If Kanhoji Angre had not imprisoned him, we would be reading a different history.

- Baji Bhiv rao Rethrekar – named by his father after Baji rao, he was his loyal aide.

- Baji rao Peshwa - The second Peshwa who was Prime Minister of a kingdom but created an Empire.

- Balaji Vishwanath Peshwa- The Brahmin from the Konkan who rose to the top by dint of hard work over decades, and laid the foundation for the future growth of Empire.

- Bankaji Naik – *Sarkhel* Sekhoji Angre's officer.

- Brahmendra swami – a seer, a money-lender, a guru to the Marathas, who influenced history by his prodding the Peshwa to do his bidding.

- Budh Singh – ruler of Bundi who lost it when he disowned his son.

- Chabila Ram – *Subedar* of Allahabad and then Awadh..

- Chandrasen Jadhav – son of Dhanaji Jadhav. Did not see eye to eye with Balaji Vishwanath and joined forces with the Nizam.

- Charles Boone – the President at Mumbai who launched a war against Angre.

- Chhatrasal Bundela – Octogenarian ruler of Bundelkhand who carved out a kingdom but needed Baji rao to help save it.

- Chimaji Appa – Younger brother of Baji rao who was as capable, if not more, than his elder brother.

- Chimnaji Damodar Moghe – One of Shahu's earliest supporters who misread the situation and joined the Peshwa's enemies.

- Dado Bhimsen – Baji rao's envoy in Delhi and Jaipur.

- Damaji Thorat – a brave man who wasted his talent by opposing Shahu and the Peshwa. His rebellion was crushed and he died in prison.

- Daud Khan Panni – a giant *pathan*. Loyal to Zulfiquar Khan. But could not face the might of Sayyid Husain Ali.

- Davalji Somvanshi – Baji rao's chief who played a pivotal part in the battle of Palkhed. Was appointed *Sarlashkar.*

- Daya Bahadur – Son of Chabila Ram who ruled Malwa with his cousin Giridhar Bahadur.

- Deep Singh Kumbhani – the shrewd envoy of Jaipur who came to assess the men in Shahu's court and realised it was Baji rao who called the shots.

- Dhanaji Jadhav – *Senapati* from *Chhatrapati* Rajaram's time. His support was crucial for Shahu.

- Dilawar Ali Khan – Led an army against the Nizam but met with a defeat near Khandwa.

- Dom Louis Botelho – the Portuguese officer who lost the island of Sashti to the Marathas.

- Dost Muhammad Khan- the Rohilla Nawab of Bhopal.

- Durjan Sal – the Rao of Kotah who chose to support the Nizam, only to regret it later.

- Farrukh Siyar – Son of the unfortunate Azim-us-shan; he came to the throne thanks to the Sayyid brothers. But he turned on his benefactors and paid the price.

- Fateh Sinh Bhonsle – The foster son of *Chhatrapati* Shahu, ruled at Akkalkot.

- Gangaji Naik – from Anjur in the Konkan, belonged to a family that was determined to liberate the *Firangan.*

- Ghaziuddin Firuz Jung – Father of Nizam-ul-mulk, the man who led Aurangzeb's charge on Golconda.

- Ghiyas Khan – The Nizam-ul-mulk's chief; helped him gain the kingdom of Hyderabad.

- Giridhar Bahadur – Twice the Mughal *subedar* of Malwa; his reign ended abruptly at the hands of Chimaji Appa.

- Govind Hari Patwardhan – An early member of a large family that gave long and distinguished service to the Maratha state from their stronghold around Sangli.

- Govind rao Chitnis – The son of Khando Ballal was a bridge between the *Chhatrapati* and the Peshwa.

- Hamid Khan – The Nizam's uncle. Governed Gujarat on his behalf for a short while before he had to flee.

- Hirde Sah – One of the sons of Chhatrasal Bundela.

- Honaji Balkavade – A valiant Maratha chief who served the Maratha state in many battles extending over decades.

- Hyder Quli Khan – Conspired to overthrow the Sayyids and was rewarded with the *subedari* of Gujarat. For a brief while.

- Inchbird, Captain - The English envoy who led negotiating teams to the Marathas and wrote detailed accounts of his experience.

- Jagat raj – Chhatrasal's son.

- Jagat Singh II – The young ruler of Udaipur when Baji rao came calling.

- Jaisingh *Sawai* – The most influential Rajput chief in early to mid eighteenth century. Built Jaipur. Favoured the Peshwa.

- John Pereira Pinto – A Portuguese General at Vasai.

- Jyotaji Kesarkar – the man who tutored Shahu in the Mughal camp.

- Kam Buksh – A son of Aurangzeb; pampered and foolish.

- Kanhoji Angre – The redoubtable Naval chief of the Marathas from 1698 to 1729. Often an autonomous power not entirely aligned with the king.

- Kanhoji Bhonsle – Persoji's nephew. For long a strong chief in Varhad. His transgressions finally ended his career.

- Kanthaji Kadam Bande – From Khandesh his roving armies went to Malwa and Gujarat. Fought with and against the Peshwa and did not realise his potential.

- Kashi bai – Baji rao's legally wedded wife, called *Tai*. A lady who kept the peace even when provoked. Had a leg ailment that needed treatment for long.

- Kavi Kalash – The Kanauji Brahmin minister with *Chhatrapati* Sambhaji, captured with his king. Doubts about his loyalty keep cropping up.

- Khan Dauran Samsam ud daulah – A minister in the Mughal court who had the Emperor's ear. Favoured the Peshwa.

- Khande rao Dabhade *Senapati*- A powerful chief from *Chhatrapati* Rajaram's time. He was Shahu's General but found the Peshwa successfully encroaching on his job.

- Khando Ballal Chitnis – The first of Shahu's loyal aides who helped him regain the Maratha throne.

- Khandoji Mankar – Chimaji's chief in the Konkan who led the invasion into Sashti.

- Khwaja Abid – The Nizam-ul-mulk's grandfather who joined Aurangzeb in 1657.

- Lal Kunwar – The dancing girl who rose to be Jehandar Shah's consort.

- Mahadeo Bhat Hingne – The shrewd Maratha envoy in Delhi.

- Mahadji Purandare – Son of Ambaji Purandare. He remained a confidante of the Peshwa in Shahu's court. A diplomat par excellence.

- Malharji Holkar – Easily one of the longest serving Maratha *subedars*. Established the Holkar dynasty at Indore.

- Malik Ambar- Abyssinian who guided the Nizamshahi of Ahmednagar and took on the might of the Mughals. Built the walled city of Aurangabad.

- Manaji Angre – A son of Kanhoji. Needed support from the Peshwa to preserve his kingdom at Colaba from his many opponents.

- Mastani – The courtesan from Bundelkhand who became Baji rao's muse.

- Mir Hasan Koka – Brash young Mughal who thought he could chase away Baji rao at Delhi.

- Mirza Raja Jaisingh – Aurangzeb's most successful General, the ruler of Amber.

- Mubariz Khan – First, a lieutenant of the Nizam, later he fought him.

- Muhammad Amin Khan – *Wazir* for a short time. Conspiracy was his forte.

- Muhammad Khan Bangash – An Afghan migrant who ruled from Allahabad. When he attacked Chhatrasal, he was defeated by Baji rao. Yet, escorted the Peshwa's mother on her pilgrimmage.

- Muhammad Shah – Known by the epithet *'Rangeela'* for his colourful life of ease. In twenty years, he presided over the fall of the Mughal Empire.

- Muizzuddin Jehandar Shah – He did more damage to the Mughal throne in one year than anybody else ever could.

- Nadir Shah – The tyrrant from Persia who ravaged and looted Delhi; for a while threatened to come to the Deccan.

- Nanasaheb Peshwa – Baji rao's eldest son and successor. He was however closer to his uncle Chimaji who taught him the nuances of war and administration.

- Nasir Jung – Nizam-ul-mulk's son who was left in charge of Hyderabad when the father went to Delhi.

- Nizam-ul-mulk *Chin Qilich Khan* – He established an independent kingdom in the Deccan that survived the Mughals, the Marathas and the British. Forever tried to extinguish the Marathas and came up against Baji rao.

- Parshuram Trimbak – The *Pratinidhi* who had to choose between Shahu and his aunt Tara bai as his monarch.

- Pedro de Mello – A brave and resourceful Portuguese General at Vasai.

- Persoji Bhonsle – Shahu's earliest supporter from Varhad.

- Pilaji Gaekwad – Managed *Senapati* Dabhade's fief in Gujarat.

- Pilaji Jadhav rao – A stalwart who served Shahu for three decades. In his lifetime was known as the *subedar*.

- Pralhad Niraji – *Chhatrapati* Rajaram's *Pratinidhi* at Jinji.

- Qaim Khan – Muhammad Khan Bangash's son.

- Qamruddin Khan – *Wazir* at Delhi during most of Muhammad Shah's reign. Wine and country houses took up much of his time.

- Radha bai – Balaji Vishwanath's wife. Matriarch in the Peshwa family.

- Rafi-ud-darjat – Short lived Mughal Emperor after Farrukh Siyar.

- Rafi-ud-daulah – His brother. Succeeded him but reigned for a few months.

- Raghuji Bhonsle – Ruler of Varhad. Owed allegiance to Shahu. His glory years began after Baji rao.

- Rajaram, *Chhatrapati* – Younger son of *Chhatrapati* Shivaji. Spent long years in Ginjee.

- Rajas bai – Rajaram's second queen who usurped power for her son in 1713 from Tara bai.

- Ramchandra Nilkanth *pant amatya*- The *Hukumat panah*. He orchestrated the entire Maratha resistance to Aurangzeb. Tara bai's chief supporter. He wrote the Adnyapatra – a treatise on administration.

- Ranoji Scindia – The founder of the house of Scindia, loyal chief under Baji rao.

- Rao Rambha Nimbalkar – he quit Shahu quite early and joined the Nizam.

- Ratan Chand – the Hindu aide of the Sayyids, much resented by the *Turani* faction in the Mughal court.

- Sadat Khan *Burhan-ul-mulk* – A migrant from Persia, proud and successful until he met a fellow Persian who brought about his downfall.

- Sambhaji, Angre – Kanhoji Angre's son who governed from Vijaydurg.

- Sambhaji *Chhatrapati*- *Chhatrapati* Shivaji's elder son and successor. He led the Maratha state in many battles and supported Aurangzeb's rebel son Akbar.

- Sambhaji of Kolhapur – The younger son of Rajaram who came to the throne at Kolhapur after 1713.

- Santaji Ghorpade – A mercurial General who had the Mughals on the run until…

- Sarbuland Khan – He was called from Kabul to take over as the *subedar* at Gujarat. Came up short against Chimaji Appa.

- Satvaji Jadhav – Pilaji Jadhav rao's son.

- Sayyid Husain Ali – The younger of the Sayyids of Barha. King-maker at Delhi. He forged a partnership with Shahu to oppose his master.

- Sekhoji Angre – Kanhoji Angre's eldest son. Supported the Peshwa in his battle at Janjira.

- Shahaji raje Bhonsle – *Chhatrapati* Shivaji's father. His quest for an independent state was realised by his son.

- Shahu, *Chhatrapati*- *Chhatrapati* Shivaji's grandson. Imprisoned for eighteen long years in the Mughal camp, he emerged to become the king of the Marathas. Had a shrewd eye for capable men.

- Shambhu Sinh Jadhav – The son of Dhanaji Jadhav who continued to serve Shahu.

- Shamsher Bahadur – The son of Baji rao and Mastani.

- Shankaraji Keshav Phadke – He was active in the battle for winning Vasai.

- Shankraji Malhar – He returned from Kashi as Husain Ali's advisor in the Deccan and helped forge a partnership with Balaji Vishwanath.

- Shankraji Narayan *Sachiv* – The founder of the Bhor state, he could not break a promise and laid down his life instead.

- Shivaji, *Chattrapati* – The founder of the Maratha state. His genius was never matched in the decades that followed.

- Shripat rao *Pratinidhi*- The son of Parshuram Trimbak. He did not agree with Baji rao and was eventually sidelined by the Peshwa.

- Siddi Abdul Rehman – Siddi at Janjira after 1733.

- Siddi Rasul Yakut – Siddi at Janjira. His death led to the Maratha invasion of 1733.

- Siddi Sat – He was fond of elephants. But when he broke the temple of Parshuram, Brahmendra swami swore to avenge his act.

- Sultanji Nimbalkar – From the illustrious family of Nimbalkar and Shahu's *Sarlashkar*. He chose to join the Nizam after 1727.

- Tara bai – The dowager queen of Rajaram who saved the Maratha state from Aurangzeb's aggression. Her opposition to Shahu led to her fall from power.

- Trimbak rao Dabhade *Senapati*- Khande rao's son. Brave and energetic, he sought the Nizam's help to defeat the Peshwa.

- Udaji Pawar – One of Malwa's foremost chiefs. He fell out with the Peshwa after 1730 and fought him at Dabhoi. Served Shahu till the end.

- Uma bai Dabhade – Khande rao's wife and fiery General who protected her fief and led armies to the field.

- Viru bai – The head of Shahu's household although not his wife.

- Vyankaji Ram – The Peshwa's envoy at Jaipur.

- Vyankat rao Ghorpade – Baji rao's sister Anu bai was married to him. Headed the minor state of Ichalkaranji.

- William Gordon – English envoy who visited Shahu at Miraj and ensured peace with the Marathas in 1739.

- Yashwant rao Dabhade – Younger son of Khande rao. Although anointed *Senapati,* he did not fulfil his responsibilities well.

- Yesu bai – The unfortunate queen of of *Chhatrapati* Sambhaji and mother of Shahu who spent long years in Mughal custody until rescued by the Maratha army under the Peshwa in 1719.

- Zinat-un-nissa – Aurangzeb's daughter. She was the guardian angel for Shahu in Aurangzeb's camp.

- Zulfiquar Khan – One of Aurangzeb's most successful Generals. Son of Asad Khan. Learnt the hard way that obeying one's father may not always be the best policy.

# Timeline

| | | |
|---|---|---|
| 1630 | – | Birth of Raja Shivaji. |
| 1657 | – | Aurangzeb becomes Mughal Emperor. |
| 1674 | – | Coronation of Shivaji as *Chhatrapati* at Raigad. |
| 1680 | – | Death of *Chhatrapati* Shivaji. |
| 1681 | – | Aurangzeb attacks the Deccan. |
| 1689 | – | *Chhatrapati* Sambhaji killed by Aurangzeb. |
| 1700 | – | *Chhatrapati* Rajaram dies. |
| 1707 | – | Aurangzeb dies. |
| 1708 | – | Shahu becomes king of Marathas. |
| 1713 | – | Balaji Vishwanath appointed Peshwa. |
| 1713 | – | Tara bai deposed and imprisoned at Kolhapur. Sambhaji II takes over. |
| 1719 | – | Balaji Vishwanath brings *sanads* from Mughal Emperor for Shahu. |
| 1720 | – | Baji rao appointed Peshwa. |
| 1728 | – | Baji rao defeats the Nizam at Palkhed. |
| 1729 | – | Chimaji appa and Baji rao defeat Giridhar Bahadur and Muhammad Bangash in Malwa. |
| 1730 | – | Baji rao begins construction of 'Shaniwar wada'. Nanasaheb married to Gopika bai. Mastani in Pune. |
| 1730 | – | Sawai Jaisingh sends his envoy Deep Singh to Satara. |
| 1730 | – | Sawai Jaisingh unseats Budh Singh, ruler of Bundi. |
| 1730-31 | – | The Dabhoi campaign. *Senapati* Trimbak rao Dabhade killed in battle. |
| 1732-33 | – | Maratha armies under Chimaji Appa in Malwa. |
| 1732 | – | The Nizam and Baji rao meet at Rui Rameshwar. |

1733    – The campaign against the Siddi of Janjira.

August 1733 – Sekhoji Angre dies.

1734    – Holkar and Scindia invade Bundi and oust Sawai Jaisingh's nominee.

1733-35 – Mughal grandees take the field against Marathas in Malwa and are defeated.

1735    – Radha bai goes on a pilgrimage to Mathura, Prayag, Kashi and Gaya.

January 1736 – Baji rao goes to Rajputana.

February 1736 – Baji rao in Udaipur.

March 1736 – Chimaji Appa descends into the Konkan and kills Siddi Sat.

March-April 1736 – Baji rao and Sawai Jaisingh meet several times.

April – May 1736 – Baji rao submits his demands to the Mughal Emperor.

June 1736 – Holkar and Scindia canton in Malwa during rains.

July-August 1736 – Muhammad Shah does not grant the *sanad* of Malwa to the Peshwa.

November 1736 – Baji rao heads north.

18 February 1737 – Ater and Bhadawar captured by the Marathas.

12 March 1737 – Malharji Holkar defeated by Sadat Khan in the *doab*.

March 29-31, 1737 – Baji rao eludes large armies to threaten Delhi.

29 March 1737 – Chimaji Appa launches an attack on Thane.

02 April 1737 – Baji rao at Kotputli.

March-April 1737 – War in Konkan. Sashti captured by Marathas.

2 July 1737 – Nizam-ul-mulk reaches Delhi.

October-November 1737 – Nizam leaves Delhi with a large army for Malwa.

November 1737 – Baji rao and Chimaji leave for Malwa.

December 1737 – January 1738 – Battle of Bhopal, Nizam defeated.

1738 – Nadir Shah captures Qandahar and marches towards Delhi.

February 1739 – Battle of Karnal.

1739 – Chimaji throws all his forces at the Firangan. Baji rao at Burhanpur.

10 March 1739 – Nadir Shah proclaimed Emperor of Delhi.

11 March 1739 – Massacre at Delhi. Looting continues for weeks.

4 May 1739 – Vasai surrenders to Chimaji Appa.

5 May 1739 – Nadir Shah leaves Delhi for Persia. Muhammad Shah placed on the throne of Delhi.

May-June 1739 – English envoys meet Chimaji Appa and Shahu.

November – December 1739 – Baji rao and Chimaji leave for the campaign against Nasir Jung.

4 to 7 February 1740 – Battle of the Godavari. Nasir Jung submits, and hands over two districts to Baji rao.

March 1740 – Baji rao to the Narmada, Chimaji to Pune.

Chimaji and Nanasaheb to the Konkan to resolve the quarrel between the Angre brothers.

28 April 1740 – Baji rao dies at Raverkhedi.

June 1740 – Nanasaheb is appointed Peshwa.

17 December 1740 – Chimaji Appa dies at Pune.

# Geneologies

## The Chhatrapatis

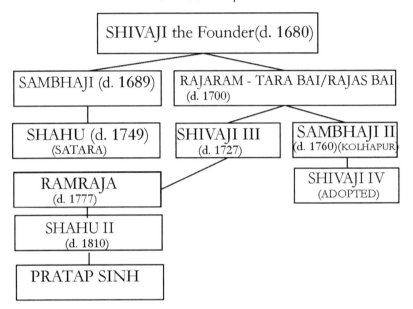

SHIVAJI the Founder(d. 1680)

SAMBHAJI (d. 1689)

RAJARAM - TARA BAI/RAJAS BAI (d. 1700)

SHAHU (d. 1749) (SATARA)

SHIVAJI III (d. 1727)

SAMBHAJI II (d. 1760)(KOLHAPUR)

RAMRAJA (d. 1777)

SHIVAJI IV (ADOPTED)

SHAHU II (d. 1810)

PRATAP SINH

## The Peshwas

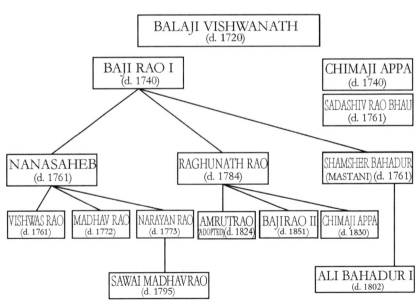

BALAJI VISHWANATH (d. 1720)

BAJI RAO I (d. 1740)

CHIMAJI APPA (d. 1740)

SADASHIV RAO BHAU (d. 1761)

NANASAHEB (d. 1761)

RAGHUNATH RAO (d. 1784)

SHAMSHER BAHADUR (MASTANI) (d. 1761)

VISHWAS RAO (d. 1761)

MADHAV RAO (d. 1772)

NARAYAN RAO (d. 1773)

AMRUTRAO (ADOPTED)(d. 1824)

BAJIRAO II (d. 1851)

CHIMAJI APPA (d. 1830)

SAWAI MADHAVRAO (d. 1795)

ALI BAHADUR I (d. 1802)

# Mughal Emperors from 1657

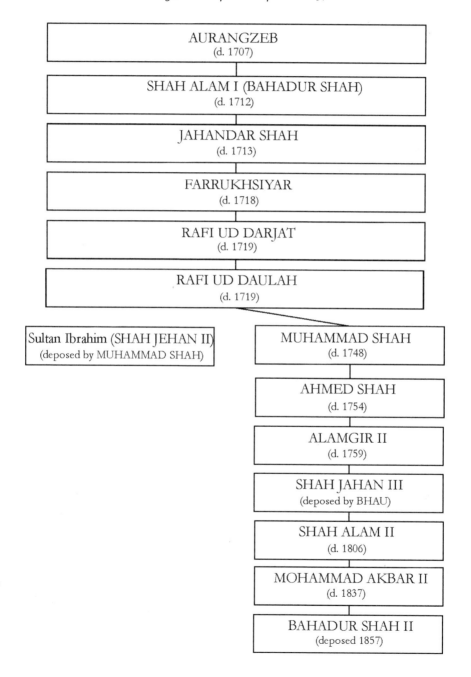

AURANGZEB
(d. 1707)

SHAH ALAM I (BAHADUR SHAH)
(d. 1712)

JAHANDAR SHAH
(d. 1713)

FARRUKHSIYAR
(d. 1718)

RAFI UD DARJAT
(d. 1719)

RAFI UD DAULAH
(d. 1719)

Sultan Ibrahim (SHAH JEHAN II)
(deposed by MUHAMMAD SHAH)

MUHAMMAD SHAH
(d. 1748)

AHMED SHAH
(d. 1754)

ALAMGIR II
(d. 1759)

SHAH JAHAN III
(deposed by BHAU)

SHAH ALAM II
(d. 1806)

MOHAMMAD AKBAR II
(d. 1837)

BAHADUR SHAH II
(deposed 1857)

# The Author's Page

It has taken a while to write this book. The work began in June 2015 and was completed by the end of November 2016. In a way it is a prequel to my first book on the third battle of Panipat, going back and covering in details the first formative years of the Maratha Empire. With 'Solstice at Panipat – 14 January 1761' coming in 2011- and enlarged the following year- the 'Bakhar of Panipat' in 2014, and then the translation of 'Solstice' into Marathi - published last year, I found time to work on this book only in mid 2015.

The original idea was to follow the Panipat story and move further after 1761. Late Ninad Bedekar, a friend and an authority on Maratha history, had suggested I should go back and write about the period of Baji rao Peshwa. However, this did not happen until May 2015 as I was busy with the translation of my first book. Then, sadly, Ninadji passed away. I returned to Baji rao after this and hope to move on with the rest of the story of the eighteenth century.

In a non-fiction account, it is essential to lay the ground work of a story, and with the very eventful seventeenth century that went before, that part of the story had to be narrated. The story therefore deals with the Mughal Maratha struggle of the first three Maratha monarchs, and then after a few chapters begins the era of Baji rao; twenty years of restless activity that transformed a kingdom into an Empire.

The book is not a biography but a narration of the unfolding of an era. A book named after a historical personality is fraught with the risk of bias and every writer of historical non-fiction is confronted with the unenviable task of smoothing the narrative to consciously keep out hyperbole and bring the story on an even keel. Baji rao's triumphant career had many opportunities for such exaggeration and it was therefore even more important to keep this aspect in mind.

This is a work of non-fiction. It has extensive references, bibliography, appendices and an index section that will help others to take up this task of relating the History of India in the years to come. Many of these references are difficult to obtain and it takes long years to gather these. Libraries and online books help to a large extent. Yet, access to libraries and proper cataloguing of their collection is something that is lagging behind and needs help.

A book of this size needs accuracy, research, and therefore a large team. I had to make do with just a few helpers. For research I had the help of Jayakar Library of the University. Dr. Trupti More from the Deccan College Library helped in obtaining difficult-to-find references. Images from the Chhatrapati Shivaji Maharaj Vastu Sangrahalay, the British Library at London, Dr Babasaheb Ambedkar Marathwada University (BAMU) History Museum, Bharat Itihas Sanshodhak Mandal (BISM) at Pune, Museum of Fine Arts, Boston, Cleveland Museum of Art, Los Angeles County Museum of Art, Yale Centre for British Art, besides some of my own photographs, helped to embellish the story telling. I used some references that I had noted during my research at the India Office Records in London that had not been published so far.

I am thankful to Dr SM Bhave of BISM, historian Pandurang Balkavade, Dr Kedar Phalke, Dr NK Bhide, and Vikramjit Singh Rooprai for their help in different areas. The copy-edit was once again done patiently and punctiliously by Soniya Khare, the lay-out of the pages by Rohinee and the printing by the team at 'Mudra' headed by my friend Sujit Patwardhan. My family helped in reading through the manuscript and giving unvarnished opinions about it.

As in my earlier book, I found it easier to draw the maps myself, adapting details from existing maps and taking the help of online maps. The dates used in the book are 'Old Style', meaning they are eleven days behind the Common Era calendar now used the world over.

The book could be published thanks to the readers who bought my earlier books, and to the booksellers – online and book shops - that stocked and sold them. If new books have to be written the scourge of piracy has to be controlled. Counterfeit books kill the book writing and publishing industry, and readers who paid and read the books are therefore the backbone for further books. Mula Mutha Publishers is committed to good non-fiction books on Indian history. There will be more in the years to come.

My dear mother was ill last year and passed away just three weeks ago. She was always been a pillar of strength to me and I am largely what I am due to her. She saw me working on this book all year and I was able to tell her it would be dedicated to her. I wish she had seen it.

Pune                                                                    Uday S. Kulkarni

12 December 2016, *Datta Jayanti.*

# Introduction

History writing is like a pyramid. At the base is the very solid foundation laid by early researchers who published original letters and documents. Then, come early histories usually of one predominant Empire and short regional narratives. These give final shape to a History of that era and a History where earlier narratives intertwine and give a story that allows you to look at the entire picture. Every writer of History owes a debt of gratitude to the early researchers who toiled without reward and gave a scaffold on which could be built an edifice. Indian history is not less than the history of a continent and as communications improved, these coalesced to form a single mainstream that can now be written.

The Indian land mass seemed to be under a stable Government until the mid seventeenth century. The Mughals had first come to India in 1526, and after a brief blip, returned to rule in 1556. The real founder of their Empire was Akbar and the momentum was so great that Jehangir and Shah Jehan could carry on without too much difficulty. By 1650 however, the first signs of a challenge began to emerge. The reasons were two fold. One, the downward push of the Mughals deeper into the Deccan and the second was the ambitious and fanatical reign of Aurangzeb.

The iron grip that the Mughals had over Hindustan, or northern India, until the end of the seventeenth century began to loosen with many adventurers moving northwards, crossing the Narmada, the river that neatly divides the country into the northern Hindustan and the southern Deccan. Once the grip was pared loose, it rapidly lost its strength and the Empire began to unravel. Aurangzeb, arguably one of the four great Mughals, with personal qualities of courage and military skill far superior to his father or grandfather, eventually became the architect of the downfall of the Mughals. It was his proactive agenda to separate the majority of his countrymen from their faith that alienated his people. His wars, and there were many of these, emptied his treasure houses. His soldiery and his chiefs grew tired of the bent old ruler perspicaciously chasing down every single detail and rebel, until the army lost its zest and the Emperor forgot his job was to govern and not oppress.

The year 1707 remains a watershed in Indian history. It marks the death of Aurangzeb and the beginning of a series of insipid rulers with no ability, who believed in nothing, and did nothing to remember them by. The twenty-six years the Mughals spent in the Deccan stamping out the Bijapur and Golconda states and fighting the Marathas, finally engulfed the Mughal Empire. Within a dozen years of Aurangzeb, Maratha armies were in Delhi.

The book begins in the seventeenth century and then moves to events after the death of Aurangzeb and release of Shahu from Mughal custody. The twenty-five-year-old king, without an army or funds, eventually gained his place as the master of the Maratha state. However, he went through a torrid time when rebellions, defections and invasions nearly brought an end to his reign. Balaji Vishwanath Peshwa, with his experience, loyalty and shrewdness pulled him out of his difficulties and set his ship on an even keel.

Baji rao inherited the charge of a small kingdom of two districts when Shahu, the Maratha king, bestowed the Peshwa's post on him. He was, as it were, on probation those first few years. He emerged from this period with a remarkable performance that sealed his place as the Peshwa. It also sealed his place in history. As Baji rao's letters show, he fought for his kingdom and his king. In the process he gained such a mastery over the Maratha state that at the end of his life, the king deferred most decisions to him.

The eighteenth century is a story of the collapse of one Empire and the rise of another. While the rulers of the Deccan began to enter the plains of Hindustan under the Maratha banner by the close of the seventeenth century, a hundred years later they were the power that held the country in their charge from Sirhind to the borders of Mysore, from Gujarat to Orissa. They were the last indigenous Empire in India, not the phantom who occupied the Red Fort at Delhi. Decisions that influenced large swathes of India for most of the eighteenth century were taken in Pune.

The motivations that guided the Marathas, their organization, the reason for their success and the collapse of the mighty Mughals have to be read with original letters that allow the men of that age to speak to us – the inhabitants of the twenty-first century. These letters are first-person accounts, the living history of the times and corroborate many of the assumptions made in the book. Therefore one will find letters written in Marathi, English, Persian and

Portuguese in this book as well as mention of what eminent historians of the past wrote about these events.

The 'Era of Baji rao' extended for longer than the time he was the Peshwa. The reason is that the consequences of his actions lived long after his death. He established an Empire from a kingdom that stood the test of time. That is the reason the first half of the eighteenth century can be called Baji rao's era. Baji rao was the single most important historical personality of that age who influenced the politics of those times.

The task of Empire-building is not the work of one man. To his credit, Baji rao created his own lieutenants from a new group of people that rose to positions of power and influence on their own merit. Baji rao was their unquestioned leader, and following him they created history.

The eighteenth century was a turbulent time for India. This is not unusual when one ruling dynasty is overturned and another emerges. What was unusual was that the successor regime continued to protect the former rulers, deriving their rights from them and keeping up the pretence of a Mughal Empire of which the Marathas appear to be a subsidiary. The appearance is far from the truth. The Marathas, having liberated their homeland and key provinces around them, began to rule and allowed the Mughal to reign. It was a rule by the Marathas in the name of the Mughals. This is often mistaken for some kind of slavery by many commentators. However, it was convenient at the time. It was convenient even when the British grabbed power after 1818 and retained the king at Delhi as their showpiece till the war of 1857. The Maratha king never wished to occupy the throne at Delhi and expressly ordered that the Mughal Empire should not be destroyed.

Let the story now speak for itself.

Emperor Aurangzeb

Emperor Farrukh Siyar and
Sayyid Husain Ali

Shrimant Baji rao Peshwa

Pilaji Jadhav rao

Book One

Dark Night

There is intelligence that the Mughal will attack your village. You should immediately evacuate the village with the women and children to a strong place below the *ghats* where the Mughal disease will not come. Do not neglect this job. Immediately you get this, move the people. If you do not do this and the Mughal takes away people, the sin will be on your head. Thinking in this manner, day and night, go from village to village and take all the people to the sanctuary below the *ghats*. Not a moment should be lost in implementing this order. You should stay alert in your place. Those who stay to safeguard the fields also you should send to the mountain tops where they will be safe. If they spot the Mughal from a distance, they should run away. You be alert at your post.

- *Chhatrapati* Shivaji's letter to Sarje rao Jedhe in 1662.

'Sambhaji will be betrayed. Rajaram will preserve the kingdom from Ginjee. Moro Pandit, Niraji Ravji, Ramchandra Nilkanth, Santaji Ghorpade, Dhanaji Jadhav will be the instruments for the growth of the kingdom. Then a king named Shiva will take the kingdom right up to Delhi.'

- *Chhatrapati* Shivaji's deathbed prophesy.

'Owing to my marching through deserts and forests, my officers long for my death'.

- Emperor Aurangzeb's letter to his son.

# Rewa Uvach [a]

The Indian sub-continent is easily divided into Hindustan and the Deccan. To the north is the vast land mass extending from the Punjab to Bengal and includes Bundelkhand, Gujarat and Malwa. In the south is the Deccan, an anglicized word for *'dakshin'* or the south, and this peninsula is bounded by the Bay of Bengal to the east, the Arabian sea to the west and the mountain range of Vindhya to the north.

The Vindhya was once a proud mountain range and according to ancient lore, grew to lofty heights. The name Vindhya itself arose from the Sanskrit 'vaindh' meaning to obstruct. The rapid rise of the Vindhya threatened Meru, mythologically the highest mountain in India. The sage Agastya then commanded Vindhya to bow before him as he had to traverse it to go south. Vindhya agreed to do so until Agastya returned. When Agastya settled in the forests of the south and never returned, the Vindhya remained a broken, not very lofty range with many forests, inhabited by men feared by the northern Aryans. For long, the peninsula in the south remained secluded and grew its own culture, traditions and languages.

From the eastern end of the Vindhya, a range now called Maikal, was born the river Rewa; also called the Narmada. From the eastern most regions to its confluence with the Arabian sea, the Rewa is a long perennial river. It is located between the mountain ranges of central India and besides the hills and forests of the Vindhya, remains the mark where Hindustan ends and the Deccan begins.

The Deccan had many rulers, many dynasties and Empires over the last thousands of years. Many have lapsed into obscurity. From the jungles of Dandakaranya where the story of Ramayana unfolded, to the modern states of the peninsula, it has been a long history. But never did a king from the south of the Rewa undertake a campaign to wage war in Hindustan. It was always the kings of Hindustan who crossed the river and ventured south: until the eighteenth century of the Common Era.

---

a.   'Rewa' is another name for the river Narmada. 'Uvach' is a Sanskrit word that means 'said'.

It was then, in the era of Baji rao, that the rulers of Deccan crossed into Hindustan and ruled over it, taking their flag to faraway lands, as far as the Indus to the north-west and the Ganga in Bengal, upto the mountain ranges of Kumaon and Garhwal and the western state of Gujarat. This is their story.

Baji rao knew the Rewa, or the Narmada, like none other. From Mandla in the east to Bharuch in the west, he crossed it in all its parts, like no other man ever did. Across a stretch of over a thousand kilometres from Mandla to Jabalpur, Damoh to Sehore; Khandwa, Khargone, Dewas, Indore and Dhar, to Nimar, Jhabua, Vadodara and at its confluence with the sea at Bharuch - at each of these places, Baji rao crossed and re-crossed the river; and the river yielded up to him her secret fords. The unfrequented jungle paths of Mandla, the flat plain of Khargone, the forests of Jhabua and the broad expanse of the river at Bharuch; Baji rao lived here for far longer than at his home. The river was his compatriot in success, his aide in quick movements, and a friend who helped him to elude an enemy. Baji rao lived his life here, and when the time came, he came to the banks of the Rewa, to die. Here, to this date, a memorial to the final abode of this great warrior lies.

This is the story of Baji rao.

I am Rewa. And I know the story of Baji rao better than anybody else. But before I narrate the story of Baji rao, I will tell you what happened before. For the future has its genesis in the past.

॥ॐॐॐॐ॥

# 1. Not a Tranquil Time

Lord Vishnu enquired of Brahma,
'Having created the world, who has been appointed to which place?'
Lord Brahma said to Jairam,[a]
'The Three People[b] are placed at appropriate places,
the Sun to the east, Moon to the west, while you sleep at the head of an ocean,
And to protect the North and the South; Here Shahaji, There Shah Jehan.'[1 c]

'…Conquests ought to distinguish the reign of a great monarch, and that I should disgrace the blood of the great Timur, our honoured progenitor, if I did not seek to extend the bounds of my present territories… You cannot with truth assert that my armies are unprofitably employed in the Deccan and in Bengal. I wish you to recollect that the greatest conquerors are not always the greatest Kings.'

– Aurangzeb's letter to Shah Jehan, after 1660CE.[2]

In India, the seventeenth century of the Common Era was not a tranquil one.

From the death of Akbar to the death of Aurangzeb spanned just over a hundred years. The seventeenth century was a period of Mughal supremacy but the years were consumed by wars and insurrection. The Mughals did not conquer the south until the last fifteen years of the century. Within a decade after this, their power receded with unexpected rapidity, so that at the threshold of the eighteenth century a new Empire arose that threatened to supplant them.

Mughal rule in Delhi, established only after the triumph of Akbar in the battle of Panipat in 1555, was the paramount power in Northern India when the Emperor died in 1605. In five decades of rule from Delhi and Agra, Akbar extended his rule all over *Hindustan* and began his push south of the river Narmada and Tapi with the invasion of the Nizamshahi[d] state of

---

a.  Jairam Pindye, the poet.
b.  Living in Heaven, Earth and the Netherworld.
c.  जगदीश विरंची को पुछत है, कहो शिष्टि रची रखे कौन कहाँ, कर जेरी कही जयराम विरंच्ये, तिरिलोक जहाँ के तहाँ ।
    ससि वो रवि पूरब पश्रिम, लों तुम सोय रहो सिरसिंधु महा, अरु उत्तर दछन रछन को, इत साहजु है उत साहिजहाँ ।।
d.  One of the five Deccan sultanates.

Ahmednagar. Chand Bibi, princess of Ahmednagar and queen of Bijapur, led the resistance to Mughal expansion, until, busy defending her city she was killed by her own officer.

Although Ahmednagar was lost to the Mughals, Bahmani rule under the stewardship of the Abyssinian '*Habshi*' Malik Ambar was established from Daulatabad. Malik Ambar laid the foundations of a revenue administration in the Deccan that lasted a long time after his death in 1626. His armies recruited many from the region who earned their spurs in battle with the Mughals. Chief of these were the Maratha father and son; Maloji *raje* and Shahaji *raje* Bhonsle. The initial tutelage gained in Malik Ambar's army led to the later guerrilla war of the Marathas. On Malik Ambar's death, Shahaji gathered the remnants of the kingdom and preserved the Nizamshahi, at one time giving shelter to Emperor Jehangir's son Khurram, the later Shah Jehan, at Junnar near Pune.

In the 1630s, during the reign of Shah Jehan, the Mughals returned, and facing more vigorous attacks on this northernmost of the five Deccani sultanates, one sees Shahaji as Regent of an infant Murtiza Nizam Shah. In 1634, Shahaji controlled nearly a fourth of the erstwhile Nizamshahi kingdom. However, an overwhelming Mughal attack in 1636 forced him to surrender and go further south to Bijapur, where he made a name for himself and created his own fief at Bangalore and Thanjavur in distant Carnatic[a] country. Shahaji's efforts at independence were the essential initial steps towards a later Maratha *swarajya*.

In this land of the Marathas, bound by the Krishna and Tapi rivers and bisected by the Godavari, the Mughals soon annexed the state of Ahmednagar, and during the viceroyalty of prince Aurangzeb threatened the Sultans of Bijapur and Golconda. Living in his *jagir* around Pune, the adolescent son of Shahaji saw the misery of the subjects. Roaming the wilds with his followers; exploring paths, hills and mountains, he gathered a following who considered him their uncrowned king. This was *Raja* Shivaji, a name that was to soon reverberate in every capital of India; from the French in Puducherry (earlier

---

a.   Carnatic is the region that includes the southern states of India; mainly Karnataka, Andhra and Telangana, and Tamil Nadu.

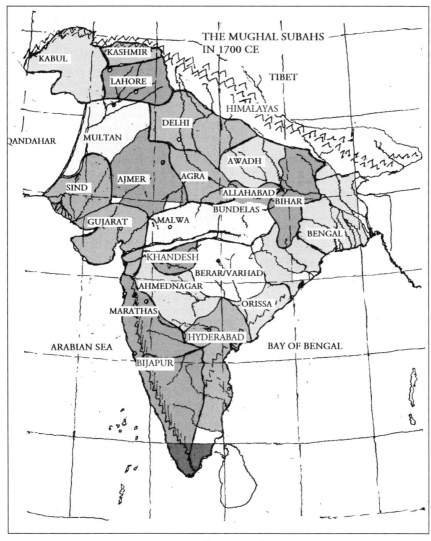

*India of Aurangzeb*

Pondicherry) to the Great Mughal at Delhi. At just sixteen he captured his
first hill fort and began to build many more along the craggy mountains
of the Deccan. Using deception and courage in equal measure, his work of
*swarajya* proceeded until it could no longer be ignored by the rulers at Bijapur
or the Mughals.

Unyielding in his core quest of independence, Shivaji did not spare the old order of landholders beholden to the Bahmani or Mughal *subedars*. If they did not help him achieve his aim, they were attacked and evicted. The imprisonment of his step-uncle Sambhaji Mohite of Supe, and the end of the Chandra rao More family of Javli, a hereditary noble from the days of the Vijayanagar kingdom, helped stamp his authority. The challenge he faced was to retain the loyalty of his followers while abolishing hereditary *vatans*. He began a system of payment to the troops from the central treasury, and the *vatan*-loving Marathas joined Shivaji's army even after he abolished their fief.

Surendranath Sen says, '*in that age the idea of nationality was yet unborn*'. Besides '*the personal magnetism of the leader*', Sen attributes the Maratha uprising to '*race and religion (that) still stirred the deepest chord in the sentiment of the rude Maratha peasant soldiery. Shivaji's conception of a Hindu empire was in no way identified with religious persecution. He enlisted in his army seven hundred pathan[a] deserters from Bijapur, at least three of his naval commanders were Muslim. He venerated the Muslim saint Sheikh Muhammad as he venerated the Hindu saints Tukaram and Ramdas.*'[3]

The nascent Maratha state emerged even stronger when neighbouring powers – the Siddi[b] of Janjira, the Portuguese at Goa and north Konkan, the Mughals surrounding Pune, and the Bijapur sultan – were played against each other. Aurangzeb, the Mughal Viceroy in the Deccan from 1653, did not quite recognize the threat posed by this new entrant on the scene, and with one eye on the throne of Delhi, soon had to leave the Deccan.

In 1657, the Mughal Emperor Shah Jehan fell ill with strangury, and florid rumours that he would not survive his illness spread through the Empire. For many days the *paatshah* did not appear in public. His favourite eldest son Dara Shukoh ran the Government at Agra, even as his three younger sons, Murad in Gujarat, Shuja in Bengal and Aurangzeb in the Deccan prepared for the inevitable battle of succession. Shuja and Murad revealed their eagerness to contest the succession while Aurangzeb displayed a clinical

---

a.   Originally residents of Afghanistan.
b.   The Siddi was of Ethiopian origin, also referred as 'Habshi' from 'Abyssinian'.

coolness that betrayed neither haste nor ambition. Joining forces with Murad and promising him help to secure the succession, Aurangzeb began to march northwards. Dara began from Agra with the imperial army to meet this threat after sending his son Suleiman Shukoh towards Bengal to stop Shuja.

Anxious about the fate of his favourite son Dara, the Emperor Shah Jehan saw the impending war of succession overwhelming him. South of Agra, at Samugarh, Aurangzeb met the imperial army and by the end of the day had won a complete victory. Dara fled the battlefield and after a pathetic meeting with his father, left with his family and whatever treasure he could carry. Murad, who now began to assert himself, was quietly lured to Aurangzeb's camp for a feast by a disloyal servant. Here after an evening of revelry, he was packed off to prison and beheaded. Dara was pursued until he was finally betrayed, brought to Delhi, humiliated, and killed for apostasy. Shuja was defeated at Khajua, and fled to Arracan in present day-Myanmar where he met his end from his own indiscretions. Suleiman Shikoh was defeated, arrested and poisoned in prison. Father Shah Jehan was imprisoned in the fort at Agra, and Aurangzeb, having eliminated all his rivals, moved on to Delhi to be crowned Emperor at the Shalimar *bagh*.

In the Deccan, the Bijapur sultanate dispatched a large army to capture or kill the 'rebel' *Raja* Shivaji. The army was led by Afzal Khan, an accomplished General. The large army meandered north, plundering temples and endeavouring to draw the Maratha king into the open. However, Shivaji only retreated further into the forested hilly region of Javli near the fort of Pratap gad. Here Afzal Khan, sure of his personal and military strength, was goaded to a one-to-one meeting with a seemingly petrified enemy. In November 1659, even as the Khan gripped the *Raja* under his powerful arm, Shivaji struck with concealed tiger claws at Afzal Khan's innards. A short skirmish between their select followers led to the beheading of Afzal Khan. Shivaji's concealed men pounced on the Bijapur army and began a fearful slaughter. They advanced, taking fort after fort from Pratap gad to Panhala near Kolhapur.

Even as Aurangzeb spent two years hunting down his brother Dara, Shivaji laid the foundations of the future Maratha state; taking on the

Portuguese at Goa and Kalyan, founding a Navy to counter the Siddi of Janjira and forcing the Bijapur state on the defensive. In 1660, when the new Mughal Viceroy and Aurangzeb's maternal uncle Shaista Khan came and occupied Shivaji's own house in Pune for three long years, he planned a bold attack. In a daring nocturnal raid Shaista Khan was attacked in his living quarters and forced to quit Pune. However, Shivaji had not quite finished. In 1664, he attacked Surat, the largest Mughal port and a rich city, looting its rich merchants leisurely over three days, before moving away to his capital at fort Rajgad as quickly and silently as he came.

The provocation could no longer be ignored. Surat was not just the principal Mughal port but also the embarkation point for the *Haj*. Aurangzeb was compelled to send a large army under *Mirza raja* Jaisingh, his most experienced Rajput General, to subdue the Maratha 'rebel'. A prolonged campaign led to a final siege to the fort of Purandar near Pune and a treaty by which Shivaji had to hand over some of his forts and accept Mughal service. Following the death of Shah Jehan, Aurangzeb was to hold a special *durbar* at Agra on his fiftieth birthday and the Maratha king was asked to attend with an assurance of personal safety. At Agra, the treatment and position in the *durbar* given to Shivaji were not commensurate with what he had been assured, and he protested loudly to *Kunwar* Ram Singh, his host and the son of the *Mirza raja*. Aurangzeb made light of this breach of etiquette but gradually imposed a house arrest on the entire Maratha delegation, which also included the young prince Sambhaji.

While Aurangzeb pondered about how he could deal with his prisoner, Shivaji escaped – a lapse Aurangzeb lamented to his dying day. Many are the conjectures about how he escaped; the most popular being in a basket of sweets meant for saints and mendicants. Fulad Singh, the *daroga* and *Kunwar* Ram Singh faced the Emperor's wrath; the latter was banished to the distant province of Bengal and Assam. The last casualty of the escape was *Mirza raja* Jaisingh himself who died on his way back from what was until then a victorious campaign.

Shivaji was a unique leader, who thought and acted at multiple levels. On the one hand we see him as a strategist founding a navy, building forts and 'managing' his enemies. As a General he micro-plans every campaign, and personally leads his army. He is conscious about the morality of his army and his subjects. He is the protector of the weak and he severely punishes the guilty. His invasions are not wanton aggressions but based on principles of freedom and justice for his people. The management of the kingdom is ahead of his time. Whether it is his letter to grow and preserve trees in his kingdom or his famous letter to Aurangzeb on the imposition of *jiziya,* he thinks and acts at different levels. The following letter of 1662 addressed to his chief Sarje rao Jedhe exemplifies his approach and concern for his people,

> There is intelligence that the Mughal will attack your village. You should immediately evacuate the village with the women and children to a strong place below the *ghats* where the Mughal disease will not come. Do not neglect this job. Immediately you get this, move the people. If you do not do this and the Mughal takes away people, the sin will be on your head. Thinking in this manner, day and night, go from village to village and take all the people to the sanctuary below the *ghats.* Not a moment should be lost in implementing this order. You should stay alert in your place. Those who stay to safeguard the fields also you should send to the mountain tops where they will be safe. If they spot the Mughal from a distance, they should run away. You be alert at your post.[4]

The concern that Shivaji had for his people was paternal and visceral. His campaign to gain *swarajya* from oppression was a mission and he used every means to liberate his land from the Mughals.

On his return from Agra, after a brief respite, Shivaji led the Marathas into an intense war with the Mughals, audaciously raiding Surat a second time in 1670. The attack was noted in English newspapers of the time, the *London Gazette* reporting a letter of November 1672,

> The English President residing at Suratte, acquaints us with the daily fears they have there, from Sevagee the Rebel, who having beaten the Mogul in several Battels, remains almost Master of that country, and takes the boldness to write to all the European Ministers in Suratte, that if they refuse to send him such and such immediate presents of Money (which as he puts them would amount to vast sums), by way of Contribution, he will return and ruin that City; That he exacts the like from the Inhabitants, who certainly would comply with his demands, but that the Officers of the Mogul hinder

them. Which puts them in an extream straight, and causes others daily to convey away their riches; many also embarking and transporting themselves into other parts, to avoid the storm they fear will fall on them.[5]

The attack reduced the importance of Surat and a fall in its commerce, as the insecurity drove away the rich merchant classes to other places.

In 1674, Shivaji crowned himself an independent king or *Chhatrapati* at his new capital Raigad in the Konkan in 1674. The English at Mumbai[a] thought it prudent to call on the king and sent an embassy under Henry Oxenden. A description of the coronation court comes down to us from John Fryer, a physician,

> …and found the Rajah seated on a Magnificent Throne, and all his Nobles waiting on him in Rich Attire; his son Samba Gi Rajah, the Pesuah, Moro pundit, and a Brachmin of great Eminence, seated on an Ascent under the Throne; the rest, as well Officers of the Army as others, standing with great Respect. The English made their Obeisance at a distance, and Narun Sinai held up the Diamond Ring that was to be presented him: He presently took notice of it, and ordered their coming nearer, even to the Foot of the Throne, where being Vested, they were desired to retire; which they did not so soon, but they took notice on each side of the Throne there hung on heads of Gilded launces many Emblems of Dominion and Government; as on the Right-hand were two great Fishes Heads of Gold, with very large Teeth; on the Left, several Horses Tails, a Pair of Gold Scales on a very high Launce's head, equally poised, an Emblem of Justice; and as they returned, at the Palace Gate stood two small Elephants on each side, and two fair Horses with Gold Trappings, Bridles, and Rich Furniture; which made them admire how they brought them up the Hill, the Passage being both difficult and hazardous…[6]

Two years later, began Shivaji's campaign to the southern-most reaches of India, establishing a chain of possessions all the way till the Cauvery. The Mughal Governor Sher Khan was ousted by the Marathas. Puducherry was given to the French to administer through a *firman* to Germain, their agent. Later, Germain described the spartan camp of the warrior king, *'without pomp, without women, no baggages, only two simple tents of simple cloth; one for himself and the other for his Prime Minister.'*[7]

The Dutch, from their post at Fort St. David, too paid a share of their revenues to the Maratha government at fort Ginjee. The English traders at

Madras (now Chennai) appeased Maratha armies with presents. At Ginjee Shivaji established Raghunath Hanumante[8] to administer Maratha territories in the south before returning to Raigad.

The death of *Chhatrapati* Shivaji in 1680, a division in his Cabinet over the succession and then the accession of his elder son Sambhaji as *Chhatrapati,* were followed by Aurangzeb himself leading the Mughal invasion of the Deccan. The Emperor was chasing his rebellious son Akbar who fled from Ajmer to seek support from the Maratha king. Although Akbar left India for Persia a few years later, Aurangzeb made the destruction of the Maratha power along with Bijapur and Golconda, his life's work. Having annexed the two southern states, and imprisoning the two sultans by 1687, Aurangzeb's *Wazir* Asad Khan petitioned him,

> Two great kingdoms have been conquered. It is now good policy that the imperial standards should return to Paradise like Hindustan, so that the world may know that nothing remains for the Emperor to do here.

Aurangzeb replied,

> I wonder how an all-knowing hereditary servant like you could make such a request. If your wish is that men might know that no work now remains to be done, it would be contrary to the truth. So long as a single breath of this mortal life remains, there is no release from labour and hard work.[9]

Jadunath Sarkar sums up the time when Aurangzeb was approaching his final triumph in the Deccan,

> When Golkonda fell to him (on 21st September 1687), a year after the conquest of Bijapur, Aurangzib's work in the Deccan seemed to have been completed. The long dream of the Mughal Emperors ever since the days of Akbar seemed at last to have been fully realised. No rival Muslim Power was left in the Deccan, and all India now bowed beneath the sceptre of Delhi. True, there was a Hindu king still unsubdued ; but he was an upstart of limited means and his soldiers no better than brigands ; their suppression, so it seemed, was only a question of time, now that the Mughal army was set free and the Marathas had no ally left to them anywhere in India.[10]

Aurangzeb then began his campaign against the Marathas.

The last of the great Maratha chiefs of Shivaji's times –Hambir rao Mohite - laid down his life fighting the Mughals at Wai in December 1687. Hambir rao was a strong voice of reason and wisdom in *Chhatrapati* Sambhaji's council. Kavi Kalash, a north Indian in Sambhaji's court, hereafter became all powerful. Historians remain divided over Kavi Kalash's role in these troubled last years. The *raja's* many enemies, some amongst his own kith and kin, passed information about his whereabouts to the Mughals. On 1 February 1689, Sheikh Nizam – titled Mukarrab Khan - marched energetically through forests and hills to capture him near the Konkan town of Sangameshwar. The Maratha king and Kavi Kalash, were taken to Aurangzeb's camp at Koregaon on the river Bhima. *Chhatrapati* Sambhaji was humiliated and, when asked to disclose his treasures and surrender his forts, let out a diatribe that singed the ears of Aurangzeb's messengers. Immediately, he was blinded and tortured; limbs were torn from his conscious body before he was beheaded many days later. Kavi Kalash too was executed.

The thirty-nine days Sambhaji *raja* was tortured in captivity are a watershed in Deccan history. Aurangzeb's almost purposeful order to kill him on the inauspicious moonless night of the Indian month of *Phalgun*, that the dead body was paraded in the chief cities of the Deccan, then torn apart and fed to animals, created a lasting revulsion against Mughal rule. At what was to be his moment of ultimate triumph, Aurangzeb unwittingly stoked the embers of a dying flame.

It was 11 March 1689. The darkest hour of the Marathas was behind them. Soon it would be first light.

༺ॐ༻ॐ༺

## 2. The Kingdom.... for a Vatan

'Sambhaji will be betrayed. Rajaram will preserve the kingdom from Ginjee. Moro Pandit, Niraji Ravji, Ramchandra Nilkanth, Santaji Ghorpade, Dhanaji Jadhav will be the instruments for the growth of the kingdom. Then a king named Shiva will take the kingdom right up to Delhi.'

*Chhatrapati* Shivaji's deathbed prophesy.[1]

The brutal killing of the Maratha king unleashed a wave of revulsion among the people. Despondency gave way to a spontaneous outburst of nationalistic fervour. The Marathas led by the veteran minister Ramchandra Nilkanth *amatya*, began a series of attacks on Mughal posts. Aurangzeb's finest hour seemed to have ended too soon.

At Raigad, queen Yesu bai released two important political prisoners. The first was nineteen-year-old Rajaram, *Chhatrapati* Shivaji's younger son, who was a virtual prisoner on Raigad for nine years. The second was Pralhad Niraji, a minister who was brought out to help in these difficult times. Sambhaji's son Shivaji[a] was just seven years old; Rajaram was therefore placed on the throne. In order to divide Mughal forces, it was decided that Yesu bai and her son would stay on at Raigad, while Rajaram would head towards the fort of Panhala near present-day Kolhapur. Raigad was considered impregnable; however, no fort can be stronger than the men responsible for holding it.

Within three weeks of Sambhaji *raja*'s death, Aurangzeb sent his *Wazir* Asad Khan's son Itiqad Khan to capture Raigad. Another army was dispatched to attack Pratap gad and yet another under Sheikh Nizam towards Panhala. On 5 April 1689, Rajaram with Ramchandra *pant amatya*, Pralhad Niraji and Shankraji Malhar slipped out of Raigad and reached Panhala. Here, Rajaram appointed Ramchandra *pant* to the new post of *Hukumatpanah* with plenipotentiary powers equal to his own. It was decreed that the orders of the *Hukumatpanah* could not be cancelled even by the king. Ramchandra *pant* was the son of Nilo Sondev, the *Mujumdar* in *Chhatrapati* Shivaji's time. As

---

a.   Whether his name was Shivaji or Shah-ji, it was later abbreviated to Shahu.

the anchor of Maratha resistance at this time, he formulated and executed Maratha strategy for three crucial decades after 1689.

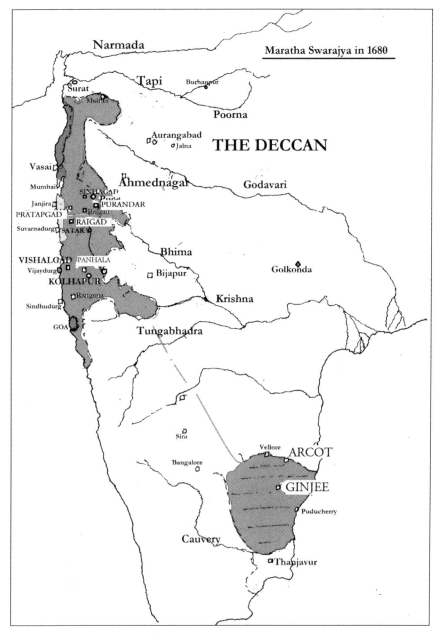

The Maratha Swarajya in 1680

The two families that had migrated to Maharashtra, claiming descent from the Sisodia Rana of Udaipur, were the Bhonsles and the Ghorpades. The Bhonsles laid the foundation of Maratha independence and the Ghorpades served with distinction as Generals of Maratha armies for a hundred years. After 1689, Santaji Ghorpade was appointed the Commander in chief. Santaji was not alone, yet, he was the key to Maratha success in these crucial times. With him was Dhanaji Jadhav, and till they were together, the Mughals could not make much headway.

From Panhala, Ramchandra *pant* dispatched Santaji to attack the Mughals. He first attacked Sheikh Nizam near Panhala and looted his army. Then, with two of his brothers and Vithoji Chavan, he executed a strike at the heart of Aurangzeb's camp at the confluence of the Bhima and Indrayani rivers. Entering the camp surreptitiously, they attacked the royal tent, cut its ropes and took away its gold pinnacle.[2] They then attacked and looted the besieging force of Itiqad Khan at Raigad before returning to Rajaram at Panhala.

These lightning attacks slowed the Mughal advance, but it was no longer safe for Rajaram to stay at Panhala. Ramchandra *pant* therefore decided to send the king to Maratha possessions in the south. Fort Ginjee, eight hundred kilometres to the south, was the strongest fort in the Carnatic. At the end of the monsoon, Rajaram with a compact group of men left Panhala and after many vicissitudes reached Ginjee by mid-November 1689. Prominent among the men who carried Rajaram was the future Maratha *Senapati* Khande rao Dabhade.

The English at Fort St. George reported Rajaram's move and the motive behind it;

> Wee haveing certaine advice that Rama Rajah King of the Morattaes is come privately from His Kingdome of Punnarree (Panhala), to the Chingye Countrey (Ginjee) leaveing his Uncle (Ramchandra pant) in charge of the Kingdome and family to manage the Warr against the Mogull, his designe of comeing hither being reported *to divert the Mogulls Army from thence*, and joine with the severall Gentue Naigues (Nayaks) & raise a considerable army to retake the Golcanda & Vizapore Kingdomes, wch there is a great probability of, both places being at present very weakly guarded. . .[3]

Meanwhile, in Maharashtra, the siege at Raigad dragged on. The fort was well chosen as a capital. It was expected to be a safe refuge for the royal family. Finding it difficult to take the fort by assault or a siege, Itiqad Khan used the services of a knowledgeable Maratha in Mughal service named Suryaji Pisal, and managed a breakthrough after eight months. A well-placed bribe probably served the Mughal cause. The *killedar*, Changoji Katkar[4] realizing he could not withstand the siege for long, sought honourable terms for the royal family. The fort surrendered and Itiqad Khan brought Yesu bai with her son and her retinue to Aurangzeb's camp. Aurangzeb honoured Itiqad Khan with the title Zulfiquar[a] Khan, a name by which he was known from then on. Inevitably, Zulfiquar Khan was asked to lead the campaign to capture Rajaram at Ginjee.

The vigorous Maratha response against Mughal invasion was tempered however, by a strong sense of self-interest. With the kingdom founded by *Chhatrapati* Shivaji apparently crumbling and Aurangzeb appearing in Maharashtra with a huge army, loyalties turned fickle and self-preservation kicked in. In the midst of two adversaries, the services of many went to the highest bidder. The Mughals lured away Maratha chiefs by liberal award of *vatans* or fiefs. This led to the Maratha king being forced to dole out similar incentives. Many bands of young men fought for their *vatan* and the king became a supplicant asking for their support in exchange for an order granting the fief. Although dictated by prevailing imperatives, the genie could never quite be put back into the bottle. MG Ranade writes,

> The main purport was that the Maratha bands should roam anywhere and everywhere, plunder the imperial treasury and territory, and harass the enemy in all possible ways. These *sanads* were nothing but promises of future reward assuring the military leaders they would be considered owners of the territory they would subjugate in any quarter of India.[5]

The Mughal Emperor and the Maratha ministers spared no effort to get men to join their cause. Suryaji Pisal exemplifies the extent to which this process could go. Pisal first helped Zulfiquar Khan capture Raigad, then went over to Rajaram at Ginjee and finally returned to the Mughal

---

a.   Zulfiquar – 'Cleaver of the spine'. Name of Prophet Muhammad's sword.

fold. Changing sides more than once, Pisal eventually converted to Islam to appease Aurangzeb. Ironically, suspecting his fidelity, Aurangzeb did not reward him for it.

Aurangzeb's was not a mere military conquest. He tirelessly strove to spread Islam in his conquests. In 1700, Manucci wrote of Aurangzeb's failed attempt to destroy Tirupati,

> In the Carnatic, inland six leagues from Madras, is a famous and ancient temple called Tirpiti (Tirupati). Here assemble many people from all parts of India. The shrine is very wealthy from the large and frequent offerings presented, and owing to the large revenue derived from it, Aurangzeb has to this time postponed its destruction. But it seems to me the reason for not doing so was his fear of renewed rebellions difficult of suppression...[6]

From Ginjee, Khando Ballal Chitnis wrote encouraging letters to men asking them to join the Maratha king,

> 'People are joining us in this region in large numbers. We have collected funds. Keso Trimal is dispatched with one lakh *hon*[a] (to Maharashtra)... Dhanaji, Santaji with five thousand troopers have reached Kopal on the bank of the Tungabhadra. So you should be loyal to the swami. Why should we worry about the ganims? When you people make up your mind, what is the *gamin*? When you people begin to worry about this kingdom, we take no account of Aurangzeb. Aurangzeb has planned to convert the people of Maharashtra and make them *Mussalman*. Accordingly Netoji and Sabaji Ghatge and Janoji *raje*, and many Brahmins have been converted. All Marathas are approaching us now with their groups. Recently Hanmant rao Nimbalkar and Satvaji Nimbalkar and Mane and other chiefs have come. Others will also join. The *ganim's* army will shrink and ours will grow in numbers.'[8]

In 1691, *Chhatrapati* Rajaram, granting yet another *vatan,* wrote to Hanmant rao Ghorpade,

> Recognising your aim to preserve the Maharashtra *dharma,* we have placed a reserve of six lakh *hon* for the army. On capture of Raigad, Bijapur, Bhaganagar[b] and Aurangabad (the four seats of power in the Deccan) a sum of three quarters of a lakh per territory amounting to three lakh *hon* will be disbursed. The remaining three lakh will be disbursed on taking Delhi.[9]

---

a.  One hon was about two and a half to three and three quarters of a rupee at that time.[7]

b.  Hyderabad

Although such large sums are mentioned, it is unlikely the besieged king had such resources. Delhi remained a distant aim for the Marathas. For the present amongst his men, the lure of *vatans* was greater. Money and land were overriding concerns.

Eminent historian GS Sardesai writes,

> An era of extraordinary chaos began. Nobody was answerable, anybody could leave and approach the Emperor, then approach Ramchandra *pant* or Shankraji, in a moment go to Ginjee and appeal to the *Chhatrapati*, speak the truth or tell a lie, by any means obtain a written order; as long as one's own interests are served, nobody cared if they did wrong things. For ten to twenty years this disorder prevailed. All discipline was lost. Behave as one pleased, obey nobody; and if a disciplinarian like Santaji tried to enforce discipline, betray him. When Shahu and the Peshwas began to rule, this indiscipline assumed huge proportions....[10]

Continuous and unremitting war had eaten into the moral fibre of a people. Baser instincts like survival and greed had come to the fore. But even that could not quite prevent the Mughals from losing the Deccan.

ॐ

# 3. The Mughals Lose the Deccan

'When the Mughal trooper's horse brought to water refused to drink, the trooper would say, 'Do you see Santaji and Dhanaji in the water?'

- Chitnis *Bakhar*.[1]

The Deccan is the region south of the perennial river Narmada that flows from the east to the west. The Narmada was the main obstacle for armies crossing from the north or south and many named crossings dotted its banks. The Deccan plateau of basalt and granite bound by the Western Ghats rising two to four thousand feet was the abode of the Marathas. The many forts in the *Sahyadri* range were their defence against powerful invaders with large armies, artillery and siege trains. The six *subah*s, or provinces of the Deccan; Aurangabad, Khandesh, Varhad (Berar), Bidar, Bijapur and Golkonda, were clubbed together by the Mughals under one Viceroy, who was first based at the walled town of Burhanpur on the river Tapi, later at Aurangabad and finally to the south east, at Bhaganagar or Hyderabad.

At Ginjee, Rajaram's chief advisor was Pralhad Niraji, now designated as the *Pratinidhi* – a title next only to the king and above the rest of the cabinet. By August 1690 Zulfiquar Khan, Aurangzeb's most successful General, reached Ginjee. Without sufficient funds or forces, he could achieve nothing that year. The following year Aurangzeb sent his youngest son Kam Buksh and his *Wazir* Asad Khan to Ginjee, but the fort could not be taken. Rao Dalpat Bundela of Orchha was an energetic supporter of Zulfiquar Khan.

Kam Buksh and the father-son duo of Asad Khan and Zulfiquar Khan did not see eye to eye. At one stage, Kam Buksh's foolish obduracy in planning a march led to unpleasantness and Dalpat Bundela dragged the prince to Zulfiquar Khan who ordered his confinement. Then a rumour of the Emperor's demise reached the camp and Kam Buksh, worried about his own future, tried to obtain the support of the Marathas. A fickle minded young man, Kam Buksh was also the Emperor's youngest and favourite son. He was born of Aurangzeb's youngest queen Udaipuri Mahal, who was once a slave girl in Dara Shukoh's harem. When the matter of Kam Buksh seeking Maratha help reached Aurangzeb's ears, he recalled Kam Buksh and exclaimed, *'A slave girl's son comes to no good, even though he may have been begotten by a King'.*[2]

Around Ginjee, the ponderous Mughal armies were no match for the quick moving Marathas. Santaji and Dhanaji's lightning raids cut off supplies to the besieging Mughal force. In 1693, Maratha attacks forced them to lift the siege. *Wazir* Asad Khan, and Zulfiqar Khan were both trapped in the Maratha counter-attack, and it was Rajaram's secret pact with them that allowed them to withdraw to safety. Santaji was unhappy that the two got away. Rajaram then confided in him and told him that Aurangzeb was not expected to live long and in the future, it was arranged that Golkonda would be administered by Zulfiqar Khan, while Bijapur would be given to Rajaram.[3] Perhaps this proposal was a precursor of the arrangement that prevailed later in eighteenth-century Deccan.

Santaji was indisputably the star in this war with the Mughals and was awarded the title of *Hindurao Mamalkat Madar.*[a] After his biggest triumph against Qasim Khan near Chitradurg, where Santaji destroyed an entire army and obtained a huge indemnity from the besieged leaders, he returned to Ginjee and demanded a status higher than Dhanaji. However, events were to take a different turn. Over the next couple of years, Santaji's irascible temper and insubordinate ways did not go down well at Ginjee. Around 1696, Santaji was removed from the post of *Senapati* and Dhanaji appointed in his place. These two then became sworn enemies. For six years from 1689 to 1695, Santaji and Dhanaji had terrorised Mughal armies. The Chitnis *bakhar* says, *'When the Mughal trooper's horse brought to water refused to drink, the trooper would say, 'Do you see Santaji and Dhanaji in the water?'*[1]

In 1695, Ramchandra *pant* sent messengers to Santaji and called him for a meeting to resolve his grievances.[4] However, Santaji remained sullen and aloof. The rivalry between Santaji and Dhanaji soon led to an open war. It also gave some respite to the Mughals. In 1696, the two chiefs clashed near Ginjee. Dhanaji's vanguard Amrut rao Nimbalkar was captured, and on Santaji's orders trampled to death under an elephant. The bond between

a.   The chief of the land.

the king and Santaji was broken and Rajaram ordered his arrest. Chased by Dhanaji's army, Santaji had to flee to Maharashtra, where he took refuge in the Mahadeo hills near Satara.

The *Masire Alamgiri*, a courtier's diary of Aurangzeb's reign, describes Santaji last days. On the run from Maratha and Mughal armies, Santaji stopped in the village of Mhaswad, abode of Nagoji Mane, whose wife was Amrut rao Nimbalkar's sister. She urged her husband to avenge her brother. Nagoji had a large area around Sholapur under his charge. He followed Santaji and found the opportunity to accost him when he was unarmed and bathing in a stream. The brave Maratha chief was beheaded. Later, his head was found by a Mughal soldier, who brought it to Aurangzeb. The relieved Emperor paraded it in the chief cities of the Deccan, and the Mughal soldier who brought the 'good news' was named Khush-khabar Khan or the *'the bearer of good news'*.[5]

Santaji's removal as *Senapati,* and later his murder, was a setback for the Marathas. Zulfiquar Khan returned to lay siege to the fort of Ginjee in 1697 with renewed vigour. Looking beyond Aurangzeb's reign, Zulfiquar was also looking to establish his own rule in the Deccan. He therefore allowed *Chhatrapati* Rajaram, a possible future ally, to escape[a] marking a safe path that he could take out of Ginjee. On Ginjee's capture, Zulfiquar Khan sent the following dispatch to Aurangzeb,

> ..the Islamic heroes, with God's help, had captured Ginjee which was situated on a high hill and enjoyed the greatest fame and pre-eminence among the forts and strong places of Carnatic in respect of height and abundance of materials of war and defence', they had 'slain large numbers of the infidels; and the wretch Rama (Rajaram) who had taken refuge in this stronghold, being frightened at seeing the valour and hearing of the assault of the ever-victorious army, had fled away from the fort, leaving his family, property and things behind. On Monday, the 7 February, 1698 /16 *Shaban*, this

---

a. Rajaram's escape was also facilitated by the diplomacy of Khando Ballal. Ganoji Shirke, related to the Maratha royal family, was part of Zulfiquar Khan's army. Ganoji had been instrumental in the capture of Sambhaji in 1689. Meeting Ganoji Shirke, Khando Ballal offered his own fief (of Dabhol) to Shirke in exchange for Rajaram's escape. Ganoji then personally escorted Rajaram and his small retinue safely out of Ginjee. Later Dhanaji Jadhav escorted Rajaram to the fort of Vishalgad in Maharashtra.

strong fortress, consisting of seven forts, was forcibly captured and annexed to the Empire. Four wives, three sons and two daughters of the luckless infidel, his dependants, friends, and assistants were made prisoners.[6]

His task in the Carnatic completed, Zulfiquar handed over military operations to his Afghan lieutenant named Daud Khan Panni and returned to Aurangzeb's camp. As the Maratha-Mughal conflict moved back to Maharashtra, the Carnatic saw a period of relative peace.

In the two years that Rajaram spent in Maharashtra before his death in 1700, he shifted his capital from Vishalgad to the fort of Satara. From the start, Rajaram maintained that he held the throne in Shahu's absence. He also made an attempt to rescue Shahu – the true heir – from Aurangzeb's camp at Brahmapuri. Rajaram's own constitution was never as sturdy as that of his brother and father. After a short illness, Rajaram died on the fort of Sinhagad near Pune. Ramchandra *pant* advocated that Shahu would be the new king, but Rajaram's dowager queen Tara bai wished to place her own five-year-old son – also named Shivaji – on the throne. Ramchandra *pant* was disheartened when his own protégés Parshuram Trimbak and Shankraji Narayan *Sachiv* too advised him to accept Tara bai's stance. Even as the new *Pratinidhi* Parshuram Trimbak began to wield greater power, Ramchandra *pant* appeared to reduce his involvement in the affairs of state.

In the face of Maratha resistance over nearly twenty years in war-torn Deccan, many of Aurangzeb's ministers once again felt he ought to patch up a peace with the Marathas. The inexorable and indefatigable Aurangzeb rejected their advice. Instead of being daunted by the failure of his Generals, he set out to personally lead his armies to capture each of the Maratha forts. Laboriously the Emperor enforced sieges, offered bribes and captured a fort, only to see it slip out of his hands when his back was turned. The last fort he captured was the *Berad* stronghold Wakinkheda in 1705. Then, nearly ninety years old, Aurangzeb fell ill and began his final retreat.

Historian Stewart Gordon says the Mughals 'lost the Deccan' as early as 1705.

> By about 1705 the Marathas had won the Deccan simply by not losing. As
> in many guerrilla wars, the Mughal defeat was not the loss of any particular

fort or town, but the loss of the will to keep chasing an enemy that struck and disappeared into the hills, or merged with the local population.[7]

Jadunath Sarkar writes,

> At the end of the seventeenth century, the great empire founded by Akbar and raised to world fame prosperity and splendour by Shah Jehan, was in a state of hopeless decay; administration, culture, economic life, military strength and social organization – all seemed to be hastening to utter ruin and dissolution.[8]

The utter desolation of the Deccan by unremitting war is brought out by Manucci, a European who spent long years in India at that time,

> Aurangzeb withdrew to Ahmednagar leaving behind him the fields of these provinces devoid of trees and bare of crops, their place taken by the bones of men and beasts. ..There have died in his armies over a hundred thousand souls yearly, and of animals, pack-oxen, camels, elephants, etc. over three hundred thousand. In the Deccan from 1702 to 1704 plague prevailed. In these two years there expired over two million of souls.[9]

In 1706, Aurangzeb, in his own words reached *'journey's end'* at the town of Ahmednagar. The twenty-six-year campaign in the Deccan, over half his reign, had ruined the Mughal Empire. Having fought till the *'last breath of his mortal body'*, he had sustained his Empire on the strength of his prestige. His Empire crumbling, treasury depleted, and life ebbing, Aurangzeb recognised his failure. In his Will, he lamented,

> The main pillar of Government is to be well informed in the news of the kingdom. Negligence for a single moment becomes a cause of disgrace for long years. The escape of the wretch Shiva (ji)[a] took place through my carelessness, and I have to labour hard to the end of my life.[10]

On 20 February 1707, Aurangzeb died and was buried by his son Azam Shah at Khultabad, near the fort of Daulatabad. Even as the mighty Emperor's death created fresh fault lines amongst the Mughals, a new entrant was eager to claim his patrimony in the Deccan.

ॐॐॐ

---

a.   The Mughals would address Maratha chiefs without the honorific 'ji' after their names and shorten even the names. Thus Shivaji was called Siva, Sambhaji as Sambha, Santaji as Santa and so on.[11]

# 4. The Prisoner of Islampuri

*'Chiranjeev* Shahu in due course, with divine help, will return to the country...what we do is all for him. The people will have to look up to him in any eventuality.'

- *Chhatrapati* Rajaram's letter to Shankraji Narayan *Sachiv.*[1]

'I am but the prince's servant; you must, it is true, give me obedience, but your loyalty and devotion you must keep for my master.'

- Rajaram *Charitra.*[2]

In 1689, Yesu bai with her son Shivaji II, her stepsons Madhav Sinh and Madan Sinh, the late *Chhatrapati* Shivaji's queen Sakwar bai and many other servants were taken prisoner by Zulfiquar Khan and conducted to Aurangzeb's camp at Koregaon. The Emperor then moved to Galgale near Bijapur to keep track of Maratha activities around Ginjee. After about three years here, in 1695, when Mughal armies had to lift the siege at Ginjee, he moved to a fortified camp at the village of Brahmapuri in a bend in the river Bhima near the pilgrim town of Pandharpur. Aurangzeb changed the name of Brahmapuri to Islampuri.

Yesu bai and her retinue were accommodated in special tents close to the Emperor's own tent within an area cordoned off by a *'circle of red canvas screen'* called *'gulal bar'.*[3] After the fall of Ginjee in 1698, Rajaram's family comprising four wives, three sons and two daughters were also lodged in the same area. Shivaji II was called Shahu in the camp, a name that may have been coined by Aurangzeb himself. The boy prince was pampered by the Emperor's unwed daughter Zinat-un-nissa. Jyotaji Kesarkar, a *patil* from the Panhala region, was employed to instruct Shahu and remained in the same camp.[4]

In 1700, on hearing of his uncle Rajaram's death, Shahu fell ill. A concerned Aurangzeb enquired the reason for his 'yellow colour'. He was informed the Raja eats only *pakwan*, as a *'Hindu does not eat cooked food in captivity'*. Both Yesu bai and Shahu walked a tightrope – on the one hand praying for Maratha success and on the other mouthing platitudes to please

Aurangzeb. The Emperor would often test Shahu by asking him questions about his uncle Rajaram, to which Shahu answered with a maturity beyond his years. Once, while rising from his throne, Aurangzeb's silk socks slipped off his feet. Shahu picked them up and offered them to the Emperor. Aurangzeb said,

> '*Raje,* your father was killed on my orders, yet you are very civil with me. Your uncle fights me. I will send you to your uncle. Will you go?' Shahu replied, 'My uncle always wanted to rule. He imprisoned my father and tried to appropriate the kingdom. When you attacked Raigad, he left us and went to Ginjee. If you hand us over, he will once again imprison us. I will sit on the throne only after you have defeated him.'[5]

Shahu was a pawn to use against the Marathas when the time was right. Shahu on the other hand had to live in fear of his life, and equally the loss of his faith. The fear that the royal captives would escape led to the Emperor deciding that he would convert Shahu to his own faith and marry off the women to his Muslim officers. Shahu was told therefore that he would have to convert to Islam. The anxious prince and his mother Yesu bai sought their benefactor Zinat-un-nissa's intervention to prevent the conversion. Aurangzeb relented but insisted that instead of Shahu, two prominent young Marathas would have to convert. Khande rao and Jagjivan, the two sons of *Chhatrapati* Shivaji's chief Pratap rao Gujar, agreed to take Shahu's place and were accordingly converted to Islam, and given the new names of Abdur Rahim and Abdur Rehman.

In 1703, Aurangzeb planned to release Shahu in the hope of dividing the Marathas. The negotiations entrusted to Kam Buksh failed, because Aurangzeb was distrustful and the Marathas were on the ascendant against Mughal forces. Interaction between Shahu and Maratha officials may have occurred at this time. Shahu continued to stay in the *gulal bar*. In the same year Shahu, who was in his twenties, was married to two girls from illustrious Maratha families. Shahu's chronicler says Aurangzeb expressed a desire to 'see' the brides. This was contrary to the tradition in the Maratha royal house. At that time Yesu bai sent forth a servant girl named Viru bai, and Aurangzeb blessed her.[6] Viru bai remained an important part of Shahu's household thereafter. The Emperor gave a *jagir* of five districts to Shahu as a wedding present. At the same time a sister and two cousins of Shahu were married to three Muslim nobles, Shamsher Beg, Raja Neknam and Muhi-ud-din – a son of the last sultan of Bijapur.[7]

The pecuniary difficulties Yesu bai faced at the time are a reflection on the financial crisis in Aurangzeb's last years. In 1705, she wrote a letter to a temple head – the Dev of Chinchwad near Pune – asking for money. The letter speaks of her stay with Shahu at the fort of Ahmednagar, her inability to borrow any more money, and asks for help in her hour of distress.[8]

In October 1699 Aurangzeb moved out of his fortified camp at Islampuri to personally lead his armies against the Marathas. Rajaram died in early 1700. Within a month of Rajaram's death Aurangzeb captured the fort of Satara. His son Azam Shah led the campaign and it was thus renamed as Azam-tara. In 1703, Aurangzeb was in Pune. In this last campaign, Aurangzeb captured ten Maratha forts over five years, some of which were retaken by the Marathas when the Emperor left for his next conquest. To his son Bahadur Shah he wrote, 'Owing to my marching through deserts and forests, my officers long for my death'.[9] Despite his own old age, till the end, none of his sons or Generals made a move against him. The Emperor dictated the pace and direction of events and with his army plodded through slush, rain, forest and hill, pursuing his fifty-year-old obsession to be the master of the entire Indian subcontinent.

The Empire was facing revolts at several places in the north. The revenue of Bengal, governed by Bahadur Shah's son Azimushan, funded the war in the Deccan for a while. Now, the Treasury was depleted. Before his death, Aurangzeb had devised a plan to divide the Empire among his three surviving sons. He allocated twelve northern *subah*s to Bahadur Shah, six to Azam Shah and two to Kam Buksh, his youngest and favourite son. At the approach of death, he dispatched Kam Buksh to Bijapur. Azam Shah remained with him till the last few days, but he too was sent away. Bahadur Shah remained in charge of Kabul. The Emperor died alone.

A denouement of Aurangzeb's reign is in the later day Persian manuscript '*Tarikh-i-shadat-Farrukh Siyar-wa-Julus-i-Muhammad Shah*', where Khan Dauran, an important noble in the Mughal court of the 1720s delivers his verdict,

Alamgir waged war with the Marathas for twenty-five years; he won only pyrrhic victories, which brought more misfortunes than benefits. Whatever had been achieved during two hundred years was undone and set at naught. All the rules and regulations established during this period were upset and thrown to the winds.[10]

On Aurangzeb's death near Ahmednagar on 3 March 1707, Azam Shah who was marching away very slowly, quickly returned, and after completing the last rites of his father, proclaimed himself Emperor. With the imperial army at his command, Azam Shah began his march to Agra just at the start of the hot Indian summer. In his army was Shahu and his family, and with every mile that the Mughals marched away from his homeland, his anxieties about his fate began to mount.

The man Shahu sought out at the time was Zulfiquar Khan. Zulfiquar Khan was the tallest General in Azam Shah's army and hoped to return to the Deccan as an independent ruler. He therefore wanted his own nominee as the Maratha king and therefore wanted to help Shahu gain the throne. Before leaving the Deccan, Zulfiquar had arranged matters to his advantage. Arcot in the Carnatic was given to Sadatullah Khan to govern and the trusted *pathan* Daud Khan Panni was appointed subedar of the six provinces of the Deccan.

Beyond Bhopal, at a place called Doraha, Shahu finally won his freedom with the help of his patron Zulfiquar and Zinat-un-nissa – his guardian angel in those difficult years – although his mother and half-brother Madan Sinh continued to be in the Mughal camp. Shahu's *bakhar* describes that he was laden with gifts and given many farewell dinners, which seems unlikely as the army was then moving north to fight the war of succession. Heading south from Doraha with a loyal band, Shahu found men joining him. In Khandesh, he had a prolonged halt at a place named Lambkani, near Dhule. He wrote to his aunt Tara bai, '*We have been released from Mughal custody and will meet you soon*'.[11]

At Lambkani, Shahu began to receive Maratha chiefs who had long waged war against Aurangzeb. The Raval chiefs there supported him. Among the first to join his standard were Persoji Bhonsle from Varhad (Berar) and Chimnaji Damodar Moghe. Recognition as the king was important to gain legitimacy and he had dispatched the trusted Jyotaji Kesarkar with Azam Shah to obtain the necessary *sanads*. Mustering his small army Shahu proceeded further, taking a detour to Khultabad to pay respects at the tomb of Aurangzeb. As he moved south, he collected taxes. At a village named Parad, the *patil* [a] who opposed Shahu was killed in the melee. In Shahu's palanquin, the *patil's* wife left her infant son saying, *'the wrongdoers are dead, but now it is for you to look after his son'*. Shahu accepted the baby, and as it was his first victory, he named him Fateh Sinh Bhonsle. Later this foster son was the ruler of the principality of Akkalkot.[12]

Shahu's first real test was Khed, just north of the river Bhima. Here, he stopped and awaited Tara bai's response.

With his eye fixed on the Mughal throne, Azam Shah began his march north. On 24 April 1707, he reached Burhanpur on the river Tapi. Marching north along a dry hot tract his army faced many hardships. His army endured many desertions. Many nobles from the Turani (or Central Asian) group suspected that Azam Shah had become a Shia. Muhammad Amin Khan therefore deserted the army. Ghaziuddin Firuz Jung and his son Chin Qilich Khan also did not join. Undeterred Azam Shah marched on, confident of his own power and eager to battle his elder brother Bahadur Shah.

Agra had the treasures that could sustain an army and an Empire, and the race to Agra was fundamental to Azam Shah's fortunes. Bahadur Shah started from Kabul in early May 1707, but his son Azim-us-shan, coming from Bengal, reached Agra first and took charge of the fort with its treasure and armament. At Gwalior, Azam Shah learnt that Agra had fallen to his elder brother. Rebuffing Bahadur Shah's overtures for peace, he continued to advance to battle. On 18 June 1707, not far from the place where Aurangzeb met the army of Dara Shukoh, Azam Shah with a tiring army on a hot day came face to face with Bahadur Shah, and was killed in the battle. Azam Shah's key aide Zulfiquar Khan had quit the battlefield and returned to Gwalior. Bahadur Shah took the army of Azam Shah in his fold and appointed Zulfiquar Khan to a high post.

---

a.  Village chief

In the Deccan, Shahu's advance towards Satara alarmed Tara bai. She declared that Shahu was an imposter and not the *'real king'*. Chitnis writes in Shahu's biography,

> Tara bai thought, 'Sambhaji *raje* was the senior. His son has now come from the *paatshah*. We will have to obey him. So far, my son has ruled with the seal of the king. My husband nurtured the kingdom, it is appropriate therefore that my son and I rule. Earlier too, an imposter had come. This must also be an imposter. We will send our army, arrest and kill him.'[13]

The dowager queen who had resisted Aurangzeb's efforts to defeat the Marathas for seven full years then asked her chiefs to take an oath with a meal of 'milk and rice' that they would never abandon her cause. This *doodh bhaat* oath was not to be taken lightly in those times. Of her chief lieutenants, Parshuram Trimbak *Pratinidhi*, Dhanaji Jadhav and Shankraji Narayan *Sachiv* promised not to switch their loyalties to Shahu. Ramchandra, however, wrote to Shahu complimenting him and encouraging his enterprise. When Tara bai heard of this she commanded that a silver shackle be placed on Ramchandra *pant's* leg and he be imprisoned in the fort of Vasantgad.[14] Khando Ballal Chitnis said, *'I am a mere clerk, the Senapati is the doer. We obey him. The swami is everything for us. What use is the oath?'* He qualified his oath saying he would not help Shahu if he was found to be an imposter.

Most of the Maratha chiefs had met and seen Shahu even when he was in Mughal custody. Therefore, when Tara bai declared Shahu to be an imposter, it did not receive universal acceptance. The first tack having failed, Tara bai wrote to her chiefs a seminal letter that defined her stance of being the founder and ruler of the then Maratha kingdom. One of these letters, written to a chief named Setavadekar Desai, says,

> Rajashri Shahu has been released from the *Tambra* custody and is on his way. However, the kingdom that the senior Maharaj (Shivaji) founded by great personal effort, was lost by Sambhaji *kaka* along with his own life. Then the late swami (Rajaram) by his own courage and gallantry created a new kingdom. Defending it, he defeated the Mughal. The kingdom began to grow. Secondly, the senior Maharaj had desired to give the kingdom to the late swami. Therefore he (Shahu) has nothing to do with this kingdom. I have dispatched my *Senapati* Jaisingh Jadhavrao, *Sarlashkar* Hambir rao Mohite and the *Pratinidhi* Parshuram Trimbak (against Shahu)...[15].

The *Pratinidhi* with Dhanaji Jadhav and Khando Ballal left Satara fort with a large army to confront Shahu and reached Khed. Dhanaji said to Khando Ballal, *'Shahu is the real king. But I have taken an oath. Khando Ballal is an old servant. Let him meet Shahu and decide whether he is the true prince or an imposter. Then we will decide our future course.'*[16] Khando Ballal, in a disguise, went and met Shahu. He ascertained the authenticity of the prince and it was decided to stage a mock battle.[a] Messages were sent to Dhanaji to stay aloof. The result of the battle was thus a foregone conclusion. The *Pratinidhi* saw that Dhanaji did not fight, and knew he could not win. He fled the battlefield. Reaching Satara, he fortified the fort.

Moving ahead, Shahu next passed Pune and reached a place named Shirwal on the road to Satara. Here he summoned Shankraji Narayan, the *Sachiv*, who was under oath to support Tara bai. Unable to find a way out of his predicament, he refused to meet Shahu. Shahu therefore moved towards the fort of Rohida to meet him, only to find the dead body of the *Sachiv* being brought down from the fort. Shankraji had preferred to take his own life than break the solemn *doodh bhaat* oath. It is said Shankraji drowned himself.[18]

The *Pratinidhi* remained Tara bai's chief supporter and made a stand at the fort of Satara while Tara bai herself moved further south to Panhala. The Satara fort was capable of strong defence. Dhanaji expressed his doubts on taking the fort. However, Shahu remarked that the fort *'will fall in eight days from now!'*

And it did. The battle for Satara after the initial siege, proved a short one. The families of Sheikh Mira Waikar, the fort's *killedar*, were arrested and brought to the fort by Shahu's forces. Sheikh Mira offered to submit, and accepting safe passage, handed over the fort to Shahu. The *Pratinidhi* was imprisoned. Hearing this, Tara bai released Ramchandra *pant* and requested him to rejoin the administration as before.

At Satara, Shahu crowned himself king. The date was 12 January 1708. The prisoner of Islampuri was now the *Chhatrapati* at Satara.

ॐ卐ॐ卐

---

a.   A letter written by Shahu in 1733 acknowledges this debt to Khando Ballal's son Jiwaji, *'Kaka saheb's* wife *Aai saheb* (Tara bai) desired to rule and sent an army with the *Pratinidhi* and *Senapati*. At that time, your father met me secretly and convinced the *Senapati* and other chiefs and brought them to my camp.'[17]

# 5. The Rise of Balaji Vishwanath

'In distant lands you will find ways to counter difficulties that you confront. The swami hardly needs to bear worry in his heart when, in you, he has a servant of incomparable ability.'

- Shahu's letter to Balaji Vishwanath.[1]

Above all, the new king needed able and loyal men to consolidate his rule. Dhanaji Jadhav and Khando Ballal had ensured he gained the Maratha throne. However, along with kingship came a host of difficulties, each threatening the extinction of Shahu's rule. The man who helped the king overcome these, with his ability and loyal service, was Balaji Vishwanath. By 1708, Balaji had spent over two decades in service to the Maratha cause. This experience was to serve the new king in good stead in the years to come.

Balaji Vishwanath Bhatt was the resident of Shrivardhan, a coastal town opposite the fort of Bankot and part of the Siddi[a] of Janjira's territory. He was the fourth of five brothers – Krishnaji, Rudraji and Janoji were older, while the youngest was named Vitthal. He also had one younger sister who was married to Bahirao bhat Mehandale, whose family featured in later history. In the Konkan region, Balaji was responsible for the collection of revenue for the Siddi, while his brother held the post of *Deshmukh*.[b]

Sometime in the 1680s, there was a mistake in the revenue collected from the salt pans harsh punishments meted out in that era, the Siddi tied Sambhaji Mokashi in a sack and drowned him at sea. The incident sparked off Balaji's migration to the Deccan plateau. Three brothers of a family surnamed Bhanu joined him. '*What I earn, I will share a fourth with you,*' is what Balaji is said to have told them.[2] The Bhatts and the Bhanus remained close to each

---

a. The etymology of the word 'Siddi' could be from the word 'Sayyid'. These were originally Abysssinians, and therefore also called '*Habshi*'.
b. The revenue head of the district.

other for nearly a hundred years from then.[a] Arriving at the town of Saswad near fort Purandar, Balaji met Ambaji Purandare who was the revenue officer or Deshpande of the area. The four of them then headed for Satara and met Dhanaji Jadhav who employed Balaji as a clerk.

In 1689, Balaji was the *mutsaddi* of Dhanaji Jadhav. Balaji Vishwanath is first mentioned in two letters written by Ramchandra *pant* to *Chhatrapati* Rajaram and *Pratinidhi* Pralhad Niraji at Ginjee. The letters were written in 1697 but recapitulated events of 1689, when Raigad was attacked and taken by the Mughals. Ramchandra *pant* wrote to Rajaram,[4]

> ....The News-writer..wrote me that when the Maharajah Sumbajee bawah[b] and Shawhoo went to hunt..., that Kabjee Boubah treacherously inviting the Moguls carried them both prisoners to Hasteenapoor; on hearing of which I sent Ballagee Veeswanada the head muttasedda of Jaudawa Raw (Dhanaji Jadhav) in pursuit....[c]

The 'Sanpuri *bakhar*', a document found in the 1940s, also gives out Balaji's close association with Shahu's welfare. The *bakhar* reports that Balaji met and made a '*nazar*' of one thousand rupees to Aurangzeb's daughter to look after Shahu. A *bakhar* at best can corroborate historical events and is thus best read with caution. If true, Balaji's later close association with Shahu may have its origins in this incident.[5]

In 1696, Balaji was again in the Konkan, as an official at Chiplun. The next mention of 1699 finds Balaji as the *sar-subedar* of Pune and in 1707, he appears as the *sar-subedar* of Daulatabad. Revenue from these regions was not easy to collect with the Mughals claiming it, but Maratha officers were nevertheless appointed to these areas and collected revenue whenever

---

a.  A poet alluding to his later career says, 'Climbing the ghat, Balaji dropped one 't' from his surname 'Bhatt' and became 'Bhat'. 'Bhatt' signifies one from the Brahmin caste, while 'Bhat' can also mean a warrior, or a person of the Kshatriya caste.

भट्ट वदे भानुसि की बाधे मज दुःख दुःसह सदैव, म्हणुनी म्हणतो पाहू देशी जाऊनी होय वश दैव,
भानुही म्हणती येऊ घरचा परिसावया मग नको र, भट्ट वदे 'या, देईन मिळेल त्यातुनी, तुम्हास चतकोर',
पुत्र महादेवाचे तीन; हरि, बाळाजी, राम भानु तिघे, घेऊनी जयासी संगे बालाजी विश्वनाथ भट्ट निघे
दैवाने दिधला जया कर तया काही नसे दुर्घट, येता कोंकण सोडूनि वरी दिसे बालाजी मोठा भट
भारे तो थकला, गमेचि चढता सह्याद्रीचा उत्तट, टाकी यास्तव भट्ट शब्दगत ट द्वंद्वातुनि एक 'ट'.[3]

b.  Chhatrapati Sambhaji.

c.  Appendix 1. The letter is only available in its translated version.

possible. During negotiations with the Mughals in these years, Balaji may
have met Shahu, probably in the *gulal bar* enclosure of Aurangzeb's camp.
Even before Dhanaji Jadhav changed sides at the battle of Khed, Balaji was
on Shahu's side. Shortly after Shahu was crowned *Chhatrapati* at Satara, Balaji
was appointed *Senakarte*.[a]

An important person in the Konkan at this time was a mystic named
Brahmendra swami. Near the town of Chiplun in the Konkan coastal strip,
a cowherd named Balu Gawli found a holy man in a cave in the forest
performing penance. He also witnessed miracles performed by him. Balu
Gawli appraised Balaji and others in Chiplun about the prowess of the swami
and they came to meet him. Later the swami stayed at Chiplun. He first met
Balaji Vishwanath sometime around 1697, and Balaji became his follower.

Brahmendra swami, besides being a holy man was also involved in the
politics of the period and was often a moneylender. The swami built the
Parshuram temple at Chiplun. His missives were obeyed by not just by the
Marathas, but also the Siddis of Janjira. Balaji believed he owed his own
progress to the swami's blessings. The swami is said to have sent his blessings
to Shahu just before he marched onto the fort of Satara. Shahu attributed
his victory and coronation to the swami and remained his devotee thereafter.
Practically every important person at the time is found corresponding with
the swami. With his mystic persona, he wielded power over the men who
ruled and this gave him a say in the politics of the day. Besides, he sought
donations and lent money to his devotees. Brahmendra swami later moved
from the Konkan to a place named Dhavadshi near Satara, where he was
closer to the king. The swami lived to a ripe old age and influenced not just
Balaji but also his sons Baji rao and Chimaji Appa.

Within days of declaring himself *Chhatrapati,* Shahu held out an olive branch
to his aunt Tara bai. The proposed treaty demarcated the boundary of the two
states. Tara bai spurned the offer and Shahu sent out his armies to take Panhala
and Vishalgad. Ramchandra *pant* remained the queen's only supporter at this

---

a.  Recruiter of armies

stage, and she took refuge in the fort of Rangana further south. Tara bai was rapidly losing followers; in just the first year, she lost the support of Dhanaji Jadhav, Khando Ballal, Balaji Vishwanath, Persoji Bhonsle from Varhad, Kanhoji Angre, Khande rao Dabhade and a stream of lesser functionaries. The *Pratinidhi* was imprisoned at Satara and the *Sachiv* had chosen death over breaking the oath of allegiance to Tara bai. Yet, Shahu generously allowed his aunt to rule and gave her the region around the fort of Panhala.

The Mughal power was still the dominant force while the Marathas were sorting out their internal problems. With his mother still hostage at Delhi, Shahu was mild in his dealings with them. Without a worthwhile army, funds, or recognition, he floundered from one crisis to another. The Maratha chiefs soon saw the king's predicament and began flouting orders and acting without restraint.

Shahu sought recognition from Emperor Bahadur Shah as the true heir of the Maratha kingdom. Although Bahadur Shah deigned to bless Shahu as his own man, and gave him a kind of legitimacy, the astute Emperor played the two Maratha factions against each other, saying that such an application had come from Tara bai also and the two factions must first decide which one is the true inheritor of the Maratha realm.

Shahu's authority still had to be backed by force and funds. In the absence of these, the grant of *vatans* was the only way to wean away adherents, and Shahu used it liberally. It was in fact the only favour he could offer to those joining him. In June 1708 his chief supporter *Senapati* Dhanaji Jadhav died, and out of a sense of gratitude, Shahu appointed his son Chandrasen in his place.

In his initial years, Shahu actively led campaigns and dispatched his commanders to collect the *chauth* he claimed on authority of the Emperor. The *chauth* was roughly one-fourth of the revenue of a province. It was claimed by the Marathas in exchange for peace in the province. If it was not paid, he even ordered that the imperial treasury be looted to make good the deficit. Chandrasen Jadhav, Rambha Nimbalkar, and Balaji Vishwanath were his chief aides. Although Rambha left Shahu quite early and joined Daud Khan Panni at Aurangabad, Chandrasen remained with Shahu for at least three years. He was unhappy with Shahu's reliance on Balaji's counsel. In 1711, a trifle became the spark that caused Chandrasen to leave Shahu and join Tara bai.

Hunting was a royal pursuit and on one such expedition, Balaji Vishwanath's soldier Piraji, chasing a deer ran into the tent of a clerk named Vyas rao in the camp of Chandrasen Jadhav. Vyas rao, a Brahmin, stood up to protect the animal. Piraji demanded his prey be given up. Vyas rao replied, '*The deer is under my protection. I am a Brahmin, I cannot give it up.*' Piraji did not relent and threw his spear at the deer. Vyas rao tried to block it and was injured. Piraji returned to Balaji's camp and informed him of what had transpired. Chandrasen too heard of it and asked Balaji to send Piraji to him to be punished.

Balaji tried to conciliate Chandrasen, '*The spear was thrown at the deer. Vyas rao came in the way. It caused an injury, but both are servants of the king, Piraji has apologized and sought my protection, please forgive him. I will punish him*'. But the *Senapati* was not satisfied. '*Send him to me*', he insisted. Balaji refused. Chandrasen then sent a posse of soldiers to arrest Piraji. At this, Balaji struck camp and moved away with the *Senapati* following closely. '*Catch them all*', was Chandrasen's terse command and he dispatched two to three thousand men after Balaji.[6]

Not having the army to confront the *Senapati*, Balaji's group broke up into smaller groups and reached Saswad. Here he sought the help of the *Sachiv* at fort Purandar. Chandrasen threatened the *Sachiv* for sheltering Balaji. Taking his wife Radha bai and sons Baji rao and Chimaji Appa with him Balaji left Purandar. Pursued by Chandrasen's men, Balaji and his family were once again on the run. Near the river Nira, Balaji sought shelter at the village of Parinche. Here, Pilaji Jadhav rao and Yamaji Dhumal came to his aid and helped Balaji escape to the nearby fort of Pandavgad. From here, Balaji sent Ambaji Purandare to Satara and obtained Shahu's protection. Chandrasen however refused to give up and challenged the king. Shahu then sent out an army that defeated Chandrasen. Tara bai had been corresponding with Chandrasen and urging him to join her.[7] In 1711, Chandrasen left Shahu and went over to Panhala but later, joined the Mughals. The son of Dhanaji Jadhav was thus lost to Shahu.

In this running battle with Chandrasen, Balaji obtained the help of Pilaji Jadhav rao. Pilaji was to be a pillar of the Maratha state for nearly three decades thereafter. The second person who won his spurs in battle was none other than the eleven-year-old Baji rao, the elder son of Balaji Vishwanath.

At Satara, Shahu's troubles seemed endless. The Mughal Viceroy Daud Khan Panni, Tara bai, and his own chiefs did not let him settle down. In an era of political instability, the advantage lay with the many players who saw an opportunity to aggrandize themselves. Around this time, Shahu released Parshuram *pant Pratinidhi* and gave him back his former titles. However, he was once again found conspiring against Shahu. An infuriated Shahu gave an order to blind him in open court. A *jethi*, or wrestler, was summoned. Forcing the *Pratinidhi* on the floor, placing a pillow on his chest and pinning him down with his knee, the *jethi* prepared to carry out the king's orders.[8]

Khando Ballal, always a close confidante of Shahu, heard of the king's harsh order when he was in his bath. Fully aware of the *Pratinidhi's* long service and capability, he rushed to Shahu's court in dripping wet clothes. Here he found the *jethi* holding down the *Pratinidhi*, poised to carry out the king's order. Khando Ballal, himself a stout man, pulled the *jethi* aside and said to the king, '*I am your culprit. First blind me, or cut off my head. Then you can order any punishment for the Pratinidhi.'* Shahu relented, the *Pratinidhi* was saved, and thereafter his family forever acknowledged the Chitnis' help. Later, the *Pratinidhi's* son Sripat rao helped Balaji in a campaign against a Mughal official of Khatav. This pleased Shahu, and Parshuram Trimbak was reinstated as the *Pratinidhi*.

In the years from 1707 to 1713, Balaji Vishwanath raised and led armies for Shahu. In 1708, Shahu transferred part of Khande rao Dabhade's lands to Balaji to help raise funds for the army.[9] In 1710, Balaji's elder son Baji rao was married to Kashi bai, the daughter of Mahadji Joshi, a moneylender. In the same year, Balaji's elder daughter Bhiu bai was married into the Naik family of Baramati, who were also moneylenders. These carefully chosen matrimonial alliances helped Balaji to raise money and recruit armies for the Maratha cause.

A new crisis confronted Shahu in 1713. Soon after Chandrasen's rebellion had been quelled, arose the far more serious challenge from the redoubtable Kanhoji Angre, *Sarkhel* or Admiral[a], of the Maratha Navy who took up cudgels on behalf of Tara bai. Chandrasen, after joining Tara bai, convinced

---

a.   Sarkhel : Persian, chief of an army.

Kanhoji to support the queen. Angre's base was on the western coast. From here, he enforced a policy of granting 'passport' or '*dastak*' to the ships plying in the Arabian Sea. Kanhoji raided ships with no permits, and this led to the Europeans labelling him a pirate. The fourth power in the Konkan was the Siddi, who took over many Mughal forts after the death of Aurangzeb; chiefly the one at Janjira, but also the Maratha capital Raigad.

Kanhoji's was not just a sea-based power. He also held many forts along the western coastal region. As a veteran chief first appointed by Rajaram in 1698, Kanhoji was thus a powerful adversary for Shahu. On declaring his support for Tara bai in 1713, Kanhoji climbed the *ghat* and took the forts of Rajmachi, Lohagad, Tung and Tikona near Pune. Shahu sent his Peshwa[a] Bahiro *pant* Pingle to stop Kanhoji's advance towards Satara. Bahiro *pant* was a son of Moro *pant* Pingle, the Peshwa in the era of *Chhatrapati* Shivaji. However, he could not match the battle skills of Kanhoji. In a short time, Kanhoji had captured Bahiro *pant* along with Nilo Ballal, a brother of Khando Ballal, and sent them captive to his fort at Colaba.

A perplexed Shahu first asked the *Pratinidhi* to go against Kanhoji, but he refused to take on the responsibility. At this time the one other person in his court who was capable of raising an army, who had just returned after a successful mission, was Balaji Vishwanath. As *Senakarte* he was not in the eight-member ministerial Cabinet. But with Kanhoji threatening a march on Satara, Shahu turned to Balaji Vishwanath.

Shahu and Balaji were then at the village of Manjari, southeast of Pune. Shahu promised Balaji rewards and higher appointments if he succeeded against Kanhoji. However, to lend weight to his position, Balaji requested his king to first appoint him Peshwa and then send him against Kanhoji. Shahu agreed, and on 13 November 1713, in a simple ceremony, he appointed Balaji as the Peshwa with the ceremonial dagger, the stamp, seal, and robes of office. Ambaji Purandare and Ramaji *pant* Bhanu were appointed as his *mutalik* and *phadnis*. Balaji Vishwanath's appointment as Peshwa at this critical juncture was supported by Khando Ballal and Parshuram *pant Pratinidhi*. Using a mix of diplomacy and aggression, Balaji met Kanhoji and agreed on terms that

---

a.   Peshwa: in Persian means foremost, or in this case, the Prime Minister.

set the stage for a rapid expansion of the kingdom. The *bakhar* tells us what transpired:

> Balaji told Kanhoji Angre, 'your father Tukaji served *Chhatrapati* Shivaji Maharaj. Now, Shahu Maharaj is the senior, the heir to the throne, is now ruling over us; instead you are serving the younger brother[a] and have turned your face away from *Chhatrapati* Shahu. Is it the *dharma* of a servant to imprison the Pradhan or take the king's forts? You should either stay aloof or please the king. If you are not prepared for either of these, the Maharaj has sent me! It will be my duty to fight with you and take your posts, forts and regions. Once the war begins, if you decide to seek the Maharaj's pleasure, it will not be granted.'
>
> Kanhoji thought, 'I have endeavoured to fulfil my promise to the queen (Tara bai). Now, even she is imprisoned.[b] It is best I serve the maharaj. I will not be called disloyal for accepting the sovereignty of the king.' Thinking in this manner, he asked Balaji to approach the fort with a small army for further talks. Balaji accordingly went forward and was received warmly by the *Sarkhel*.[10]

Balaji gave Kanhoji autonomy to rule in the Konkan as long as he swore allegiance to Shahu. Shahu appointed Kanhoji as the *Sarkhel,* and the Peshwa agreed to help him in his campaigns in the Konkan against his enemies. Kanhoji then returned all the captured forts to Balaji save the fort of Rajmachi. The Maratha kingdom found a secure western border at the sea.

At Panhala in the next few months, a palace coup saw Tara bai out of power. Supported by Ramchandra *pant*, Rajaram's second queen Rajas bai and her son Sambhaji II took the reins of power. Tara bai and her son were imprisoned.

Shahu had every reason to hope that his troubles were behind him. With his benefactor Zulfiquar Khan's deputy Daud Khan Panni agreeing to pay *chauth*, and Tara bai deposed, Shahu began to feel secure. However, dramatic events in Delhi soon cast their shadow on the Deccan.

ॐक्षॐक्ष

---

a. Rajaram's Queen Tara bai.
b. Tara bai was deposed in 1713-4.

# 6. The Rise and Fall of Zulfiquar Khan

'Farrukhsiyar and Jahandar Shah both fought for the throne in front of Agrah,

The conqueror beat his drums, the defeated fled,

The warriors forgetting all, turned their bridle-reins,

Resolutely, verily diverting rivers, did Azam Khan,

Strong and loyal, uphold the cause of his king,

As in the Mahabharat, the weak king was chased away by Bhim,

Strong of arm, at Kurukhet.'

- *'Jangnama'* of Farrukh Siyar and Jahandar Shah.[1]

After a brief five years on the throne, Emperor Bahadur Shah died in Lahore on 28 February 1712. His reign merely put off the anarchy in the Mughal Empire. Unlike his father, he kept his four sons with him in Lahore. Influenced strongly by the Shia faith, Bahadur Shah had introduced changes in the Islamic prayer that met with protests throughout the Empire, forcing him to withdraw them. Months before his death, his mental state was suspect. He earned the epithet *Shah-i-Bekhabar.*[a]

The Emperor's four sons Muizzuddin, Azim-us-shan, Jahan Shah and Rafi-ushan, each began preparations for the inevitable battle of succession. Azim-us-shan, who was expected to succeed his father, adopted an expectant approach. His advisors told him to arrest Zulfiquar Khan, with whom he was never on cordial terms. However, Azim-us-shan demurred, and felt *'Zulfiquar Khan could do but little.'*

Azim-us-shan lost his opportunity. The veteran campaigner that he was, Zulfiquar forged an alliance of the other three brothers against Azim-us-shan. So, while Azim-us-shan assumed regal insignia, Zulfiquar visited Muizzuddin and coaxed him to fight for the throne. However, Muizzuddin had neither wealth nor an army. Zulfiquar Khan alone had a larger army than all the princes combined. Offering his own money, Zulfiquar raised an army against Azim-us-shan.

---

a. Be-khabar - one who is unaware of what is happening around him.

The battle was fought between Azim-us-shan's depleted army and the three brothers led by Zulfiquar Khan. Azim-us-shan was killed when his elephant was hit on his nozzle with a musket ball and the animal went out of control and jumped into the river. The next morning, Zulfiquar Khan crowned Muizzuddin as Emperor, titled Jehandar Shah. He appropriated Azim-us-shan's carefully collected treasure trove. In a few days the three brothers disagreed over the partition of the Empire and the treasure. In a contest that dragged on for nearly a month in the environs of Lahore, Muizzudin Jahandar Shah emerged victorious after killing his brothers. Zulfiquar Khan, who led him to victory, became his *Wazir*.

Jehandar Shah, already over fifty years of age, began his reign with a spate of executions. Ridding himself of potential rivals, Azim-us-shan's eldest son Karim Khan was dragged to court and handed over to Zulfiquar Khan. Two days later, ignoring his pleas for food and water, he was killed. Of Azim-us-shan's surviving sons, Farrukh Siyar was on his way from Bengal to Azimabad, or modern-day Patna. Jehandar Shah sent orders to Bengal that Farrukh Siyar should be eliminated. The young prince got wind of this order at Patna and panicked, even contemplating suicide. His force numbered just four hundred men and he had no treasure. Murshid Quli Khan, the *diwan* of Bengal, refused to help him.

At this time, Sayyid Husain Ali was the Governor of Patna and his brother Abdullah Khan was at Allahabad. Both owed their position to Azim-us-shan's patronage. The desperate Farrukh Siyar, who had contemplated suicide or fleeing by sea, in *humility 'unbecoming of one from the dynasty of Timur'* approached Husain Ali with entreaties for help. His daughter, the future queen Malika zamani, his mother, and other women made similar entreaties to Husain Ali. When Farrukh Siyar tied his own sword to Husain Ali's side, the overwhelmed Sayyid changed his mind and agreed to undertake the perilous venture of opposing the imperial forces. He also convinced his elder brother Abdullah Khan to join him.

In this manner, of the men his father had helped, only Husain Ali and Abdullah Khan, the Sayyids of Barha, came out to help Farrukh Siyar. At Husain Ali's prodding and with his own mother's support, Farrukh Siyar declared himself Emperor.[2] A happy omen for the Sayyids was the arrival at Allahabad of one crore rupees as the annual tribute of Bengal. Abdullah Khan took charge of it and used it to pay his troops. When Chabila Ram, a local chief from the region joined him, Farrukh Siyar's hopeless cause began to gain strength.

In Delhi, Jehandar Shah and Lal Kunwar continued to shock the elite with their drunken sorties in the city. The mad outrages of the royal twosome crossed all limits of reason. The reign of the 'Lord of Misrule' and collapse of the Mughal court at the time is described in the *Jangnama*, collectively written by poets of the time:

> 'Here Muizuudin, puffed up, maddest of the mad, goes on drinking,
> All the musicians are made nobles, they do what their heart desires,
> At every moment in their mind arises joy for some brother,
> Who has got fish-dignity, flag, hand, yak-tail, and kettledrums.
>
> They load with wine, their bullets are opium pills,
> Long and short drums are their cannon, long horns replace muskets,
> Instead of a gun-match they fill cups, they conquer floods of *bhang*,[a]
> Night and day are thus noised abroad their plans for war and battle-field.
>
> All the lily-eyed, pain-quelling beauties are collected.
> The cleverest dancers wave in the ball their dusky locks,
> Passion kindles by their songs, he bears sweet poet's rhymes,
> He beholds attentively the dances of the pretty juggler boys.
>
> Here a group of drunken players, there the overtures of loose women,
> Here dance joyous eunuchs, moving with great quickness,
> There boys run about, making the *durbar* a sodomites' resort,
> This is Muizuddin's madness, he attends to nothing else...' [1]

As Farrukh Siyar advanced towards Delhi, Jehandar Shah ordered his son Azziuddin against him from Agra. Azziudin began the campaign half-heartedly and reached Khajua, where he entrenched himself, placed his guns around his camp, and waited. Here, Muhammad Khan Bangash, an Afghan soldier of fortune in these parts, joined Farrukh Siyar with about five thousand

---

a.  Made of cannabis

Afghans. Farrukh Siyar attacked Azziuddin's camp with a cannonade on the entrenchment and the imperial army shut itself behind a trench.

Farrukh Siyar's final assault was planned for 29 November 1712. However, the preceding night the Mughal grandees with the army decided to flee and convinced the reluctant prince to do likewise. Frantically gathering what treasure he could get, Azziuddin fled from Khajua towards Agra, meeting an astonished Chin Qilich Khan who stemmed the flight by a Mughal *shahzada*. The next morning Farrukh Siyar's army looted the imperial camp at leisure. Azziuddin joined the army of Chin Qilich Khan which returned to Agra.

Placing the old Asad Khan in charge of Delhi, on the cold misty night of 9 December 1712, Jehandar Shah with Zulfiqar Khan leading his vanguard began his march from Delhi. Money was short, so the Mughal treasure houses were opened, *'gold vessels from Akbar's time broken down, gold from the palace ceiling removed.'* [3] They reached Agra on 29 December and Samugarh on 30 December. Although the army presented a grand spectacle, Zulfiqar Khan was the only General who had experience in battle. Chin Qilich Khan and his cousin Muhammad Amin Khan decided not to fight on the day of battle. Jehandar Shah grabbed all the boats in the river Yamuna to prevent Farrukh Siyar from crossing, but Abdullah Khan found a ford near Emperor Akbar's tomb at Sikandra and brought the army to face Jehandar Shah.

Although it was the month of January, it was raining in Agra and the river was in spate. The sun came out on 10 January in the afternoon and Abdullah Khan began the attack on the imperial forces. Husain Ali attacked precipitously but was wounded and fainted on the battlefield. The imperial army commanded by Zulfiqar Khan seemed to be winning the day. Azam Khan, Governor of Agra, supported Jehandar Shah and acquitted himself well. Abdullah Khan tactically moved away, which led Zulfiqar to think he was abandoning the battle. Even as Zulfiqar ordered drums to be beaten signifying victory, Abdullah Khan attacked him from the rear. Jehandar Shah's elephant went out of control, forcing him to get on a horse. Lal Kunwar rushed him out of the battlefield and brought him to Agra on her own elephant. With his veterans around him, Zulfiqar stood alone on the battlefield as darkness fell, but so great was his reputation in war, that none dared attack him. Unable to find the

Emperor on the battlefield, he made his way back to Delhi. The old war horse had erred; grievously, as it turned out.

At Agra, Jehandar Shah shaved off his beard and taking Lal Kunwar and one attendant in a bullock cart, travelled at night to reach Delhi in two days. Dusty from travel, he reached the mansion of Asad Khan to seek shelter. Here Zulfiquar and his father were in disagreement over their future course of action. Zulfiquar wanted to move to Multan or the Deccan where he could build an army to challenge Farrukh Siyar. However, Asad Khan, the old *Wazir* of Aurangzeb, felt they ought to hand over Jehandar Shah to Farrukh Siyar and seal their place in the new Emperor's court. Asad Khan's view prevailed and perfidiously imprisoning Jehandar Shah, they sent him in chains to the fort.

At Agra, Chin Qilich Khan and Muhammad Amin Khan were prominent amongst those who changed sides and joined Farrukh Siyar. Husain Ali Khan was brought from the battlefield and his wounds nursed. Asad Khan's letter, saying Jehandar Shah was imprisoned, was the signal for the end of the war. Abdullah Khan marched to Delhi and on the outskirts, was met by an apprehensive Zulfiquar Khan. Abdullah Khan reassured Zulfiquar Khan that he would be safe.

Farrukh Siyar was however, burning with revenge against the man who engineered his father Azim-us-shan and elder brother Karim's death. Asad Khan, on the other hand, was confident that his long service in the Mughal court would see his family emerge unscathed. Soon, he was to be disillusioned.

Sending for both father and son, promising their safety, Farrukh Siyar made a great pretence of receiving them kindly at his camp and awarding them with ceremonial robes of honour. Asad Khan murmured, *'I have brought a culprit with me, may I hope for the pardon of his offences?'*[4] Zulfiquar was then ushered in, his hands tied in front. The Emperor ordered these to be released, at which Zulfiquar fell at Farrukh Siyar's feet, was raised up and reassured. Then, stating he had to leave to visit a shrine, the Emperor bid Asad Khan to leave, and asked 'brother' Zulfiquar to stay. Served a meal, Zulfiquar was then trapped between two screens of the royal tent and surrounded by two hundred heavily armed soldiers. From an adjacent tent, Farrukh Siyar sent messengers to Zulfiquar questioning him about his past acts including the imprisonment of Kam Buksh at Ginjee and the deaths of Azim-us-shan and Karim.

The stars of the great warrior had turned away from him. Zulfiquar realised it was the end. He replied to Farrukh Siyar, *'if you want to kill me, kill me in any way you like, what is the use of all this talk?'* The assassins 'fell upon him, threw him to the ground, twisted the strap from a shield round his throat and strangled him.' Thus ended the life of Zulfiquar Khan, conqueror of Raigad and Ginjee, and benefactor of Shahu.[5]

The assassins next went to Jehandar Shah's prison cell and extricating him from Lal Kunwar's arms, beheaded him. The bodies of Zulfiquar and Jehandar Shah were thrown before the Delhi gate of the Red Fort and buried several days later. Asad Khan was forced to follow his dead son's disgraced body in a procession through Delhi.[6] Officials were deputed to confiscate the houses and property of both father and son. Several other princes, including the Emperor's own younger brother were blinded. The purges took away princes, nobles, and old Generals, who once formed the backbone of the Mughal Empire.

New appointments followed. Abdullah Khan titled Qutb-ul-mulk became the *Wazir*, and Husain Ali, the *Amir-ul-Umara* and *Mir Bakshi*. Chin Qilich Khan replaced Daud Khan Panni as Viceroy of the Deccan with the title Nizam-ul-mulk. The year 1713 thus saw a thorough change in the Mughal court.

It was not more than six years since the death of Aurangzeb. The death of Bahadur Shah marked the end of rule by the Mughal Emperor; from then on, real power was to shift to the *Wazir*. Although Farrukh Siyar reigned, the Sayyids of Barha ruled. Therein lay the nub.

༺ဝ❧ဝ❧༻

# Book Two

First Light

'Our fathers in the past did great deeds, if we cannot do them, what use are these glorified ranks and posts? Give us the order. I will bring armies and treasure and place it at the feet of the swami. I will counter the Nizam's threat and campaign in Hindustan....'

- Baji rao Peshwa to *Chhatrapati* Shahu, 1721.


'I have, with God's help, called to my side Raja Sambhaji – who is Shahu's rival – conciliated him and engaged him in punishing and destroying Shahu.'

- Nizam-ul-mulk's letter to Sawai Jaisingh.

# Rewa Uvach

From my vantage point at the divide between Hindustan and the Deccan, I could perhaps see events and appreciate their significance better than most others. It is said one can miss many things when one is too far or too close to the places where events occur. At the waistline of India I was perfectly placed. It was clear to me that the apparent peccadilloes in Delhi were actually catastrophes of a high order that finally ruined the Empire as much as any invasion did. Unless good men are in places of governance, no state can survive. The accumulated wisdom of five generations can dissipate in a year of wanton living. Perhaps Jehandar Shah, whose reign was erased from Mughal court records, did more damage to his patrimony than any other later Mughal.

There was also a certain finality about the end of the Mughal monarchy. If 1707 saw the death of the last autocrat, the death of his son Bahadur Shah ended what remained of the all powerful central figure of the monarch. Jehandar Shah, in just one year reduced the Mughal court to a circus and it never quite recovered from this shock. The ascent of Farrukh Siyar and the many succession battles fought in a matter of half a dozen years resulted in massive erosion in Mughal battle-hardened veterans. Many of these were killed in battle and many afterwards in the purges that inevitably followed. The result was a rule by the *Wazir* and a cabal of nobles who held the effete Emperors in thrall with the Mughal court reduced to complex alliances to serve the interests of rival nobles.

Provincial satraps began to call the shots and resisted imperial *firmans*. The Emperor became a supplicant and the powerful Sayyids took over the reins of Government. The Emperor, although impotent, devised new ways to eliminate the check they placed on him and plots and counterplots took precedence over governance. The Deccan and Bengal, placed furthest from Delhi, became the first provinces to begin a drift away towards autonomy. Rebellions that had always been a feature of Mughal rule became even more common. The Marathas crossed into Hindustan with increasing frequency and although their king professed allegiance to the Mughal Emperor, the Maratha chiefs did not hesitate to raid Mughal territories.

On either side of the Rewa, the divide became apparent year after year. The Sayyids sat on a shaky perch and faced eternal strife in the years they spent in Delhi. The Emperor and the *Turani* party conspired against them until finally the brothers had to separate. The twists and turns of events in Delhi affected Maratha fortunes and paved the way for an Empire of their own.

But I am getting ahead of the story. Right now, the era of the Sayyids had just begun. How they played their cards and where they went wrong is what we will see in the coming pages.

☙❧☙❧

# 7. The Sayyids Become All-Powerful

'It is necessary however, to be very cautious of the Sayyids of Barha…'

- Aurangzeb's Will.[1]

The Sayyids of Barha came to India many centuries ago from Iraq. For over a hundred years the family had fought for Mughal Emperors from Akbar to Bahadur Shah. Classically they fought on foot, sword in hand, at the front of their armies, surrounded by thousands from their clan. In the Deccan, Zulfiquar Khan once recommended the Sayyid brothers Husain Ali and Abdullah Khan, then junior officers in Aurangzeb's army, for promotions and rewards. The Emperor had replied to Zulfiquar,

> To relax the reins to the Sayyids of Barha is to bring on final ruin, because these people on getting the least prosperity and promotion boast, 'There is none like me'. [2]

The close-knit loyalties among the clan made them powerful allies and dangerous enemies. Again, in his Will, Aurangzeb stated,

> It is necessary, however, to be very cautious of the Sayyids of Barha, and without abating any internal regard for them, not to advance them according to their dignity, as they will confederate, not only with the most powerful, but the tyrant of the country. If the rein therefore, is once slackened, repentance will be in vain. Repentance will not avail when the thing is done.[1]

Husain Ali had fought for Bahadur Shah in the battle for succession, where a younger brother was killed. The Sayyids commanded loyalty from their kinsmen, and fought bravely with scarce regard for their own safety. Of the two, Husain Ali was more impulsive and intrepid. His elder brother Abdullah Khan was more patient and fond of the good life, although he could acquit himself well on the battlefield.

Delhi has been the hotbed of politics from time immemorial. Within days of assuming power, Farrukh Siyar began doubting the fidelity of those who had placed him on the throne. The contrary pulls of the *Turani* and *Irani* groups at the Delhi court; broadly from the Sunni and Shia sects or from Central Asian Turkish and Persian ancestry, began to influence the vacillating Emperor. Even as Husain Ali, his original supporter, still lay injured at Agra and Abdullah had taken the capital, Farrukh Siyar found men warning him against the two brothers. One of these was Mir Jumla of Dhaka, and he formed the nucleus of resistance to the triumphant Sayyids. Swayed easily, the new Emperor began to find ways to remove their influence from his counsel. Petty quarrels and even superstitions strained relations between them within a month in power.

Removing rivals from Delhi, *Wazir* Abdullah Khan appointed Chin Qilich Khan as Viceroy of the Deccan and Zulfiquar Khan's confidante Daud Khan Panni was moved to Gujarat. Abdullah Khan honoured Chin Qilich Khan with many titles; Khan Khanan, Bahadur, Fath Jung and the Nizam-ul-mulk, the title by which he was commonly referred to from then on. He did not look favourably upon the Sayyids of Barha. Schooled under Aurangzeb, the Nizam found the arrangement with the Marathas quite disagreeable. In May 1713, the Nizam left Delhi for the Deccan and began measures to oppose the Marathas and challenge their collection of *chauth*.

*Chauth* was not an invention of the Marathas. Documents show it was paid by the Portuguese residents of Daman to the Rajput raja of Ramnagar (now Dharampur) 1579 onwards.[3] When Ramnagar was conquered by Shivaji, he demanded the same *chauth* be paid to him. The idea was developed so that money to wage war was generated by war, which explains the Maratha '*mulukh-giri*'—raids to collect money in the course of a campaign. However, once *chauth* was paid, *mulukh-giri* and the depredations ceased. The rationale for *chauth* is mentioned in this letter sent from Surat to Mumbai in 1672, two years after the city was sacked for the second time. Shivaji made clear to the Mughal Governor of Surat,

> as their king had forced him to keep an army for the defence of his people and country, so that army must be paid, and if they send him not the money speedily, he bid them make ready a large house for him, for he would come, and sit down there, and receive the rents and customs; for there was none now to stop his passage.[4]

Surendranath Sen says,

> the chauth in Shivaji's time was therefore a military contribution paid by
> defenceless subjects of enemy kingdoms and territories, for the protection
> of their lives and properties from the invading Maratha army.[5]

In Shahu's time, it remained for the Mughals the price to purchase peace
and security; in Aurangzeb's time it was collected in defiance of imperial
authority. Unlike Shivaji, in Shahu's case, he sought imperial sanction to levy
*chauth*.

The collection of *chauth* and other dues was not an easy task. First, there
was the civil war between Satara and Kolhapur and later, the difficulties
posed by Mughal officers who did not pay the revenues without a strong
Maratha army to enforce payment. This dual role persisted for a fairly long
period, a settled government did not exist and the Mughal-Maratha struggle
continued. The policy dictated by Shahu to remain as an *Amir-ul-Umara*[a]
to the Mughal Emperor did not help matters at all. Zulfiquar Khan and his
protégé Daud Khan had accepted the 'arrangement'. However, with the fall
of Zulfiquar Khan and the imminent arrival of Nizam-ul-mulk, the policy
was set to change.

The Nizam-ul-mulk's father and grandfather had served the Mughal crown
before him and fought in Aurangzeb's armies in the Deccan. In the mid-
seventeenth century, Khwaja Abid, the Qazi of Bukhara in Central Asia,
passed through India to Surat, from where he embarked for the pilgrimage
to Mecca. Around 1657 he returned, just when Prince Aurangzeb was setting
out from the Deccan to fight the war of succession. Abid joined his army and
was successively rewarded with high posts. When Aurangzeb descended into
the Deccan in 1681, Khwaja Abid accompanied him. For his bravery at the
siege of Golkonda in 1687 Aurangzeb titled him Qilich Khan.[6] His eldest son
Mir Shahabuddin, later Ghaziuddin Khan Firoz Jang, came to India around
1668, joined Mughal service, and like his father became a trusted servant of
the Emperor. His son, Qamruddin Khan, born in 1671, was awarded his first
*mansab* at the age of six. His loyal service led to the title of Chin Qilich Khan

---

a.   Commander of Commanders or equivalent

in 1691. After Aurangzeb's death, Ghaziuddin Khan and his son Chin Qilich Khan did not join the battle for succession.

The dynasty of Khwaja Abid was *Turani* – or those who were of Turkish ancestry – and of the Sunni faith. Bahadur Shah appointed Ghaziuddin to Gujarat, a less important appointment. Ghaziuddin became blind for the last twenty years of his life and died in 1710 at Ahmedabad. Chin Qilich Khan was *subedar* of Bijapur and Bahadur Shah moved him to Awadh in the Gangetic plains. Within a year however, Chin Qilich Khan resigned from his post and for the next two years saw no active service. At the end of Bahadur Shah's reign he was given his father's titles. In the war of succession, he was in favour of Azim-us-shan, but Zulfiquar Khan – as we saw earlier – prevailed and Jehandar Shah became the next Emperor. On Jehandar Shah's defeat at Agra, Chin Qilich Khan joined Farrukh Siyar.

Chin Qilich Khan, now titled Nizam-ul-mulk would not admit the Marathas to be the rightful claimants of the *chauth* of the Deccan. In this first stint as the Viceroy of the Deccan, he rewarded Maratha rebels such as Chandrasen Jadhav with estates, awarded the title of 'Rao Rambha' to Rambhaji Nimbalkar, and encouraged them to oppose Maratha officers who attempted to collect revenues. Rao Rambha himself was a great grandson of *Chhatrapati* Shivaji and Pune district was placed under his charge. The arrival of the Nizam in the Deccan thus posed a fresh challenge for Shahu.

The Emperor and Sayyids' factions continued to clash in the turbulent court of Farrukh Siyar. Taking advantage of this, the Rajputs led by Ajit Singh of Marwar took the city of Ajmer. Gathering at Pushkar, the Rajputs vowed never to give their daughters in marriage to the Mughals. To put down this revolt, Husain Ali marched from Delhi against Ajit Singh. Farrukh Siyar took this opportunity and wrote to Ajit Singh to do away with the overbearing Sayyid. In the event it was Husain Ali who subdued Ajit Singh and among the terms imposed, was a clause that his daughter Indra Kunwari be given in marriage to Farrukh Siyar.

With the Emperor's many plots against him, Delhi did not seem safe for Abdullah Khan. He called back Husain Ali, stopped attending the court, and delegated day to day administration to his trusted aide Ratan Chand. The two factions finally agreed on a compromise. Mir Jumla, the Sayyids' chief opponent, and Husain Ali were both asked to go to a *subah* away from Delhi. Husain Ali decided to replace the Nizam as Viceroy of the Deccan. After the celebrations of Farrukh Siyar's wedding to Indra Kunwari in 1715, he left for the Deccan. However, before his departure he warned the Emperor, *'if in his absence anything should be attempted against his brother, he could be assured he would quit everything and be back in the capital within twenty days, at most.'*[7]

The Nizam, annoyed at his recall from the Deccan, passed within a few miles of Husain Ali but ignored him and did not pay him the customary courtesy visit. On his part, Farrukh Siyar once again tried to eliminate Husain Ali and wrote a secret letter to the veteran Daud Khan Panni to kill him in battle. Accordingly, Daud Khan came from Ahmedabad, occupied Burhanpur and refused to recognize the authority of Husain Ali as Viceroy of the Deccan. He also enlisted a large army that included the Maratha chief Nemaji Scindia.

The armies of Husain Ali and Daud Khan clashed near Burhanpur on 12 October 1715. Daud Khan, a towering *pathan* on his elephant, presented a fearful sight to the Sayyid's army, and as he charged he was *'preceded by three hundred Afghans armed with battle axes.'* Husain Ali's army scattered before Daud Khan, who shouting *'where is Husain Ali?'*, came searching for the new Viceroy. The battle seemed to be going against Husain Ali when, in full flow, Daud Khan was hit by a musket ball and killed. The Sayyid emerged victorious. A vengeful Husain Ali then ordered Daud Khan's corpse to be tied to the foot of the dead man's elephant and had it dragged through the streets of Burhanpur.[8]

The Emperor lamented the death of Daud Khan Panni. He said to Abdullah Khan, *'it was a pity that so heroical a man as Daud Khan should have been slain; he had been unworthily used'*. The angry Wazir retorted, *'had his brother been slain by that savage of an Afghan, his death, he supposed, would have appeared very proper, and at any rate, would have been more welcome to His Majesty'.*[9]

Husain Ali took over as Viceroy of the Deccan at Aurangabad. Shankraji Malhar, who had been *Sachiv* during Rajaram's initial stay at Ginjee, had come back from Kashi with Husain Ali and became his advisor on affairs of the Deccan. Naturally, there was increased interaction with the Marathas. With the Emperor himself plotting against the Sayyids, Husain Ali's policies were necessarily governed by the need for survival and the Marathas became his natural allies. The Mughal policy in the Deccan was thus to change once again, but this time it was to prove favourable to Shahu.

꧁꧂꧁꧂

# 8. The Marathas go to Delhi

'I much fear, lest under the appearance of these dissensions, ruin and desolation should have crept under the pillars of the Timurid throne.'

- *Wazir* Asad Khan on his deathbed to Farrukh Siyar.[1]

Relations between Farrukh Siyar and the *Wazir* did not improve. The Emperor was fearful that the Sayyids would remove him from the throne. Sometime in 1716, hearing that the old *Wazir* Asad Khan, father of Zulfiquar Khan, was on his deathbed, he sent a trusted man to seek his advice. Apologising at first for the ill treatment Asad Khan's family endured, the Emperor's emissary said,

> Now, we repent, and regret, and sob: but all these came too late, and prove of no avail. Nevertheless ….we flatter ourselves, that you shall not deny us some piece of advice on what we are to do with the Sayyids…

The old man of eighty-eight lunar years, who had reconciled to the murder of his son and confiscation of his property, heard Farrukh Siyar's message and replied,

> You have committed a grave error, but such doubtless was our destiny; and you were yourself under the actual impulse of fate – but now the day of retribution, I am afraid, seems at hand; you are full in its way – and I much fear, lest under the appearance of these dissensions, ruin and desolation should have crept under the pillars of the Timurid throne. Now that you have so unfortunately given up your throne and your authority into the hands of the Sayyids, it is too late to retrograde; on the contrary spare nothing to keep them easy and satisfied, lest these dissensions, by being protracted to a length, should give birth to matters of a high nature, and reduce you to the necessity of suffering the reins of your liberty to slip absolutely out of your hands.[1]

The Emperor did not keep the Sayyids 'easy and satisfied'. The attempts to eliminate Abdullah Khan did not end. By directly appointing lesser officials to the Deccan, Husain Ali was constantly embarrassed.

The Emperor called several nobles in the hope that they would destroy the power of the Sayyids. Nizam-ul-mulk was called from Muradabad, but he discerned the Emperor's enterprise to be hopeless and merely played with kind words. Farrukh Siyar's father-in-law, Ajit Singh of Marwar, too decided to support the *Wazir*. The final straw was when Mir Jumla came to Delhi and chose to meet Abdullah Khan first. The *Wazir* felt a showdown was near. He recruited fresh troops and wrote to Husain Ali to return to Delhi forthwith.

Unknown to them, fate had dealt the Marathas a good hand. The time for their first big move was closer than they realised.

Sometime in 1716 an incident became the catalyst for the unlikely alliance between Husain Ali and the Marathas. Shahu had to counter many rebels, one of which was Damaji Thorat. The Thorat family was earlier with Tara bai, and was opposed to Shahu. Damaji had built a small fort at Hingangaon near Patas. Shahu first sent the *Sachiv* Naro Shankar against him, but he was defeated and imprisoned. It was then decided that Balaji would visit Damaji at his village. Although accompanied by just a small army, Balaji felt he would achieve the same success with Damaji as he had with Kanhoji Angre.

In those days, the Marathas considered an oath called the *Bel-bhandar* as ample security and guarantee of good conduct. The oath was taken using leaves of the *Bel* tree, a pot of water, turmeric and some grain on an old blanket.[2] Damaji swore on the *Bel-bhandar* that Balaji would not come to harm when he came visiting to his house. Reassured, Balaji with his wife and two sons visited Damaji, but were promptly imprisoned. Damaji not only demanded a ransom for their release but ridiculed the oath, stating it was just leaves of a tree and some items of food.[3] Leaving his family hostage, Balaji obtained funds from Shahu and paid Damaji the ransom. Damaji then used Pilaji Jadhav rao's fortified house at the foot of Purandar fort to create havoc in the region between the fort and Pune.

Damaji later met Shahu, but refused to heed his call for peace. Damaji's fort at Hingangaon could easily withstand attacks by Shahu's fledgling army; Balaji therefore sought Mughal guns through Shankraji Malhar. A letter written by Pilaji Jadhav rao's mother mentions this episode; *'The Prime Minister (Peshwa), chiranjeev[a] Pilaji and brother Mughal have thrown a cordon*

---

a.   One with a long life

*around Hingangaon*.[4] The Mughal artillery helped storm the fort and Damaji was taken prisoner.[5] Damaji's fort at Hingangaon was destroyed, and later, he died in captivity. *Sachiv* Naro Shankar too was freed, and he gave the fort of Purandar to the Peshwa for his help.

Husain Ali, fully posted of the events in Delhi, was making his own plans. To counter the Emperor, Shankraji Malhar advised Husain Ali to seek Shahu's help. Shankraji himself approached Shahu and Balaji Vishwanath, and soon a treaty was drawn up for Husain Ali to sign in return for Maratha help. The main points of the treaty were the acceptance of Maratha rights of *chauth*, *swarajya* and *sardeshmukhi* in the six *subah*s of the Deccan, in return of which Shahu would maintain an army to keep the peace. He would also pay an annuity to the Emperor. The other major demand was that Shahu's mother Yesu bai and half-brother Madan Sinh would be released from Mughal custody.[a] A large Maratha contingent would be part of Husain Ali's army to Delhi. Husain Ali promised to fulfil these demands and undertook to pay the Maratha army for its sojourn north of the river Narmada on a daily basis. In November 1718, the combined army began its march to Delhi.

Husain Ali also remembered that there was a young man named Muezzeddin[6] living in Shahu's court, purportedly the son of Prince Akbar and thus grandson of Aurangzeb. Husain Ali wrote to Farrukh Siyar that the Marathas had in their custody the son of Akbar and would hand him over to the Emperor if he accepted their demands. A 'pompous retinue' accompanied Muezzeddin in the camp, impressing upon all the importance of the young man. Nobody could meet him and he was kept in a private tent befitting his status. Farrukh Siyar sent an order to dispatch this mythical Mughal prince to him. Husain Ali however, wrote back that the Marathas would hand over the prince only in exchange for Shahu's family in Delhi and were accompanying him for that purpose.

Leading the Maratha contingent was the Peshwa Balaji Vishwanath, *Senapati* Khande rao Dabhade, Pilaji Jadhav rao, Balaji Mahadeo Bhanu, and the Peshwa's elder son Baji rao, then eighteen years old. Also accompanying

---

a. Appendix 2.

the Maratha army was the young Malharji Holkar, at that time living off the land with his men. Husain Ali appointed his nephew Alam Ali in his place at Aurangabad and the army began from Ahmednagar in mid-November, reaching Delhi on 16 February 1719.

The Rajput prince Sawai Jaisingh, Farrukh Siyar's only supporter, recommended stern and immediate action against Husain Ali, but the Emperor could not muster the courage to take a bold stand. The Emperor meekly complied with the *Wazir's* demand to send away Jaisingh. The *Wazir* then replaced the troops in the fort with his own men. Husain Ali chose this moment to make his grand entry into the city and visit the Emperor. Some more concessions were extracted from the Emperor who anxiously enquired about the 'son of Akbar'. A bare minimum of courtesy was extended to the Emperor and Husain Ali departed from the *durbar* with *'so careless a bow that it gave general offence',*[7] but Farrukh Siyar had by now, lost his ability to act.

The Sayyids then entered the palace and hot words were exchanged. Itiqad Khan, the last imperial faithful, panicked at the scene and ran out of the *durbar*. Farrukh Siyar went to the women's chambers and took shelter there. The night was spent in posting the *Wazir's* troops all over the capital, the entire Maratha army and officers remained awake and on horseback.

The morning brought a rumour that the *Wazir* was killed. Suddenly Sadat Khan and two more officers rode with their armies to help the Emperor, while Amin Khan came out in support of the Sayyids. The Marathas stopped some of the troops from going further and found themselves caught in the narrow streets of the city – a place where they did not wish to stay and fight. They therefore decided to leave and in the melee some were caught by armed men and disbanded soldiers, who had been offended by their presence, and put to death. Every street and door the Marathas turned to, had men who turned out to be their enemies. In the end fifteen hundred of them died on the streets of Delhi.[8] The violent mob even found gold in some of the saddles. Persoji Bhonsle's son Santaji[9] was one of those killed, as was Balaji Mahadeo Bhanu, grandfather of the later day statesman Nana Phadnis. William Irwine, who researched Mughal history extensively in the nineteenth century says,

> This, the first armed Maratha appearance in Delhi, where in forty years time they were to be lords and masters, was not of happy augury. They

were not accustomed to street fighting and were, no doubt, overtaken by irresistible panic.[10]

A general fight began in the streets between Husain Ali's troops and other factions still loyal to the Emperor. It was soon learnt that the *Wazir* was safe. Sadat Khan and Itiqad Khan then retreated. Farrukh Siyar was dragged out of the harem and blinded in his own *durbar*. Rafi ud darjat, a son of Rafi-ushan, was placed on the peacock throne. The next day, the *Wazir* appeased the Hindus by revoking the levy of the *jiziya*.

Balaji Vishwanath, with the *sanads* promised by Husain Ali left Delhi at the end of March 1719. He returned to the Deccan along with Shahu's family and the promised *sanads* for collecting *chauth* and *sardeshmukhi* in the Deccan as well as in sixteen districts of the region known as *swarajya*, with some exceptions in the south and the *subah* of Khandesh. The rights for Gujarat, Malwa and parts of Varhad were not granted then. Balaji reached Satara on 3 July 1719 and Shahu came forward to welcome him. The biographer of Emperor Muhammad Shah who came to the throne at Delhi a year later, says,

> The formal grant of *chauth* and *sardeshmukhi*, obtained by the Peshwa Balaji Vishwanath Bhatt in 1719, marked a decisive advance in the rise of Maratha power. It raised the status of Raja Shahu and established his supremacy in Maharashtra. The Peshwa, by his tact and devotion, surmounted innumerable difficulties which had beset the early career of Raja Shahu and succeeded in placing the Maratha kingdom on a firm foundation.[11]

That year, in the monsoons, Balaji implemented the revenue system of the Marathas, later improved over the remainder of the eighteenth century. The king was assured of income through *sardeshmukhi* and some other heads, while the chiefs who would collect the revenue from the *subah*s had their own share of the revenue to keep. The system lasted a hundred years with some modifications by later Peshwas; but the mould of the confederacy was set.[a]

The Nizam was appointed the *subedar* of the crucial province of Malwa, and left Delhi by the middle of March 1719. With the Sayyids ordering Alam Ali, the Viceroy of the Deccan, to cooperate with the Marathas it seemed as if

---

a. Appendix 3.

Shahu's rule was finally here to stay. Minor revolts were put down and Balaji Vishwanath was busy till the early months of 1720 campaigning to implement the system he had created. Balaji set up an elaborate distribution of revenue among the various arms of the Maratha power, which lasted for many years. In 1719, the framework of the arrangement led to a rapid expansion of the kingdom and an equitable distribution of revenue besides an assured income for the king. It achieved some of its aims, in a few others it fell short.

The towns of Kalyan and Bhiwandi in the Konkan were taken in 1719 and the district of Pabal to the north of Pune soon after. At the end of the year Balaji had gone as far south as Belgaon. His last battle with Sambhaji of Kolhapur was on 20 March 1720. He then retired to his home at Saswad with an ailment, and there on 2 April 1720, he breathed his last.

Balaji's role in Shahu's success can scarcely be exaggerated. The 'Cambridge History of India' a trifle bombastically states,

> Balaji Vishvanath may without exaggeration be termed the second founder of the Maratha Empire. Without his directing brain, Shahu Raja, enervated by his upbringing in the Mughul court, would not have survived for a year.[12]

At Balaji Vishwanath's death after seven years as Peshwa, Shahu was secure in the Deccan, the Sayyid brothers called the shots in Delhi, Sambhaji of Kolhapur was considerably weakened and the Mughal Viceroy Alam Ali allowed the Marathas to collect the *chauth* of the six *subah*s of the Deccan. What remained was to assertively stamp Maratha supremacy over all of Hindustan.

The era of Baji rao was about to begin.

ᘒᑫᘓᘒᑫᘓ

# 9. Downfall of the Sayyids

'Behold the inconstancy of fortune, and the end of all earthly greatness.'

- Abdullah Khan, battle of Hasanpur, November 1720.[1]

Just when it appeared that the Sayyid brothers had firmly taken control of the throne of Delhi and displayed their ability to change Emperors at will, a series of events led to their downfall.

The deposition of Farrukh Siyar by his ministers was the first in the Mughal dynasty. His subsequent death in captivity made the Sayyids suspect in the eyes of the people. That they had sidelined the existing *Turani* and Irani nobility, abolished the *jiziya* and favoured the Rajputs was cause for quiet resentment among those who held power during Aurangzeb's rule. Jaisingh in Malwa and Ajit Singh at Ajmer governed over a large contiguous part of north India. In these *subahs* cow slaughter was banned and temples were being built and repaired. Lastly, the Sayyids had a cosy relationship with the Marathas. In the Deccan they were already collecting *chauth*, while their request to extend this privilege to Gujarat, Malwa and parts of Varhad was being actively considered. Alam Ali, who was almost like a son to Husain Ali, was guided at Aurangabad by Shankraji Malhar, the former Maratha minister.

The appointment of Muhammad Amin Khan, a cousin of Nizam-ul-mulk, as the second *Bakshi* and the appointment of the Nizam to Malwa were steps taken to appease the old nobility, but in the process they were put in positions of power. When the Nizam was asked to go to Malwa, he asked that he should be allowed to remain there and not moved quickly. Malwa was a crucial province as it was the chief link between Hindustan, or northern India, and the Deccan. After this was accepted, the Nizam moved with his family to Malwa in March 1719. Amin Khan remained in Delhi to discreetly oversee the Nizam's interests.

Husain Ali and Abdullah had to face two rebellions after deposing Farrukh Siyar. The first was at Agra, where a Mughal prince named Neku Siyar, a son of the unfortunate Prince Akbar was released from Agra fort prison by an obscure fortune-teller named Mitr Sen and proclaimed Emperor. Husain Ali marched with an army, laid siege to the fort and captured Neku Siyar. The treasure at Agra was appropriated by Husain Ali. Abdullah Khan came towards Agra with the Emperor Rafi ud daulah but stopped when he heard the fort was taken. On the way back, Rafi ud daulah fell ill and died near Fatehpur Sikri, and a new prince was called from Delhi and enthroned. This was a grandson of Bahadur Shah named Roshan Akhtar, who ascended the throne as Muhammad Shah.

The second revolt was by Chabila Ram, an adherent of Farrukh Siyar, who refused to vacate the fort of Allahabad and move to Awadh. After his death, his nephew Giridhar Bahadur – of whom we shall hear later – led the fight. Ratan Chand was dispatched with an army and using diplomacy rather than force, he succeeded in getting Giridhar Bahadur to hand over the fort and assume charge as the *subedar* of the province of Awadh.

The bickering amongst the two Sayyids led to Husain Ali's decision to take charge of Malwa. The brothers felt the unwieldy Empire would be better managed by such an arrangement. The Nizam was summarily ordered back to Delhi. Simultaneously, Husain Ali sent a force under his kinsman Dilawar Ali Khan to the northern border of Malwa, and wrote to his nephew Alam Ali in the Deccan, to trap the Nizam between their armies.

Under the pretext that he needed more men to face Maratha incursions into Malwa, the Nizam had begun recruiting men for his army. On receiving the recall to Delhi, he dutifully began the journey to Delhi, and then suddenly turned south, crossing the Narmada in early May 1720. The Nizam's first winning move was to gain the garrison of fort Asir gad, north of the river Tapi and considered the 'key to the Deccan'. Next, his officer Ghiyas Khan occupied Burhanpur, south of the Tapi, without a fight.

As a battle with the Nizam seemed inevitable, Abdullah Khan wrote to Shahu asking for help from the Marathas,

> At this time, Nizam-ul-mulk, the dismissed Nazim of *subah* Malwa, due to his adverse destiny, has raised his head from obedience to the Supreme Sanctuary. He has come to the Deccan without orders, and is bound to fail ('he wears the garland of failure'). In view of this, we had urgently written to

you earlier about your joining Alam Ali Khan., Since that seditious person (Nizam) has evil intentions, we are confident that you will join Alam Ali, and give him the fullest help.[2]

Unaware of Balaji Vishwanath's demise, the *Wazir* sent a separate letter to him dated 25 May 1720,

You should yourself take command of the army that may be appointed, and reach the worthy Khan (Alam Ali) with all haste, and block the road of that short-sighted person (Nizam).[3]

Barely two months after assuming the robes of office, on 9 June 1720, Baji rao fulfilled the task asked of his father and met Alam Ali in his camp.[4] The Nizam had decided not to fight in the rains and camped to the east of Burhanpur. There he heard that Sayyid Dilawar Ali Khan had crossed the Narmada and was just twenty-eight miles away. Quickly crossing the Tapi, the Nizam came out to face Dilawar Ali. First, he sent messages of peace that were rebuffed by the hot-headed Sayyid. On 19 June 1720, the two armies met near Khandwa and the battle began in the afternoon with the Nizam's lieutenants Aivaz Khan and Ghiyas Khan in the vanguard. Dilawar Ali personally led the attack on the Nizam's centre when a single bullet found its mark and ended the battle in favour of the Nizam.

In Delhi, as news of the Nizam's victory reached the Sayyids, there was consternation at Dilawar Ali's defeat, and lamentation at the loss of a fine army manned largely by their own clan. Husain Ali's first instinct was to jump on a horse and rush with his army to confront the Nizam. However, soon it was decided that the Nizam should be appeased. A *firman* formally appointing him as Viceroy of the Deccan was drawn up. Husain Ali added his own letter to the *firman*, in which he said Dilawar Ali had been merely sent to escort his own family back to Delhi, but had 'interfered with the Nizam' and 'received what he deserved'.

The *firman* changed the Nizam's status from a rebel to the Emperor's representative. To Husain Ali, the Nizam wrote a friendly letter saying it was Dilawar Khan who attacked him when he had come to the Deccan in order to bring the Maratha raids under control; and ended with, '*my feelings of friendship to you remain unchanged*'.[5]

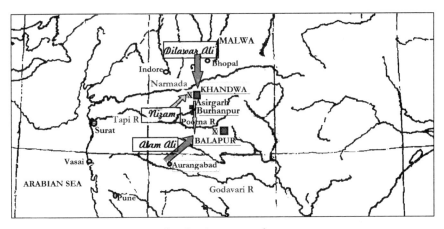

*Battles of Balapur and Khandwa*

The Nizam received the *firman* appointing him to the Deccan and urged
Alam Ali to disband and accept the order. But Alam Ali would not retreat.
The Nizam then moved away from Burhanpur and wrote to Alam Ali that
he intended to go to Mecca and was not interested in power. He made a big
pretence of disbanding his army and moving towards Surat. The Marathas
advised Alam Ali to retreat to Aurangabad or Ahmednagar and await the
arrival of Husain Ali. However, the hot-headed young man considered this
advice a disgrace. Soon the Nizam and Alam Ali, with Marathas in tow, were
camped not far from each other across the river Purna.

In mid-July the Nizam decided to cross the river Purna and finding a
ford near Balapur brought his entire army to the south of the river, camping
at Shegaon. The Marathas with Baji rao, Khande rao Dabhade, Kanhoji
Bhonsle, Shankraji Malhar, and nearly seventeen thousand men, hovered
around the Nizam's camp, attacking his baggage and plundering a treasure
of gold coins.[6]

The battle of Balapur was fought on 10 August 1720. Alam Ali made
fierce charges, all the while looking for the Nizam. In the early part of the
battle the Nizam's centre was broken. Alam Ali was wounded as he fought
from the front. The arrows on his howdah were exhausted and it is said Alam
Ali pulled out those which were sticking out from his wounds to attack his
enemy. His elephant was also hurt and began to flee the battlefield. Turning

round his elephant, Alam Ali exclaimed that it was strange that the Nizam was hiding and did not appear in the thick of battle. Hearing this, suddenly the Nizam rose with his bow and arrow pointed at Alam Ali, and shouted, *'I am Nizam-ul-mulk'!* The arrow found its mark. Alam Ali's head was cut off and sent to the Emperor. Shankraji Malhar died a few days later due to injuries sustained. Mubariz Khan, the Governor of Hyderabad, joined the Nizam. With Alam Ali's death all Mughal officers of the Deccan joined the victorious Nizam. Of Alam Ali's death the *Jangnama* says,

> Friends have told us, clear of mind,
> That on his body, were thirty-six wounds,
> Nine were gashes of spear and sabre,
> He paid no heed to these hurts,
> Fountains of blood began to spurt,
> Came out of the howdah and flowed onward.
> This was one man, they a crowd of thousands,
> In battlefield, the head was severed from its case.[7]

The Nizam made a report to the Emperor mentioning the role of the Marathas in the battle:

> Shankaraji, Baji, the son of Balaji Vishwanath and the Peshwa of Raja Shahu, Khandoji Dabhade *Senapati*, Kanhoji Bhosle, Tukoji Gurjar, Pilaji Jadhav, Davalji Somavamshi, Chimnaji Damodar, Mankoji and other Maratha chiefs were on the left wing of the army. In the battle the guns were soon given up and both sides took to swords. The enemy tried to attack from the left wing. They attacked our rear guard. But they were repulsed. Alam Ali Khan had decided to sacrifice his life. He stood his ground stoutly. Heavy fighting continued for two *gharis*. Our army fought gallantly. The enemy too did not spare any effort. At last the grace of God was on this servant. Alam Ali Khan with some of his chiefs and many of his colleagues was killed. Many were wounded and captured. Shankaraji Malhar was captured alive.[8]

The Nizam's victories at Khandwa and Balapur were a major jolt to the power of the Sayyids. A campaign to subdue the Nizam was needed. Husain Ali decided to lead the army and planned to take friendly Rajput chiefs with him. Accordingly, Husain Ali set out with the Emperor and Amin Khan towards Ajmer. Abdullah Khan remained at Delhi. Hyder Quli Khan, an erstwhile resident of Persia, wormed his way into Husain Ali's confidence and was appointed as chief of the artillery. Sadat Khan, a new comer from Persia and a Shia, had been appointed the *faujdar* of Hindaun, and made a big display of his loyalty.

Amin Khan had to play his part well to save his own life as well as that of the entire *Turani* faction. He began to explore the minds of other nobles and the Emperor. One day, in the *durbar*, Amin Khan spoke to Muhammad Shah in Turki, a language known only to the two of them and hinted at moves to eliminate Husain Ali. When Husain Ali asked the Emperor what Amin Khan had said, the Emperor replied he had just said he had some stomach pain and had to leave. This gave Amin Khan a clue that Muhammad Shah himself was not unfavourable towards a plot against the Sayyids. Amin Khan soon found a willing assassin named Mir Haider Beg who was himself from the Sayyid clan. The plot ripened on the way to Ajmer. The army was camped at Toda Bhim near Hindaun on 7 October 1720 when it was set in motion.

The next morning, just after Hussain Ali had seen off the Emperor to his tent and turned around with Amin Khan, the latter pretended to faint and fell to the ground. Husain Ali arranged to shift him to Hyder Quli Khan's tent. Then Hyder Beg, the chosen assassin, attracted Husain Ali's attention by shouting for justice and saying Amin Khan had embezzled his money. Husain Ali bid him come closer, whereupon he told the guards that he would personally hand over his written complaint against Amin Khan. Husain Ali knew the man by sight and told the guards to allow him to come closer. Taking the written complaint, Husain Ali began reading it, and as his servant gave him the hookah, he turned away from the would-be assassin. Hyder Beg seized the moment, drew a butcher's knife from his waist and stabbed the Sayyid in his side. In his death throes, Husain Ali kicked the assailant to the ground, but Hyder Beg pulled Husain Ali out of his palanquin by his feet and sitting on his chest began to cut off his head. A young cousin of the Sayyid fired at the assassin and killed him. Some Mughal soldiers nearby killed the boy.

Hearing the commotion, Amin Khan emerged from Hyder Quli's tent and saw the dead body of Husain Ali. He rushed to inform Muhammad Shah, bidding him to come and take charge. The Emperor's mother and other women held him back but Sadat Khan, throwing protocol to the winds, rushed in, pulled the Emperor away and brought him to Amin Khan. Muhammad Shah was then forced onto an elephant, while Husain Ali's head was stuck on a long pole for all to see.

A short battle followed. Husain Ali's supporters were cut down and his camp thoroughly plundered. The Sayyid's loyal aide Ratan Chand was roughed up and arrested, but not before he had dispatched a fast camel rider with a note to Abdullah Khan. The news reached the *Wazir* near Agra at midnight, eighteen hours after the murder. He sent a letter of protest to Muhammad Shah and simultaneously picked a new prince to install as Emperor. This was Ibrahim, the elder brother of Rafi ud daulah and Rafi ud darjat. Then, assembling the best army he could, he marched to meet the advancing army of Muhammad Amin Khan.

At Hasanpur near the Yamuna, on 13 November 1720, the battle raged all day, and the next morning, Abdullah Khan had only a thin army of loyal supporters left around him. Ibrahim, the chosen 'Emperor', had already quit the battlefield. Najmudddin Khan, a younger brother of the Sayyids, went in search of Abdullah Khan and *'found him standing on the ground... still fighting like a lion'*. Anguished at the turn of fate, Abdullah Khan called out to him, *'Behold the inconstancy of fortune, and the end of all earthly greatness'*.[1] Just then, Hyder Quli Khan reached the spot and saw the bare-headed *Wazir* surrounded on all sides. Hyder Quli humbly approached Abdullah Khan, *'Was he not a well-wisher, and was not his life one with his? Except to set forth for the presence of the Emperor, what else is left?'* It was indeed the end.

Abdullah mounted the elephant that was brought for him. Hyder Quli Khan threw a shawl to the Sayyid to wrap round his bare head and then conducted his prisoner to Muhammad Shah. Ibrahim was captured and brought before Muhammad Shah who spared his life and sent him to prison.

Muhammad Shah made a grand entry in Delhi and was congratulated by the entire Mughal and Rajput nobility. The old faithful were given gifts, titles, and promotions. Sadat Khan was rewarded with the *subedari* of Agra while Muhammad Khan Bangash was given Allahabad. Haidar Quli Khan, who took the lead in the assassination of Husain Ali, was awarded the *subedari* of Gujarat. Muhammad Shah at this time married Malika zamani, the daughter of Farrukh Siyar, who played a long innings in later Mughal history. Muhammad Amin Khan was appointed the new *Wazir*. He lived just a few months to enjoy his office, dying of an abdominal complaint in January 1721. The huge estate he had collected was passed on to his son Qamruddin. Abdullah Khan was kept in relative comfort in prison till October 1722, when the Mughal faction obtained the Emperor's consent to poison his food and kill him. This was duly done.

The rule of the Sayyids was over. It was time for Nizam-ul-mulk, now the tallest noble in the Mughal realm, to return to Delhi as the new *Wazir*.

༄༅༄༅

## 10. Baji rao Pandit Pradhan : Early Days

'Our fathers in the past did great deeds, if we cannot do them, what use are these glorified ranks and posts? Give us the order. I will bring armies and treasure and place it at the feet of the swami. I will counter the Nizam's threat and campaign in Hindustan....'

- Baji rao Peshwa to Shahu, 1721.[1]

The death of Balaji Vishwanath in April 1720 propelled his elder son Baji rao to his place as the Peshwa. Baji rao Ballal, as he was called, was born in August 1700 and Chimaji was about six or seven years younger.[a] Besides Baji rao and Chimaji Appa, there were two sisters; Anu bai and Bhiu bai. Baji rao was born when his father must have been nearing forty years of age, and becoming a parent for the first time at that age was unusual at the time.

The *Chhatrapati* does not seem to have spent much time in making his choice. Just after the mourning period for Balaji was over, on the fifteenth day, at a place called Masur near Umbraj in Satara district, Baji rao was appointed *Pandit Pradhan*, or the Peshwa, and Chimaji Appa was accorded the title of *Pandit*. There were many elders in the king's court who opposed the decision, and a *haqiqat* or narrative of the time gives Shahu's argument for appointing Baji rao over other aspiring candidates in his court,

> When his father died, Baji rao was twenty years old. Chimaji Appa was about twelve years old. Ambaji Purandare was the *karbhari*. ..... At this time Baji rao met the king at Satara. The appointment of the Peshwa was discussed. At that time Baji rao was of an arrogant disposition, constantly immersed in soldiering, with no patience that is needed to run a Government. So, many advised Shahu that he was not suitable for the post of Peshwa. After hearing them all, the king replied, 'Balaji Vishwanath put his life and all his hard work into sustaining this kingdom but did not live to enjoy the

---

a.   The etymology for the suffix 'Ballal' is explained by a look at the Peshwas who were known by this name. So, Baji rao, Madhav rao and Narayan rao had 'Ballal' after their names as their father's name was 'Balaji'. Similarly 'pant' signifies a Brahmin clerk or karkun, while 'rao' signifies a person with martial pretensions.

fruit. Hence for now, I will award the post to him (Baji rao). If his fortune is good, the Lord Sri Shambhu will bless him. If it is found he is of no use, we can rethink later.' In this manner, praying to the Lord, the king gave the robes of the appointment to *Raosaheb*.[a] Chimaji Appa was honoured and given the robes of the *Diwan*. [2]

Jadunath Sarkar, the eminent historian of the twentieth century, writes,

> When Baji rao, a youth of nineteen, was appointed by Shahu as Peshwa in succession to his father, it was not really a case of hereditary succession to offices, which had now become a fixed practice in the Maratha kingdom. Young Baji rao had given evidence of his precocious ability in his father's campaigns, and Shahu was a good judge of character, who followed the wise rule of choosing the ablest instruments and allowing them full initiative without himself interfering...[3]

True to his nature, Baji rao did not tarry at Satara. He left for Khandesh where the confrontation between the Nizam and Alam Ali loomed large. The war had resulted in a drop in revenue. A letter from Khandesh said,

> Qilich Khan has come to Burhanpur. He has won Asir gad. .. Khandesh has changed. No *taka* is to be had. God has disturbed this season of collecting large amounts as revenue. The (Peshwa's) army must reach soon, else the strategy will suffer.[4]

Baji rao met Alam Ali on 9 June and promised him help. However, the battle ended badly for Alam Ali and Baji rao was back in Satara in early September 1720. In October 1720, Husain Ali was assassinated. The news reached the Maratha envoy Malhar Dadaji Barve in Delhi and within a week he wrote to Ambaji Purandare to act and take advantage of the situation. He wrote,

> While we waited for a treaty through the Sayyid, came news that Amin Khan killed Husain Ali Khan. This district is ours...if the treaty happens soon it is good. But make sure that success does not slip away.[5]

However, it was not yet time to take up distant campaigns. The Mughal collectors of the Deccan had to be tamed. The upheaval at Delhi led to minor skirmishes around Pune and Satara during collection of revenue. Thus, in Baramati, in a battle in December 1720, a son of Krishnaji Dabhade was

---

a.  Baji rao

killed.[6] Ranoji Scindia fought the *Bhils* and lost some horses. The Nizam arrived in the Deccan. His lieutenants Aivaz Khan at Burhanpur, Ghiyas Khan at Aurangabad and Mubariz Khan at Hyderabad began a concerted effort to stop the Marathas from collecting the revenues promised by Husain Ali Khan. The *sanad*s from the Emperor were thrown to the winds. The Nizam blocked them at every stage. Even when the Nizam left for Delhi as the next *Wazir*, these three officers continued to resist Maratha efforts in the Deccan.

In this manner, the year 1720 was spent skirmishing for control in areas from Khandesh to the Tungabhadra. In the last months of the year Baji rao convinced Shahu to give him a free hand to negotiate with the Nizam, and take up the task of advancing Maratha interests in the north. On 4 January 1721 therefore, Baji rao met the Nizam for the first time at Chikhalthan near Chalisgaon. The meeting was reported as 'successful' and Baji rao was congratulated by his mother Radha bai as well as Shahu.[7] The young Peshwa was keen to understand what the Nizam proposed and the meeting helped him gauge his opponent.

The first murmuring of a caste divide among Brahmins in Shahu's large family began with the appointments of Balaji Vishwanath and Baji rao as the Peshwa. Balaji Vishwanath had migrated from the Konkan coastal strip and belonged to a sub-caste named *Kokanastha* or *Chitpavan*. The *Deshastha* Brahmins who attained positions of power in the Maratha court hailed from the plateau to the east of the Sahyadri mountain range. These two communities, speaking the same language and hailing from contiguous regions had however, startlingly different appearances and behavioural patterns, many of which persist to the present day. Although there were other castes like the *Prabhu*s, *Shenvi*s and Marathas in the government, the Brahmins held many of the key posts.

The Peshwa and the *Pratinidhi* were naturally placed in adversarial positions due to their appointments. The Peshwa had been the Prime Minister in the eight-member Cabinet in the reign of the first two monarchs. In Rajaram's reign, the *Pratinidhi* emerged as a parallel power centre. Besides, Balaji Vishwanath Peshwa was *Kokanastha*, and Shripat rao *Pratinidhi* was a *Deshastha* Brahmin. These two therefore came to lead rival caste factions in Shahu's court. In early days, Balaji was among the very few who hailed from the Konkan. But soon, many of his kinsmen began to come to Satara in search of better prospects. The Bhanu, Mehandale, Patwardhan, Joshi, Barve and other families that came from the Konkan soon rose to positions of influence and power. The sudden rise of the *Kokanastha*s in affairs of state led to mutual jealousy that persisted for many decades after.

In those early days, the divisions within Shahu's court are described in the Chitnis *bakhar*. Shripat rao *Pratinidhi* and Baji rao had a sharp difference of opinion in Shahu's court and the king ruled in favour of the path advocated by Baji rao.

> Shripat rao *Pratinidhi* said, 'We have an agreement with the *paatshah* and the Nizam, whose army is here. If we break the peace, we will be saddled with a campaign and a war. The swami (Shahu) is keen to conquer Hindustan, and it will be done. But first, let us conquer the Carnatic which the senior Maharaj (Shivaji) had already achieved in part. Then we can turn northwards.'

> To this, Baji rao answered, 'How does the *Pratinidhi* suggest such a course of action? The *paatshahi* is weak, has no life left in it. Many disputes exist. The *paatshah* desires to preserve his rule with our help. While doing this, we should resolve the disputes. We ought to take our *swarajya* to newer regions. Qilich Khan is nearby, and breaking an agreement will cause a clash, (but) why should we take any account of him? Then, how can we rule and govern? Aurangzeb took the *subah* of Daulatabad, and later brought Bijapur and Bhaganagar under his rule. When Sambhaji lost the kingdom, Aurangzeb took both the kingdoms and caused a fatal situation (for us). The Maharaj (Shahu) was imprisoned by him. He took the entire kingdom, brought an army of two hundred thousand from Delhi and stayed here. Rajaram fought from Ginjee. When Ginjee fell, he came here, attacked Aurangabad and enforced his rule. The kingdom that was lost, by the grace of God, has been regained. The swami returned from the *paatshah*, employed good people and began to help the *paatshah*.

> Our fathers in the past did great deeds, if we cannot do them, what use are these glorified ranks and posts? Give us the order. I will bring armies and treasure and place it at the feet of the swami. I will counter the Nizam's threat and campaign in Hindustan. I will complete both the tasks. The Carnatic is not with the *paatshahi*. Bijapur and Bhaganagar have already been threatened by us. These conflicts are within our own house. Dispatching the *Huzurat* and some senior chiefs will easily complete the task there. Let

the *Pratinidhi* handle it. The senior Maharaj's (Shivaji's) wish to capture Hindustan remains incomplete. It is for this purpose that the swami has risen to power. The *paatshah* is calling us for help these days. Therefore this task must be taken up and completed. Balaji *pant* Nana (Balaji Vishwanath) had already been in touch with the kings of Hindustan for this very purpose. The Maharaj's fame is such that what he desires will be implemented. So it is the best time to implement this strategy now.'

Shahu replied, 'It is appropriate that you are Balaji *pant*'s son. With such men in my service I can take the boundaries beyond the Himalayas into the land of the *kinnara*s. Then what is difficult in this campaign? You go to Hindustan! The chiefs here and the army will manage the Nizam if he indulges in any excess, and we can invade the Carnatic.' [1]

The long discussion set the direction for future course of action by the Maratha chiefs and the Peshwa.  Baji rao's later actions show that he acted on what he said in Shahu's court and concentrated on expansion towards the north.

A later poet encapsulates Baji rao's statement,

> 'Just one strike with an axe,
> Will cut the foot of the tree at Delhi,
> With an awl the trunk will splinter to pieces,
> Then the branches will easily fall in one's hands'. [8]

In 1722, Baji rao campaigned in Malwa, the province sought by many including the Nizam and Sawai Jaisingh. Baji rao met the Nizam at Bolasha and later sent a small army to help him fight the Nawab of Bhopal. After the monsoon months, he burst into Malwa in 1723 with Malharji Holkar and a twelve-thousand-strong army. He had been in secret communications with Sawai Jaisingh of Amber and with Nandlal Mandloi, a *chaudhary* of Indore. Securing help from disaffected local elements, Baji rao advanced and defeated Azimullah Khan, the *subedar* of Malwa, who was also a cousin of the Nizam. The capital city of Ujjain was plundered. Before returning to Satara, he campaigned in western Malwa and adjoining parts of Gujarat, giving him firsthand knowledge of the terrain and river crossings in the region, besides helping to consolidate Maratha presence in the region. [9]

Knowing that the old order would not heartily support him, Baji rao looked for support elsewhere. Besides Pilaji Jadhav rao and Udaji Pawar, he found support in young and dynamic men like Malharji Holkar and Ranoji Scindia; and it was with their help that his future plans were crowned with success.

Pilaji Jadhav rao was senior to Baji rao, and had helped Balaji in his first struggle with Chandrasen Jadhav. No relation to Dhanaji Jadhav, Pilaji is sometimes considered a mentor to the young Baji rao. He was from Wagholi, north of Pune and also had a *wadi* near the fort of Purandar where he later built a small fort. In 1724 for some reason Shahu ordered the confiscation of Pilaji's estates and confined him for a while. Later Pilaji accompanied Baji rao and Chimaji on almost all their campaigns.

Udaji Pawar was from an old family that had served the Maratha cause since the capture of Torna fort in 1647. Serving under all the Maratha kings, the family was a large one in the early eighteenth century. Of the various branches, Udaji began early by attacking the Mughal posts at Mandavgad (or Mandu) in 1709. In 1718-9, he was part of Balaji Vishwanath and Khande rao Dabhade's army that went to Delhi.[10] He captured some posts in Gujarat over which he had a few clashes with another chief named Pilaji Gaekwad. In 1722, he came into prominence when Baji rao Peshwa awarded him half the *mokasa*[a] of Malwa.

Ranoji Scindia's family came from Kanherkhed, a village near Satara. He was the son of Jankoji. Ranoji began as an ordinary soldier and was noticed by Balaji Vishwanath who promoted him to be a *khijmatdar*. His progress continued in Baji rao's era and he was given charge of a '*paga*' or command of a cavalry unit and finally became a chief.

Malharji Holkar was born near Pune in 1693. As a child he went to Khandesh where he grew up and took up employment with Kadam Bande – another distinguished name among Maratha leaders of those early days. Malharji joined Balaji Vishwanath's army going to Delhi, where Baji rao first saw him with his men.

Holkar was bold and irreverent from his early days. During the Delhi

---

a.   The balance of *chauth* after the deduction of the king's share.

campaign, it was ordered that farms in a village will not be touched. However, Malharji's men entered the field, cut the corn and gave it to their horses. The matter reached the Peshwa. Baji rao was sent to attend to the matter and he beat one of the culprits with a stick. Malhar was sitting outside his tent twining a rope. From there, he abused Baji rao and threw a lump of wet mud on him. *'Are you giving us pay that you are beating us with a stick?'* he demanded of Baji rao. The next day hearing that the Peshwa had plans to castigate him, he left all his horses in the camp, burnt his tents, applied ash on the body and with his men went and sat atop a hill. Balaji Vishwanath then collected the horses, called his men back and gave them clothes.[11]

On the way back from Delhi, Baji rao was sitting by a stream. Having bathed, he was sitting in the shade having his food. Malharji appeared with five hundred troopers from the forest. Sitting on his horse, he placed his lance on Baji rao's chest. *'The other day I threw a lump of mud at you. Now should I pass this lance through your body? Is there anybody here who can save you?'* Baji rao rose, brought Holkar down from his horse and praised his swordsmanship. *'In each battle,'* said Baji rao, *'I saw your flashing sword. Come join me for lunch'.* Holkar said, *'Your mind is not clear about me , how can I sit for a meal with you?'* Then Baji rao said, *'I take an oath on this food,'* and touched the food; *'the next time we campaign, you will have a command of five thousand horse.'*

In a letter seeking employment with the Peshwa in 1721 Malharji says, *'wherever the master keeps me I will stay without protest. (But) the master who employs the servant must treat him with respect'.*[12] In the years to come, Malharji proved a dependable aide for Baji rao and served the Maratha state for over four decades.

Besides these loyal aides, Baji rao had other associates like Avaji Kavade and Baji Bhivrao Rethrekar who figured prominently in many battles. Baji Bhivrao was named after the Peshwa and had a younger brother named Chimnaji. The two brothers fought loyally in Maratha armies from the Konkan to the *doab* of the Ganga and Yamuna.

But above all, Baji rao depended on his brother Chimaji Appa. Chimaji in the initial period was with Shahu at Satara. The reason was two-fold. The need to represent the Peshwa at the king's court was an important function.

But the unstated need was to keep track of the varied moves to turn the king's mind against the Peshwa. A member of the Peshwa family was always at Satara, besides trusted associates like the sons of Khando Ballal and Ambaji Purandare.

With the death of *Wazir* Amin Khan in February 1721, Muhammad Shah asked the Nizam to come and take over the post. Unwilling to leave his interests in the Deccan, Gujarat and Malwa, the Nizam tried to avoid the move. However, in October 1721, he had to move to Delhi. His heart was not in the job and he did not like the easygoing Muhammad Shah. Leaving Mubariz Khan in Hyderabad and Aivaz Khan in the Khandesh region, the Nizam once again left the Deccan. In the Nizam's absence, Mubariz Khan resisted Maratha collection of revenue and the *sanad*s awarding the six *subah*s to Shahu remained worthless.

It was becoming clear that it would only be by strength of arms that the Mughals would concede the demand for *chauth* and the young Peshwa began to prepare for the inevitable struggle that was to follow.

# II. Nizam's 'Fateh' at Sakharkherda

> '*Shahmatpanah* Baji rao, *Tahavvur dastagah* Sultanji, *Jaladat intibah* Pilaji performed extremely well to destroy the enemy. Their prowess in war was a reflection of your love…'
>
> -Nizam-ul-mulk's letter to Shahu, October 1724.[1]

The Nizam was called to Delhi as the new *Wazir*, but was preoccupied in the Carnatic area, and his arrival in Delhi was delayed. Much older than the other Mughal nobles, the Nizam arrived in Delhi with plenty of pageantry, and took over as the new *Wazir*. He found the Mughal court in disarray with rival factions conspiring against each other. Ajit Singh of Jodhpur at this time once again took the town of Ajmer, representing to the Emperor that he had given up Gujarat but Ajmer ought to be left in his charge.[2] No expedition could be sent against him with the Khan Dauran Samsam-ud-daulah and Qamruddin Khan quarrelling with each other, and the treasury quite empty.

Described as '*a man of much gravity, of a reserved behaviour, but also fond of power*', the Nizam advised the Emperor to '*assume in public an air of gravity and seriousness, to correct his morals*' and so on. The Emperor did not relish this advice.[3] With each passing day, the Nizam grew increasingly uneasy in the Delhi court and longed for the independence he enjoyed in the Deccan.

The Nizam effected another reshuffle in the provinces; Sadat Khan being put in charge of Awadh while Giridhar Bahadur was shifted to Malwa and Sawai Jaisingh placed as Governor of Agra. Hyder Quli Khan, who had challenged the Nizam, was dismissed from Gujarat. The Nizam himself set out for Gujarat in November 1722 to assume charge. The Nizam's march so affected Hyder Quli Khan that he ran away to Delhi. The Nizam placed his uncle Hamid Khan there as *subedar*. He then removed Giridhar Bahadur who had spent barely a year in Malwa and appointed his cousin Azimullah Khan before heading back for Delhi. On the way, taking some Maratha troops along, he chastised Dost Muhammad Khan of Bhopal for having helped Dilawar Ali against him in 1720.

In the years 1722 and 1723, Baji rao was always on the move in Khandesh, Malwa and Gujarat countering Mughal moves. In February 1723, he met Aivaz Khan and the Nizam for the second time at Bolasha.[4,a] While the Nizam returned to Delhi, Baji rao came back to the Deccan. The outcome of the meeting is not recorded and can only be surmised from the future course of events. Shahu's envoy Anand rao Sumant also met the Nizam and Mubariz Khan.

Soon, Muhammad Shah became known for a life of ease, earning the sobriquet *Rangeela* or colourful. Besides hunting, good wine, dance and music, the Emperor also enjoyed idle talk with frivolous young men, and did not give the Empire the attention it deserved. The Nizam, from the old school, wanted the Emperor to commit time and energy to the administration.

A new twist in the politics at the Mughal court appeared when Rahim-un-nissa, later called Kuki Jiu,[b] worked her way into the fancy of Qudsia Begum, the Emperor's mother. A bright daughter of a geomancer named Jan Muhammad, the girl gained such influence that she was given Muhammad Shah's writing desk and private signet. She undersigned various petitions that she took with her to the seraglio and soon became a power unto herself. She also recited poems about the decadence at the Mughal court, and one of these said,

> The sceptre of command has now passed from the Imperial cocks to the hens,
> And there is between them a contest for superiority and power.
>
> Possibly we may see the foolish fellow's bucler dance in a fit of intoxication,
> And women exchange their *dhol* for his flaming sabre.[5]

The Nizam's efforts to reform the Emperor and shift his focus to the business of governance brought scorn and contemptuous remarks from the Emperor's favourites. Kuki Jiu was often behind these moves, and the Nizam in anger is said to have composed a satirical poem that ended with, *'today a filthy woman is in the place of Alamgir'*.[6,c] The fifty-year-old Nizam's 'old school' manners were a source of amusement to the young men in the court. A simple matter of bowing to the Emperor was ridiculed.

---

a. Bolasha : Co ordinates 22⁰ 53' 11" N, 74⁰ 52' 58" E.

b. Means 'Madam foster sister' of the Emperor.

c. Aurangzeb.

The *Siyar-ul-Mutaqherin* describes it,

> Nizam-ul-mulk always dressed in the ancient mode, with a *jubba*, or short surcoat with short sleeves over his *jama*, always made his obeisance to the Emperor in the old-fashioned manner used at the late Aurangzeb's court, to wit, thrusting both hands into the opposite sleeves of his *jama* and carrying them both upon the navel, and then inclining the body at the same time, profoundly. This Chinese or Tartarian obeisance was ridiculed by the courtiers of Muhammad Shah's palace, who liked only the Hindustani manner, to wit, putting the four fingers of the right hand upon the forehead, and inclining the body very low. So that when Nizam-ul-mulk came to court with his three old-fashioned bows, he was sneered at by the young courtiers, who used to point to him with the finger and say: 'Look at the old baboon of Deccan; look how he dances', – a raillery which doubtless gave more offence than would have done his dismission from the high office.[7,a]

Soon the Nizam began to wish he was someplace else and looked to find a way to go back to the Deccan. The Emperor however, sent him to Awadh instead. The Nizam therefore left Delhi by the end of 1723 heading

---

a. Tilak Das, a chronicler of those times, puts the history of Muhammad Shah in a poem, and to the Nizam's insult here, he attributes the later tragedies of the Mughal Empire.

'Once a week all men did homage to the king,
Each, in his own fashion, always used to come.
When the noble, Nizam-ul-mulk, came before the king,
On seeing him the king forthwith laughed, looking on him as his servant:
Look you, how with a monkey's gait he comes,
Adorned with a nice, pretty-coloured green turban.
Seeing his strange gait, they burst into hoarse laughter.
His shoes sounded nicely 'thump, thump.'
The king declared, 'Many come, but no one's walk has so delighted me.
A great noble, he looks like a black monkey;
On seeing him my heart o'erflows with joy.
He is noble and great, he looks like a black monkey;
To a him is a pleasure, know this is my delight,
No other noble is so lovely, he goes tinkle-tinkle, his gait is a joy to behold.
See, clever one, the shining of the lamp-black on his eyes,
He sounds like drum-beating, how he jingles as he goes,
Such is this noble, named Nizam-ul-mulk,
He who is called the greatest of all the nobles.'[8]

Tilak Das says the Nizam nursed this wounded pride for long and called the Persian king Nadir Shah to punish the Mughals. (see Ch. 29.)

for Moradabad saying the air of Delhi did not suit him. He sent a stream of reassuring messages to Delhi, even as he changed direction for Agra. As soon as he reached Ujjain the Nizam threw away all pretence of where he was headed.

In February itself, seeing the Nizam's rebellious attitude, the Emperor appointed Mubariz Khan as Viceroy of the Deccan. Mubariz was a man of sixty by then, an old man by the standards of the age. However, he was a veteran in the south and was vehemently opposed to any move by the Marathas to collect *chauth*. Chandrasen Jadhav, working for him, had raided Maratha territory in 1722.[9]

The Deccan was in for a few turbulent years. A mixed picture of Marathas skirmishing with Mubariz Khan's men while talking to the Nizam's officers emerges from the correspondence of the time. A battle for possessing the Deccan was in the offing and the situation was still quite fluid. Baji rao remained in touch with the Nizam and his aide Aivaz Khan from 1723 onwards.[10] Meeting opposing rival chiefs without adequate safeguards was fraught with danger in those times as the niceties of diplomatic immunity were not always followed. A letter from his father-in-law at this time asks Baji rao to be on his guard when visiting Aivaz Khan.[11] One letter mentions a clash near Tasgaon with the Mughals.[12] Chimaji Appa met Turktaz Khan at Kharadi[a] while Holkar and Ranoji Scindia were hovering near the Godavari.[13]

Once Muhammad Shah learnt that the Nizam had reached Aurangabad, he sent him a soothing message that Mubariz Khan had only been appointed to the Deccan since he was headed towards Muradabad, and if the Nizam had communicated his wish to go the Deccan, it would have been granted. These messages had no effect on both the Nizam and Mubariz Khan who prepared for a trial of strength. A battle became inevitable. The Nizam had already obtained support from Sawai Jaisingh, Chhatrasal Bundela and some Maratha chiefs.

The Emperor and his court threw their weight behind Mubariz Khan. Muhammad Shah sent a letter to Shahu seeking Maratha help to defeat the

---

a.   Near Aurangabad

Nizam. Shahu and Baji rao took this opportunity to once more press their claims on the Deccan as well as Gujarat and Malwa. A long list of demands was sent to the Emperor in return for help to put down the Nizam.[14] The wish list helps us understand what the Marathas were fighting for at this time. Broadly, compared to the agreement of 1718, Shahu sought exemption from paying a tribute, grant of Gujarat, Malwa and Tanjore, the restoration of seven forts including Shivneri and Miraj, that the protection to Sambhaji of Kolhapur be withdrawn, and fifty lakh rupees be paid by the Emperor for Maratha assistance. The demands were considered too high and not accepted by the Emperor.

Since Mubariz Khan had been rigidly opposing Maratha rights in the Deccan after the fall of Husain Ali, and the Nizam had more or less the same policy, Shahu himself was confused about where his army should go. His envoy Anand rao Sumant first met Aivaz Khan. After he did the groundwork, it was time for Baji rao's meeting with the Nizam.

Baji rao left Satara in January 1724, crossed the Narmada, and reached Nalchha, where he met the Nizam on 18 May.[15] In this third meeting in three years since 1720, many unrecorded discussions took place between the two; one, an experienced and crafty General and the other, an ambitious man of twenty-three. It appears that a decision was taken to help the Nizam and extract concessions from him at the meeting.

The Nizam, on his part, believed he had obtained the cooperation of the Marathas. In a conversation with his *Bakshi* Muhatsham Khan, he said,

> I have won over these people (Marathas). Otherwise they were the zamindars of this country. The Emperor Alamgir with his immense army and the expenditure of the entire treasure of Hindustan could not defeat them. Many families were ruined and no benefit came out of this campaign. I have made them faithful and obedient to me through diplomacy.[16]

It was to be another couple of years before he was to be disabused of this notion.

While Baji rao was busy in Malwa, Shahu was annoyed that the Peshwa had not met him despite sending him summons. Calling Baji rao 'lazy' and 'negligent', Shahu reprimanded him for not taking adequate care to protect the kingdom. Shahu added,

> In future, if I find you are unable to deliver, I will have to rethink my decision (to appoint as Peshwa). You will find that day difficult and you will run around; hence this admonition. Your late father served us loyally and the result is for you to assess.[17]

The letter gives an idea of the relations between the monarch and his Peshwa, who until then, was not entirely trusted and continued in office due to the good work of his father Balaji Vishwanath. Baji rao had to spend time away from Satara but Shahu expected a personal visit, which was not always possible. With many opponents in the *durbar*, men like Ambaji Purandare, Chimaji Appa and even the veteran Khando Ballal at Satara were thus engaged in removing some of Shahu's apprehensions about the new Peshwa.

The Emperor, at this stage, supported Mubariz Khan. He reappointed Giridhar Bahadur to Malwa in place of the Nizam's appointee. Nobody yet knew what the Marathas planned to do. While Baji rao had met the Nizam, Kanhoji Bhonsle had offered help to Mubariz Khan.[18] However, Shahu wrote to Kanhoji to stay away.[19]

Once the Nizam reached the river Tapi, the adversaries began moves to acquire an advantage. Depending on his deputy Aivaz Khan to hold Aurangabad for him, Mubariz made the first move from Hyderabad to Burhanpur. This gave an opening to the Nizam to take Aurangabad. Aivaz Khan openly declared his support to the Nizam and welcomed him to the city in July 1724. Mubariz therefore left Burhanpur and marched south towards Aurangabad. Baji rao in turn, wrote to his brother Chimaji to go to Burhanpur and stay strongly entrenched there.[20] Mubariz was thus between Maratha forces at Burhanpur and the Nizam at Aurangabad.

The Nizam, as was his wont, now wrote to Mubariz of the inadvisability of infighting as both served the Emperor and would shed the blood of fellow Muslims.[21] Mubariz paid scant attention to these messages and gathered all the Nawabs of the Deccan under his banner. He began approaching Aurangabad from the east, hoping to surprise the Nizam. On a thundery day in raging monsoon rain, the Nizam advanced from Aurangabad with Baji rao. Seeing the city undefended, Mubariz Khan turned west and made a dash to capture it. In early September, he was intercepted by the Nizam at the village of Sakharkherda,[a] about one hundred and forty kilometres from Aurangabad, and they blocked each other's paths. The monsoon months were thus spent by the protagonists in jostling for a better position.

With the end of rains, the battle was joined on 30 September 1724 near Sakharkherda. Mubariz advanced and attacked Aivaz Khan. A pitched battle was fought. By late afternoon Mubariz's sons, Asad Khan and Masaud Khan, were killed. Mubariz lost heart and said,

> Thanks be to the Almighty, from my first youth until now, I have never been defeated; wounds and death are our portion, to die unshrinking on the battlefield is our salvation; Asad and Masaud have gone from this earth; of what longer use is my valour? [22]

By the end of the day, Mubariz was dead on his elephant. The victory of the Nizam was complete. Complimenting Baji rao, the Nizam honoured him with an elephant and jewellery besides the command of 7000 *zat* and 7000 *swar*, effectively meaning he was a first-class sardar paid to maintain a cavalry and an army of 7000 each. The Nizam wrote the entire narrative of the battle to Shahu and ended with,

> *Shahmatpanah*[b] Baji rao, *Tahavvur dastagah*[c] Sultanji (Nimbalkar), *Jaladat intibah*[d] Pilaji (Jadhav) performed extremely well to destroy the enemy. Their prowess in war was a reflection of your love…[1]

The Nizam also appeased Muhammad Shah with sweet words. The Emperor accepted the fait accompli. Wrote the victorious Nizam,

> Mubariz Khan, infatuated by the dotage incident to old age, having taken the resolution of advancing hostilely towards Aurungabad at the head of a body of regular troops, (who had strayed from the 'path of gratitude), about 25,000 horse, and an innumerable host of Carnatic infantry—it was in vain that I remonstrated with him upon so improper a proceeding. In vain was it that I exhorted him against engaging in a seditious enterprise that could not

---

a.  20° 13' N., 76° 27' E.                    b.  The epitome of bravery.
c.  Best of braves.                           d.  Who knows bravery.

but be fatal in its consequences to many true believers, as well as infidels. Disregarding my authority and his own duty, he persisted in his design, and with his own life sacrificed the lives of three and thirty other gallant and distinguished noblemen.

Of the particulars of this bloody action (the parallel of which no age has produced) Your Majesty will no doubt have been fully apprised. As to the rest, it being my duty to obey Your Majesty's orders, let it be communicated to me wherein I can execute your royal pleasure. Having represented what was proper, I conclude.[23]

From the time of this victory, the Nizam became virtually independent. To commemorate his victory, he renamed Sakharkherda as *Fateh*-kherda. He also shifted his capital from Aurangabad to Hyderabad at this time, putting some distance between himself and the Maratha territories.

Having obtained Maratha help in this crucial battle, the Nizam believed he had finally mastered the Maratha 'problem'. Speaking to his officers he said,

I consider all this army (Marathas) as my own and I will get work done through them. It is necessary to take our hands off Malwa. God willing I will enter into an understanding with them and entrust the *mulkhgiri* on that side of the Narmada to them.[24]

The Nizam settled in the Deccan and his dynasty at Hyderabad properly began after his victory at Sakharkherda. Baji rao, after four years of constant campaigning, was gaining in maturity and stature. The stage was set for a prolonged rivalry in the Deccan. For now, the two protagonists circled each other, like two pugilists in what would be a long match.

# 12. Kanhoji Angre's War in the Konkan

'What to write on these things, we are at a great loss... we think you should take the best care you can to preserve these estates.'

- EI Co., London, to the Governor of Mumbai.[1]

In early eighteenth century, four powers jostled for control of India's western sea coast. The Portuguese at Goa and at Vasai in north Konkan, Kanhoji Angre from his sea forts Colaba and Vijaydurg, the English from the island of Mumbai, and the Siddi who operated from the island fort of Janjira and a large stretch along the coast including the erstwhile Maratha capital Raigad. The English were a late entrant, having secured Mumbai when Portuguese princess Catherine of Braganza married Charles II of England and brought the marshy rocky group of islands as dowry. In 1675, Mumbai was awarded to the East India Company. Until well into the eighteenth century however, the Portuguese remained the chief power in the Konkan, and were somewhat derisively called the '*Firangis*'. The region they occupied was called *Firangan*.

The word '*Firangi*' probably originated from the Franks, and came via Arabic and Persian to India. It referred to Europeans, of which the Portuguese were the first to come, and generally came to be associated with them. There was a contemptuous quality in the word as used in India and it was considered a derogatory reference to the Portuguese. From *Firangi*, arose the word '*Firangan*', meaning the land ruled by the *Firangis*.

The Portuguese came to India in 1500 CE, took the port of Kochi and gradually worked their way up the coast so that they became masters of large swathes of India's western coast, displacing existing small kingdoms, tribal kings and so on. The entire sixteenth century was one of uninterrupted growth for the Portuguese, and after a few decades of peaceful administration the ugly aspects of their rule comprising the Inquisition and forcible conversion of people as well as destruction of temples and mosques in the coastal region became a prominent feature.

The chief centre of the Portuguese remained Goa, but northwards they had strong forts all over the Konkan up to Gujarat. The strongest was at Vasai, at the north end of the mouth of a creek through which the river Ulhas joins the Arabian Sea.

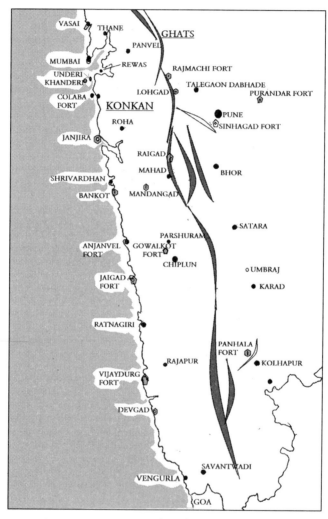

Map of Konkan

Until challenged at sea by the English in 1612, the Portuguese pretty much had their way. The Haj pilgrim ships in the reign of Emperor Akbar had to obtain a Portuguese *cartez* to ply unmolested in the Arabian Sea.[2]

The advent of Maratha rule under *Chhatrapati* Shivaji was to be the first real threat to the Portuguese in India. The last decade of Shivaji's life was one of continuous war in the Konkan to push back the *Firangis*. Kalyan was captured, and that is where began the work of building a Maratha navy to challenge Portuguese domination at sea. The Portuguese demand for a passport to ply the Indian seas became a sore point for most seafaring vessels. In course of time, the Maratha navy found its feet and began to enforce passports issued by them. Just a year before his death, Shivaji captured the island of Khanderi that became an important base at the mouth of Mumbai harbour for the Angres later on. The Siddis took the neighbouring island of Underi a year later and it remained with them till 1759 when the Marathas took it.

The next twenty years saw many battles between the Marathas, Portuguese, Siddi and the Mughals; even the Arabs of Muscat attacked the Portuguese-ruled island of Sashti[a] next to Mumbai and took prisoners. The Arabs were expert seamen and their enmity with the Portuguese flared up over the issue of giving passports to other vessels. For a while the Marathas recruited Arabs for their cause and used them to attack the Portuguese. People in the Konkan were often the victims in these struggles that were part economic and partly fed by religious fervour.

In 1713, Kanhoji Angre headed the Maratha navy, and there were intermittent battles between him and the Portuguese. After Kanhoji's treaty with Balaji Vishwanath, he secured the help of the Maratha king and Peshwa. The northern *Firangan* that stretched from Sashti to the port of Daman, an uninterrupted stretch of nearly one hundred and seventy kilometres, remained under Portuguese occupation. Although the Peshwa received many complaints about Portuguese harassment, until the 1730s, he had no opportunity to look into these matters. Ramchandra Chaskar Joshi had taken Kalyan in 1720 from the *Firangis* and among the Hindus living there, the Anjurkar family was in the forefront of the battle to liberate the Konkan from the Portuguese.

The Portuguese and the English in those early years were collaborators as well as competitors. However, an effective combine against the Marathas

---

a. Sashti comes from *sahasasht*, or sixty-six, the island of sixty-six villages, styled Salcette by the western traders.

never came into being. Matters continued in this state for another decade, before the Marathas could intervene in a decisive manner.

The English in Mumbai were at the time mainly interested in trade and securing a *firman* from the Mughal Emperor and local Governors had cost them a lot of money. Having secured it, they felt they ought to be allowed to trade without any disturbance. However, the country was torn by war and it was difficult to be neutral in those turbulent times. The Marathas on the mainland were a market and also a source for supplies, while the Mughal armies were still able to threaten the traders. The Portuguese were neighbours, being in possession of the island of Sashti. The Marathas could get to Mumbai either through Sashti, or through a wide creek. The Siddi had a colony at the village of Mazgaon and was known to threaten the English settlement at the southern end of Mumbai. The castle of Mumbai was poorly defended with walls barely eleven feet high. The complicated situation led to Mumbai asking for guidance from London, but the Company's Directors confessed their inability to give any advice. In a letter of 1713, they recommended discretion and bribery,

> ..what to write on these things, we are at a great loss..we think you should take the best care you can to preserve these estates, and if you can by private methods and at an easy charge recommend the English to the new Mughal, you may do it, but in such a manner that if a superior power should know what you have done,… lest this provoke them and force you to buy your peace with a second and much larger *peshkash*.[1]

Kanhoji had in his possession the island of Khanderi off Mumbai, given to him by Shahu in 1713, that the English claimed was part of Catherine's dowry. The English labelled him a pirate, while Shahu titled him as the *Sarkhel* or Admiral of the Maratha navy. Kanhoji had at this time demanded that the English obtain a *dastak*, or passport, to ply the seas and trade from the western coast. Papering over differences and deep-rooted animosity, a treaty was signed with the English in 1713.[3] The English began hiring local vessels to carry their freight to avoid paying Kanhoji's levies. Kanhoji argued that country crafts hired by the English would be captured if they did not have his *dastak*. This led to yet another war.

In 1715, a vigorous Governor named Charles Boone was appointed at Mumbai and he began the construction of a defensive wall and the building of new frigates. The Portuguese signed a treaty to support him, but eventually did not do so. Angre captured some English ships in 1718, and Boone felt he was strong enough to declare a war on Angre and even plan an attack on the Angre sea-fort Vijaydurg. At the same time he wrote to Kanhoji,

> The condition of my Government is to observe the orders and interest of my sovereign and Rt. Hon. Company, and in this again, yours is different from us, since though you acknowledge a prince (Shahu), who is actually in peace with us, you act in opposition thereto, following the dictates of your ambition....[4]

The letter emphasises the dual nature of the Maratha state and the relations between the sovereign and his confederates – who did not entirely follow the king's orders, and also acted on their own account. Kanhoji, first pronounced *Sarkhel* as early as 1698, had always followed a policy of opposing the English, and his alliance with Shahu in 1713 was not sufficient reason to deviate from past practice.

Charles Boone made strenuous efforts to counter Angre. He began by an expedition to capture Khanderi in 1718. Being very close to Mumbai it was a constant irritant to the English. Boone set out on 1 November 1718 with a large flotilla of six grabs, a gully, three ketches and forty-eight gallivants.[5] An intense assault on Khanderi from 3 to 8 November, and a chase in the high seas, failed to yield a result. English marines who attempted to land on the island were forced to leave. Kanhoji unfurled his 'red flag' as a sign of victory. The English had an untrained army under a civilian leader and failed.

There was a lull for a while after this. The support Kanhoji might obtain from Shahu always intrigued the English. Relations between Shahu, the Peshwa and Kanhoji, was another matter they wanted to know more about. The English therefore sent an envoy to Shahu in August 1718 with detailed instructions. One of these said,

> You will also note whether Balaji Vishwanath, and his other favourites unreservedly obey him (Shahu) or there is misunderstanding between them; also observe whether Balaji and Angria have friendly relations or they pretend to be friends and ascertain whether Balaji will or will not send

Angria any succour if he asks for it...and if you find Balaji happens to be
Angria's friend, you will conduct your business with all care and prudence.[6]

At this time Balaji Vishwanath was preparing to join Sayyid Husain Ali's
march to Delhi and he had little time for any interaction with the English
envoy.

In October 1720 Boone once again began a campaign against Angre with an
attack on Vijaydurg. However, Kanhoji stood firm and the English had to call
off the attack. The English forged a fresh alliance with the Portuguese in June
1721. In September, a 'Royal squadron' sent by King George I of England
reached Mumbai to reduce Angre's fort of Colaba. The Portuguese joined the
English. Baji rao, who was the Peshwa, hearing of this alliance sent an army
of six thousand men to help Angre.[7] The combined English and Portuguese
forces failed to dent Angre's defences and the Peshwa asked them to come to
terms with Kanhoji.

The Portuguese had in the meanwhile signed a separate treaty with the
Marathas at Versauli. The English then sent Robert Cowan to Baji rao asking
for reparations, threatening that the war would otherwise continue. This was
accompanied by a 'friendly letter' from the Governor to Baji rao. Cowan
reached the port of Chaul and asked Baji rao to send a person *with full power
and instructions to adjust the peace without delay.'*

Baji rao brushed aside the English request. On receipt of Cowan's letter,
Baji rao, replied,

> I take notice of what you write concerning the peace. That point was fully
> discussed when we made peace with the Portuguese, no person being
> present for the English was reason why they were not included. You desire
> me to send a person with full powers and instructions, but what has been
> already proposed (with the Portuguese) is sufficient and to talk of more is
> not convenient. If you have anything further to offer, you may send one
> with sufficient powers, and when I know your pretensions, I'll send a person
> if I think proper.[8]

Baji rao's firm reply put a damper on English hopes. He refused to discuss
reparations or a fresh treaty and *'complete freedom of trade on the basis of
mutuality'*. The conflict between Angre and the English lingered on. Beyond

a point Shahu did not involve himself with resolving matters between the two. The English propped up the Siddi against Angre but decided never to break with Shahu, whose power was considered too big to trifle with. The Marathas continued to raid areas around English possessions and the anxious merchants at Mumbai sought advice from London:

> The unsettled condition of the kingdom of Indostan continues, and the *Ganim*s appear in great bodies from places adjacent to Surat, robbing and plundering what they can, insomuch that it causes a general damp on trade… and..no measures from Court are taken to prevent these incursions…which interrupts all trade from Surat…[9.]

An uneasy peace prevailed between Angre, the English, Baji rao and the Portuguese. In 1725, the English exchanged prisoners with Angre. However, the war that Boone started in 1718 went on till 1756. In time these matters reached a threshold where they had to be acted upon. For now, with Shahu's attention drawn to the Nizam's machinations, the affairs on the coast became a sideshow.

ॐ卐ॐ卐

# 13. Rivalry in the Carnatic

'Moving by the way of Mudgal and Gadag I will outflank Baji rao. If you from that side drive Baji rao before you, and if that wretch is hemmed between our two armies and is captured, it will be a good fortune of ours.'

- Nizam-ul-mulk's letter to a *pathan* chief.[1]

'I have, with God's help, called to my side Raja Sambhaji – who is Shahu's rival – conciliated him and engaged him in punishing and destroying Shahu.'

- Nizam-ul-mulk's letter to Sawai Jaisingh.[2]

Having met Baji rao thrice and seen his intense activity, the Nizam realised that the truce with Shahu would not last. Baji rao was seen as ambitious, not amenable to any control by his king and desirous of founding an Empire. His demands were growing in conjunction with his military abilities. While the Nizam desired to have the Maratha army with him and was prepared to pay its expenses, he did not want the Nawabs and Rajas of the south to pay any tribute to the Marathas. Here, he found Baji rao blocking his path and aspiring to extend Shahu's kingdom to the south.

Shahu's court had seen the first confrontation between Baji rao and Shripat rao *Pratinidhi* over the 'north or south' debate. Shahu had largely separated the two areas of influence thereafter, sending the *Pratinidhi* with Fateh Sinh Bhonsle to campaigns in the Carnatic, and Baji rao to the north. Many Maratha chiefs, once unified under a strong king in *Chhatrapati* Shivaji's time, now offered their services where they found better prospects. Outside powers such as the Nizam were always looking for opportunities to drive a wedge in the confederacy. Many restless Maratha chiefs such as Udaji Chavan, Chandrasen Jadhav, Rao Rambha and the sons of Santaji Ghorpade had already joined either *Chhatrapati* Sambhaji of Kolhapur or the Nizam. The lack of a strong central authority to ensure cohesive action was the need. However, with the monarchy itself divided between Satara and Kolhapur, this was a big ask.

In 1725 a seven-point treaty was signed between Shahu and Sambhaji pledging to support each other in their fight with the Mughals. However, the arrival of the Nizam changed political equations in the Deccan. There was a short period of amity between Baji rao and the Nizam; their interests, however, soon drew them apart. The first theatre of conflict was the south, in the Carnatic.

Shahu set his sights on the south and the possessions his grandfather had gained in the last years of his reign. The Nizam-ul-mulk had already decided to campaign in the same region and asked Shahu and Sambhaji to send troops to support him. Shahu, to maintain peaceful relations with the Nizam, sent Shripat rao *Pratinidhi* to the Carnatic after the festival of Dassera. Khande rao Dabhade, Kanhoji Bhonsle, Sultanji Nimbalkar were ordered to join him at the pilgrim town of Pandharpur with their armies. Later he asked Baji rao to join them.[3] The *Senapati* being unwell, sent his son Trimbak rao Dabhade[4] – a man who figures in later history. The army assembled by the end of 1725 and headed south collecting tribute on the way. They passed Galgali and Mudhol and camped at Bedhatti, where the Nawab of Savanur Abdul Ghaffar *Pathan* met Baji rao.[5] The Marathas crossed the river Tungabhadra and reached Chitradurg, a strong fort in western Carnatic.

At Sira the army joined the Nizam. The Nizam camped with troops of Shahu on one side, and of Sambhaji on the other. In his letter of April 1726 he describes his happiness at seeing the open divide between Shahu and Sambhaji;

> Baji rao and Shripat rao saw me on the 29th of *Rajab* (March 23, 1726). Neela Prabhu, the Chief Minister of Raja Sambhaji, (was) already in my camp. On seeing them, Shripatrao and Baji rao were confused. Their bewilderment cannot be described. They were full of pride and had aimed at making great demands on me (bring pressure on me). By God's grace, wolf and lamb lay together. Both these troops were camped on both the sides of my army. They were not favourably inclined towards each other. It was all God's grace.

The Nizam's meeting with Baji rao – his fourth in a span of six years – and the impressions the two carried of each other's intentions were to leave their mark in the years to come. The Nizam followed the old Mughal line of fomenting dissension between the two Maratha kings while drawing their chiefs into his fold. Baji rao understood that Shahu's policy of accommodating the Nizam would be at the cost of their own kingdom. He resolved therefore to resist the Nizam's endeavours to engulf the Maratha state.

The Nizam concludes his letter about the Carnatic campaign of early 1726, claiming success:

> During these days our army had turned its attention to set the affairs of Carnatic in order. So great was the impression created by the army of Islam that all pride evaporated from the haughty chiefs. Shripat rao, Sambhaji Nimbalkar, Baji rao, and other chiefs of Raja Shahu joined me with ten to eleven thousand cavalry. Hindurao, Narsinghrao and Neela Prabhu on behalf of Raja Sambhaji joined me with a considerable army. By God's grace a strong and numerous army was collected. The Raja of Mysore and the Raja of Bidnur were the two important chiefs in this region. They were proud of their army, and their inaccessible territory. They had not submitted even during the reign of *Hazarat Khuld Makan*[a]... On the news of the arrival of the army they submitted and vied with each other in paying tributes.[6]

The next year saw a change in the Marathas' attitude towards the Nizam. Shahu sent a second expedition to the Carnatic after the rains in 1726, which did not co-operate with the Nizam. The Nawab of Savanur, who had met Baji rao the previous year, was attacked by his neighbours and Shahu ordered Baji rao, Khande rao Dabhade and Sultanji Nimbalkar to set out to the south to protect him. Fateh Sinh Bhonsle also joined the campaign. They began their march from Pandharpur; Baji rao and Trimbak rao Dabhade joined, however, Sultanji did not. By February 1727, the army stood before Srirangapatnam, the capital of the king of Mysore – a residual state from the old Vijayanagar Empire. Although they resisted the Nizam's efforts to increase his influence in the Carnatic, the Maratha army was plagued by illness and had a difficult time in the campaign.

The Nizam sent a letter to Shahu where he complained about Maratha support to *pathan* chiefs in the south. The letter tells us more about Maratha

---

a.   Aurangzeb - 'he whose abode is eternity'

activities in that campaign:

> Prior to my departure from Hyderabad to put the affairs of Carnatic in order, letters had been addressed to Shripat rao, Sultanji Nimbalkar and Baji rao asking them to join me on the way. They did not come. Their arrival was delayed beyond measure. This was against agreement and friendship. They conspired to raise commotion on all sides and to disturb my plan. Your chiefs co-operated with my opponents; I would have destroyed them. It was only out of regard for you, who is considerate and not in favour of such improper acts, that I ignored the manoeuvres of your chiefs.

He ended the letter with a peace offering to Shahu,

> It is our duty to settle the country and be considerate to people who are the creation of God. I have sent trusted officers to you to express my sincere regards for you and stress the need for settling the country. This is due to the firm alliance which I have with you.[7]

The Carnatic became a region of conflict between the Nizam and Baji rao. The Nizam found Sambhaji of Kolhapur to be the more pliant and declared his support in his favour to become the unchallenged king of the Marathas. He marched out of Hyderabad on 4 March 1727 towards Malkhed, where the troops of Shahu and Sambhaji had gathered. Marching nearly thirty kilometres on the first day, he rushed to help Sambhaji. He wrote to a *pathan* chief attacked by Baji rao,

> From your writings it appeared that the depredations of Baji rao had spread in that region. God willing, this victorious army will rush in all haste in that region to assist you. It was necessary to assist Sambhaji. With this view … trusting in God we left Hyderabad on Saturday the 21 of *Rajab* (4 March 1727). Today is the 22 of *Rajab*. I have marched a distance of 12 *kos*. My aim was to move by forced marches. I will take the army (of Sambhaji) with me and move in all haste to punish Baji rao. Moving by the way of Mudgal and Gadag I will outflank Baji rao. If you from that side drive Baji rao before you, and if that wretch is hemmed between our two armies and is captured it will be a good fortune of ours.[1]

Baji rao was the one person the Nizam wanted to remove from the scene. His moves from here on were towards achieving this. Taking Sambhaji with him, the Nizam embarked on the task of chastising Baji rao and threatening Shahu, and moved towards Satara.

At Srirangapatnam, Baji rao and Khande rao received an urgent summons from Shahu,

> A consideration has arisen here. The *Pradhan* (Peshwa) and the *Senapati* are ordered to return to the capital. This should be done without delay; it takes time to raise troops for a campaign. You are beholden to the king. Your loyalty has pleased the king. You are ordered to return with your army and to start immediately you receive this command.[25]

Baji rao started from Srirangapatnam on 8 March 1727 and was in Satara on 27 April 1727. The Nizam had thrown a gauntlet and it was for Baji rao to take up the challenge.

# Book Three

## The Rising Sun

'The sword is the decisive argument and dispels the darkness of useless disputation, the opener of the gates of victory. Its studded hilt in the hand of the most devoted servant has established imperial sway in seven climes and raised aloft the banner of sovereignty in the whole world.'

- Nizam-ul-mulk's reply to Muhammad Shah.


'Thus Baji Rao, unaided, had brought to his knees the foremost soldier of his time. It was a feat of arms of which any commander might well have been proud.'

- The Cambridge History of India.

# Rewa Uvach

From here, a new chapter opened.

Baji rao's first seven years as Peshwa saw him playing bit roles in many campaigns, meeting the many powerful chiefs of the Deccan and building his own loyal team. In Pilaji Jadhav rao, Malharji Holkar, Udaji Pawar, Davalji Somvanshi and Ranoji Scindia, he had the best team any army commander could hope for. In his brother Chimaji Appa he had a firm base on which he could work his plan. In diplomacy he had the wise counsel of Ambaji Purandare. In the familiar terrain of the Deccan and parts of Malwa, he had a battlefield he knew better than anybody else.

The Nizam had begun with his well-equipped army towards Shahu's capital and the Peshwa's *jagir* at Pune. The king of Panhala was in his camp. The aim was clear – to uproot Shahu's rule. Once earlier too in the Deccan a powerful chief had entered Maharashtra to eliminate a Maratha king. The year was 1659. Afzal Khan, a General in the Bijapur army, started with a mission to 'catch' and exterminate Siva. Many *firmans* were sent to the Deshmukhs in the Maval area commanding them to leave Raja Shivaji and come over to the Mughal side. Those who did not do so were served with threats. Save one or two, they all remained faithful to their king. Afzal Khan was gradually drawn into the hilly forested area near Pratapgad, and on 10 November 1659, he was killed. The story is well known and does not bear repetition. The situation in Maharashtra in 1727 had similar aims. The Nizam wished to remove Shahu and place Sambhaji on the Maratha throne. This was achievable once he removed the young Peshwa Baji rao from his path.

Baji rao had men he could depend on, and a large mobile cavalry that could move quickly, but not stand the fire of the Mughal artillery. The Nizam-ul-mulk, on the other hand, was considered the tallest General of the Mughal Empire. He was crafty and had been victorious in all the battles in which he had led his armies. At Khandwa, Balapur and Sakharkherda he won famous victories consolidating his hold on the Deccan. However, despite the Nizam's record of victories and his claims to have been trained by Aurangzeb, he lacked the personal courage the late Emperor was known for.

The Nizam's demand for the *subedari* of Malwa and Gujarat along with the Deccan had been turned down by the Emperor. Thereafter he had established his rule in the south disregarding the Emperor's orders. His survival depended therefore on how well he marshalled his forces in the Deccan, where even Aurangzeb with his great resources had failed. He began by questioning the basis of Shahu's right to claim the *chauth* of the Deccan, summoned the representatives of Shahu and Sambhaji, and arrogated to himself the arbitration of this old question about who was the 'true heir'.

The Nizam first succeeded in corrupting some of the officers of Satara, but realised that his chief obstacle was Baji rao, who was not only steadfast in his aim of supporting Shahu but also on establishing a Maratha Empire. Like Dilawar Ali, Alam Ali, the Sayyids and Mubariz Khan, it was Baji rao who now had to be removed from his path. The Nizam-ul-mulk - Baji rao confrontation in 1727-28 occupied the entire territory of Maharashtra, Khandesh, and parts of Gujarat. Its narrative is not easy to piece together given the length of the campaign, its many characters and the huge area of operations.

The long-drawn battle of nearly six months over an area more than a thousand square kilometres could have been the end of the Maratha story. The finale in February 1728 was at the end of a series of strategic manoeuvres and the battle at Palkhed is therefore deservedly called a 'masterpiece in strategic mobility'.

Baji rao was on the banks of the Rewa for many days during this campaign, and it was here that he decided on the strategy.

# 14. 'A Masterpiece in Strategic Mobility'

'The sword is the decisive argument and dispels the darkness of useless disputation, the opener of the gates of victory. Its studded hilt in the hand of the most devoted servant has established imperial sway in seven climes and raised aloft the banner of sovereignty in the whole world.'

- Nizam-ul-mulk's letter to Muhammad Shah.[1]

The Nizam's juggernaut rolled towards Pune with Sambhaji of Kolhapur, aiming to install him as the true king of the Marathas in place of Shahu.

*Raja* Sambhaji joined the Nizam in his camp some time after June 1726, possibly in early 1727. Leaving the administration of his kingdom to his mother Rajas bai, Sambhaji, believing the Nizam's promise to place him on the throne as the only king of the Marathas, joined the Mughal Viceroy. Chandrasen Jadhav helped bring Sambhaji to the Nizam's fold. Sambhaji had written to Shahu that he was meeting the Mughal Viceroy for some discussions. A report from Shahu's court dated 9 June 1726 to Chimaji Appa said,

> Raja Sambhaji's letter reached *Rajashri* swami (Shahu)...Sambhaji raje wishes to resolve the matter of outposts at Nargund and Torgal[a] with the Nizam, and for this reason will go and meet the Nizam; his servant said to the *Rajashri* swami. *Rajashri* said to the servant, it is inexpedient for the king himself to go and discuss matters relating to some minor outposts. It is necessary to be firm with the Mughal. If one becomes soft, the Mughal becomes more powerful. Therefore you should tell him once, not to go.[2]

The reason given for meeting the Nizam was a cover; in fact, Sambhaji was joining forces with the Mughals. For the next two years, Sambhaji remained in the Nizam's camp. Besides Sambhaji, Shahu's *Sarlashkar* Sultanji Nimbalkar also joined the Nizam. The Nizam gave his plan in a letter to Sawai Jaisingh:

> These misguided people (Marathas) have spread through the provinces of Malwa and Gujarat...the Emperor has sent me his royal letters to prevent this. I have again and again written to Shahu giving him the counsel that

---

a. Two places about two hundred kilometres southeast of Kolhapur.

it is not good that the Marathas should go out to plunder the countries of Malwa and Gujarat..it was displeasing to the Emperor – so that Shahu should urge his troops not to cross the Narmada. Although he was pressed and thus threatened, nothing at all resulted from it, and the soldiers of Shahu, who do not listen to his words nor are under anybody's control, did not give up their raids.

Therefore with a view to carrying out the Emperor's order, and pleasing you my friend and increasing the power of the Maharana, I have, with God's help, called to my side Raja Sambhaji – who is Shahu's rival – conciliated him and engaged him in punishing and destroying Shahu.[3]

A letter from Sambhaji to Chandrasen at this time says,

The Nizam has sent a message to be prepared and break the treaty with the Satara king. You should come and meet me immediately. There are other people like Morarji (Murar rao Ghorpade) and Udaji Chavan Himmat Bahadur, who are with me.[4]

By the middle of 1726, Shahu got the first inkling of a grand conspiracy to unseat him. His chiefs were deserting him. One of Shahu's earliest supporters, Chimnaji Damodar was sent to Bhaganagar[a] to agree on dues from that province. The Nizam turned Chimnaji Damodar to his side and made him the Peshwa at Kolhapur. Shripat rao *Pratinidhi* would have no part in the venture against the Nizam. Earlier, he had urged Shahu to accept the Nizam's offer to exempt his capital Bhaganagar from *chauth* in exchange for a *jagir* in Pune district. This ran contrary to Baji rao's aggressive policy.

Once the Nizam began marching from Hyderabad towards Satara, a flurry of activity began. Funds were the first requirement for war. A sum of two thousand rupees came from Kanhoji Angre as part of the dues from Kalyan and Bhiwandi regions in the Konkan.[5] Kadam Bande and Pilaji Gaekwad had held back some of the tribute due from Gujarat and an army was to be sent to collect it. This was then postponed to a later date and the army recalled for the defence of the *swarajya*.[6] Chimaji Appa began an incantation of the *Ati Rudra* by Brahmins at Harihareshwar, in praise of Shiva, the Lord of destruction in the Hindu pantheon.[7] Letters were sent to all the forts to reinforce their defences.[8] At the end of the monsoon, it was clear that Sultanji Nimbalkar too had gone over to the Nizam, so his brother Sidhoji was appointed the

---

a.   Hyderabad.

*Sarlaskhar.*[9] Shahu urged Ambaji Purandare – who was in Malwa to return, while a letter from Baji rao to Ambaji said, *'Come at once. Do not let me down'.*[10] Shahu sent letters to Kanhoji Angre, Kanhoji Bhonsle, Davalji Somvanshi, Kanthaji Kadam and Pilaji Jadhav rao; *'Take your armies and go after Qilich Khan (Nizam). Arrest his progress, teach him a lesson and please me'.*[11] Fateh Sinh Bhonsle wrote to Baji rao that the Nizam was approaching and asked what steps were intended.[12] To Baji rao, Shahu wrote,

> I have sent you letters from time to time about the Nizam-ul-mulk's armies. The latest is that they have come three stages beyond the fort of Dharur. The enemy is in a hurry. You must have attacked his city (by now). How far have you gone, what are you thinking, how big is your army; write to me in detail.[13]

All eyes were on Baji rao. The survival of Shahu's regime depended on what the young Peshwa planned to do.

Proceeding from Beed, the Nizam camped at Dharur for the three monsoon months. He then headed for Pune, the district given to Baji rao as his *jagir*. The Nizam had a powerful artillery with him, which the Maratha forces lacked. From Satara Ambaji Purandare wrote to Bajirao that the enemy was coming towards the capital. *Senapati* Khande rao Dabhade sent his son Trimbak rao to join Shahu's forces. However, Trimbak rao headed for Malwa and began raiding and looting the Peshwa's territories.[14] Minor grievances between Maratha chiefs such as Kanthaji Kadam Bande and Udaji Pawar were, however, tackled at this time with Baji rao warning them that they should focus on the job and not quarrel over inconsequential issues.[15]

Since Satara was deemed unsuitable to withstand a siege, Chimaji Appa escorted Shahu to the strong fort of Purandar. While Chimaji directed operations from here, Baji rao was on the move from the end of August 1727. Baji rao sent out his chiefs to face the Mughal onslaught. The Nizam's lieutenants Aivaz Khan and Ghiyas Khan were at Junnar, north of Pune. Tukoji Pawar faced Aivaz Khan near Nashik. However, Turktaz Khan reached Parner near Ahmednagar and occupied it. Chandrasen Jadhav's advance was blunted by Fateh Sinh Bhonsle and Raghuji Bhonsle. Ranoji Scindia defended Patas valiantly for a while.

At this critical juncture, the Maratha armies were not well provisioned with supplies or funds. Each chief had to use his own initiative and raise troops; sometimes on specious promises. While some persevered for their king and state, others who enjoyed the perks of their *jagirs* barely stirred out of their homes. Ranoji Scindia, forthright and loyal, suffered severe privations from lack of funds and food. He sought urgent relief when defending the villages around Patas and wrote,

> We are unable to arrange for our food. I have gathered five hundred men. But just a hundred rupees a day are not enough. I have about two hundred with me now. We will die of hunger. The master orders me to fight and save the boundaries and places. We boasted and made a mistake. When the campaign was planned, those who were close to the swami, whom you gave a thousand or more rupees, those so dear to you, have all gone! I have no weapons. But we are still doing what we agreed to do and are campaigning here. Thinking of those people – who commit incest with their mothers– (in contrast) we have been speaking half truths but we gathered some people. These people have *saranjam*s of over a lakh, but do not keep even a few hundred soldiers... However, I gathered a hundred and fifty men. But the swami does not realise this. There is no food. Villages are all in ashes. There is no place to get money. You ask us to keep five hundred men. But a day or two of fasting and the men will go away... Send me funds that will last a month.[16]

Ranoji's rant shows the constraints that the Maratha army was facing. The fight against the Nizam was sustained by loyal chiefs like Ranoji. At another place Ranoji complains about Malharji Holkar, who did not show up at the designated place, leaving him alone to face the enemy. One finds Ranoji's sense of service to the state, and specifically to the Peshwa, in his successors through the eighteenth century.

Baji rao began from Satara in the last week of August 1727 and spent a month at Saswad making his plans, collecting an army and observing the Nizam's movements. He then passed through Loni and Vadzire near Parner[17] before crossing the Godavari at Puntamba. He camped at Yeola, then moved east and passed north of the walled Mughal city of Aurangabad. He looted the business towns of Jalna and Sindkhed further east. He lay waste the entire territory belonging to the Nizam, returning in kind the damage done to the Pune region. He then sped towards the *pargana* of Sindkhed and reached Washim deep in the Nizam's territory. Plundering Mangrul Pir, and heading for the river Tapi, gave out that he was attacking the imperial city of Burhanpur. The feint towards Burhanpur brought the Nizam furiously out of Pune.

To save the prestigious Mughal city, the Nizam sent Aivaz Khan's men after Baji rao. They had a skirmish at Jalna where Aivaz Khan seemed to have the advantage, but Baji rao moved away towards Burhanpur. West of Chopda, Baji rao crossed the Tapi, and turned north towards the river Narmada. Here, he crossed by the Baba Piara ford near Bharuch and camped on the bank of the Narmada for a week. He came south to Songad near Surat after this and spent a fortnight there. On 21 January he met Udaji Pawar at Songad.[18] From here he once again crossed the Narmada and stayed in the Chota Udepur – AliMohan (Ali Rajpur) region for four or five days. Here, he learnt of the Nizam's depredations in Pune and started towards Khandesh.

The Nizam had followed Aivaz Khan and hurriedly crossed the Godavari to defend Burhanpur, but there he heard that Baji rao had departed for Gujarat. He began towards Surat. The Mughal *Subedar* Sarbuland Khan was ill disposed towards the Nizam, and could not understand Baji rao's sudden arrival in his province. Baji rao informed Sarbuland that the Nizam was following, and together they planned to attack him. As Sarbuland Khan prepared to face the attack, the disheartened Nizam returned to Pune. Here, he formally crowned Sambhaji as the *Chhatrapati* on 8 February 1728. He also arranged his marriage with the Sisodia princess of Ramnagar state.

Chimaji Appa witnessed the tremendous Mughal invasion of Pune district. Turktaz Khan, Rao Rambha, Thorat and Dhiraji Pawar spread out in Pune district. The Mughals faced stiff resistance at the fort of Lohagad. From Junnar in the north to Shikrapur towards the east, the Mughals surrounded Pune. The Nizam, with Sambhaji, made Pune his headquarters.

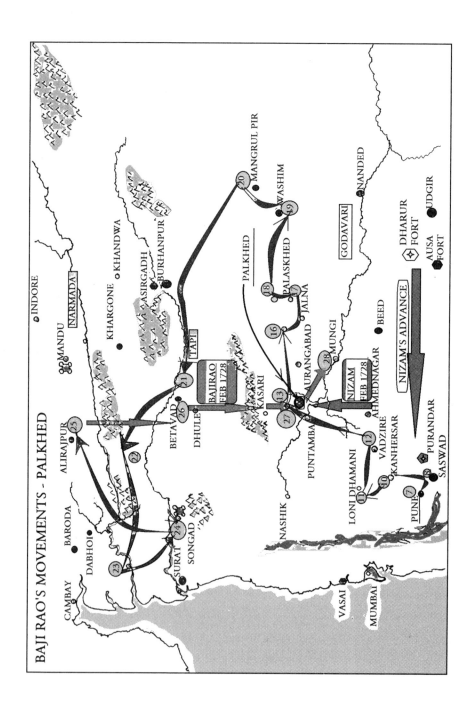

BAJI RAO'S MOVEMENTS - PALKHED

Baji rao's *movements before Palkhed*[32]

| | Place | Hijri date | Old style (Julian) | New style/Common Era |
|---|---|---|---|---|
| 1. | Satara | 17-21 Jilkad, 1139 Hijri | 25 to 29 June 1727 | 7 to 11 July 1727 |
| 2. | Bhuinj, Satara | 22-24 Jilkad 1139 Hijri | 30 June to 2 July 1727 | 11 to 13 July 1727 |
| 3. | Saswad | 26 Jilkad to 29 Jilhej, 1139 Hijri | 4 July 1727 to 6 August 1727 | 15 July to17 August 1727 |
| 4. | Saswad | Muharram 2 to 5 1140 Hijri | 9 to 12 August 1727 | 20 to 23 August – 1727 |
| 5. | Supe | 6-12 Muharram 1140 Hijri | 13 to 18 August 1727 | 4 to 19 August 1727 |
| 6. | Saswad | 15 to 27 Muharram | 21 August to 3 September 1727 | 2 to 14 September 1727 |
| 7. | Pune | 29 Muharram to 4 Safar 1140 Hijri | 5 to 10 September 1727 | 16 to 21 September 1727 |
| 8. | Saswad | 6-11 Safar 1140 Hijri | 12 to17 September 1727 | 23 to 28 September 1727 |
| 9. | Loni Kalbhor | 29 Safar 1140 Hijri | 5 October 1727 | 16 October 1727 |
| 10. | Kanhersar, Pabal | 4 Rabilawal 1140 Hijri | 8 November 1727 | 19 November 1727 |
| 11. | Loni Dhamani | 5-7 Rabilawal 1140 Hijri | 9 to11 November 1727 | 20 to 22 November 1727 |
| 12. | Vadzire, Parner | 8 to 9 Rabilawal 1140 Hijri | 12 to 13 November 1727 | 23 to 24 November 1727 |
| 13. | Andarsul, Yewale | 13 to15 Rabilawal 1140 Hijri | 17 to19 November 1727 | 28 to 30 November 1727 |
| 14. | Yewale | 17 Rabilawal 1140 Hijri | 21 November 1727 | 2 December 1727 |
| 15. | Borsar, Vaijapur | 18 Rabilawal 1140 Hijri | 22 November 1727 | 3 December 1727 |

| Place | Hijri date | Old style (Julian) | New style/Common Era |
|---|---|---|---|
| 16. Dongargaon Dabhadi | 24 Rabilawal 1140 Hijri | 28 November 1727 | 9 December 1727 |
| 17. Palaskhed Malakdeo | 28 Rabilawal 1140 Hijri | 2 December 1727 | 13 December 1727 |
| 18. Jafarabad | 29 Rabilawal 1140 Hijri | 3 December 1727 | 14 December 1727 |
| 19. Washim | 5 Jamadilawal 1140 Hijri | 8 December 1727 | 19 December 1727 |
| 20. Mangrul Pir | 6 Jamadilawal 1140 Hijri | 9 December 1727 | 20 December 1727 |
| 21. Kusumbi, Chopda | 15 Jamadilawal 1140 Hijri | 18 December 1727 | 29 December 1727 |
| 22. River Tapi | 16 to 21 Jamadilawal 1140 Hijri | 19 to 24 December 1727 | 30 December 1727 to 4 January 1728 |
| 23. Bank of the Rewa | 1 to 6 Jamadilakhar, 1140 Hijri, | 03 to 8 January 1728 | 14 to 19 January 1728 |
| 24. Songad | 10 to 23 Jamadilakhar 1140 Hijri | 12 to 25 January 1728 | 23 January to 5 February 1728 |
| 25. Mohan/Alirajpur | 29 Jamadilakhar to 3 Rajab 1140 Hijri | 31 January to 3 February 1728 | 11 to 14 February 1728 |
| 26. Betavad | 13-14 Rajab Hijri 1140 | 11 to 12 February 1728 | 23 to 24 Feb 1728 |
| 27. *Palkhed* | 30 Rajab, 1140 Hijri | 28 February 1728 | 9 March 1728 |
| 28. Mungi Shevgaon | 10 Shaban 1140 Hijri | 11 March 1728 | 22 March 1728 |

Chimaji wrote to Baji rao about the loss of Pune district to the Nizam's forces in February 1728,

> To sum up, first Turktaz Khan, Rambhaji Nimbalkar, Thorat and Dhiraji came and caused chaos, they went till Lohagad, but were beaten by the soldiers on the fort. They came to Chinchwad. Then Nizam came here and stayed at Anjanapur (?near Shirur). Chimnaji Damodar took over the post here. They also took over Talegaon and Shikrapur. They took Udapur (near Junnar, north of Pune). Narayan gad accepted Sambhaji's flag. Then they came to Pune. Sambhaji's marriage to the (daughter of) Ramnagarkars was solemnised. Fazil Beg was appointed to govern Pune. Rambhaji took Supe and Thorat took the town of Patas…Janoji Nimbalkar was appointed to Baramati….[19]

From Gujarat, Baji rao came back to Khandesh and on 14 February 1728 camped at Betawad near the city of Dhule. The Nizam was near Ahmednagar at this time. He interpreted Baji rao's move as an impending attack on Aurangabad and began moving north with his entire army to intercept Baji rao. The best place to cross the river Godavari was the town of Puntamba, where it was fordable. It was decided that a camp with provisions and a bazaar would be set up at the village of Palkhed before the Nizam crossed over, blocking the Peshwa's path to Aurangabad.

Baji rao was observing the Nizam's moves. Realising that his cavalry-borne force will not be able to stand against the Nizam's heavy guns, he anticipated his adversary's moves and deployed his commanders with simple instructions on his strategy. Passing through a hill range by the Kasari *ghat*, he descended onto a flat plain to the north of the Godavari, just a day's march from Palkhed.

As the Nizam crossed the Godavari, the Marathas chased away the *banjaras* who brought food to the camp at Palkhed. They burnt the fodder and laid the province waste. Kasari *ghat* and Puntamba are roughly equidistant from Palkhed. The Nizam headed north east towards Palkhed, hoping to block Baji rao's path to Aurangabad. The Nizam's artillery had not yet crossed over. The two adversaries came close to each other at Palkhed, near Lasur.

Baji rao asked for intelligence in a letter,

> Is the Mughal coming today? Should I come forward or stop here for the day? Gather good people around the flag. I am without a horse, so

Anandrao Pawar's horse Kotwal and Rangaji Jadhav's horse named (once again) Kotwal should be procured and sent to me. Rambhaji Kadam and Davalji Somvanshi should be to my Left and Pilaji Jadhav rao should be to the Right. The *Sarlashkar* (Sidhoji Nimbalkar) is here, but has many doubts; so go tell the men – that with the pride and courage of the Nimbalkars, the Mughal ought to be shamed at your hands. Preserve your presence of mind. The Mughals' camp followers have gone into the village. Did they all go or have some stayed behind? Send me the news. The Mughal continues to march ahead. Send me both the horses.[20]

With the Godavari thirty kilometres away, a small tributary named Shiv about six kilometres to the west and his artillery still south of the Godavari, the Nizam found his force encircled by the Maratha horse. The Marathas had blocked the fords on the rivers and access to water-bodies in the region. Supplies to the Nizam's army stopped suddenly and completely. Baji rao, Pilaji Jadhav rao, Malharji Holkar, Davalji Somvanshi, Ranoji Scindia, Baji Bhiv rao and Udaji Pawar enforced a siege, rapidly bringing the Mughal army to suffer extreme privations.[21] In a matter of days the Nizam realised he had no way out. He sought terms on 28 February 1728. The Cambridge History of India says, '*Thus Baji Rao, unaided, had brought to his knees the foremost soldier of his time. It was a feat of arms of which any commander might well have been proud*'.[22]

The Nizam's army was intact, but he had been cornered and brought to his knees. Facing the first defeat of his long career, he met a generous adversary in Baji rao, and Shahu, who allowed him to survive. Aivaz Khan, who had met Baji rao in the past, was sent to negotiate. The Peshwa took hostages, and under the escort of Malharji Holkar, allowed the Nizam to move towards Mungi Shevgaon near the Godavari where water was provided to his army. Baji rao first demanded the surrender of Shahu's cousin and rival Sambhaji. However, the Nizam did not feel it was 'chivalrous' to hand over an ally who was under his protection, to the enemy. Other than this, writing under his own hand, the Nizam agreed to the rest of the terms.

Grant Duff, who accessed many Maratha *bakhars* and letters based on which he wrote his History of the Marathas, describes the Palkhed finale in these words:

> Nizam Ool Moolk recrossed the Godavery, when the Peishwa, after some days' skirmishing, drew him into a situation favourable to his purpose, set fire to the grass, destroyed the forage, and effectually straitened his supplies. Tlie Marattas suffered severely by the fire of the artillery, but they cut off such detached parties as they could overpower, and drove off the draught cattle. At last, in some broken ground, around which, for several miles, there was no water, the Mahrattas completely surrounded the Nizam's army, and so effectually impeded his march, that night closed before he could extricate himself from his embarrassing situation. Nizam Ool Moolk had foreseen that this species of warfare would be practised, and in entering upon the campaign, expected that the part of light troops should be performed by his associates. He had reproached them with their want of vigour, and recommended their adopting the same system against their countrymen, as Bajee Rao was practising. But Chandrasen Jadow represented that most of his troops were Moghuls; and Sumbhajee acknowledged, not only that his numbers were inadequate, but that he suspected his *karkun*s were in league with the enemy.[23]

Grant Duff further elaborates on the nature of relations between Sambhaji, his ministers, and *karkun*s, saying their mutual suspicions were such that both begged the funds be handed over directly to their own selves.

In early March 1728, in the treaty that was signed at Mungi Shevgaon on the Godavari, the Nizam agreed to give the *chauth* and *sardeshmukhi* dues of the six *subah*s of the Deccan to Shahu and issued letters to the chiefs of the six provinces to pay it to the Marathas without any obstruction.[24] Sambhaji was escorted back to Panhala and the Nizam promised not to support him against Shahu in future. The parts occupied by the Nizam in the late war in Pune district were to be handed back. Further minor reparations were also agreed to by the Nizam. The entire *swarajya* of *Chhatrapati* Shivaji was liberated at Palkhed. The Nizam honoured Baji rao and his chiefs. Reciprocal gifts were given to the Nizam. The two opponents then returned to their capital. Baji rao's place in Shahu's counsel rose even as his opponents in the court lost face. Baji rao awarded Malharji Holkar many new districts of Malwa and Gujarat as his *saranjam* and shared the revenue of the province with Scindia and Udaji Pawar.[25]

A few weeks later, Chandrasen Jadhav sent a complimentary letter to Chimaji on the victory at Palkhed. *'I am pleased by the success of Raya (Baji rao). The Nizam is on the way to Aurangabad now,'* he wrote.[26] The Nizam was not at peace, however. The defeat *'utterly prostrated him.'* Qasim Aurangabadi has written, *'for some days he gave up taking meals.'*[27] In a letter to the Emperor, the Nizam anguished,

> The resources of the Marathas have doubled since the death of Aurangzeb; the affairs of the Empire on the contrary have fallen into disorder;... Many forts and posts once under Mughal control have passed into the hands of the Marathas. Raja Shahu receives large collection of *chauth* and *sardeshmukhi* from the imperial Deccan.[28]

Eminent historian Jadunath Sarkar states,

> This heaven born cavalry leader by his Palkhed campaign led the Nizam through a devil's dance for three months from Ahmednagar to Gujarat, and at last manoeuvred him into an utterly untenable position at Palkhed, where the new Lord of the Mughal Deccan was forced to make a complete surrender. The Nizam agreed to allow the Marathas a free hand in Hindustan and a free passage through Berar (Varhad) and Khandesh in their northern march, while Baji rao promised to spare the Nizam's own domains in return for the stipulated *chauth*. Thus the way was cleared for Baji rao up to the Narmada and a permanent Maratha camp was planted just beyond the southern frontier of Malwa.[29]

Field Marshal Bernard Montgomery after defeating the German Erwin Rommel at Alamein in October 1942 was called 'Montgomery of Alamein'. Using a strikingly similar strategy of starving the enemy of supplies, he defeated his famous adversary. He writes, *'Success in the war in the African desert depended more than usual extent on the factors of equipment and supply... the Germans had an advantage in equipment but not always in supply'.*[30] Something quite similar happened at Palkhed.

About the battle of Palkhed, Montgomery writes,

> They (the Marathas) were at their best in the eighteenth century, and the Palkhed campaign of 1727-8, in which Baji rao outgeneralled Nizam-ul-mulk, is a masterpiece in strategic mobility. Baji rao's force was a purely mounted force, armed only with a sabre, lance, a bow in some units, and a round shield. There was a spare horse for every two men. The Marathas moved unencumbered by artillery, baggage, or even handguns and defensive armour. They supplied themselves by looting.

Baji rao resented the Nizam's rule over the Deccan and it was he who struck the first blow. In October 1727, as soon as the rainy season ended, Baji rao burst into the territory of the Nizam.... The lightly equipped Marathas moved with great rapidity, avoiding the main towns and fortresses, living off the country, burning and plundering. They met one reverse at the hands of the Nizam's able lieutenant Aivaz Khan at the beginning of November, but within a month they had fully recovered and were off again, dashing east, north, west, with sudden changes of direction. The Nizam had mobilised his forces, and for a time pursued them, but he was bewildered by the swift unpredictable movements of the enemy, and his men became exhausted. At the end of January the Nizam changed his strategy; he gave up the pursuit of the elusive Maratha forces and instead made direct for their heartland around Poona, which he captured and ravaged. But Baji rao resisted urgent calls to come back, and instead countered the Nizam's move by in turn threatening his capital Aurangabad. The Nizam predictably evacuated the Poona district and returned to rescue Aurangabad. As the Nizam once again endeavoured to catch Baji rao, the Marathas harried and circled round his forces. The Nizam preserved his army intact, but in March 1728 he gave up. The Marathas returned home laden with plunder, and by the peace terms some of their territorial claims were conceded.

Palkhed was a watershed in Maratha history as, for a while it ended the question of the *chauth* of the southern provinces and recognised Shahu as the true heir of the Marathas. The Nizam was allowed to survive.[26]

In the nineteenth century a poet wrote,

Both went; One with his lustre extinguished,
The Other, with Victory in battle accomplished.

# 15. Across the Narmada

'You fill your stomach there, I will fill it here. Do not let egoism enter your mind. Do what is essential to earn money and pay off debts. Safeguard your prestige and reputation and do what is needed to complete the job.'

- Baji rao's letter to Chimaji Appa.[1]

The province of Malwa, nearly at the centre of the India, was not just the pathway from the north to the south but also a rich province that yielded considerable revenue to the Mughals. The first Mughal province to the north of the Maratha *swarajya*, Malwa was raided from the last decade of the seventeenth century onwards by Maratha adventurers like Nemaji Scindia and Udaji Pawar. Successive Mughal Governors were hard-pressed to stop the incursions that grew as the Mughal state became weak and indolent.

The year 1720 saw Baji rao appear on the scene and some of his first moves were in the province of Malwa. The local landlords were tiring of Mughal rule and had sent feelers to the Marathas. A *jagirdar* from the region of Mandu sold a part of his fief to Baji rao citing the breakdown of rule of law, huge debts and no security of life and property.[2] The Mandloi family from Indore were one of the first to switch allegiance to the Marathas. In a letter to Mandloi in 1720 Holkar says,

'You are aware of our differences with the king of Badwai. You are close by. Give him some good advice. Else I am capable of teaching him a lesson.'

In another he writes,

'the agreement is to pay four thousand rupees. You should pay the amount to Naro Shankar. Do not prevaricate. If you prevaricate, in a day or two I will come and call on you. Let it be known.'

In 1724 Baji rao wrote to Mandloi,

'You have not sent an emissary with the *khandani* of the region as promised. It is not as if you have behaved correctly. I am coming there. Do not pay the amount to Keso Mahadev who is in that region. If you do so, it will not be counted in your account.'[3]

The takeover of Malwa was a process that went on for many years. Effective Mughal authority in the province dipped with successive Maratha incursions. In 1724 Holkar had a post in Indore and two years later Udaji Pawar captured the fort and town of Dhar, which infuriated the Emperor. He commanded Khan Dauran's son and Sawai Jaisingh to evict the Marathas.[4] The pretence of authority and the appointment of *subedars* by the Emperor carried on for long after effective control slipped out of their hands. The actual cession of the province to the Marathas by a helpless Emperor, however, was still some distance away.

Although Malwa had seen Maratha attacks even during Aurangzeb's lifetime, since 1720, the number and intensity of these attacks increased. The Marathas gained support of the local *zamindars*. Baji rao was involved in the battle of Balapur in 1720 and was again near Burhanpur in 1722. He met the Nizam at Bolasa in February 1723, crossed the Narmada and campaigned in places such as Hoshangabad, Mandu and so on. Later, the Peshwa's forces joined the Nizam in punishing the Nawab of Bhopal for opposing him at Khandwa.

Besides the Peshwa, Malwa was invaded by Raghuji Bhonsle of Varhad.[5] Raghuji was the nephew of Shahu's earliest supporter Persoji Bhonsle. In 1724, Baji rao had written a stern letter to Raghuji to desist from taking any revenue from Malwa, *Do not take a single rupee. If you take it you will have to pay it. Let it be known.*[6] Despite this, Raghuji had gone campaigning to Malwa in 1726, when Baji rao was campaigning in Carnatic. Trimbak rao Dabhade also raided areas of Malwa under Baji rao and Shahu sternly reprimanded him in a letter of May 1728.[7]

Malwa was eyed not just by the Marathas but also Sawai Jaisingh who wished to use the weakness of the Mughals to expand his own kingdom from the Narmada to the river Chambal. Mughal grandees like the Nizam and Muhammad Khan Bangash were also interested in governing the contiguous provinces of Malwa and Bundelkhand.

In the aftermath of Palkhed, Maratha *vakil* Dado Bhimsen, conversant with politics in the Delhi court, wrote to Baji rao that Sawai Jaisingh favoured him, and felt that the presence of Maratha forces in Malwa at this time will strengthen his case and force the Emperor to cede the province.[8] Dado Bhimsen also asked the Peshwa to write to Chhatrasal Bundela, the ruler of Bundelkhand, that he would come there to help him against Mughal invasions after the festival of Dassera.

The Nagar Brahmin family of Chabila Ram were old imperial servants, having served in Allahabad and Awadh as Governors. On Chabila Ram's death, his nephew Giridhar Bahadur was first appointed as *subedar* of Awadh. Giridhar was moved to Malwa on 30 August 1722, replacing Nizam-ul-mulk and Sadat Khan was appointed at Awadh. Giridhar Bahadur saw a flurry of Maratha incursions in Malwa. However, in 1723, the Nizam, as the *Wazir*, took direct charge of Malwa and handed it over to his relative Azimullah Khan. The next year saw the momentous battle of Sakharkherda that established the Nizam firmly in the Deccan.

After Sakherkherda, the Emperor once again appointed Giridhar Bahadur as *subedar* in Malwa. His cousin Daya Bahadur joined him. The Mughal position in Malwa was shaky at best. Giridhar Bahadur and Daya Bahadur earned the opprobrium of the landowners of Malwa but got little help from Delhi. The next two years were spent by these two in fending off the Marathas while strengthening their own position in the capital city Ujjain.

With Sawai Jaisingh's ambition to be the master of Malwa with Maratha help, and Baji rao's own aim to conquer Malwa, a storm was soon to burst over the province. Sawai Jaisingh did not wish that anybody else should succeed in holding the province. The Marathas, encouraged by Jaisingh, but short of money, had to find ways to repay the debts of their king Shahu and the Peshwa. The campaign in Malwa therefore aimed to retire some of these debts. Baji rao in his letters instructed Chimaji repeatedly to get enough money to repay debts wherever he went. From Ranoji Scindia's plea for funds before Palkhed to Baji rao's own letters over the next decade, one sees the Peshwa perpetually in debt.

Baji rao's many debts had a strong bearing on his career and his worries. With every year, these debts reached astronomical proportions, so that the Peshwa was worrying as much about his finances as his military campaigns. Grant Duff wrote,

> Bajee Rao, owing to the vast army he had kept up, both to secure his conquests and to overcome his rivals, had become greatly involved in debts. His troops were in arrears; the *sovkars*, to whom he already owed a personal debt of many lakhs of rupees, refused to make any further advances, and

he complained bitterly of the constant mutinies and clamours in his camp, which occasioned him much vexation and distress.[9]

Baji rao's mother Radha bai's family were moneylenders and when Chimaji was campaigning in Malwa, Bajirao's maternal uncle Malhar Dadaji Barwe wrote to him,

> May the Lord always bless you with success in all your ventures. The swami had promised at Pune that I should not worry about the money I lent - the earlier loan of five thousand taken while at Pune, and the one before; the swami will gain in his campaign from this good fortune. Day after day the swami earns *taka* and money. Always remain successful.[10]

Brahmendra swami, the spiritual guru of almost the entire Maratha establishment, functioned as a moneylender himself. The money he lent was considered a loan from God and called 'Shri's money' or in Marathi, 'श्रीचा ऐवज '.[11] He not only lent money to Baji rao, but also urged where military force ought to be directed.

By the middle of the 1730s, Baji rao, vexed over demands from several quarters, poured out his angst in several letters to Brahmendra swami. Bajirao writes in one letter,

> You have asked for repayment of five thousand rupees. I have sent two thousand. I will repay the remaining three thousand in the months of *Shravan Bhadrapad*. I have obtained the fruit of serving loyally in every way. I have repaid from who I borrowed. I will repay. But the debts have drowned me. It was better to lose my life instead. Die by poison or sit by the swami's feet; just this much is left to be done. .. I will not go to Satara. What shall I do there? I will have people trampling my chest with their feet. Hence am sitting here. Everybody has brought me to the same state as of a woman who has lost her husband.[12]

In another letter,

> The debts do not get over. What use is it to live now? I will sacrifice my life. If you are giving me advice that is not practical, I do not wish to listen. If you convey a solution about how to get rupees, in four five days, it will be good. Else, we will find our own way.[13]

The victorious Peshwa's anguish comes through in these surviving letters, which he addressed the swami, who he reveres, in intemperate language over his demands for repayment of debts. He also compares his sad state to other chiefs who have grown wealthy without having the same loyalty to the king that he practises. In yet another letter, Baji rao writes to the swami,

> Why should I worry? You have become a saint and you have made us a householder. In the bargain, I have landed with a debt of twenty lakh rupees. Last year I handed over everything to you and decided to spend time worshipping God, but out of kindness you said, 'Bhargava[a] is with you'. Now every day I get up and fall at the feet of the debtors. Falling at the feet of the *silahdars* has split my forehead. Now I do not want these 'pleasures'. When I am still alive, who worries about money? I will repay it. Right now all I have is my own life. Either you come here and take it or I will come there and give it up to you. ... I have drowned in Hell with debt and debtors. If you liberate me from debt this year, I will give my life to God. If there is anything I have written that is false, I may be cursed. What kind of a god are you that you do not understand whether I am spotless or a liar? My destiny is in ruins. Why do you curse poor people like us? Today Dabhade, Gaekwad, Bande have treasures of crores of rupees; my serving my master loyally and sitting at your feet has made it difficult to even satisfy my own needs.[14]

The burden of debt followed Baji rao through his entire reign as Peshwa. In Shahu's court there were whispers about the Peshwa's financial situation. One day in 1735 Shahu summoned Mahadji Purandare who stayed at Satara as the Peshwa's *mutalik*. The letter throws more light on the desperate financial straits the Peshwa faced. Shahu said to Purandare,

> Today by the grace of God, Baji rao's progress is all round. Success and fame, loyalty to me and his service, stand without blemish. But in one matter his behavior is inappropriate. To earn money...(*missing words in the letter*).. so he should protect his reputation a little more. In the past, Dadoji Konddev[b] was a small Brahmin man, but the justice he delivered were revered even by Emperor Aurangzeb.

Baji rao replied to this criticism asking Mahadji to say to the king,

> 'We are the children of the king. Who other than him will correct us with affection? In the past too the Maharaj said such a thing. If he points out where an injustice was seen to have been done, we will make amends as per the Maharaj's desire.'[15]

---

a. Another name for Brahmendra swami.
b. He was appointed administrator of Pune district by Shahaji raje in 1636, and continued in his post till his death in 1647. He was known for his probity and strict administration.

Grant Duff feels Baji rao ran up huge debts as he had to 'outbid' the Nizam to get the best soldiers of the Deccan to join him. Be that as it may, Baji rao had to face a vexed time all through his career due to high debts for his many campaigns which often did not yield sufficient returns to be able to repay them.

The warrior Peshwa seems lost in the world of commerce and finance. Besides, his scrupulous conduct and unflinching loyalty towards his king are underlined in these letters. In contrast, other Maratha chiefs are accused of aggrandising themselves at the cost of the king and the state. It would appear therefore that the chiefs would keep back much of what ought to have been transferred to the central treasury into their own account and armies raised by the Peshwa had to be funded by debt.

In October 1728, Chimaji Appa along with Udaji Pawar and Malharji Holkar and a large army began the Malwa campaign. Nandlal Mandloi, who was responsible for guarding the fords on the Narmada, let the Marathas pass freely. The Marathas were at Dharampuri to the north of the river on 24 November 1728. From here they passed the fort of Mandu and camped at Nalchha.[16]

From Nalchha, two routes lay before Chimaji Appa in his pursuit of mastery over Malwa. One was the more direct route that would take him to Amjhera across the Mandavgad, or Mandu, hills. The second took him to the east of Mandu to Dhar, and then towards Amjhera, where Giridhar Bahadur was based at the time. Giridhar Bahadur had just chased Kanthaji Bande out of Malwa towards Gujarat. As a result, he was camped at Amjhera. Chimaji decided to divide his forces and send part of the army to block the advance of Daya Bahadur, who was at a place between Dhar and Amjhera called Tirla, and another on the *ghat* road to Amjhera. The main force went with him towards Dhar and then west to Amjhera.

Giridhar Bahadur and Daya Bahadur at this time were just north of the hills and on the road between Dhar and Jhabua. The Tanda *ghat* to the west of the fort of Mandu was the expected path of Maratha advance. However, Chimaji took the eastern route round the hills, and passing Dhar, approached

Amjhera. On a hunch, Daya Bahadur felt the approach would be made from the east and turning his army, he began moving from Amjhera towards Dhar. On the way, the two cousins suddenly encountered the Marathas.[17]

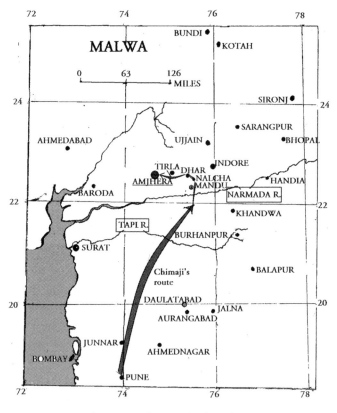

*Chimaji's Path to battle of Amjhera*

A severe engagement broke out between the two forces. Giridhar and Daya Bahadur both fought in an engagement that lasted two *prahar*, or six hours. Both were killed and their entire camp looted. Chimaji's victory at Amjhera and the death of the Mughal *subedar* sent shock waves across the Mughal Empire. The Jaipur *daftar* has a letter from Sawai Jaisingh's agent Keshav Ram that describes the battle,

> Kanthaji Kadam was plundering in Malwa with ten thousand men, so Giridhar Bahadur attacked him and he fled to Banswara in Gujarat.

Then Giridhar Bahadur camped at Amjhera. Just then Baji rao's brother Chimaji and Udaji Pawar with twenty-two thousand men suddenly crossed the Narmada and marched thirty *kos* a day to attack Giridhar Bahadur. Muhammad Umar Khan was at Dhar, so Chimaji kept a small force to prevent him from coming to Bahadur's help, and on 29 November 1729 he suddenly surrounded Bahadur's camp. Rao Gulabram and Salabat Khan came out to fight the Marathas, but both were unfortunately killed. Raja Anandram sustained two bullet wounds and the Marathas caught him and his brother Shambhuram. Giridhar Bahadur himself rode on an elephant and began to fire arrows at the Marathas killing many in the Maratha army. All four quivers of arrows on the elephant were exhausted. Just then an enemy bullet hit him in the chest and he was killed. He served the *sarkar* loyally and gave his life for his master. His family should now be looked after.[18]

On 30 November 1729, Chimaji set up camp at Amjhera, resting his victorious army. Before Chimaji's own letter reached him, Baji rao heard of the battle when he was near the Godavari. On 20 December 1728 he paid forty-eight rupees to two messengers who brought him the good news.[19] The Peshwa wrote to his brother, *'if what we hear is true, proceed to Ujjain and settle matters there before going to an empty district to let the army recover. Take sufficient money from Ujjain.'*[20] Congratulatory letters were sent to Chimaji. One letter says, *'Daya Bahadur was no ordinary pawn. Now the world is on the swami's side.'*[21]

Chimaji next headed for Ujjain and finding it difficult to breach the city walls enforced a siege. Chabila Ram's son Bhavani Ram held the walled city of Ujjain. Bhavani Ram, sent piteous letters seeking help from Jaipur. He wrote,

> The brother of Baji rao and other sardars attacked the city of Ujjain on all sides many times with a view to enter it; a fight ensued and bows and muskets were used in such a way that all villains were either killed or wounded, while on our side too some were killed and wounded. At last they were ashamed and returned to their homes (camp). In this way more than one month has passed since the villains first besieged the city and the fight is on daily. So far none of the imperial servants have reached the city.[22]

When Bhavani Ram, titled Chimna, weathered the siege and the siege at Ujjain seemed to drag on, Baji rao wrote to Chimaji to not waste any more time but send money from other sources to Satara for Shahu.[23] The Peshwa also asked Chimaji to plan his moves independently, while his own plans were to go from the Godavari towards Varhad, (although Shahu at this time had ordered him *'not to go into the province of Varhad'*) the territory of the Bhonsles.[24] The Peshwa signed a treaty with Ranoji Bhonsle to allow his army to traverse his territory.

The invasion of Malwa was Chimaji's first independent campaign. The Peshwa therefore kept himself posted of his brother's progress. He also advised and cautioned him about handling his men and what his aims should be. He wrote to Chimaji,

> I plan to go to Bundelkhand via Chanda and Devgad. I am heading for Chhatrasal's territory.[1] You fill your stomach there, I will fill it here. Do not let egoism enter your mind. Do what is essential to earn money and pay off debts. Safeguard your prestige and reputation and do what is needed to complete the job.[25] Be very cautious; execute such plans as will bring money, don't be guided by only one man's advice. Keep Udaji Pawar entirely pleased. Use discretion and be alert, without considering ease or comfort. If I send any urgent call for you, come away instantly.[26]

In yet another letter he repeats his caution and adds,

> Ranoji Bhonsle who was to join me, has gone to Nemad and Malwa. If he enters Malwa, loot his army. Use sweet words and keep Udaji and Malharji Holkar happy.[27]

Chimaji continued the siege of Ujjain for a while longer but when it failed to make an impact, he moved to Sarangpur, Bundi, Kota and collected dues from these places. From here he began his return journey and reached Pune before the monsoons in May 1729.

Even as Chimaji began withdrawing from Ujjain in January 1729, Baji rao had begun his approach to Chhatrasal's kingdom of Bundelkhand.

# 16. 'Our Realm has Reached the Yamuna'

'We have encircled Bangash and food is at three rupees to a seer in his camp. We have blocked all supplies. In the coming eight days we will sink him or come to an agreement and return home. With the swami's blessing our realm has reached the Yamuna.'

- Pilaji Jadhav rao to Narayan Dixit.[1]

'Cows, horses, and asses came soon to be eaten; things horrid became food; and a dead beast attracted a thousand eyes.'

- *Siyar-ul-Mutaqherin* on the siege at Jaitpur.[2]

The region of Bundelkhand is south of the river Yamuna, stretches to the south to the Narmada and includes the important towns of Orchha, Jhansi, Banda, Kalpi, Sagar and so on. Some of these places rose to prominence after 1730 or so. The name Bundelkhand is said to have come from a legend, where a medieval king was deprived of his kingdom and prayed to the goddess of the Vindhya mountain range – often called *Vindhyavasini* – using his own dagger to shed his blood as a sacrifice. Just as he wounded himself, the goddess appeared and blessed him. The drops – or in Hindustani, 'बूंद', led to the province being called 'Bundel-khand'; *'khand'* meaning a block of land. The land has many rivers like the Chambal and the Yamuna, the Betwa, the Sone and Ken. A hilly forested province, the people living there have been called the 'Bundelas'. Contiguous with the province of Malwa to its west, Bundelkhand is nearly placed at the centre of India.[3]

In the seventeenth century, Champat Rai, the ruler of Bundelkhand helped Aurangzeb win the battle at Samugarh against Dara Shukoh, who had wronged the Bundela king. Champat Rai's help was soon forgotten, and when Aurangzeb turned against him Champat Rai returned to his land and began to assert his own independence. The fight with the Mughals finally culminated in his death in 1661, and his son Chhatrasal took the reins of the province. Although the flame of independence continued to burn bright, Chhatrasal had to accompany Mughal armies to the Deccan where he met and asked *Chhatrapati* Shivaji for help. Shivaji advised him to return to Bundelkhand, fight for his people and gain freedom. This Chhatrasal did with some success when Aurangzeb was embroiled in the long Deccan war. Briefly around 1700, he joined the Mughals in the siege of Satara but returned to Bundelkhand in 1705.

The Afghan adventurer Muhammad Khan hailed from the town of Kohat in eastern Afghanistan and belonged to the Bangash tribe of Pashtuns.[4] His father first came to India in Aurangzeb's reign and made his mark in the Mughal army. Muhammad Khan Bangash first rose to prominence when he helped the Sayyids in their battle with Jehandar Shah. He named his stronghold Farrukhabad after Farrukh Siyar. After Farrukh Siyar was deposed and the Sayyid brothers also dispensed with, he was appointed Governor of the province of Allahabad. Parts of the the Bangash *jagir* lay in Bundelkhand and he began to claim it. From 1721 onwards, Mughal forces attacked Bundelkhand. The defeat of a Mughal chief at Kalpi at the hands of Chhatrasal precipitated the invasion. However, Chhatrasal stoutly opposed his armies, killing Bangash's General Dalel Khan in a fierce battle. Despite the defeat, the heroic fight put up by Dalel Khan is remembered in Bundelkhand to this day.[5]

It was in 1726-7 that Muhammad Shah once again sent Bangash to occupy Bundelkhand with an allowance of two lakh rupees a month. Many Bundela rivals of Chhatrasal also helped Bangash. His son Qaim Khan crossed the Yamuna into Bundelkhand, and father and son began operations in different quarters. For long, Qaim Khan was employed in reducing the fort at Tarawan and could not join his father. In the hilly forested regions between Jaitpur and Mahoba, Chhatrasal struggled against the invaders for two years, until in December 1728 the Bundelas surrendered the fort of Jaitpur. The victorious Bangash sent messages to Delhi seeking permission to bring in his prisoners, and waited for the Emperor's reply.

Three months passed in this state with both armies camped in the jungles of Bundelkhand. Gradually it became clear that Bangash was out of favour in the Mughal court. The Emperor's suspicions about Bangash's motive, a possible coup, prevented any help going to him from Delhi. Nor was he called to Delhi for a personal meeting with Muhammad Shah. Sadat Khan at Awadh too conspired against him. During this lull in activity, the Bundelas began to quietly gather an army again. In February 1729, Chhatrasal, nearly eighty years old was brought to meet Bangash in a palanquin and described as 'extremely ill'. Lest he die in the forest he was allowed to be taken to a nearby town. His sons were allowed to move away from the Mughal camp to celebrate the festival of Holi with the family.

Contrary to popular belief, the Maratha invasion of Bundelkhand had been planned some months earlier. After Palkhed, Baji rao returned to Satara and after the celebrations over his victory were on, there were bills to pay and debts to clear for the king as well as the Peshwa. A fresh campaign had to be planned after the monsoons. This was the genesis of the Bundelkhand campaign, where Chhatrasal was facing invasion by Muhammad Khan Bangash, the *subedar* of Allahabad. Baji rao was by this time in the Varhad region and heading for Bundelkhand via the forested and hilly regions of Garha and Deogarh. In August 1728, Dado Bhimsen, the Peshwa's vakil in Delhi had already asked Baji rao to write a letter to Chhatrasal saying *'our forces will come there after Dassera and help you'*.[6] Dado Bhimsen's letter also mentions that Chhatrasal had sent a family retainer named Durgadas to meet the Peshwa. It was therefore always the Peshwa's intention to head for Bundelkhand as seen in his letters to Chimaji in December 1728 and January 1729.

Baji rao crossed the Narmada at Garha near Jabalpur, accompanied by Pilaji Jadhav rao and *Sarlashkar* Davalji Somvanshi. On 23 January 1729 at Deogarh, Bajirao subjugated the Gond king Chand Sultan. He obtained a tribute of sixty thousand rupees, a fine horse and an elephant. At this time, in extremis, the proud Chhatrasal is said to have sent his famous appeal of ninety-nine stanzas to Baji rao. Chhatrasal was a poet and could well have composed these verses himself. Sending the appeal through Durgadas, Chhatrasal emoted,

'जो गत ग्राह गजेंद्र की, सो गत भई है आज
बाजी जात बुंदेल की, बाजी राखो लाज.'[7]

'I am in the same sad plight,
As the famous elephant when caught by a crocodile,[a]
My valiant race is on the point of extinction,
Come and save my honour.'

Moving through hilly and forested regions, not often used by armies going north, and crossing the Narmada at Garha, Baji rao covered a distance of nearly five hundred kilometres to meet Chhatrasal at Dhamora about forty kilometres west of Shivpuri, on 13 March 1729.[8] Chhatrasal made an offering of four thousand nine hundred eighty-nine rupees and fifty paise while Baji rao honoured him with an elephant and a horse. The combined army then headed for Mahoba, about one hundred kilometres away and reached in its vicinity in three days.

As the *bakhar* says, 'on the twenty-second day' of getting Chhatrasal's message, Baji rao was near Jaitpur.[9]

Having defeated Chhatrasal after a campaign lasting two years, Bangash was able to send away some of his troops to their homes and retain just a small force of four thousand with him. His son Qaim Khan was at Tarawan, near Karwi, with a large army of thirty thousand men. After the triumph at Malwa, rumours of the Marathas approaching Bundelkhand began to fly, but Bangash would not believe them. Baji rao was approaching the region by a forested unfrequented route and until the Marathas reached twenty kilometres from his position, Bangash did not believe the news. Then, he hurriedly mustered his army and began organising a defence at Jaitpur. Hirde Sah, who had given Bangash his word, remained aloof and did not join the Marathas against Bangash.

As they approached Jaitpur, Baji rao, Pilaji Jadhav rao, Tukoji Pawar, Vithal Shivdeo, Davalji Somvanshi and other Maratha chiefs began spreading

---

a.   In the *Bhagawata Purana*, an ancient Hindu text, is the story of Gajendra *moksha* that Chhatrasal alludes to in his letter. A great elephant was once bathing in a lake near his abode by a mountain named Trikuta. A crocodile in the lake grabbed the elephant's leg and began dragging it into deep water. The elephant – Gajendra – prayed to Lord Vishnu, who appeared before him and saved him by cutting off the neck of the crocodile.

their troops to encircle Bangash's camp. On 22 March 1729, the Marathas were just three kilometres away from Bangash.

Qaim Khan heard of his father's plight and came as far as Supa, a place about twenty kilometres north-east of Jaitpur with a large army of thirty thousand. Pilaji Jadhav met them in battle and describes the action in his letter,

> We had encircled Muhammad Khan Bangash's position when suddenly we heard that his son was coming with an army of thirty thousand. We fought with him. By God's wish, he was sunk along with his army. We took three thousand horses and thirteen elephants...[10]

Taking advantage of the diversion, Bangash moved off to the fort of Jaitpur further south-east. At Jaitpur he took a strong defensive position and sent urgent messages to the Emperor for help. Muhammad Shah ordered Khan Dauran to head for Bundelkhand. However, this noble merely sat in his camp outside Delhi setting a fresh date for departure every morning and evening without actually embarking on the campaign. On the contrary, he sent messages to the Bundelas that they ought to finish Bangash now, and send his head to the Emperor who would be pleased as the *pathan* was plotting to take the throne of Delhi. Qaim Khan met Sadat Khan at Awadh and sought his help, only to find he was himself in danger of being detained. He got some help from Ali Muhammad Rohilla, a fellow Afghan, and he raised money from his home district of Farrukhabad. Finally, raising a fresh army of thirty thousand, he began his return journey to Jaitpur to succour his father.

At Jaitpur, in the meanwhile, the Marathas besieged Bangash and cut off all supplies to the garrison. On 4 April 1729 Pilaji Jadhav rao wrote to Narayan Dixit,

> We have encircled Bangash and food is at three rupees to a seer in his camp. We have blocked all supplies. In the coming eight days we will sink him or come to an agreement and return home. As per the swami's blessing our realm has reached the Yamuna. Many people have gone on a pilgrimage too.[1]

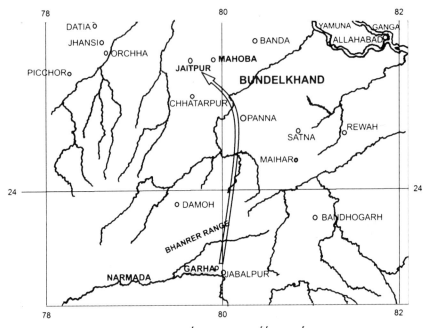

*Baji rao's dash to succour Chhatrasal*

William Irwine, from neglected original letters and notebooks lying in dust at the Bangash capital of Farrukhabad in 1879, pieced together an account of the campaign:

> The Maratha army was commanded by Baji rao and Pila Jadon and others, twelve leaders in all. No account could be got of the force they had when they started, but on the way they had been joined by turbulent spirits among the zamindars, who came in the hope of plundering and laying waste the imperial territory. The total force had thus swelled to nearly seventy thousand men besides an equal number of Bundelas.

> On Wednesday, the 22nd *Sha'ban* of the 11th year (1141 H = 12 March 1729), the Marathas sent out a party to the hills of Ajhnar, who came within one *kos* of Muhammad Khan's encampment and reconnoitred the position. They fell on the grazing cattle of the camp followers, but were soon driven away by the Muhammaedans, who brought in three heads and some horses.

> The next day, before sunrise, the Marathas advanced by the right and the left to the rear of the camp, where they cut off the camels and other beasts of burden, when going out for grass. Troops were sent out to recover the

camels and the fighting went on till midday. The same tactics were repeated on the 24th (14 March 1729), and the enemy were again repelled, twenty heads being brought in.

On 25th *Sha'ban* (15 March), Muhammad Khan made a sortie and all day the enemy hid themselves in the hills. Near sunset they suddenly rushed out, but were driven back with the loss of five men and four horses. After the first watch of the night, when it was very dark, the contest began again on the right wing and *'the fire was like the fall of leaves from trees'*. Four of the enemy were killed and some horses and camels captured. It was now reported that Baji rao had sent for his brothers who were then on a plundering expedition towards Kotah and Bundi.

Gradually the Marathas succeeded in closing round the camp, and placed outposts to the rear where they kept up the most vigilant outlook. In all directions the roads were blocked, prices rose very high, mahrwah or mandwa, an inferior grain, cost twenty rupees the seer, and other grain could not be procured. All, great and small, endured the greatest privations for two months (15 March to 15 May 1729), sustaining life on the flesh of camels, horses and cows. Nor were they left in peace by night and day: they were in action often five or six times a day. Each day the enemy *'like the multitude of the stars before the rising sun'*, fled into the rocks and hollows of the hills.[11]

The siege of Jaitpur lasted from the middle of May till as late as the end of August 1729 as per Persian *tawarikh*s, but Marathi letters state the task was complete when Baji rao left for the Deccan on 9 June. The narrative in original Marathi letters, and the story as gathered by Irwine therefore has some differences. Pilaji Jadhav rao's letter says that Qaim Khan with thirty thousand soldiers was 'sunk' before the siege at Jaitpur, while Irwine says, Qaim Khan returned with thirty thousand men after collecting troops at various places. Irwine's account says that in the first skirmish Qaim Khan had barely one thousand men with him and was repelled by the Marathas.

Irwine continues his narration,

> The Marathas, having defeated Qaim Khan soon returned, and completely invested the town and fort of Jaitpur, into which Muhammad Khan had withdrawn with his men and had closed the gates. A cannonade from both sides began and Akbar Khan, the Nawab's son (Bangash's son), who was renowned for his strength, threw down heavy stones from the fort wall and killed many of the Marathas. When the besiegers found they could not take the place by assault, they decided to starve out the garrison. Jaitpur was strictly

invested for several months till there was no longer any grain for food. Then the soldiers began to slaughter their horses and bullocks. Flour could not be procured even at hundred rupees the seer. Some of the Marathas used to come at night with supplies of flour, half of which was made up of ground bones. Those inside let down their money by a rope, flour was attached in its place at the rate of a seer for a hundred rupees, and the rope was then drawn up. Many of the soldiers died of starvation, and many more leaving the Nawab to his fate escaped from the fort. Baji rao's orders to his guards were that any of Muhammad Khan's men who gave up their arms should be allowed to pass unmolested. Many having no food preferred to give up their arms and get away. Only some thousand or twelve hundred remained with the Nawab.

The *Siyar-ul-Mutaqherin* says,

> Cows, horses, and asses came soon to be eaten; things horrid became food; and a dead beast attracted a thousand eyes.[2]

A terrible epidemic is also said to have spread in the Maratha camp and many thousands died. The rains were setting in and they were anxious to return home. Muhammad Khan Bangash soon came to terms and was allowed to leave unharmed on condition that he would never again enter Bundelkhand while the Bundelas would remit the yearly tribute as agreed. Bangash left Bundelkhand in October 1729, kept his word, and never entered the province again.

Baji rao was given a third of Chhatrasal's kingdom and became the third son of the aged king. At the conclusion of the war, Chhatrasal held a *durbar* and invited the Peshwa. Baji rao stood before Chhatrasal, and the old king asked him to be seated.

Baji rao said, 'Give me a place to sit and I will do so.'

Chhatrasal said, 'You are a son to me.'

Baji rao said, 'You have two legitimate sons, besides which you have fifty-four other sons. In this, I will get a place worth just two lakh rupees. I have exhausted fifteen to twenty lakh rupees over the last six months. If this is not resolved, when I return, Maharaj Shahu will be displeased. Therefore if you give me a place that befits me, I will take a seat.'

The Raja then answered, 'I have two sons; Hirde Sah and Jagat raj. You are my third son. I will make three parts of my kingdom and divide them as per seniority.'

महाराजाधिराज श्रीजयसिंघराजाजी घजीश्रीजयसिंघीरानो

Sawai Jaisingh of Amber (on left) with Maharana Sangram Singh of Marwar

Malharji Holkar

Nizam-ul-mulk Asaf Jah

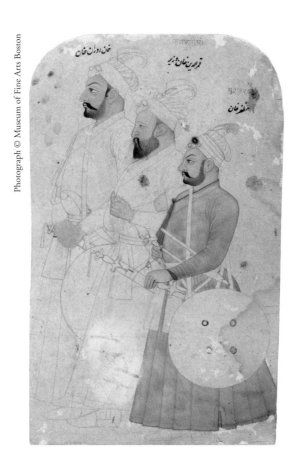

خان دوران خان

قمرالدین خان وزیر

مظفر خان

Left to right : Khan Dauran, Wazir Qamruddin Khan and Muzaffar Khan

Shaniwar wada

Saying this, Raja Chhatrasal rose, held Baji rao's hand and gave him the seat next to Jagat raj. Baji rao and Hirde Sah exchanged turbans. The kingdom was divided as decreed by the raja. Out of the total value of one crore and eleven lakh, Baji rao was given an estate worth thirty-six lakh rupees.[12] The yield from the diamond mines of Panna were also distributed accordingly. Mastani, the daughter of Chhatrasal from a Muslim lady was presented to the Peshwa as a 'gift' and stayed in Pune from then on. Baji rao then appointed his own officers in the newly acquired territory and returned to Pune. Chhatrasal died soon after in 1731 at the age of eighty-one.

Baji rao reached Pune in July 1729 and spent the monsoon months at his capital. The town on the bank of the river Mutha had been given to Baji rao as his *jagir* in 1726. The Peshwa preferred to make Pune his headquarters over the town of Saswad as it was a place that had a better water supply and was better located. On 10 January 1730 he began construction of a permanent abode at Pune called the *Shaniwar wada*.

The *Shaniwar wada* was built by Shivram Krishna Khasgiwale, and although the amount spent is mentioned as sixteen thousand one hundred and ten rupees, it was possibly more than that.[13] Many other buildings of Baji rao's aides were built nearby. Shahu did not like any fortification around the *wada*, arguing it would be used against the Marathas if anybody else occupied it. The town was never fortified, but Nanasaheb Peshwa built a wall around *Shaniwar wada* at a later date. The *Shaniwar wada* was completed in 1732 and the buildings within were added as time went by.

Successive victories at Palkhed, Malwa and Bundelkhand had changed the Indian political scene. The Mughal Emperor's court, divided as always, furiously began to devise ways to control the Marathas from spilling into the north and ravaging Mughal territories. Principal among these worthies were two groups of courtiers led by Sawai Jaisingh and Khan Dauran on the one hand and *Wazir* Qamruddin Khan with Sadat Khan on the other. These led to events in the north that forever stamped the name of Baji rao in Indian history.

≷ঔৎ≷ঔৎ

# 17. Sawai Jaisingh sends an Envoy

'Baji rao*ji* is the only one who can be described thus. There is none other
who is honest, or mature, or capable of raising large armies at short notice.'

- Deep Singh's answer to the Nizam.[1]

The Kacchhwa Rajputs of Jaipur were for long close allies of the Mughal
Emperor. In the days of *Chhatrapati* Shivaji, *Mirza raja* Jaisingh had led a
campaign to the Deccan that forced the Maratha king to sign a treaty and
agree to meet Aurangzeb at Agra. Shivaji's sensational escape from Agra led
to a fall in the Kacchhwa influence in Delhi. Sawai Jaisingh therefore began
his career in the Mughal armies under Aurangzeb as a relatively modest
*mansabdar* of 2000 *zat* and 2000 *swar*. This was a major climb-down from
the 7000 zat 7000 *swar* that Mirza raje Jaisingh held under Aurangzeb. In
1701 Sawai Jaisingh, at the age of fourteen, took part in the siege of the fort
of Khelna in the Deccan, and it is surmised that he must have met Shahu at
the time as he had to move with Aurangzeb's camp.

On Aurangzeb's death, Azam Shah started from the Deccan and on the
advice of Zulfiquar Khan, promoted Jaisingh to the customary rank of 7000
*zat* and 7000 *swar*. The reign of Azam Shah ended shortly thereafter in the
battle against his brother Bahadur Shah, who became the next Emperor.
Jaisingh was once again demoted and Bahadur Shah even tried to remove him
from the throne of Amber.[2] In 1709, the Rajputs perceived the Emperor to be
weak and a semblance of unity appeared among them. Ajit Singh of Marwar
and Jaisingh made demands on Bahadur Shah to get back their hereditary
*vatan*s. Bahadur Shah, with his eye on the Sikh uprising raging in the Punjab,
made peace and Jodhpur was returned to Ajit Singh after a thirty-year-long
struggle.

Once the Mughals' war with the Sikhs was over, Jaisingh feared the
Emperor would march against him, and in 1711 sent letters to the Marathas
asking them to come to Malwa and Gujarat thereby diverting imperial
resources. However, the Emperor did not invade the Rajputs. Azim-us-shan

also approached the Marathas in 1711, to create such disturbances as would disturb Zulfiquar Khan's deputy Daud Khan Panni in the Deccan. The Marathas were thus seen by the Rajputs as well as the Mughals as a means to further their own interest after the death of Aurangzeb.

In 1712, Zulfiquar Khan once again rose to power as the *Wazir*, and Jaisingh was promoted to the high rank he aspired for. In the reign of Farrukh Siyar, Jaisingh remained loyal to the Emperor and in 1713 was rewarded with the *subedari* of Malwa, when he even won a major battle against Maratha forces. Ajit Singh, whose daughter was married to Farrukh Siyar, was given the province of Gujarat. The power struggle at Delhi during the Sayyid supremacy, led to Jaisingh being recalled from Malwa in 1717, and after a brief reappearance in imperial affairs in 1721, he remained aloof for half a dozen years when he was building his new capital city of Jaipur. Rajput politics struck a new low in 1724, when Ajit Singh was murdered by his own son Bakht Singh purportedly on the orders of his elder brother Abhay Singh, at the instigation of the Mughal court.[a] Ajit Singh's part in the deposition of Farrukh Siyar still rankled, and by his elimination, the Mughals felt they had meted out justice.

Jaisingh had by 1725 gauged the power of the Marathas and advised the Emperor to come to terms with them by giving them some *jagirs* in Malwa and Gujarat and satiate their desire for conquest. He also advised Sarbuland Khan, the then *subedar* in Gujarat, to concede the Maratha demand for *chauth*.

In the aftermath of Chimaji's victory at Amjhera, Jaisingh was reappointed as *subedar* of Malwa. When he took over in October 1729, Jaisingh tried to have an agreement with Shahu and wrote a note to the Emperor explaining his approach to the Maratha invasions,

> Marathas had tasted Malwa for long. By our heavy concentration of troops this year we prevent their entry into Malwa or chastise them when they enter, we will know the expenditure needed for this purpose every year. Since Raja Shahu is a *mansabdar* from the days of Aurangzeb, I propose Your Majesty should give him a *jagir* of ten lakh in the name of his adopted

---

a. It is not quite clear if this was indeed the case.

son Khushal Singh,[a] on condition that he prevent any further disturbance in
Malwa and an auxiliary contingent of his troops should attend the *subedar*
of that province. This will give peace to the land and save us the expense of
campaigning every year.[4]

Jaisingh requested Shahu to return the fort of Mandu and establish a
good basis for further negotiations. Shahu accordingly ordered Chimaji and
Udaji Pawar to return the fort to Jaisingh.[5]

Then Shahu came to an agreement with Jaisingh to stop incursions into
Malwa in exchange for a *jagir* of ten lakh rupees in the name Khushal Singh,
the Rajput prince who Jaisingh tried to have Shahu adopt as his son. However,
on returning from Bundelkhand, Baji rao opposed the agreement as it would
mean foregoing the entire enterprise of northward expansion. The agreement
therefore was abandoned.

Given the convoluted politics of the Delhi court, Sawai Jaisingh did not last
long as the *subedar* in Malwa. Muhammad Khan Bangash, who had faced
defeat and disgrace in Bundelkhand, promised the Emperor that he would
throw the Marathas out of Malwa. The Emperor thus replaced Jaisingh with
Bangash as the *subedar*. However, he was poorly equipped and financed for
his mission. Obtaining what guns and soldiers he could at Agra, Bangash
finally made his way to Gwalior.

Jaisingh, on his way back to Jaipur, began to devise ways to reconcile
the Emperor with the Marathas, and if possible, recruit them in the imperial
cause. Khan Dauran was Muhammad Shah's favourite, and was also in favour
of such a policy. Jaisingh therefore decided to send some emissaries to the court
of Shahu to hold talks and find out how the Marathas could be persuaded to
stay south of the Narmada. A clever diplomat named Deep Singh Kumbhani
and Mansa ram Purohit were sent to Satara. Vyagharaj (called 'Bagaji' in
Marathi papers) of Mewar also accompanied them.

Deep Singh reached Satara on 22 May 1730, but as Baji rao was
indisposed no discussions were held till 20 June. During his stay at Satara

---

a.  The identity of Khushal Singh is not known. Shahu did show an inclination to adopt
    Nathji who was the younger son of Maharana Sangram Singh of Mewar.[3]

in the monsoon months, Deep Singh met all Shahu's ministers. Jaisingh sent Shahu a studded crest[a] while the Peshwa was given gifts for a wedding in the family.[6] On behalf of Jaisingh and the Emperor, Deep Singh made an offer to pay the Marathas eleven lakh rupees for Malwa and fifteen lakh for Gujarat against their claim for *chauth*, in exchange for their promise of not crossing the Narmada. The Maratha response is not available to us.

From Satara, after the rains, Deep Singh proceeded to Aurangabad to meet the Nizam and sound him out about the proposals in hand. The Nizam in general deprecated any agreement with the Marathas saying any such treaty is not worth a '*kowrie*.'[7] After reaching Hyderabad, Deep Singh's first meeting with the Nizam took place on 22 October 1730. The Nizam's conversation with Deep Singh is described by the Maratha *vakil* in considerable detail, and throws light on the prevailing situation in Satara and the Deccan,

> Deep Singhji has arrived. The Nizam has given him robes of honour. The Nawab greeted Deep Singhji and held him close. Then sitting with him, the Nawab asked him, 'Sawai Jaisingh is a great prince, he specifically sent you to Shahu; what could be so important a task? It was hardly appropriate for a great person like yourself coming for this.' Thus the Nizam began to woo Deep Singh.
>
> Deep Singh answered, 'Jaisingh did not send me of his own accord. The Emperor ordered him to go and take back Mandavgad (Mandu) and to send a respected diplomat to Shahu Maharaj to arrange matters related to Gujarat and Malwa, and to prevent the Marathas from crossing the Narmada. Hence I came on the orders of the Emperor.'
>
> Then the Nawab asked, 'So how did you do when you were there?'
>
> Deep Singh said, 'I offered them the *khandani* of Malwa at eleven lakh and of Gujarat at fifteen lakh, so that the Marathas will leave those provinces.'
>
> The Nawab said, 'Malwa is not in your hands. Bangash is sitting there.'
>
> Deep Singh said, 'Bangash should pay this amount, if he does not, the Marathas will see what to do.'

---

a.  Its value is given as nine hundred and seventy rupees.

The Nawab said, 'In this manner you have tied the amount of eleven lakh around Bangash's neck and drowned his house. What is profitable for him in this deal? When I was *subedar* of Malwa I realised revenue of thirty to forty lakh. Then, in Gujarat, Bande and Gaekwad will create havoc, what about them? Will they accept the treaty you have made with the *Pradhan*?'

Deep Singh said, 'Bande, Gaekwad, Dabhade will be censured by Chimaji Appa and Jaisingh together.'

Nizam said, 'Do you trust Chimaji Appa or the *Pradhan pant*? I have no faith in them.'

Deep Singh answered, 'I have complete trust in them. They are known to us as family friends from my father's time. They will not go back on their word.'

Then leaving all these things aside, the Nizam repeatedly began to ask, 'Who did you find with the Satara Maharaj who is eminent, and capable of strategic planning, and trusted by the Raja?'

Deep Singh replied, 'It was to find this that Maharaj Jaisinghji mainly sent me; that Baji rao Pandit *Pradhan* is renowned for his bravery in the land, but who is it that is capable of managing affairs, known for diplomacy, and respected and honoured in the kingdom, and a mature administrator; such a person I should identify in my mind. So I have fulfilled that task and identified such a person.'

Then the Nawab began to ask, 'so, who did you identify in the Satara court as eminent, mature, efficient, confidante of the king?'

Deep Singhji answered, 'Baji rao*ji* is the only one who can be described thus. There is none other who is honest or mature or capable of raising large armies at short notice.'

The Nawab then asked, 'How is the Raja himself?'

Deep Singh said, 'The king also has many nuances.'

The Nawab asked, 'We have heard he is gullible and hears gossip.'

Deep Singh said, 'If the king does not take advice of all the courtiers then how could such a large kingdom have survived? The king is clever, mature and wise. He is a good interlocutor.'

Thus they talked to each other.[8]

The embassy of Deep Singh paved the way for further interactions between the Rajput princes and the Marathas. The impression that an envoy of Jaipur conveyed about Shahu and Baji rao in the Nizam's court would be a fair reflection of their power and personalities.

However, the Nizam was still smarting from his defeat at Palkhed. He could not have been pleased to hear Deep Singh's answers, for at that very time he was busy putting together the finishing touches to another grand campaign. Once again he found an aggrieved and willing Maratha chief to take up cudgels against the Peshwa.

It was to be a stern test of Baji rao's abilities.

# 18. The *Senapati's* Revolt

'You may not be wrong, but you should take care that it does not appear
as if you are causing the kingdom's Marathas to desert Shahu. Be very
cautious that no untoward event that besmirches your reputation or appears
repugnant to the public occurs.'

- Naro Ram to Baji rao, December 1730.[1]

When the Nizam arrived in the Deccan in 1724 in defiance of Muhammad
Shah's orders and fought Mubariz Khan, he also appointed his uncle Hamid
Khan as *subedar* of Gujarat. The Emperor then called Sarbuland Khan from
Kabul and appointed him in Gujarat. This worthy did not go there at once
but sent his lieutenant Shujaat Khan instead. Hamid Khan, finding himself
unequal to face the challenge, summoned Kanthaji Kadam Bande to help
him. In the battle that ensued Kanthaji defeated and killed Shujaat Khan and
Hamid Khan gave Kanthaji the *chauth* of Gujarat.

Shujaat's brother Rustam Ali Khan was then at Surat. He obtained the
help of Pilaji Gaekwad and rushed to give battle to Hamid Khan. However,
when Pilaji saw Kanthaji in Hamid Khan's army, he deserted Rustam Ali who
was killed in the ensuing battle. As a prize for abandoning Rustam Ali Khan,
Hamid Khan gave Pilaji *chauth* of the region south of the river Mahi while
Kanthaji was awarded the region to the north.

On hearing of the defeat of Shujaat Khan, Sarbuland Khan finally came to
Gujarat, but was completely overpowered at Ahmedabad by thirty thousand
Maratha troops. Offering the Marathas large sums of money he succeeded
in bringing them to his side. For Hamid Khan, it meant an end to his rule.
Fleeing Gujarat, he went to the Nizam.

Sarbuland Khan's troubles were not over. Finding that Pilaji Gaekwad
and Kanthaji Kadam Bande had secured the *chauth* of Gujarat, the Peshwa
sent Chimaji Appa, who attacked Gujarat in 1726, and once again in 1730.
Chimaji forced Sarbuland Khan to concede the *chauth* of Gujarat to the
Peshwa and signed a treaty. This led to disgruntlement among Dabhade,

Kanthaji Kadam Bande and Pilaji Gaekwad. Gujarat was, until then, a province delegated to *Senapati* Khande rao Dabhade and although Shahu gave it to Chimaji in 1726, he was told to give half of the province back to the Dabhades.

The Peshwa, as Prime Minister of the kingdom, wished to have a part of Gujarat under his jurisdiction and offered Dabhade some part of Malwa in exchange for a share in Gujarat. However, this was not acceptable to Dabhade. A few years preceding 1729, Khande rao Dabhade himself was unwell and many of his duties were performed by his son Trimbak rao. Relations between Baji rao and Trimbak rao Dabhade were far from satisfactory. The Peshwa's military success had reduced the *Senapati's* authority. During the battle at Palkhed, Trimbak rao, instead of helping the Peshwa was raiding his territories in Malwa. Shahu had served a severe reprimand to Khande rao,

> You have plundered Malwa and taken *khandani* from there. Rupees 1,13,000 from Dongarpur, 50,000 from Banswada, 80,000 from Jhabua. You took money and about two hundred and fifty horses too. In other places too you took a ransom. People ran away out of fear. You burnt their houses and broke down the walls. The region was made desolate. What is the need for you to plunder Malwa and take tribute? Now, whatever money you have taken should be sent to Baji rao Pandit *Pradhan*. You should not plunder Malwa ever again. I should get no complaints about this.[2]

The conflict over the *chauth* of Gujarat further strained relations between the Peshwa and the *Senapati*. This intelligence reached the Nizam, and around the time Deep Singh was visiting the Nizam, he set in motion a broad-based strategy to check the Peshwa.

The Dabhade *bakhar* is a chronicle giving the history of the family based in Talegaon near Pune. In the seventeenth century, Yash Patil Dabhade, the *mukadam* of Talegaon, had taken employment with *Chhatrapati* Shivaji as an ordinary attendant. Later he was said to be a 'tutor' to the two princes, Sambhaji and Rajaram, while his sons Khande rao and Shivaji Dabhade worked as pages.[3] When in 1690 Rajaram had to flee from Panhala to Ginjee in the south, the two brothers physically carried their king forty miles in one

day. Shivaji Dabhade is said to have died of fatigue in the journey.[a] Rajaram
was pleased and gave Khande rao *jagir*s in Kolhapur, Indapur and Junnar,
besides Baglan and Khandesh. Khande rao was titled *Sena Khaskhel*, or
Commander of the Royal Guards, and held important positions in Rajaram's,
and later, Tara bai's administration.

In 1707, Shahu's return led to a split in the Maratha nobility and Khande
rao initially joined Shahu, but a year later he rejoined Tara bai. Shahu took
away his *jagir*s around Kolhapur and gave them to Fateh Sinh Bhonsle.
Shahu's award to Fateh Sinh said,

> If any one were to disturb the possession, his act, were he a Hindu or of the
> Bhonsle family, would be deemed as heinous as if he had killed both a cow
> and a Brahmin at Benares and were he a Musulman as if he had taken an
> oath on the *Kaaba* and broken it.[4]

In the same year, Shahu also took away half of Khande rao's *mokasa*
around Nashik and handed it over to *Senakarte* Balaji Vishwanath.[5] Two years
later Khande rao once again returned to Shahu, and was given the old rank
of *Sena Khaskhel*.[6] However, the very next year, he was part of the group of
Maratha chiefs who joined Tara bai with Chandrasen Jadhav.[7] He returned
to Shahu a few years later and on 11 January 1717 was appointed as the
*Senapati*. However, Khande rao's *jagir*s were not restored to him. Khande rao
wrote to Shahu in 1721 asking for the *jagir* required to maintain his troops
and *'if there be any stigma attached to the post of Senapati, it should not be
transferred to him'.*[8][b] The *jagir*s were however, not restored in full.

Khande rao could not cope with the needs of his post and after 1725,
his sons fulfilled his commitments. Khande rao wrote several letters to Baji
rao asking for money to pay his troops and for a share in the revenue of the
districts of Ramnagar and Jawhar in the Konkan.[9] In two separate letters to
Ambaji Purandare and Baji rao, Khande rao and his wife Uma bai accuse the
Peshwa of not keeping his word and remitting dues from places under their
jurisdiction. To resolve these problems Shahu sent emissaries to Talegaon
asking the Dabhades to come to Satara for a reconciliation with the Peshwa,

---

a.   Rajaram *Charitam* says it was Bahirji Ghorpade who took Rajaram on his shoulder and
      safely to Ginjee.
b.   He was probably referring to the rebellion of Chandrasen Jadhav.

but this did not happen,[10] and efforts to mend relations between Dabhade and the Peshwa did not bear fruit.[11] Baji rao, as Prime Minister, stood on the principle that all provinces must have the presence of the *Chhatrapati* and the Peshwa. Dabhade's interest was more personal; to regain his patrimony.

The dispute remained unsettled when Khande rao Dabhade died on 27 September 1729. On 8 January 1730, his eldest son Trimbak rao was appointed the *Senapati*. Simmering anger over loss of their huge *jagirs* over the years, coupled with the growing power of the Peshwa and fall in prestige of the *Senapati*, gradually came to a boil. Trimbak rao was young and active, and a brave soldier, and felt his grievance could only be addressed by opposing the Peshwa. He believed the king was no longer free to take his own decisions and the Peshwa's overpowering influence had to be cut to size; if necessary by force. With the Nizam's encouragement, once again, a Maratha chief was to tread the familiar path of joining Shahu's enemies.

Even as Trimbak rao was taking over his father's mantle, Chimaji Appa was campaigning in Gujarat. Chimaji entered the province in December 1729 and took the fort of Pawagad from Kanthaji.[12] Sarbuland Khan was away in Kutch and could not face the fresh aggression. In March 1730 Chimaji plundered Petlad and Dholka near Ahmedabad, forcing the embattled Sarbuland Khan to concede the *chauth* of Gujarat to the Peshwa. As Kincaid and Parasnis write, Sarbuland Khan looked upon Pilaji Gaekwad and Kanthaji

> ..as little better than bandits, but Chimaji Appa had behind him the authority both of the king and the Peshwa. To Chimaji Appa, therefore, the distracted Sarbuland Khan addressed himself and offered to give him the *chauth* and *sardeshmukhi* of Gujarat, if he would protect him from other Maratha marauders.[13]

Ranoji Scindia and Malharji Holkar attacked Kadam Bande and forced him to seek protection in the walled village of Ranala near Nandurbar.[14] Chimaji also collected tribute from Cambay (Khambayat) before returning to Pune. The monsoon months were spent by both camps planning a stormy campaign after the festival of Dassera. The Jaipur envoy Deep Singh was in Satara and Pune at this time. By the time Deep Singh visited the Nizam in October 1730; large armies were already on their way to Gujarat.

The rivalry between Shahu and Sambhaji was a festering sore in the Maratha state. In the year 1730, a conflict between the two in the environs of Satara and Kolhapur occupied many Maratha chiefs and the two kings. One of Sambhaji's principal supporters was Udaji Chavan, who had an estate at Athni near Bijapur, and he had always been a thorn in Shahu's side. For a while he did come to terms with Shahu. However, in early 1730 Udaji began collecting revenue from villages around Shirol, calling it Chavan *patti*. Shahu had greater resources and strength; it was thought, perhaps the matter could be resolved without coming to the battlefield.

An interesting anecdote of Shahu precedes the main battle between the two cousins. Shahu was hunting in a forest and had spread out his men. Alone in a palanquin with just a stick, he saw two burning wicks and guns behind a tree.

'Who is it?' Shahu called out.

Two men came before him, bowed their heads before him and said, 'we are assassins.'

'Then why did you not kill?' Shahu asked.

The assassins said, 'seeing you, we lost our courage and the heart to do the deed.'

'Who sent you?' Shahu then asked.

'We are from Panhala[a]', the men answered.

'Leave your guns, and run away,' Shahu advised them, 'if the *Pratinidhi* finds you, he will kill you.'[15]

After this, Shahu bestirred himself to lead a campaign against his cousin. The *Pratinidhi* and Shambhu Sinh Jadhav, a son of Dhanaji Jadhav, were called. Baji rao was told not to go too far away. Trimbak rao Dabhade, Davalji Somvanshi, and Sekhoji Angre were also summoned. However, not all these took part and essentially Shripat rao *Pratinidhi* and Shambhu Sinh led the campaign. A few skirmishes put an end to Udaji and Sambhaji's pretensions and they fled to Panhala. Their whole camp was looted and many of Sambhaji's family members were also caught in the swoop. Tara bai, Sambhaji's mother

---

a.   Kolhapur

Rajas bai, his wives, Ramchandra *pant*'s son Bhagwant rao *amatya*, and Baji rao's brother-in-law Vyankat rao Ghorpade of Ichalkaranji were all taken prisoner. The *Pratinidhi* escorted Rajas bai and Sambhaji's queens to Panhala, and returned to Satara with the others.

Tara bai, who had opposed Shahu during her reign, was welcomed warmly at Satara and honoured with many gifts. Shahu offered to take her to Kolhapur if she so desired. However, Tara bai said, *'if it is prison that I have to endure, it does not matter where I stay. I will prefer living at Satara'*. From that time for the next three decades Tara bai was a resident in the fort at Satara. In August 1730, Sambhaji conceded defeat and agreed to sign a treaty. The two cousins signed the 'Treaty of Warana', and Sambhaji visited Satara in early 1731 where he was received and treated honourably. Boundaries between them were adjusted. Bhagwant rao was released on Sambhaji paying his ransom; however, the *Pratinidhi* would not release Vyankat rao Ghorpade. It was only after Baji rao paid ten thousand rupees to the *Pratinidhi* that Ghorpade was released.

The Mughal court did not like Sarbuland Khan's capitulation to the Marathas in Gujarat. The Emperor decided to send Abhay Singh from Jodhpur to Gujarat as the new *subedar*. On 28 October 1730, Abhay Singh entered Ahmedabad, imprisoned Sarbuland Khan and dispatched him to Delhi.[16] Although Abhay Singh promised to remove the Marathas from Gujarat, he could not achieve much. The Maratha armies were already on their way to his province.

Matters between Dabhade and the Peshwa continued to escalate through the monsoon months of 1730. Baji rao decided to adopt an aggressive attitude. He lured away several of Dabhade's men by giving them the *mokasa* of various places. Dabhade's step-uncle, Bhavsingh Toke, was given a *jagir* in November 1730.[17] Toke was to play a seminal, even errant, role in the days to come. Malharji Holkar and Ranoji Scindia had been awarded large parts of Malwa and Udaji Pawar's share had been reduced. Udaji therefore fell out with the Peshwa in October 1730, and joined Dabhade. Along with Udaji, Kanthaji and Pilaji Gaekwad, Trimbak rao made common cause with the Nizam to form a front against the Peshwa. The alliance grew further when Chimnaji Damodar and Muhammad Khan Bangash joined them.

On 8 October 1730 Trimbak rao left his home at Talegaon with a large army, heading towards the Nizam's territory. Baji rao and Chimaji left two days later for Gujarat via Nashik, crossing the Tapi and Narmada. Chimaji, along with Pilaji Jadhav rao, stayed in the Khandesh region to keep a watch on the Nizam. Baji rao laid a siege to Pilaji Gaekwad's stronghold, the city of Vadodara. Chimaji found the Nizam heading north, and guessing he would go to help Dabhade, went towards Gujarat to reinforce Baji rao. At the same time he posted Holkar and Ranoji Scindia in Malwa.

Letters of the period show how Dabhade and his allies stitched together a coalition against Baji rao. The confederates met each other in the run-up to the campaign. A letter of 28 October 1730 from Govind Ballal reports that Udaji Pawar and Kanthaji Bande met the Nizam at Sakharkherda. The letter also says that Chimnaji Damodar is expected to meet the Nizam.[18] This meeting was followed by the Nizam's meeting with Dabhade.

The Nizam marched to Khandesh with his well-equipped artillery. Trimbak rao headed for Sangamner and met Turktaz Khan. He then met the Nizam at Chalisgaon, and after deliberations headed for Gujarat. Kunwar Bahadur from Sinnar joined him as did Shahu's former aide Chimnaji Damodar. Near Surat, Trimbak rao's army swelled further when Udaji Pawar and Pilaji Gaekwad joined him. They crossed the Narmada on 26 March 1731 and camped at Karnali at its confluence with the river Orsang.

Earlier at Ahmedabad, Abhay Singh the new *subedar*, had heard Baji rao had laid a siege to Pilaji Gaekwad's stronghold at Vadodara. Abhay Singh sent Baji rao a message inviting him for talks. Baji rao accepted the invitation and the two met at Ahmedabad's Shahi *bagh*. The Peshwa's demand of *chauth* was accepted in exchange for his help to clear the province of other Maratha chiefs such as Gaekwad and Kadam Bande. Abhay Singh suggested to the Mughal court that conceding some demands and bringing over Baji rao to the imperial side would help restore order in Gujarat. He complained that instead of doing this, the Nizam was encouraging others like Gaekwad and Kadam Bande, thereby provoking Baji rao to act against the Emperor.[19]

A major flash point began to devolve on Gujarat. Abhay Singh favoured Baji rao. The Nizam along with Bangash was engaged in helping Dabhade. Dabhade himself was fighting to win back his patrimony and *mokasa* in Gujarat.

A combative Chimaji Appa's letter of 12 November 1730 laments that the entire revenue of the harvest that year was already taken by Gaekwad. Writing to Baji rao, he says,

> It seems the king's desire is to give the *mokasa* of Gujarat to Dabhade, and give us some money in exchange and create a conflict between us. Let me know whether the *sanad*s are to be accepted or the money is to be accepted. The year's revenue was wholly taken by Pilaji, so you have to factor that in case you decide to take money. If Dabhade causes a conflict, I will take care of it; there is no cause for worry. But if Dabhade goes and meets the Nizam, he should be removed from his post. The king should agree to this, and only then the *sanad*s accepted.[20]

Mediation to resolve the differences between Baji rao and Dabhade were afoot for long. Even late in December 1730, Shahu's emissaries were scurrying between Satara and Talegaon to bring about a conciliation. Naro Ram *Mantri*, who had met the Dabhades at Talegaon, wrote to the Peshwa in early December 1730 and cautioned him against an untoward event:

> The situation here (Talegaon) is that there are extreme demands. They wish to be given the old *jagir*s without reducing a single village from it. I requested them to come with me to the king, but none of them is willing to accompany me. Ambaji (Purandare) was with me. If the dispute enlarges further it is not good for the kingdom. If you were here, we could have found a way out. I have taken Krishnaji Dabhade with me. The *ganim* is near you (in Gujarat). This has created a domestic dispute. To irritate them for trivial issues is not good. Matters should not come to a head, and the public perception should remain positive. You may not be wrong, but you should take care that it does not appear as if you are causing the kingdom's Marathas to desert Shahu. Be very cautious that no untoward event that besmirches your reputation and appears repugnant to the public takes place.[1]

As a final measure, on 15 December 1730, Shahu decided to give Dabhade the entire state of Gujarat. He asked Dabhade to be loyal and wrote,

> It does not behove you to take the help of others and harm the kingdom. This is being treacherous and disloyal and you know what the consequence will be.[21]

Shahu also wrote to Baji rao,

> The *mokasa* of half of Gujarat given to Chimaji is revoked and awarded
> to *Senapati* Trimbak rao Dabhade. You should not interfere with the
> province.[22]

However, it was too late. The die was cast.

꒰ꕤ꒱ꕤ꒰ꕤ꒱

# 19. Battle of Dabhoi

'Fight like this with the enemy and please the king. I will stop the battle and come and meet you.'

- Baji rao to Dabhade during the battle of Dabhoi.[1]

Muhammad Khan Bangash had been appointed *subedar* of Malwa and was at Gwalior awaiting funds from Delhi. In December 1730, Khan Dauran sent him a letter to urgently go and stop the Marathas from crossing the Narmada. Bangash who was keen to avenge his defeat at Bundelkhand, moved towards Ujjain. At Sarangpur, Malharji Holkar began harassing his army. The Nizam, who was still considered a rebel by the Delhi court, wrote to Bangash that they should meet on the Narmada and *'concert common measures against the enemies of Islam'.*[2] Bangash agreed, and headed for Dhar while he sent his son Ahmed Khan to face Holkar. However, Holkar followed Bangash to Dhar and throughout February 1731 kept him busy with sporadic attacks around that city. The new confederate against Baji rao was thus unduly detained in Malwa.

The Nizam marched leisurely to the ferry of Akbarpur near Mandu on the Narmada by the end of February 1731 to meet Bangash, who was delayed. Sometime after 26 March 1731, the two met and spent the next three days in discussing how to defeat the Peshwa. While this leisurely meeting was on, Baji rao was already moving rapidly against this growing coalition. The three days that Nizam and Bangash spent at Akbarpur eventually proved fatal for Dabhade. On 1 April, the Nizam was still on the north bank of the Narmada when he heard that Baji rao, having fought a battle, was rapidly moving towards Surat. The startled Nawab hurried to intercept the Peshwa.

Amongst the earliest histories of the Marathas was the one written by Grant Duff after referring to original documents he found at Satara, many of which now do not exist. In 1825–6, he wrote a three-volume history of the Marathas.

About the Peshwa-*Senapati* conflict he writes,

> Ever since the Peishwa had obtained the deeds (of *chauthai*) from Sur
> Boolund Khan, Dhabaray had been negociating with the other Mahratta
> chiefs, and assembling troops in Guzerat. At length, finding himself at the
> head of thirty-five thousand men, he had resolved to march for the Deccan
> in the ensuing season. Bajee Rao was well aware of the Senaputtee's enmity,
> but was not alarmed by his preparations until he discovered that Nizam
> Ool Moolk was to support him in the Deccan. Immediately on being
> apprized of their intention he determined to anticipate them; although,
> when joined by all his adherents, his army did not amount to above half
> that of Dhabaray. The latter gave out that he was proceeding to protect
> the Raja's authority, and was supported by Peelajee Gaekwar, Kantajee, and
> Rughoojec Kuddum Banday, Oodajee, and Anund Rao Powar, Chimmajee
> Pundit (Damodar), Koor Buhadur, with many others. Bajee Rao proved that
> Dhabaray Senaputtee was in alliance with Nizam Ool Moolk, and declared
> that he was leagued for the purpose of dividing the Mahratta sovereignty
> with the Raja of Kolapoor, a measure inconsistent with sound policy, and
> contrary to the divine ordinances of the Shastras.[3]

Duff sums it up rather well.

The *Senapati*'s alliance with the Nizam and Bangash was held by the Peshwa
as being inimical to the Maratha Empire. While he continued to send messages
to Trimbak rao Dabhade to come to terms and avoid war, in his mind he knew
he had to prepare for war. With Scindia and Holkar in Malwa, Pilaji Jadhav rao
in Khandesh and Chimaji Appa by his side, Baji rao was not deterred.

The *bakhar* of Shahu says,

> Trimbak rao became *Senapati* and felt 'despite having Malwa with him, these
> people are invading this province'. He became friendly with the Nizam. Baji
> rao learnt of this. Despite being an eminent officer, the *Senapati* is doing
> this, he informed Shahu. Shahu wrote to Baji rao, 'You should speak some
> words of wisdom to the *Senapati* and bring him to me and I will effect a
> conciliation.' Then, when Baji rao was coming back that way, the *Senapati*
> blocked his path and said, 'you should not come this way.' At the same time,
> the Nizam was coming towards that area. Baji rao therefore hurriedly came
> forward. The *Senapati* had forty thousand while the Peshwa had twenty-
> five. 'How does one resolve this? The *Senapati* along with the Nizam will
> defeat our force. A defeat is bad for the reputation of the Government.
> Therefore it has come to this; if the *Senapati* comes to battle, one has to

fight him first. There is no time to bring an order from the king.' Saying this, Baji rao mustered his army. 'The *Senapati* has become disloyal to the king; he will thus never be successful. We do not cause depredations in the king's province. The Nizam is approaching us in this area, so we have to go by this path,' Baji rao wrote to Trimbak rao. However, Trimbak rao, fully intending to fight, marched on Baji rao's force.[4]

Leaving Ahmedabad, Baji rao began his approach to Vadodara. Seeing that Trimbak rao with a large army of nearly forty thousand was in his way, and the Nizam with his army was to join him, the Peshwa realised the gravity of the situation. A part of the Nizam's army under Momin Yar Khan had already joined Dabhade.[5] On 25 March 1731, Baji rao reached Savli and had intended to lay siege to Pilaji Gaekwad's stronghold at Vadodara. Now, he changed his plans and approached the town of Dabhoi. The *Senapati* had moved from his last camp at Karnali, crossed the river Orsang and camped between Dabhoi and Bhilapur.

The *Senapati*'s army began crossing the Orsang, and the Nizam was approaching with his large army. Trimbak rao was barely a few *kos* away from the Peshwa's camp. The *Senapati* would come to the field on an elephant every day, ready to fight. However, Baji rao felt the place and the time was not yet right for a battle. He therefore moved forward to Thuvavi,[a] nearer Dabhoi. Finding the time and the place appropriate, on 1 April, Baji rao made a frontal attack on Trimbak rao.

Shahu's *bakhar* describes the battle eloquently,

> Trimbak rao came with an intention to fight astride an elephant. The battle was fought for nine hours (three *prahar*). Many people were killed on both sides. The *Senapati* shot arrows from his elephant until the skin of his fingers peeled off. The battle was intense. Baji rao rode a horse and fought with his sword along with his men. With trusted men around him, he approached the *Senapati*'s elephant. The *Senapati*'s men began to flee. However, Trimbak rao himself did not yield. His mahout was killed so he drove the elephant himself and shot arrows at the same time. Baji rao sent a messenger to him; 'Fight like this with the enemy and please the king. I will stop the battle and come and meet you'. But caught in the moment and with courage, the *Senapati* drove his elephant forward. Baji rao warned his

---

a.  Thuvavi : about 9 kilometres from Dabhoi.

men that none should harm the *Senapati*. But just then, a bullet struck the *Senapati's* forehead. He died. Baji rao immediately ordered his troops not to plunder or chase the remnant of the army, that nobody should take any horses or elephants and to release the prisoners.[1]

The Dabhade *bakhar* names Trimbak rao's step-uncle Bhavsing rao Toke as having ordered a musketeer to aim and fire at Trimbak rao, in contravention of Baji rao's specific order not to attack him.[6] It also says Trimbak rao had just five thousand men and his brothers were forty miles away. However, the fact that they were injured and ran away contradicts this assertion. Baji rao's own letter to Brahmendra swami said that the *Senapati* '*came with thirty to thirty five thousand men to battle us*'.[7]

Baji rao wrote on 2 April to Krishnaji Kadam who was near Surat,

> 'Trimbak rao Dabhade with Bande, Gaekwad, Udaji Pawar and Nizam-ul-mulk's army came to Dabhai. I camped for two days at a distance of two *kos*. Daily the *Senapati* would come and stand to give battle. This was not a good place so I marched towards Thawai in Dabhai district. The *Senapati* came with his entire army to give battle. The battle took place. The *Senapati* was killed. Maloji Pawar and Javaji Dabhade were also killed. Pilaji Gaekwad's son died, Udaji Pawar and Chimnaji Damodar were caught. Bande, Gaekwad and Anand rao fled. Kunwar Bahadur is injured but ran away. Mustifa Khan[a] and Pilaji's forces are there (Surat). Defeat them.'[8]

Baji rao handed over Trimbak rao's body to his brothers Yashwant rao and Babu rao. He then left Dabhoi, crossed the Baba Pir ford on 9 April and reached Ankleshwar. From here he traversed a hilly forested region to reach Dhargaon north of Junnar in exactly thirty days. Six days later, on 15 May 1731, he was in Pune and after a short stay here, reached Satara on 2 June. Some part of Baji rao's army was intercepted by the Nizam's troops north of Surat.

The Nizam gave a long description of his campaign in a letter [b] of 3 May to a Abdun-nabi Khan, and summed it up with,

> The accursed Baji rao, finding the province of Gujarat unoccupied by defenders, laid siege to Baroda...I reflected that if, God avert it, the rebel got Baroda, it would be a great disgrace and loss, and our work would be ruined while his intrigues would become perpetual in that *subah* and the

---

a.  Governor of Surat
b.  The complete letter in Appendix 4.

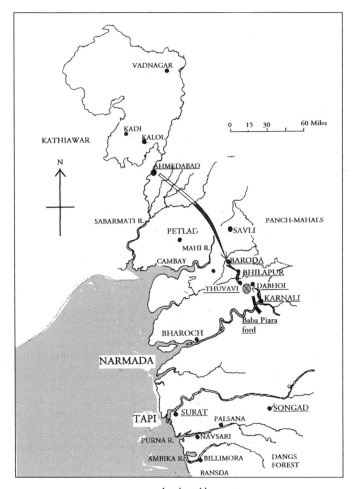

Battle of Dabhoi

ways of the followers of Islam would be completely upset. Therefore, out of the spirit and pride of Islam and fidelity to salt, I decided upon this religious duty, that after crossing the Narmada I should engage at full gallop in rooting this dark-natured wretch out, and thus perform the tasks of holy war in cutting off the roots of disturbance.

Therefore to put it briefly, the Islamic army from the Akbarpur ferry, by forced marches traversing the wildness of Khandesh, Surat and Konkan, owing to the abundance of trees, seldom found any path to take, but just in the nick of time arrived near Surat and drove the Marathas away to the neighbourhood of Daman, which is a Portuguese possession and a city of

Konkan or the extreme western limit of the Deccan; and these beasts, like ants and snakes took refuge in narrow places with dense trees and strait paths into which imagination cannot penetrate.[9]

One week after the battle, the English described it, naming Chimaji instead of Baji rao as having fought the battle although both were present at Dabhoi,

> Some days since they came to an engagement within three or four miles of Baroda, wherein Chimnaji[a] had the advantage. Kanthaji fled, Pilaji is wounded and run into Dabhoi fort with two or three thousand men; Trimbak rao, a great General, is killed, Pilaji's son is killed, four or five thousand men are killed of Pilaji or Kanthaji; and Chimaji is said to have lost not a thousand men. Seventeen elephants, it is said, Chimaji has taken with ten camels of treasure and four or five thousand horses without their riders….. Khan's son, nephew to Chin Qilich Khan Nizam-ul-mulk, who it is said commanded five thousand Moor men belonging to Chin Qilich Khan, he is likewise said to be killed. Udaji Pawar, a commander of fifteen thousand horse, is taken prisoner…..what makes the action greater is that Chimaji had but fifteen or sixteen thousand horse, and the joint forces of Pilaji and Kanthaji are said to have been upward of fifty thousand..'[10]

Baji rao released Udaji and Chimnaji Damodar with robes of honour and an elephant each. Udaji continued to serve the Maratha state thereafter but his relations with Baji rao did not return to normal.

A short narrative of the Dabhades says Yashwant rao and Babu rao Dabhade chased the Peshwa right up to the gates of Satara. There, the Dabhade brothers were greeted by Shahu himself. The *Rajashri* said *'Cut my throat first, then you can kill the Brahmin. I am the culprit'*. Hearing this, the Dabhades returned to Talegaon.[11]

At Satara, Baji rao explained his position to Shahu. Shahu said, *'The Nawab has been unwise. With evil intentions he created a rift among two of my chiefs.'*[12] After a long stay at Satara, Baji rao returned to Pune towards the end of 1731. Uma bai was aggrieved. Shahu therefore went to Talegaon and met Uma bai. He appointed Yashwant rao as the *Senapati* and her youngest son Babu rao as *Sena Khaskhel*. Yashwant rao was considered too young, and the

---

a.  Chimnaji or Chimaji, both names were used. Chimaji is a pet name, as his real name was Antaji.

duties were managed by his mother Uma bai. Shahu once again gave half
of Gujarat's *mokasa* to Dabhade and arranged the distribution of revenue.
However, Yashwant rao became addicted to spirits and Uma bai effectively
took charge, guiding Pilaji Gaekwad to manage her affairs in Gujarat. The
Dabhade *bakhar* describes Shahu bringing Baji rao to Uma bai, giving her a
sword and placing the Peshwa's head on her feet. He then said, '*You cut his
head with your own hands*'. At another place Uma bai and Baji rao with his
two sons Raghunath and Janardan appear before Shahu who orders Baji rao
to give these boys to Uma bai. He then tells her, '*these two boys are given to
you. They are yours. Bring them up and call them your own. Now have the sweets
with your meal and give up the animosity towards each other*'.[13] The deep fissures
were papered over for now, but the *Senapati's* family remained inimical to the
Peshwa thereafter.

Krishnaji Dabhade wrote to Brahmendra swami from Satara,

> Maharaj swami and his chiefs went to Talegaon and satisfied the mother
> Uma bai and took her to Satara with the army. He resolved outstanding
> issues.[14]

The bitter fallout of Dabhoi was felt by the Maratha confederacy. On
the one hand the Peshwa was an aggressor in Gujarat. On the other hand,
Dabhade, by his alliance with the Nizam was clearly a rebel. However, both
claimed to be loyal to Shahu and the fight was over their status vis-à-vis each
other. Where Trimbak rao erred was to seek Mughal assistance against the
Peshwa which lost him any sympathy from the Marathas. Baji rao on his part
held his hand until there was clear evidence that the *Senapati* was aligned with
the Nizam. The Nizam of course, was fishing in troubled waters.

In the years to come, the Dabhades did not quite accept the Peshwa's
preeminent position in the administration. Although they had half the share
of Gujarat, they did not co-operate in his future ventures and gradually the
post of *Senapati* lost its importance. Among other chores of the *Senapati* that
Baji rao took over was the practice of *dakshina*, first begun by *Chhatrapati*
Shivaji. Grant Duff writes,

> It had been a custom to feed some thousand Bramins for several days every
> year at Tullygaom near Poona, the Inam village of Dhabaray ; this charitable
> practice Bajee Rao continued at Poona, and gave sums of money, at the

same time, to the assembled *Shastrees* and *Waeedeeks* (Vaidiks). This festival, continued by his successors, was known by the name of *Dukshina*.[15]

The battle of Dabhoi gave out a stern message that dissidence within the Maratha fold would not be tolerated. At the same time, there was a change in the Maratha command structure. The king was seen as weaker than the Peshwa. Despite Shahu's desire to bring Dabhade and the Peshwa before him and conciliate the two, Dabhade was killed in a battle. Shahu supported the Peshwa and this pre-empted further dissidence in the Maratha confederacy. Sorely dependent on Baji rao and Chimaji Appa for his military needs, Shahu was unable to chastise them. In the Maratha court, an irreversible power shift from the *Chhatrapati* to his Peshwa began.

A letter written by Manaji Jadhav to his uncle *Chhatrapati* Shahu shows this change. Manaji was the son of *Chhatrapati* Rajaram's daughter Ambika bai. After the battle of Sakharkherda, he came to stay with Shahu for some time before returning to his village. In a letter written on 17 November 1731 to Shahu he complains about Chimaji Appa's overbearing attitude. He claims Chimaji sent Pilaji Jadhav rao to bring him to his presence, and when he refused Pilaji marched with two thousand men and coerced him to come. At the meeting, Chimaji said to him, *'you have been disobeying me and sheltering behind the Maharaj. If you do not listen, you will be plundered. Trimbak rao Dabhade was killed. What did the Maharaj do to us?*[16] For long, Manaji longed to get back his old estate near Sindkhed. Later, in 1738, one finds Baji rao writing to him promising him all help in the matter.[17] The incident illustrates the tough measures the Peshwa and his brother took, with the help of officers like Pilaji Jadhav rao, to enforce orders. On the other hand, it reflects the reality of the turbulent eighteenth century, when force was often the determinant for real executive power.

Following the battle of Dabhoi, and with Sambhaji and Shahu signing a peace treaty in 1731, the Nizam found it was not in his interests to obstruct Baji rao. He wrote to Shahu earnestly soliciting a meeting with Baji rao. This, their fifth meeting, would determine the events of the coming years.

꒰ꕤꕥꕤꕥ꒱

# 20. Entente at Rui Rameshwar

'It is the opinion of all concerned that he should not go for the meeting. The Peshwa's rank is such that once ordered by *Rajashri* he must go. But now the news on everybody's lips is that the Mughal has given the *Rajashri* Shahu two crore rupees…'

- letter discouraging Baji rao from meeting the Nizam.[1]

There was a lull for a while. The peace between Shahu and his cousin Sambhaji and the battle with Dabhade had reduced internal dissensions, Deep Singh's embassy and the failure of the Nizam to unseat Shahu — all contributed to a feeling of stability in the Maratha state. Maratha forces had spread out in Malwa and Bundelkhand, Gujarat was managed by the Peshwa and by Dabhade through his manager Damaji Gaekwad, while Sawai Jaisingh was trying to convince the Mughal Emperor to come to an agreement with the Marathas. Abhay Singh of Jodhpur sent an assassin who murdered Pilaji Gaekwad in 1731, and this led to an expedition led by Uma bai Dabhade and Kadam Bande attacking Ahmedabad. Holkar and Scindia followed, capturing Champaner and the fort of Pawagad. Udaji Pawar, Holkar and Ranoji Scindia countered the feeble attempts of Muhammad Khan Bangash to combat the Marathas in Malwa. Before Dabhoi, Udaji fell out with Baji rao and his brother Anand rao was therefor appointed in his place. Udaji thereafter claimed to be Shahu's servant and served the Maratha state only on the orders of the *Chhatrapati*.

Malharji Holkar at one stage did try and resolve the differences between the Peshwa and Udaji, who was far older than Baji rao. The Holkar *kaifiyat* says,

> At the bank of the Godavari, Holkar met Baji rao and decided to resolve Pawar's dispute with the *Shrimant*. Pawar was at Sendhwa, north of Dhule. He suggested to the Peshwa to go there and the three of them would resolve all the problems. Baji rao and Holkar then went to Sendhwa and met Udaji. But Pawar would not agree. He was proud of his swordsmanship. 'What can the Brahmin do without him', was his belief. Finally Baji rao removed his

own turban and placed it before Pawar. However, he still would not relent. Then Malharji became angry, and taking Baji rao's hand he pulled him away, 'After so much persuasion he does not understand! If one farmer[a] does not come, why should we worry? Our destiny is with us'. He lifted Baji rao to his feet and without taking the customary betel leaf, departed.[2]

The share in the revenue of Malwa that went to the Pawars reduced thereafter and Holkar and Scindia became the principal stakeholders in the region.

The monsoon months over, Chimaji Appa left for a campaign in Malwa and Bundelkhand. On Bangash's failure, Sawai Jaisingh had once again been appointed the *subedar*, and leaving Jaipur he came with a large army towards Ujjain in December 1732. The Marathas opposed the Mughals under Jaisingh; Scindia and Holkar were at the time in Gujarat and promptly rushed to meet the new threat.[3] At Mandsaur, just north of Ujjain, Chimaji with Holkar and Scindia surrounded his army. Sawai Jaisingh tried to wean away the Pawar brothers, but Holkar prevailed and forced Jaisingh to pay an indemnity of six lakh rupees besides a charge on twenty-eight districts before he was allowed to go.[4]

The defeat of his *subedar* at the hands of the Marathas bestirred the Emperor. Emerging from his life of luxury in Delhi, he threatened to lead a campaign personally. He travelled not more than sixteen miles before his equally inept *Wazir* Qamruddin Khan took over the responsibility and started for Agra where Muhammad Khan Bangash joined the Mughal army. Chimaji settled the terms with Chhatrasal's sons about Baji rao's *jagir* in Bundelkhand. As Chimaji retraced his steps, Holkar and Scindia began campaigning against the Mughals. Before long, the ambitious Mughal attack petered out. Muhammad Shah sent a message recalling his *Wazir*, '*With you wine is lawful; without you, water prohibited*'. Without further ado, the *Wazir* turned back for Delhi.[5]

The defeats of Bangash, Jaisingh and Qamruddin Khan revealed that the Mughals were a hollow power – a shell without a soul. The Nizam, having

---

a.   Uttered in contempt

tasted defeat, began to find a way to protect his own kingdom and pursue some limited goals in the Deccan. From the earlier aim of removing Baji rao from his path, he now moved to attempting an adjustment with him. He therefore wrote to Shahu that he earnestly desired to meet the Peshwa.

Baji rao was at this time without any of his loyal lieutenants and his brother, all of who were in Malwa. That the Nizam's request for a meeting came within days of their departure led to a suspicion that foul play was planned. Shahu insisted the Peshwa should meet the Nizam and for a while, there were rumours that Shahu was collaborating with the Nizam to get rid of his powerful Peshwa. The Peshwa's mother Radha bai, a lady with great stature in the Maratha state wrote to her son,

> I heard of *Rajashri's* letter to you. You should not go to meet him (the Nizam). You should advance reasons that in the absence of Shambhu Sinh Jadhav and Anand rao Somvanshi, it is not appropriate for me to go. If after meeting Turktaz Khan and Rambha Nimbalkar, the meeting fizzles out, it is good. You should think and do something by which this plan of meeting him falls through.[6]

The Peshwa's aunt wrote to Radha bai as well as the Peshwa in similar vein,

> I have heard *Rau* is going to meet the *Tambra*. It is the opinion of all concerned that he should not go for the meeting. The Peshwa's rank is such that once ordered by *Rajashri* he must go. But now the news on everybody's lips is that the Mughal has given the *Rajashri* two crore rupees. ..if he has to go, he should wait for Chimaji Appa to return with his army. Do not let him go until then. Once Chimaji is back, they can both decide how to act.[1]

Giving vent to his own apprehensions, Baji rao replied to Brahmendra swami, who also advised him not to go,

> Many have said you should not go to meet the Nawab; and they are right. But what does one do when the king orders? We try our best not to go. Whatever is to happen, will happen. God is capable of protecting from all calamities. It appears I will have to go as it is what the king desires. I am not keen to go. I have nothing to discuss and I don't trust him. I am facing a calamity due to this order that I should meet the Nawab. I cannot see a way out. I wonder what lies in store for me.[7]

The matter began to be openly discussed and reached Shahu's ears. Seeing the Peshwa was without any of his loyal sub-ordinates and reluctant to go,

Shahu wrote to the *Sarlashkar* Anand rao Somvanshi that he must accompany the Peshwa.[8]

The Nizam had planned a meeting at an unusual place called Rui Rameshwar[a] near the town of Latur on the river Manjara. Along with Davalji Somvanshi, who had an estate near Beed and Shambhu Sinh Jadhav, Baji rao reached the Nizam's camp on 27 December 1732. The Nizam received the Peshwa with every mark of respect and presented him an elephant, two horses, many robes and ornaments.

The meeting did not yield a written document. Baji rao wrote a detailed account to Chimaji[b] on 12 January 1733 where he described all that passed between them. Summing up, Baji rao wrote, *'we exchanged pleasantries rather than have a specific discussion on issues. We had two or three meetings recently and the suspicions we harboured of each other in our minds were cleared while affection increased.'*[9] The importance of the meeting and its possible outcome can only be seen in the light of future events; the Nizam and the Peshwa did not obstruct each other's path for the next few years. This allowed the Nizam to survive and consolidate in his dominion, while he gave the Peshwa a free hand to achieve his northern ambitions.

Historian Jadunath Sarkar comments on the change after Palkhed,

> ...by 1728, his victory was complete and his position unassailable; and the shrewd Asaf Jah was the first to recognise this historic fact and to promptly abandon his policy of double-dealing and to form a secret but cordial *entente* with Baji Rao as the best means of securing the west and south flanks of the Hyderabad state.[10]

GS Sardesai points to a list in the Peshwa archives that Baji rao may have presented to the Nizam on this occasion, about several outstanding demands.

> The list that Baji rao *pant Pradhan* gave the Nizam-ul-mulk:
>
> 1. The Kingdom of Thanjavur and Ginjee belonged to Raja Shivaji. It must be made over to Raja Shahu.
>
> 2. The *Pradhan pant* should be given a *jagir* of fifty lakh from the *subah*s of Khandesh, Bijapur and Aurangabad.

---

a.  $18^0$, 31' 29"E, $76^0$ 26' 10"E.

b.  Appendix 5.

3. The Deccan's *sardeshpande* tax should be paid to the *Pradhan pant* at five per cent of the revenue and administrative arrangements made through him.

4. The *Pradhan pant* has many debts. These should be relieved by contributing to the expenses.

5. The fort of Shivneri should be given to the *Pradhan pant*.

6. Many villages should be given as a gift.

This was discussed verbally.[11]

Most of these clauses were never accepted by the Nizam. However, it is indicative of what the Marathas wanted at this stage.

The peace at Rui Rameshwar silenced one enemy. There was no respite however. Before the monsoon set in, there was trouble in the Konkan and the Peshwa had to attend to it.

༄༅༅༄༅

# Rewa Uvach

The Nizam-ul-mulk patched up a peace with a warrior he could not overcome. He first tried to obtain his cooperation, then, to defeat him, before finally accepting that he would have to live with him. The unsigned treaty opened more doors for the Peshwa than for the Nizam. The Nizam's aim was to protect his realm, Baji rao aimed to expand northwards and knock on the doors of Delhi. With the treaty, the Peshwa freed himself somewhat from his southern entanglements and in the years to come enlarged his footprint on the Indian landscape.

The open plains and hot dusty plateaus of the north afforded Baji rao the terrain he relished, and the use of cavalry, the arm he desired. The cavalry was the Peshwa's forte, however he now had to undertake a campaign in a terrain restricted by hills and interrupted by the sea. For too long the western coastal strip of the Konkan had been neglected. From Balaji Vishwanath's forced migration to Pune fifty years ago, the Siddi of Janjira had enforced a tyrannical rule on the residents of the region. When complaints came to Shahu and to the Peshwa, all they could do was offer some sympathy and some aid. The threat to the survival of the kingdom itself had to be tackled first. By 1732, these had been overcome. There was no power in the land that would look at Shahu's realm with an evil eye; there was no power that could face the might of Baji rao, Chimaji, Holkar, Scindia and Pilaji Jadhav rao.

It was time; time to delve into affairs of the Konkan. Shahu himself took the lead and the reins of the campaign in his own hands. No longer did the king wish to wait for news of battles fought far away, for the Konkan was near his capital. Brahmendra swami, the seer, once lived in the Konkan and became the prime mover of a campaign against the Siddi.

In war, in politics and in the lives of nations, the campaign has to be fought when the opportunity is right and the year 1733 gave the right mix for just such a move. The Peshwa and many other chiefs spent long months in the Konkan, braving its monsoon, the sea, the hills and rivers.

Baji rao did not have the time to move north that year, and did not cross the Rewa, so that year's campaign in the Konkan was something I only heard of. Yet, the following narrative is true. In the beginning, they did not achieve the result everybody wished for. Long months and valuable resources were poured into the campaign. The end was a long time coming. And when it came, surprisingly, the man at the helm of the campaign was not Baji rao.

Yes, the success that came finally liberated a long-oppressed people; as it emerged, for evermore.

❦❦❦

# 21. The Campaign in 'Habshan'

'You have got your elephant. However, you have unwisely harmed the deity and Brahmins. Hereinafter, you will soon be utterly destroyed.'

- Brahmendra swami to Siddi Sat.[1]

'The Siddi has two powerful arms; one is Anjanvel, the other is Underi.'

- Baji rao's letter to Ambaji Purandare.[2]

## The Swami and the Siddi

The Konkan coastal strip has been the landing place for many trading communities from across the Arabian Sea. It had many trading ports from times immemorial. India was a giant medieval economy and a rich trading partner for Europe and Africa as well as Arabia. The Abyssinians, present-day residents of Ethiopia, were also among those who came by sea to trade with India. They were excellent sailors but perhaps not quite as good traders. In course of time, they found better employment in the army and administration of the Bahmani kingdoms of Bijapur and Ahmednagar, and rose to powerful positions by their ability as well as loyalty to the monarch. Followers of Sunni Islam, they were labelled Siddis; a name that may or may not have arisen from Sayyids. Remarkable men like Malik Ambar in Ahmednagar and Ikhlas Khan in Bijapur rose to fame and left their mark on the administration of their kingdoms. When Akbar, Shah Jehan, and finally Aurangzeb annexed the Bahmani kingdoms, the Siddis joined the Mughals.

The Siddis ruled over the Konkan from their sea fort of Danda Rajpuri, often just called Janjira, derived from the Arabic 'jazira', or an island. The entire region they controlled came to be called 'Habshan' after 'Habshi', the name they were called by in that region. The fort of Janjira was separated from the mainland and surrounded by fairly deep water, making access difficult at all times of the year. The fort was originally built probably during the rule of the Yadava dynasty between the ninth to the fourteenth centuries. Legend has it that around 1489, a few Siddi traders sought permission to stop at the fort with their cargo which was in the form of some three hundred crates.

Brahmendra swami

Janjira fort

Emperor Muhammad Shah

Seals of Baji rao Peshwa and Sripat rao Pratinidhi

Permission granted, the cargo was brought in, and from each of the crates emerged a fully armed soldier.[3]

Once the island was taken, the Siddis did not let go. *Chhatrapati* Shivaji tried to capture Janjira for most of the 1660s, when even the English took a liking for it; at one time preferring it to Mumbai which they got in 1668.[4] However, an attack from sea was always difficult and a blockade from land would not work otherwise. A cannonade was not quite enough due to its strong walls and distance from the shore. The Dutch, the Marathas and the English– all failed to win the place. From here, the Siddi ruled not just the island but also a good part of the coastal strip and a few forts; prominent among them the erstwhile Maratha capital Raigad. Siddi Yakut's petition to Aurangzeb to be

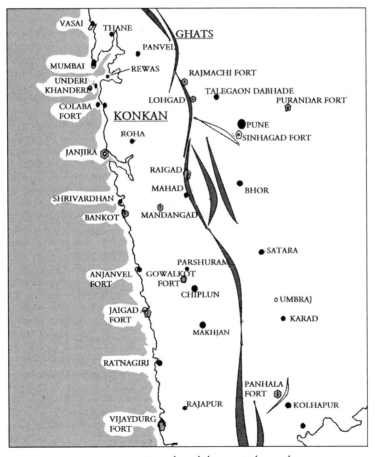

An *Overview of 'Habshan' and the Konkan*

appointed as *mutsaddi* of Danda Rajpuri had the Mughal Emperor write on it, *'for a long time I have known of this aggressive and self-willed spirit of Siddi Yakut Khan'.*[5] In the 1690s the Siddi spread his wings in the Konkan, and *Chhatrapati* Rajaram appointed Kanhoji Angre as the *Sarkhel* to deal with them.

The '*Habshan*' was a stretch of two hundred kilometres of broken coastline in the Konkan. It began just south of Bombay harbour with the tiny island fort of Underi near Alibag and extended to the southern bank of the river Vashishthi where Siddi Sat ruled from his stronghold of Anjanvel. Underi was close to Colaba and Khanderi, two forts held by Kanhoji. From here coming south along the coast one came to the fort of Chaul at the northern end of the mouth of the river Kundalika. Upstream of this river, around the town of Roha were the four forts of Avachitgad, Birwadi, Tala and Ghosale. Going further south, the coast once again makes way for the broad creek of the Danda Rajpuri river. The island fort of Janjira is to the north of this creek but separated by half a mile of deep water from the coast. Further south, the fourth puncture in the coast is where the river Savitri joins the sea. On its northern end lie Shrivardhan and Harihareshwar, the native places of the Peshwas and on the southern bank lies the fort of Bankot. Going upstream from the Savitri, one encounters the fort of Mandangad. The last break in the coastline comes from the river Vashishthi. Anjanvel lies on its southern bank, and upstream, the fort of Govalkot is surrounded by the river on three sides. Not far from Govalkot is the town of Chiplun. The terrain in the Konkan was not just broken by rivers but also several hills and forts making cavalry operations nearly impossible. The heavy rains from June to September were a further deterrent to continue operations in this period. Into this region, suited for operations of the infantry, the Peshwa was soon dispatched to deal with the Siddi.

The Konkan had an important place in Maratha strategy in the era of *Chhatrapati* Shivaji and Sambhaji. However, since Shahu's return, the region had not been given the attention it deserved. It was under undisturbed occupation by not only the Portuguese but also the English and the Siddi. Once the home of Balaji Vishwanath, the Peshwa could give it his attention only after facing challenges from elsewhere. In course of time, Siddi Sat, who ruled at the fort of Anjanvel, emerged as a powerful enemy for the Angres.

Kanhoji asked for help from Shahu in 1726, but beyond sending a letter assuring help, he could do nothing.[6]

The people of Konkan learnt to live with the Siddis and their periodic cruelty, although they waited for the day when they would be delivered. As the naval arm of the Mughal, the Siddis were protected in the seventeenth century from land. When the Mughal power weakened, the Siddis had to defend themselves from their enemies. In 1715, Peshwa Balaji Vishwanath had gone to the Konkan and signed a treaty with the Siddis, and peace prevailed for a while. While the Siddi in the Konkan spread from Anjanvel fort in the south to the island of Underi off Mumbai harbour, another branch of the Siddis ruled from Surat and helped their brethren in Janjira when they were in distress. So far, the Marathas had concentrated on growing inland and not taken much notice of the Siddis' kingdom in the Konkan.

All this was to change, and the catalysts were an elephant and a saint.

Brahmendra swami once helped *Chhatrapati* Rajaram in his southern sojourn, and the king gave the swami the village of Dhamani in the Konkan area. Here, his divine powers were discovered by a cowherd. He came into prominence when he blessed Shahu and Balaji Vishwanath who rose to become the king and the Peshwa. The belief in his powers was widespread and along with royal patronage he became known for his capability to help his devotees resolve their earthly problems. Many were the requests he received and reciprocally the swami made many demands on his royal devotees. Maratha chiefs from the Peshwa, *Pratinidhi* and Angre to Shahu's queens, and even the Siddis, believed in the swami, and helped him in his worldly and celestial pursuits. In 1708, Siddi Yakut gave two villages as a gift to the swami.[7] The *Pratinidhi* also gave two more villages. In this manner his influence across powers in the Konkan grew year after year.

Brahmendra swami soon built a temple to Parshuram, the Lord of the Konkan, near the town of Chiplun. Legend has it that the entire coastal strip of Konkan is a gift from Parshuram, who pushed back the sea and reclaimed this land. The temple of Parshuram along with many small temples was built by donations from all the swami's influential devotees including the Siddi. In 1725, Brahmendra swami visited Shahu and was given three villages including Dhavadshi, near Satara. Baji rao also awarded him a village the following year. By 1726, the swami earned an income from eight villages.[8]

In 1726, Siddi Sat, was presented an elephant by the Nawab of Savanur in the Carnatic. That year Maratha armies had gone as far south as Srirangapatnam. There were many Maratha check posts between Savanur and the Konkan, a distance of over five hundred kilometres. Transporting the elephant safely across these posts was not possible without permissions and passes. Siddi Sat, realising the hold Brahmendra had over the many potentates, requested him to arrange for the transport of the animal. The swami, who was visiting the Carnatic that year, agreed. Siddi Sat sent ten *pathan*s with the swami for this purpose.

Completing his trip in the south, the swami travelled back with the elephant via the fort of Vishalgad. The *Pratinidhi's* men stopped him, but the swami intervened and obtained their sanction. The Siddi had also written to the *Pratinidhi* about this. After a long journey, the group reached the village of Makhjan, about seventy kilometres short of Anjanvel. Here, the elephant reached a check post manned by Kanhoji Angre's men. The swami was not with the group and was following a few days after. Knowing Kanhoji to be his follower, the swami did not expect any trouble here. However, Angre's men stopped the elephant and took it to the coastal fort of Jaigad.

Meanwhile, news reached Siddi Sat that Angre's men had taken the elephant to Jaigad. He was furious. He suspected the swami was complicit in the affair and had deliberately given the elephant to Angre. Taking three hundred soldiers he attacked the swami's Parshuram temple on 8 February 1727, the festival day of *Maha Shivratri*. He looted the temple and the houses of the priests and other men staying in the premises. The temple itself was damaged. All Brahmins in the temple and the villages nearby fled to save their lives. The Siddi's men mercilessly beat three attendants of the swami to force them to show the location of any valuables.

The swami reached a few days later and heard that the temple he had built and nurtured was desecrated, and his men beaten up. He wrote to Kanhoji, *'Your men took away the elephant. Using this pretext, the Siddi Sat desecrated the temple, tortured the Brahmins, and took away many items. They are still beating up the clerks. On receipt of this letter, you must release the elephant and send it to me.'* Taking custody of the elephant from Jaigad, the swami went to Anjanvel. He summoned Siddi Sat and gave him the elephant. The Siddi apologized for his actions. The swami was not appeased and his imprecation was immediate; *'You have got your elephant. However, you have unwisely harmed the deity and Brahmins. Hereinafter, you will soon be utterly destroyed.'*

The swami then went to the Parshuram temple and saw that the idols had been thrown away, the temple dug up and his *karkun*s injured. He went and met Siddi Yakut of Janjira and angrily cursed him. Yakut expressed regret and promised to send back the items Siddi Sat had looted.

Matters did not improve. Siddi Sat continued harassing the people around the temple of Parshuram. Brahmendra swami approached Kanhoji Angre as well as Shahu. The swami finally wrote to Baji rao listing his troubles. Baji rao, who was facing invasion by the Nizam, wrote back, asking him to leave the Konkan and come to the plateau, and stay at Dhavadshi. In 1728 therefore, the swami leaving his belongings with one of Angre's officers, left Parshuram for Dhavadshi. On hearing this, Siddi Sat's attitude towards the swami became openly disrespectful. *'He is a gosavi. He will go where he pleases. What about him?'*, he wrote.[9]

Years passed. Baji rao and Chimaji were busy with the battles of Palkhed, Malwa, Bundelkhand and Dabhoi. In 1732, the Nizam and Baji rao met and agreed on peace. The swami had always urged the Peshwa and Shahu that the Siddi be punished. The opportunity finally arose the following year.

In February 1733, Siddi Rasul Yakut, who ruled from Janjira, died and his sons began to quarrel over the succession. Abdullah, the eldest took over his father's responsibilities. However, before he settled down, he was murdered. His son Siddi Abdul Rehman came to cremate his grandfather on the mainland but did not return to Janjira and stayed at Danda Rajpuri. The divisions among the Siddis gave the opening the Marathas were looking for, and the Janjira campaign finally began. It was a campaign entirely directed by *Chhatrapati* Shahu from Satara, and it stretched for three long years.

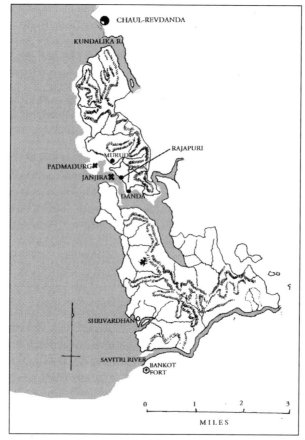

*The Janjira Region*

## The Janjira Campaign of 1733

For thirty years Kanhoji Angre had led the Maratha navy; from the era of Aurangzeb to his death in July 1729. He left behind three wives and six sons, all valiant and capable. On Kanhoji's death, his eldest son Sekhoji was appointed as the *Sarkhel*. Sekhoji's younger brother Sambhaji did not get along with him. There were four other brothers– Manaji, Tulaji, Dhondji and Yesaji. The brothers disputed the distribution of assets but Sekhoji succeeded in keeping a check on them and preserved their power at sea.

Sekhoji, like his father, was a devotee of Brahmendra swami. In February 1732, Baji rao went to the Konkan and met Sekhoji.[10] Sekhoji wrote about the meeting: *'Baji rao Pandit Pradhan came to Colaba. We met each other. We struck an excellent rapport'.*[11] After Siddi Yakut's death, Shahu sent Baji rao along with Fateh Sinh Bhonsle to the Konkan to capitalise on the divisions among the Siddi brothers. Shahu's agent, named Potnis, was already in the Konkan. Potnis recruited Siddi Abdul Rehman and a koli chief named Sheikhji, who had converted to Islam, to help the Marathas. Sheikhji was promised help including money and custody of some forts.

Baji rao quickly reached the Konkan and captured the four forts of Birwadi, Tale, Ghosale and Avachitgad from the Siddi. Sheikhji joined the Peshwa and guided him towards Khokhari, a place where many of the Siddi rulers have their tombs, and from where he could easily capture Danda Rajpuri town right opposite the Janjira fort. Within days of his arrival in the Konkan, on 2 May 1733, Baji rao was camped at the Bal Roza mosque of Danda Rajpuri.

Meanwhile, Sekhoji's armies led by Bankaji Naik won the forts of Bankot and Mandangad further south. Their armies then attacked Govalkot. Manaji Angre, a younger brother of Sekhoji also attacked Janjira from the sea. Siddi Raheen from Janjira landed with some troops and attacked Baji rao at Rajpuri, but they were beaten back with slaughter, in which Raheen was among the killed. At Danda Rajpuri, the Siddi's fleet in harbour was taken over by Baji rao and given to Manaji. Some supplies from Siddi Masud of Surat were still reaching the fort and Shahu asked Dabhade and Gaekwad to stop them, however, they did not cooperate.[12]

Baji rao's immediate success within days of his arrival there was a happy omen. He wrote of it to his mother Radha bai, and she replied,

> You have written about the capture of Danda Rajpuri, Rajkot, Bal Roza and Khokhari. This is excellent news. That Sekhoji has come and met you is very good. Keeping him contented you should act in a manner that will help achieve success in your coming endeavours. You are in a foreign place, so do not trust anybody. Be very careful. You should protect your body (from any attack) and stay there with abundant caution.[13]

Sekhoji met Baji rao on 6 May, and they discussed how Janjira could be captured. There was barely a month left before the monsoons to launch any attack from the sea when any action would be impossible. Sekhoji's fleet was away at the time, so it was not possible to blockade the fort from the sea.

Baji rao with his land-based army could not capture it without this crucial naval help. The four monsoon months therefore delayed the action, which eventually never took place.

While supporting Siddi Abdul Rehman at Danda Rajpuri, Baji rao was also keeping an open channel of communication with the Siddi's men on the fort of Raigad. In a letter to Ambaji *pant* Purandare on 24 May 1733, Baji rao explained the situation for the king's benefit;

> The senior *khanzada*[a] died. His son[b] was outside, he is now with us. There are six younger brothers. This boy is clever. Siddi Samul and Siddi Ambar Aflani are in the fort (Janjira). Twelve hundred men are on the fort, earlier there were just a few. Recently they had help from Anjanvel and Underi. Anjanvel is strong; so is Underi. All four forts have watchful Muslims in them. Anjanvel may have some Marathas. Vijaygad and Govalkot are also with them. They have grabbed Mandangad. Raigad has three to four hundred Muslims and four to five hundred Marathas. The fort is strong; they are fighting. Some messages have also gone up.[14]

Then Shahu decided to send more help. He ordered the *Pratinidhi* with the new *Sarlashkar* Anand rao Somvanshi and Shambhu Sinh Jadhav to go to the Konkan. The *Pratinidhi* reached the Konkan on 20 May 1733, but refused to meet Baji rao at Rajpuri. He camped at Mahad, south of Raigad, nearly ninety kilometres away. On 26 May 1733 Baji rao once again wrote to Purandare explaining how the campaign can end successfully,

> *Pratinidhi* has come to Mahad, but it is of no use. If he goes to Anjanvel and enforces a siege it will immobilise the *Habshi*. The *Habshi* is not an ordinary enemy. Earlier, he had just Janjira, but could not be defeated. But if he has to be destroyed completely, it will need lot of hard work, a blockade from all sides with an armada, lot of money will be spent. An army of at least fifteen thousand with five to seven thousand having guns..... if all this is done, in a year or two, Janjira will be captured. In the fort, they have the material needed for ten years, but a blockade and not allowing his ships to go out alone will help us succeed. The master's destiny is great, but if there is an obstacle to this, it may take longer. The Siddi has two powerful arms: one is Anjanvel, the other is Underi. It will be good if the *Pratinidhi* goes to Anjanvel, then the *Sarkhel*

---

a.  Siddi Yakut
b.  actually his grandson

can do something at Underi. Once these two are captured, his morale will be low. Raigad also has to be captured and one and a half to two thousand men will be needed there. This is the overview of this entire campaign.[2]

The Peshwa was also strapped for funds. Explaining that a salary of five rupees has to be paid in the Konkan against three on the plateau, the Peshwa wrote to Purandare,

> Huge expenses are needed here. The work is the master's, the kingdom belongs to the master, and therefore the expense will also have to be borne by the master. I cannot take debts to run the campaign. If the master provides funds, I will stake my life to gain success in the campaign. If the kingdom is lost it will be the master's. From my side there will be no deficiency of service.[15]

Sekhoji had sent Bankaji Naik from the fort of Suvarnadurg to attack the two southern forts of Anjanvel and Govalkot. Bankaji first captured Bankot and Mandangad to his north and then headed south towards Anjanvel. He now proposed to the *Pratinidhi* that they should each attach the two forts and they will be rewarded with success.

The *Pratinidhi*, sitting close to Raigad, was confabulating with the Siddi's men on the fort. These talks led to a breakthrough and the impregnable fort of Raigad was handed over to the *Pratinidhi*'s men on 8 June 1733. There was widespread jubilation at this stupendous success. Shahu's joy knew no bounds. However, the *Pratinidhi*'s refusal to join forces for unified action had angered the Peshwa. There was rivalry, and an unstated contest between the Peshwa and the *Pratinidhi* to take Raigad. A letter to Baji rao's son Nanasaheb from Shahu's court dated 30 May 1733 says,

> It is reported to the court that *Pant Pratinidhi* has gone to Mahad. About seven to eight hundred people of the Prime Minister and Fateh Sinh baba were camped at Pachad[a]. They were negotiating (with those on the fort). The *Pant Pratinidhi* sent a letter to the swami (Shahu) that some people have approached him (for the fort), and wanted to know what was the order? To this *Rajashri* replied that he should go ahead, and after deliberations with the people on the fort, take possession of Raigad. The *Pratinidhi* then rode from Mahad to Pachad. We will now inform you about who conducts negotiations for (the surrender of) the fort.[16]

---

a. Village at the foot of Raigad

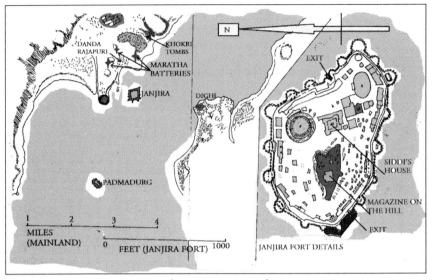

*Map of Janjira and Maratha Positions*

Meanwhile, Bankaji Naik had come to Chiplun and attacked Govalkot. He killed a hundred soldiers of the Siddi and besieged the place. Fresh from his success at Raigad, the *Pratinidhi* moved to Chiplun where he hoped for another diplomatic triumph. Worried about Bankaji Naik's attack, Siddi Sat saw the coming danger and began parleys with the *Pratinidhi*, with whom he had maintained good relations in the past. Siddi Sat promised the *Pratinidhi* that he would peacefully hand over his forts and accompany him to meet Shahu provided Maratha forces were withdrawn at this time. The *Pratinidhi* believed him and asked Bankaji to withdraw from Govalkot. Once Bankaji moved away, Siddi Sat broke his word.

Raghunath Hari, who was Bankaji's aide, wrote to Baji rao and said they were leaving the campaign due to the *Pratinidhi's* interference,

> When we were at Chiplun, *Pratinidhi* was wooing us. But we came away. Siddi Sat came to meet him. The Siddi met and deceived the *Pratinidhi*. Now he (Siddi Sat) has made preparations to fight. The *Pratinidhi* is gradually learning what the *Habshi* is like. Eight days later, the *shamal* attacks him now and then. Anjanvel is a distant affair, now even Govalkot looks difficult (to get). Earlier the Siddi had no help. If the *Pratinidhi* had not interfered, we would have won both forts in fifteen days or so. The rains are very heavy. It takes three to four days to cross one river.[17]

Kanhoji Angre's wife Mathura bai also complained to Brahmendra swami about Bankaji's withdrawal from Govalkot,

> Siddi Sat was pushed back into the fort. Then the *Pratinidhi* came to the spot and saw the battle situation. Cannons had been brought from Jaigad with reinforcements. But the *Pratinidhi* began talks. He told Bankaji Naik that he will obtain the fort by peaceful means; there is no reason to fight. Bankaji said, 'you should go to Anjanvel, I will take Govalkot'. The *Pratinidhi* would not agree. He met Siddi Sat.... [18]

Another letter to Brahmendra swami by his clerk Ganesh Ballal says,

> *Pratinidhi* and Siddi Sat met this Saturday at Kashi *bundar*. A horse was presented to the Siddi. The Siddi said I will settle matters relating to Anjanvel if you ask Angre to withdraw his troops. I will then accompany you to meet *Rajashri* Shahu. They dispersed thereafter. Then he (the Siddi) began preparing for war. Bankaji Naik has come to *Rau* (Baji rao). They have agreed to fight together. The coming days don't look good. [19]

The immediate danger before Siddi Sat passed, and before long heavy rains began lashing the Konkan coast. This gave Siddi Sat the respite to build his army and attack the *Pratinidhi*. The outcome of differences between the Pratindhi and Bankaji was that the latter left the campaign and returned to Sekhoji. Sekhoji and the *Pratinidhi* did not see eye to eye after that and the *Pratinidhi* had to face Siddi Sat's aggression alone. The embattled *Pratinidhi* asked Shahu for help. Shahu in turn wrote to Chimaji Appa to go to the Konkan. However, Chimaji did not do so. An angry Shahu wrote, *'if you do not go, I will'*.[18] Finally, Pilaji Jadhav rao was asked to go. Not much was achieved though, and the *Pratinidhi's* campaign ended inconclusively.

Although help from Surat did not reach Janjira till September 1733, Baji rao was worried that the English might send help to the Siddi. He therefore wrote a letter to the English at Mumbai that they would not permit their fleet to interfere with his operations; and shortly afterwards he invited them to mediate between himself and the Siddi, sending an envoy to them, and another to Rajapur.[20] The English of course, did not help him as he was allied with Angre, their arch enemy. In fact, soon after, they sent four 'cruisers' against Angre and in the following year, they also managed to send the Siddi some gunpowder.

By June 1733, Sekhoji had taken Chaul's Rajkot, the fort of Rewas in the Pen river near Mumbai, and the fort of Thal. He was poised to mount an attack on the Siddi's island of Underi which stood at the centre of these three forts. Mortified at such a possibility, the English sent their troops under Captain Holden in July 1733 to Underi. Captain Inchbird and MacNeal met the Siddi and prevailed upon him to fly the English flag on the island.[21] Although the Marathas fired on Underi from the fort of Khanderi, the island could not be taken.

The Siddis at Janjira had also sought help from the Mughal Emperor and the Nizam. The Khan Dauran sent an appeal to the English at Mumbai to help the Siddi. The English, as businessmen, asked the Mughal Emperor to defray the expenses and send an army to help them. They also added that it was their main business to trade and, *'not to increase our charges, we keep up such number of troops only as are capable of defending and protecting our commerce'*. The Nizam sent robes of honour to Siddi Sat and began planning a diversionary raid on Shahu's territories.

Conspiracies and rivalries are the essence of politics, and the English felt that Siddi Masud of Surat was actually on the Peshwa's side and acting against the Siddi of Janjira, his grouse being against Siddi Yakub of Underi. In a letter of September 1733, Henry Lowther, the Governor of Surat, wrote that Masud had confessed to him that the report of his treaty of friendship with Bajirao was true to fact. The English wrote that it was *'now clear that Siddi Masud being for a long time at variance with the Siddi Yakub'*, had been chiefly instrumental in first stirring up the Marathas against his own countrymen. It was practically due to him that the Siddis had lost their fleets and many of their forts.[22]

In July 1733, Shahu heard that the Nizam planned to invade him from the west and had begun with an army from his capital. In August, Shahu wrote to Baji rao asking him to return and face the Nizam. Baji rao replied to Shahu that Chimaji, Pilaji or Ambaji Purandare, who were with Shahu, could replace him in the Konkan, in which case he would come up the *ghat* to fight the Nizam. Alternatively, he would remain in the Konkan and the Nizam's army could be stopped by any of the three chiefs at Satara.

This letter of 10 August 1733 finds the Peshwa explaining to his king the finer points of the entire campaign. Pained by Shahu's aspersions on his integrity, Baji rao wrote,

> To defeat the Nizam and capture Janjira (at the same time) is not possible. It is difficult to manage two fronts. It is better to come to an agreement with the Nawab and let him keep the places he has taken. It is best to extinguish that fire. You have asked me to write my thoughts. But when I write I need more money, I am accused of looking after my own interests and am labelled a coward. It is therefore difficult to write what I think. Success depends on the Maharaj's destiny. We servants will do our duty keeping the Maharaj's reputation in mind.

Pointing to the galaxy of chiefs who were enjoying the benefits of their fiefs without doing sufficient service, Baji rao wrote,

> If the Maharaj wants us to manage both fronts, then what is impossible for the Maharaj? He has many chiefs like the *Senapati*, Sambhu Sinh Jadhav rao, Kanhoji and Ranoji Bhonsle, Udaji Pawar, Bhuinjkar Jadhav and so on. Let all the forces of the kingdom combine and march on the Nawab. Those who come with their armies should be honoured. Those who don't come should have their 'business' taken away and given to others.[23]

Baji rao was until this time keen to complete the campaign in the *Habshan* and win the battle. Sambhaji Angre from Vijaydurg was also keen to join forces with Baji rao, but eventually did not come. He wrote on 11 August that he was prevented from coming due to torrential rains.[24]

Finally, fate lent a hand to the Siddi and Janjira was saved. In August 1733 the Janjira campaign received its death blow. Sekhoji fell ill. *'I have high fever for nine days. Blood is flowing from my nostrils. Send Pilaji to me urgently'*, Sekhoji wrote to Baji rao.[25] Sekhoji's illness crippled the mission against Janjira. Pilaji Jadhav rao reached Colaba at midnight on 27 August and met Sekhoji. However, by sunrise the next day, Sekhoji was dead.

After Sekhoji's death, Shahu appointed Sambhaji Angre as the *Sarkhel*. Sambhaji had stayed aloof so far, and with the fraternal clash with his brother Manaji taking precedence, the plan of a sea blockade against Janjira receded. The four forts of Janjira, Anjanvel, Govalkot and Underi remained in the Siddi's possession. The Marathas had to accept the situation.

Before leaving the Konkan, Baji rao tried his best to prevent a treaty between the English and the Siddi. The English felt that the Siddi's defeat would mean being neighbours with the Marathas, and this they considered was a situation to be avoided at all costs. The English therefore finally formalized their alliance and signed an offensive and defensive treaty with the Siddi of Janjira on 7 December 1733.[26] With the Siddi and the English navy together, after Sekhoji's death Baji rao realised the campaign would not make any headway.

Making the best of the situation, in consultation with the English, Baji rao installed Siddi Abdul Rehman at Janjira and negotiated a peace. On 11 December 1733 Baji rao returned to Pune. He had spent seven months in the Konkan and felt he had other matters to attend to. *Habshan* was largely won and Janjira itself rendered innocuous. However, Siddi Sat remained at Anjanvel and lived to fight another day.

ॐॐॐ

# 22. The End of Siddi Sat

'You have been successful like *Hanumant*. Your letters of success are as if *Raghuvir* has placed a garland of gems around Hanumant's neck. You have killed a demon like *Ravana*.'

- Brahmendra swami to Chimaji Appa.[1]

The death of Sekhoji Angre was a severe setback to completing the mission at Janjira. Sambhaji and his brother Manaji were always at odds with each other. Although a division of their patrimony by awarding Vijaydurg to Sambhaji and Colaba to Manaji was attempted, it did not quell the dissensions. For the English it was a heaven sent opportunity. They had feared that with the Siddi's defeat, Angre would be all powerful on the coast and their trade would become extinct.

Anderson, an English official, wrote,

> Emboldened by success, and looking for support from the Raja of Satara, the Angrias aspired to bring all the Siddees' territories under their subjection, and possess themselves of every port on the coast between Bombay and Goa. Nor, in all probability, would their efforts have been fruitless, if family dissensions, which so often thwart the best matured designs of Native powers, had not intervened. Manajee and Sumbhajee became estranged from each other, to the great satisfaction of the President and Council, who at once resolved to foment their disputes.[2]

The fragmented command structure in the Konkan with Shahu sitting in distant Satara led to a dilatory campaign against the Siddi. However, mutual antagonism and jealousy between the Peshwa and the *Pratinidhi* were equally the cause.

Baji rao had come to the Konkan region and after taking a few forts camped opposite Janjira. When Shripat rao *Pratinidhi* came later, Baji rao called him for a meeting so a campaign could be planned. However, the *Pratinidhi* camped at Chiplun, and ignoring the Peshwa began an independent campaign wherein he obtained the possession of Raigad.

The Peshwa's annoyance grew when he found the *Pratinidhi* conducting a negotiation with Siddi Sat. Bankaji Naik was carrying out a siege at Govalkot near Chiplun and in a couple of engagements had got the better of the Siddi. These reverses forced the Siddi to talk to the *Pratinidhi*, who felt it was yet another opportunity to win a fort by negotiation.

Baji rao at this time wrote to Bankaji to withhold his cooperation with the *Pratinidhi*. Bankaji quotes Baji rao in his letter of 11 July 1733:

> You wrote that I have not written about the siege at Anjanvel and that I will make all the efforts and the *Pratinidhi* will take all the credit; therefore I should not do such a thing. I agree with this thought of the swami.[3]

Eight days later Bankaji wrote to Baji rao that he had a disagreement with the *Pratinidhi* and had returned to Suvarnadurg. On 18 July 1733, he once again quoted Baji rao's orders:

> You have written 'Shripat rao *Pratinidhi* has come there while I have laid siege to Anjanvel. It seems you two are operating in unison. This is not good. One should not allow another person to take advantage and enter the political field one operates in.
>
> I have never allowed it to happen before this. I took up this campaign by your orders; I have now informed the *Pratinidhi* that I will not stay, and have come away. I will join you in four or five days and will consider your orders as well as those of the *Sarkhel*.[4]

Sekhoji ordered Bankaji to return from Govalkot and follow Baji rao's instructions.[5] Further, Sekhoji wrote to his brother Sambhaji not to join the *Pratinidhi*.[6] A letter from Laxmi bai Angre, Kanhoji's eldest widow, to Baji rao also recapitulates the entire episode and describes how Bankaji refused to cooperate with the *Pratinidhi*.[7]

Whether the Peshwa's moves caused the *Pratinidhi* to return with failure, or the *Pratinidhi* showed poor judgement and chose the wrong tack when he accepted Siddi Sat's word and asked Bankaji Naik to stop the war against the Siddi, will be debated. Events of the period show that the success in the Konkan in 1733 accrued from the combined effort of Sekhoji and Baji rao. The *Pratinidhi* captured Raigad but let the Siddi escape and paid the price when Siddi Sat returned and attacked him.

The historian Grant Duff has remarked on the rivalry between the Peshwa and the *Pratinidhi*,

> The rivalry of Sreeput Rao tended to preserve the Raja's ascendancy, as head of the state for a longer period than it might otherwise have existed; but whilst it usefully controlled the conduct of Bajee Rao and Chimnajee Appa, both of whom are safely said to have been naturally domineering, it also, for some years, cramped the efforts of the Peishwa, obliged him to return to Satara more frequently than was conducive to the success of distant expeditions, and aided Nizam-Ool-Moolk in his endeavours to excite internal dissensions amongst the Mahrattas.[8]

The Nizam-ul-mulk was anguished to see the Siddi defeated and the fort of Raigad return to Maratha control. Since he defeated Mubariz Khan in 1724 and appointed himself Mughal Viceroy of the Deccan, he was in the bad books of the Emperor. However, that did not prevent him from sending letters to Muhammad Shah about various events in the Deccan. At the defeat of the Siddi in 1733, he wrote:

> Siddi Yaqub Khan was appointed the Governor of Danda Rajpuri and other places. His son was killed. As a result, disturbances broke out. The following were the forts in that region. Suras gadh, Avachitgad, Birwadi, Mankot, Ghosala, Malpan, Madangadh, Karwah, Mank and Rajkot. These were the forts of the Empire. There were some other forts too. The Marathas seduced the *Habshi*s. They seized the opportunity and took possession of the forts. The fort of Raheri (Raigad) known as Islamgad is one of the strong forts. It is the capital of Konkan. It was in the possession of Raja Shahu's ancestors. During the time of *Hazrat Khuld Makan* it had been captured after a great struggle. The Marathas seduced the garrison with inducement of money and captured it.[9]

The Nizam ended his letter warning the Emperor of bad days ahead,

> They (the Marathas) will spread to other provinces of northern India. It will be very difficult to put down the Marathas. Nobody will be able to contend against them.

Baji rao's departure from the Konkan was a signal for Siddi Sat to begin reclaiming his losses. He began by attacking the fort of Bankot, which he quickly captured. His next target was the prestigious fort of Raigad. Shahu, alarmed at this fresh aggression, dispatched Baji Bhivarkar, the Somvanshi brothers, and Udaji Pawar to the Konkan. A fierce fight ensued at Pachad with the Siddi's forces, almost to the gate of the fort. In a fierce battle on 10 January 1734, Udaji Pawar killed Siddi Ambar Afwani. Shahu wrote, *'You have cut off the head of Siddi Ambar Afwani. Send it to me'.*[10] With this battle, the Siddi once again retreated in the face of Maratha forces. Bankot was retaken by Baji Bhivrao on 8 March.

The Marathas had been fighting in this area for four years now. Kondaji Shinde, one of Shahu's chiefs, wrote to him emphasising their valour in protecting Raigad and winning back Bankot, ending the letter asking for leave: *'many of my men have to get married and have not been home for many years, they know not the poor state of their homes.'*[11] In April 1734, Baji Bhivrao also wrote to the Peshwa, *'We have been ordered to go to Govalkot after winning Bankot. Many of the Kannadas cannot tolerate the Konkan. Many others are also not happy. I am aware you are not in charge of this campaign now (but) who else can I write my woes?'*[12] In May 1734, Baji Bhivrao was still fighting at Govalkot: *'Eighty men are killed. Babu rao Vaidya died. Many of his men were destroyed. Sambhaji Angre is sitting comfortably at Vijaydurg and does not come to fight. In the rains, the shamal takes away our pride.'*[13]

While the English kept up the pretence of friendship with the Marathas they surreptitiously helped the Siddi. Many Maratha prisoners had been with the English for long. Baji rao's *vakil* visited Captain Inchbird[a] in his garden house in Parel at Mumbai in September 1734, and reported how he took the Governor to task for helping the Siddi against the Marathas;

> Baji rao's *vakil* said 'You are using Underi to send your ships to loot villages so you are not implicated. People are saying this is a breach of faith. Do you understand this? The *Pant Pradhan* has written to me in anger. If you say Underi is not yours, then why have you kept your flag there? You think we don't understand this? You and the *Habshi* are together. We have lost faith in you. Who is the loser; ask your General to write an answer'. The next day the General met me and ordered Siddi Masud (of Surat) be taken in custody and sent out of the city. I said that the Siddi's word cannot be trusted. It is not enough to send the Siddi away. The one who acted stupidly

---

a.  Captain Inchbird was the foremost English diplomat of the day. Anderson describes him as 'who had become better acquainted with the customs and languages of the Natives than all his contemporaries, and was in consequence the favourite diplomat of the day.'

(*'bewaqoofi'*) must be punished so it does not happen again. They are now going to release our men.[14]

The *vakil* also met Siddi Masud the next day and advised him that pride will bring about his downfall. *'The Peshwa wished him well, but if you do not act faithfully, how will you be benefitted?'*[15] From this letter it appears that Siddi Masud had promised to help the Peshwa against Siddi Yakub of Underi, but had gone back on his word.

In December 1735, Siddi Sat retook the fort of Bankot. On hearing this, the *Chhatrapati* ordered Chimaji Appa to take charge of the campaign against the Siddi. Shahu remarked to Mahadji Purandare,

> 'On losing Bankot, I spoke with so much vigour, but you have said nothing.' Mahadji said, 'it is the practice with others to do just a little but speak a lot. But my swami (Peshwa) has a rule; to talk little but do a lot – and the Maharaj knows this. The *shamal* may have taken Bankot, but will not be able to digest it.' The king said, 'you write this to Chimaji Appa, and don't write what I said. He will take it to heart and do what is required. He is a man after my heart. Chimaji is a noble person. He will definitely go to Bankot. He has shown his swordsmanship in distant provinces, (but) who saw it? If he takes Bankot, it will add to his reputation.'[16]

At that time Chimaji was unhappy that his labours were not recognised by the king. On 4 December 1735 an aggrieved Chimaji Appa wrote a long letter to Shahu clarifying how he had been directing the campaign at Konkan. He mentioned the huge debt he had incurred raising armies – which no other member of the confederacy did – and pointed to the fact that he had not been given a '*vatan*' to raise funds. He asked the king not to believe false stories being spread about him by others and to see his performance in loyal service to the kingdom. The long letter ends by requesting Shahu to make proper enquiry about where a battle was fought and who was fighting it and then he would not need to write him such a letter.[17]

Shahu had also asked Sambhaji Angre to help in the war against the Siddi. Sambhaji wrote a reply in early December 1735, where he described the barren state of the land, shortage of funds, the help the Siddi was receiving from the English and the Portuguese, and the strong defences of Govalkot and Anjanvel. If Shahu could send funds, food, and fodder from the plateau, the campaign could be taken up after the monsoons. However, according to Sambhaji, the navy had a small part to play in reducing these forts.[18]

With Baji rao away, the onus for undertaking the campaign fell on Chimaji Appa. Within a few days came news that the Siddi had taken Mandangad and was advancing on Mahad.[19] Soon after, Shahu consulted his ministers and decided that before Chimaji himself goes to the Konkan, it would be proper to send a good army with supplies there under Pilaji Jadhav rao. Chimaji would remain ready to move, and when the time was right, descend the *ghat*s to the Konkan. Rumours also flew that the fort of Bankot had been demolished and then it would be pointless for Chimaji to proceed there. Soon there was news to the contrary; that the Siddi was in fact strengthening the fort and any delay would make it more difficult to capture it.

On 17 December, Nanasaheb wrote to Chimaji that Shahu had summoned him one evening and asked him whether Chimaji planned to go to the Konkan. His spies had informed him that Chimaji's tents have been put up, but not much else seems to be going on. Shahu then wrote a letter to Chimaji and Pilaji and demanded immediate replies. Nanasaheb suggested to Chimaji to not go *'unless his own army is ready. Depending on others is not a good idea.'*[20] By the end of December came news that Siddi Sat himself had come to Bankot.

The paralysis of December 1735 eased when Pilaji Jadhav rao took back the fort of Bankot in March 1736, and stayed there till he was recalled to Satara.[21] After meeting Chimaji and Shahu, he returned to begin the campaign against Govalkot. Chimaji's mother Radha bai wrote to her son to avoid taking too many tasks on hand when Baji rao was away in the north. In April, came fresh intelligence that Siddi Sat was moving out of his forts and heading further north. The Siddi with his fleet went towards Underi and entering the creek took the fort of Rewas. The entire Maratha garrison at the fort was put to the sword. He then began plundering that region and headed towards Manaji's stronghold of Colaba. Manaji Angre, already in the area, sent urgent summons to Chimaji.

After the capture of Rewas, Siddi Sat began depredations in the area. Manaji's defeat at his hands was widely expected. Chimaji had been waiting for just such an opportunity when the enemy would come out of his forts into the open. He quickly moved from Satara in mid-April and within two days had reached the Konkan. Chimaji camped at a place named Charhai near Colaba where Manaji Angre joined him.

On 18 April 1736, Siddi Sat, as yet unaware of Chimaji's arrival in the region, attacked Manaji. In the midst of battle, he was surprised to find himself face to face with the elite Maratha cavalry commanded by Chimaji. Undeterred, Siddi Sat fought bravely in a fierce battle that raged for nearly four hours. Chimaji describes the action in a letter to Baji rao,

> Siddi Sat with his fleet came to the fort of Rewas. There were sixty men in the fort, who were killed. Then Manaji Angre went against him. A severe fight ensued and many good people were killed. There were more fights and fifty or fifty-four men from Manaji's army were killed. The victorious *shamal* began burning villages and advanced. He wanted to capture the fort of Thal. He had the support of *Sarkhel* Sambhaji Angre. This news came to me in Satara. Immediately, I left with the army, and on the sixth day reached Poyenad(?). The next day Siddi Sat with select one and a half thousand men and all his chiefs attacked Charhai. I attacked him. The battle was fierce. Siddi Sat is by nature a brave man. He had a strong artillery and had prepared well. He fought very well. From our side many men and horses were killed, but with the blessings of the swami, Siddi Sat was killed. On his side, men like Davakod Naik and Subhan Ghatga, Phaim and Balaji Shenvi were also killed. Thirteen hundred men were killed from his army. Manaji Angre also reached the spot. His men also fought hard. Many of the enemy ran away naked, and jumped in the sea. The *shamal* has been taught a severe lesson.[22]

In addition to Siddi Sat and the thirteen hundred, Siddi Yakub of Underi was also killed in the battle. Chimaji lost sixty horses while seventy-five were injured, four hundred foot soldiers were killed along with another four hundred from Manaji's army. Manaji himself sustained a bullet wound in his chest.[23] Nanaji Surve braved twenty-seven wounds to kill Siddi Sat and was awarded the village of Kusgaon for his valour.[24]

Chimaji's triumph reverberated in the Deccan. A euphoric Brahmendra swami, who had initiated the Janjira campaign after his temple was burnt by

Siddi Sat, wrote to Chimaji,

> You have been successful like Hanumant.[a] Your letters of success are as if
> Raghuvir[b] has placed a garland of gems around Hanumant's neck. In future
> too, you will have success right from Delhi to Rameshwar. You have become
> like Ram. See my greatness! I gave your family money and spiritual powers
> and success. The temple of Bhuleshwar[c] is on, and two thousand (rupees)
> should be immediately given to Naruji. Even if a ten-crore-strong army had
> gone to the Konkan, this task would not have been completed. Understand
> this. You have killed a demon like Ravana'.[1,d]

Shahu was away on a royal hunt. Hurriedly returning to Satara, he ordered
that every gun in the city be fired in celebration. He sent robes of honour to
Chimaji Appa and Manaji Angre. He repeatedly said, *'it is not an ordinary
thing to kill a chief like Siddi Sat'.*[25]

Janjira remained with Siddi Abdul Rehman. The forts of Govalkot
and Anjanvel also remained with the Siddi as the treaty signed by Baji rao
came into force. These two forts were taken nine years later by Tulaji Angre.
Brahmendra swami lived to see these forts captured by the Marathas.

The war in Konkan was over for now. In these two years Baji rao had
taken huge strides on the national stage. Towards this part of the story, we
shall now return.

꒰ꕤ꒱ꕤ꒰ꕤ꒱

---

a.   The term alludes to Maruti or Hanuman, Lord Rama's disciple and lieutenant from the
     Ramayana.
b.   Another name of Lord Rama.
c.   Yadav era temple fifty kilometres south-east of Pune.
d.   King of Lanka in the Ramayana

# 23. Rajput Affairs, Mughal Wars, ... and a Pilgrimmage

'For years it had been the custom at Court, when the Dakhin intelligencers reported the invasion of Gujarat and Malwa to send out Muhammad Shah on long visits to the various gardens round the capital, or to distract his mind by hunting and shooting expeditions in the many royal preserves.'

- Shafi Warid Tehrani (*Mirat-i-Waridat* or History of Occurrences).[1]

## *L'Affaire* Bundi

The entry of Marathas in Rajput affairs began with a murky domestic dispute in the minor Rajput state of Bundi. The details of the episode are symptomatic of the mores the royalty of the eighteenth century lived by and the sordid story bears narration.

Budh Singh, the ruler of Bundi, was married to Sawai Jaisingh's sister and had a son named Bhawani Singh by her. Budh Singh also had another wife, who was his favourite and he wished to have her child as his successor. A proposal for marriage for Bhawani Singh came from the small Rajput state of Salumber ruled by a branch of the Sisodias. To this Budh Singh objected and declared that Bhawani Singh was not really his son. An infuriated Jaisingh asked Budh Singh why the child was not killed at birth if it was believed that the child was ill-gotten.

Jaisingh's ambition to expand his kingdom led to a series of consequences leading to the first Maratha entry into Rajputana. Setting his heart on securing complete control over the state of Bundi, he set in motion a plan by which the next ruler of Bundi would be his own nominee. Jaisingh first obtained the written consent of Budh Singh that Bhawani Singh would be killed for being an imposter (thereby protecting their 'honour') and then Bundi's successor would be nominated by him. To this, Budh Singh agreed. The matter was next sanctioned by the Maharana of Udaipur. On his return from Udaipur, Jaisingh met his sister and told her that her child Bhawani Singh was declared an imposter. The lady angrily left Jaipur with her son. Jaisingh then sent his minister Ayamal to bring her back with specious promises. When the lady returned, Jaisingh had Bhawani Singh killed.

The sordid episode did not end there. Budh Singh's favourite wife, named Chundavat, soon gave birth to a son who was named Umed Singh. Jaisingh demanded the child be handed over to him, and as agreed, Jaisingh would nominate a successor. Budh Singh refused. However, Jaisingh went ahead and anointed Dalel Singh, the son of a Bundi vassal named Salim Singh Hada, on the throne of Bundi. Jaisingh then gave his daughter in marriage to Dalel and declared him successor to Budh Singh. Budh Singh's resistance was soon broken by Salim Singh Hada and he had to take asylum in Udaipur. In 1730 Dalel Singh became the ruler of Bundi. Effectively Bundi became a part of the state of Jaipur.

Dalel Singh had an elder brother named Pratap Singh, and the young man travelled to Pune and approached the Peshwa for help on behalf of Bhawani Singh's aggrieved mother, the sister of Jaisingh. In 1733, Holkar with Ranoji and Pilaji Jadhav rao were in Malwa. On the Peshwa's orders, in April 1734 Malharji Holkar and Ranoji Scindia with Pratap Singh in tow, attacked Bundi and captured Salim Singh Hada. The fort of Bundi was occupied. Budh Singh's wife called Malharji her brother, tied him a *rakhi*[a] and paid him a sum of six lakh rupees. However, as soon as the Marathas departed, Jaisingh deposed Pratap Singh. The Bundi affair strained relations between Malharji Holkar and Sawai Jaisingh.

The Maratha invasion of Bundi spurred the Rajputs led by Maharana Sangram Singh of Udaipur to unite against the Marathas, and they met on 16 July 1734 at Hurda near Ajmer. Since Sangram Singh had died shortly before this, his son Jagat Singh II presided over the meeting. They decided to fight for each other, assemble after the rains and begin their campaign against the Marathas. However, this never came to pass due to rivalry and suspicions between the main confederates of Udaipur, Jaipur and Jodhpur.[2]

The situation at Bundi remained in the same state until much later, when after the death of Jaisingh, Budh Singh's son Umed Singh returned to take his place on the throne of Bundi.

---

a. A coloured thread tied on the brother's wrist as a symbol of his protection.

## Mughal Wars

By 1733, the Mughal court found that its chief grandees—Nizam, Bangash and Jaisingh— had all faced defeat at the hands of the Maratha power that seemed to be spreading rapidly in newer territories of Hindustan. The previous year they had spread over a three-hundred-kilometre wide front from Gwalior to Ajmer, approaching Agra. Jaisingh had gone forth to meet the challenge but was soon locked up in his fort while the Maratha troops had the run of the country.

A Mughal commentator named Warid has commented on the events of the period. Sawai Jaisingh, who collaborated with the Marathas, comes for special mention. Accusing Jaisingh of doing nothing when he was master of the entire region from Agra to the Narmada, Warid says he received huge amounts of money from the Emperor which he shared with the Marathas and sent them back to their homeland. *'After two or three years of this procedure, the Mahrattas began to expect their "breakfast", as Warid styles it, and every time grew greedier and more avaricious.'*[1]

The Nizam, who understood the Marathas better than any other Mughal grandee, wrote to the Emperor in 1733,

> The aggressions of the Marathas are increasing day by day. They are extending to northern India. They have penetrated into the important provinces of the empire. There is not much distance between Akbarabad (Agra) and Shahajahanabad (Delhi). In spite of this, people have become very heedless. They do not understand the disaster which is in front of them.[3]

The pusillanimous courtiers and apathetic chiefs of the Mughal court emboldened the Marathas to return every year while Baji rao raised his demands with every victory. Jaisingh having failed, Muhammad Shah commanded the boastful Samsam-ud-daulah Khan Dauran to set out with an army to expel the Marathas from Malwa. However, Khan Dauran was unwilling to move out of Delhi while the *Wazir* wanted to lull the Emperor with the pleasures of life so that he could retire to his own country home for a life of repose. Warid comments,

> For years it had been the custom at Court, when the *Dakhin* intelligencers reported the invasion of Gujarat and Malwa, to send out Muhammad Shah

on long visits to the various gardens around the capital, or to distract his mind by hunting and shooting expeditions in the many royal preserves. Meanwhile the *Wazir* sought relaxation by a visit to his country house on the canal about twelve miles from Dihli, where he would remain a month or longer. His time was taken up with fishing or hunting deer. All business was suspended, and the country remained practically without a Government. The pious Muhammadan could do no more than raise his helpless hands to Heaven.

Warid quoted the proverb,

> The earth dried up, the clouds without dew,
> Alas! for the poor handful of grass.[4]

*Mir Bakshi* Samsam-ud-daulah Khan Dauran could not put off a campaign for long. He was ordered to go to Malwa in June 1733; he eventually rode out in February 1734 when Baji rao had just returned to Pune from his Konkan campaign. In March, the grandee moved another six miles outside the capital and stopped there.

Much used to the easy life of the Mughal capital, Khan Dauran sent his brother Muzaffar ahead, who led the army as far as Sironj. Here, '*the Marathas returned, surrounded his camp, and by continual skirmishes, so straitened his quarters, that provisions and necessaries became scarce in his army; but he contented himself with conserving his person, and waiting for orders from his brother and the Emperor.*' Thus ended Khan Dauran's campaign and he returned to his life in the palace, distributing alms for '*extricating so illustrious a General from the manifold dangers of that mighty expedition*'.[5]

In 1734, the Mughals once again threw large armies in the field to push back the Marathas. A two-pronged Mughal campaign, led by *Wazir* Qamruddin Khan and Khan Dauran started from Delhi. Qamruddin Khan started on 20 November 1734 and headed for Bundelkhand. This year Baji rao sent Pilaji Jadhav rao with Nanasaheb to face the *Wazir*. On 26 November, Pilaji started from Loni near Pune and crossed the Narmada by the end of the year. Malharji Holkar, Ranoji Scindia had already gone ahead and Anand rao Pawar was following Pilaji. By February 1735, Pilaji was in Narwar after which he confronted the *Wazir* in Bundelkhand. Many skirmishes between the two forces are described in Marathi letters addressed to the Peshwa and Chimaji:

> On 15 February 1735, we are at Hategaon, near the province of Vodse.[a]
> *Wazir* Qamruddin is after us. We left the *bunagas* in Bundelkhand. Two
> days back we had a battle. We attacked and brought one hundred or one
> hundred twenty-five camels. We camped a kilometre from the Mughal.
> Next day was *Id*, but the Mughal moved out of camp early in the morning.
> We encircled his army with the *Huzurat,* Satvaji Jadhav[b], Govind Hari and
> many others. We pushed Qamruddin into the fort of Orchha, crossed river
> *Betravati[c]* and reached Jatwada, Bhadawar and Gwalior. The Mughal has no
> energy to come after us.[6]

Vyankat rao Ghorpade wrote to Chimaji, '*with your blessings, we have
taught Wazir Qamruddin Khan a lesson and achieved success.*' Pilaji wrote on 2
March 1735,

> The *Wazir* came at us with twenty-five thousand troops from Delhi. We
> fought two or three battles. We took two to three hundred camels from
> him. We have come to Sipri. Qamruddin is willing to pay five lakhs, but I
> have not agreed. He is twelve *kos* from us. We will soon return via Devgad.[6]

At the same time, another army led by Khan Dauran passed by the westerly
route. Joined by Jaisingh and Abhay Singh the huge army traversed through
the Mukandara pass which links Rajputana to Malwa. Near Rampura, the
Mughals faced Ranoji and Malharji, who surrounded them and harassed
them until finally, '*the imperial army was unable to move to break the cordon*'.[7]
and a nearly lakh-strong imperial army was brought to its knees by twenty
thousand Marathas. Naro Shivdeo sent a report from Dhar,

> Khan Dauran and Jaisingh and Abhay Singh and Maharao of Kotah with a
> huge army of two lakh men, artillery and soldiers that cannot be counted,
> passing through the Mukandara came to Rampur. Malharji Holkar and
> Ranoji Scindia came from this side and confronted them. In eight days
> they cut off all food and fodder to the huge army, took their camels and
> horses. Then using guerrilla tactics, they went to Bundi and Kotah, and
> into Jaisingh's territory, so the Mughal force turned back. Khan Dauran is
> at Bundi, Sawai *ji* has gone near Jainagar. Holkar is ten *kos* ahead of him.
> Pilaji met Qamruddin Khan's army. Chhatrasal's son Hirde Sa joined Pilaji.
> Qamruddin is willing to pay five lakhs..[8]

---

a.   Orchha                   b.   Pilaji's son                 c.   Betwa

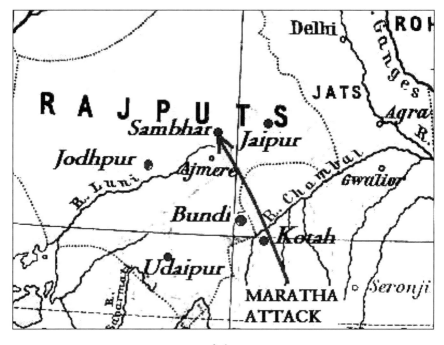

*Mughal Wars*

When Holkar launched a counter-attack and entered the vacant Jaipur territory, the Rajputs were forced to turn back. The city of Sambhar was looted. The terror-stricken *Qazi* there killed his womenfolk with his own hands.[9] Jaisingh rushed back to Jaipur to save the city. Khan Dauran met Holkar and Ranoji and was forced to concede a *chauth* of twenty-two lakh rupees, signing a treaty on 24 March 1735 near the town of Kotah.[10] Ramchandra Shenvi conducted the negotiation on behalf of the Marathas. Mahadeo bhat Hingne, the Maratha envoy at Delhi, was entrusted with the responsibility of collecting the money.

Muhammad Shah was annoyed with the *Wazir* and the *Mir Bakshi* for not only failing to push back the Marathas but paying them large amounts of money. A crestfallen Khan Dauran explained to the Emperor that he had convinced the Marathas to not disturb the Emperor's possessions. The failure of the *Wazir* and Khan Dauran's campaign added strength to Jaisingh's advice to the Emperor to come to terms with the Marathas and recruit them in the imperial cause.

Holkar, Scindia and Pilaji Jadhav rao returned home in July 1735. The Peshwa came forward nearly two miles to ceremonially receive his victorious chiefs. However, Shahu was worried. The expeditions to the north and the intense mobilisation of Mughal armies led to the king once again urging a rethink on whether it was not better to go to south, to the Carnatic, to earn money, where *'one town pays as much as one parganah in the north. Besides, there was always a chance of a tragedy in expeditions to the north and especially involving Delhi...'*.[11]

When Pilaji, Malharji and Ranoji were fighting the Mughals in the north, Baji rao spent the months of February and March 1735 in the Konkan. After the death of Sekhoji, his brother Sambhaji was appointed as the *Sarkhel*. He handed over some responsibilities to younger brothers Manaji and Dhondji at the fort of Colaba. Sambhaji along with Tulaji had gone in early 1734 to attack the Siddi's strongholds of Anjanvel and Govalkot. On his return, he found Manaji and Dhondji to be inefficient and removed them from their posts. Manaji then began confabulating with the Portuguese and this annoyed Sambhaji further. While Sambhaji was trying to capture the forts from the Siddi, Manaji also began talks with the English, who were helping the Siddi. Fearing Sambhaji's wrath, Manaji ran away to the Portuguese fort at Revdanda. This festering feud weakened the Angre power.

Manaji requested Baji rao to come to the Konkan, and the Peshwa reached the town of Pali in early February 1735. He stayed there for two months and divided the Angre patrimony between Sambhaji and Manaji. Sambhaji was given Suvarnadurg and Vijaydurg with the higher rank of *Sarkhel*, Manaji was given Colaba and was titled *'Vajaratmab'*. Baji rao felt he had resolved the issue, but in the years to come it only became more acute. The Peshwa had to repeatedly prop up Manaji's weaker party against Sambhaji. Naturally this turned Sambhaji against the Peshwa. Tulaji, another brother, was to later carry the Angre grievance against the Peshwa over the next two decades.

Shahu's court was also divided in its support to the Angre brothers; while the Peshwa supported Manaji, the *Pratinidhi* supported Sambhaji. However, Shahu finally divided the Angre possessions as per the Peshwa's decision.

How events unfolded over the next two years, we will see shortly. First, in the midst of these turbulent times, Baji rao's mother Radha bai embarked on an astonishing journey across war-torn Hindustan, as she left for her pilgrimage to Kashi. The lady's iron will and Baji rao's own power and prestige when his armies were fighting the Mughal nobles were tested to the full.

## Radha bai's Pilgrimmage

In the eighteenth century, Kashi, Gaya, Prayag, and Mathura were places in North India that Hindus strived to visit at least once in their lifetime. The journey was arduous and a person going for the Kashi *yatra* moved in large groups or accompanied armies going on campaigns. The holy places were under Mughal rule and without adequate safeguards, it was scarcely possible to return unharmed due to the thick forests and insecure roadways all through the journey. Kashi *yatra* was sometimes considered the last journey, from which one may never return. Death in Kashi was considered a path to salvation, a belief that endures to the present day.

Radha bai, wife of Balaji Vishwanath and mother of Baji rao and Chimaji, now in her late sixties, expressed a desire to visit the places of pilgrimage in the north. For one and a quarter year from February 1735, through a war-torn hinterland, a small contingent comprising Radha bai, her daughter Bhiu bai, her husband Abaji Naik Joshi and his brother Babuji Naik traversed the length and breadth of the country.

After leaving Pune, the first halt where the security of a Maratha administration began to wane was the town of Burhanpur on the Tapi. A worried Babuji Naik wrote,

> It was unwise of us to leave. The path is distant. Politically there is war all round. If we face a dangerous situation, how will we reach home? If we go to Bundelkhand, there is risk from Qamruddin Khan, we cannot go to Sawai *ji* as he has gone far. To do what is ordinarily not done, unnecessarily take risks, when the swami's name is so very respected... but the swami is blessed, so why worry? The *avindh*[a] here has given an escort of a couple of hundred men till the Narmada, so we will proceed.[12]

---

a. *Avindh* = one whose ears are not pierced, a Muslim.

Taking all possible care, the group crossed the Narmada, traversed Malwa and reached Udaipur by 18 May. The Rana of Udaipur received Radha bai warmly and urged her to stay for eight or ten days. Babuji Naik, pleased at the reception, wrote that the Rana took the mother to the palace, gave many jewels, an elephant cub and five thousand rupees. Biharidas, the *diwan,* presented another thousand rupees.[13] From here, the party left for Jaipur.

The reception at Jaipur was equally warm. Sawai Jaisingh left no stone unturned to ensure that their stay was comfortable. The entire period of the four monsoon months was spent here. This stay was soon to evolve into a diplomatic exchange between Jaisingh and Radha bai's entourage. In the monsoons months of 1735, a proposal for a treaty with the Marathas was initiated by Jaisingh, first with the Peshwa's mother Radhabai, and then with Baji rao's agent. From Jaipur, the Peshwa's agent reported his talks with Jaisingh in his letter of August 1735,

> Khan Dauran and the *Rajadhiraj* (Jaisingh) are of one mind. They applied to the Emperor that if we fight with the Deccanis, we will not be able to match them. If we have a treaty, either Baji rao or his brother will serve us. They will not disturb our territory. If Sadat Khan and the Nizam come together they will raise a new Emperor to the throne. The *paatshah* understood this, and is still thinking, but he is fickle minded. Sawai *ji* said, 'bring an army of five thousand and come here. We will pay the money from Malwa onwards. We will pay twenty lakh rupees. We will give five thousand rupees as a *rozmura.* When the swami (Baji rao) comes, if we have an agreement and if Khan Dauran can assure security on oath, he can meet the Emperor. Otherwise he should go back (to Pune). If the revered mother (Radha bai) and Babuji Naik feel this is a good idea, let me know.' However, they (Radhabai and Naik) said they have come on a pilgrimage. Politics should be discussed by those who are handling these issues. Then Sawai *ji* asked me, whether Baji rao will agree to come. I replied that it is a major proposal...the swami is wise. Please let me know how we should proceed.[14]

Jaisingh was at his hospitable best. In the months that Radha bai spent in Jaipur, his minister Raja Ayamal was in Delhi arranging security and passports for her pilgrimage. Jaisingh personally saw her off, gifting an elephant, dresses and twenty-five thousand rupees for expenses. Radha bai gave gifts to Jaisingh's queens and his sons Ishwari and Madho Singh. Ayamal's brother Narayan das, who was at Agra with Bangash, accompanied her. On her way

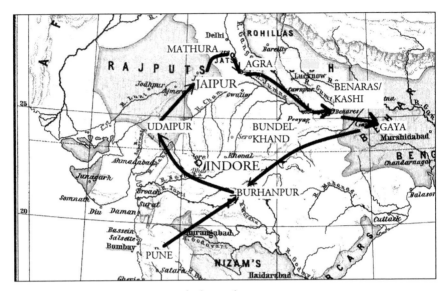

Radha bai's Pilgrimmage

towards Agra, Jaisingh sent an escort of a thousand horse and three thousand archers.[15]

Radha bai first proceeded to Mathura. Here Baji rao's old adversary Muhammad Khan Bangash came forth and escorted the group to Agra. Bangash's minister was related to Jaisingh, and he ensured the group travelled securely and with adequate funds. The Bangash Nawab said the Peshwa's mother was *'no different from his own'*.[16] The Peshwa's envoy Sadashiv Ballal wrote,

> At Agra, *Raya* Shivdas, the *Naib* and brother of Ayamal took care of us. Shivdas discussed with me for four hours saying the prestige of the *Raya* (Baji rao) is such that if he desires to take the kingdom of Hastinapur (Delhi) and give it to the *Chhatrapati*, it will be possible.[16]

On the festival day of *Dassera*, they crossed the Yamuna. Bangash also asked that a message of friendship be conveyed to Baji rao, with whom he had a treaty. *'Together we will secure Malwa and share the revenue'*, Bangash said. Jaisingh too seemed keen to be in Baji rao's good books, and voiced the hope that should Sadat Khan oppose him, the Peshwa will defeat him.[16]

In Delhi, there were two opposing parties in the Emperor's court. The Emperor himself was unable to make up his mind on the strategy to

adopt with Baji rao. The Peshwa's *vakil* Mayaram wrote from Delhi on
21 October 1735,

> The Emperor has conciliated Abhay Singh and Qamruddin Khan. Akbarabad
> (Agra), Malwa and Gujarat were placed in charge of Qamrudddin Khan.
> The Emperor was unhappy that Jaisingh and Khan Dauran paid money and
> came to a truce with the Marathas. Khan Dauran explained that he has an
> agreement with the Marathas that they should not harass Malwa, and that
> he has only given them territory occupied by Rohillas and brigands. 'Baji
> rao will serve the Emperor. He is sending pilgrims for bathing in the Ganga
> from the south. He has already sent his mother for this purpose.' Sadat
> Khan was then summoned. He said Allahabad should be given to Bangash
> so he will teach Chhatrasal[a] a lesson. He asked for Patna and said he will
> give loyal service. The Emperor himself may come after the water in the
> rivers recedes. Khan Dauran and Jaisingh will come south from Jaipur and
> Qamruddin Khan, Sadat Khan and Abhay Singh will come from Gwalior.
> The revered mother has been given passports to go to the three holy places
> with a thousand armed men and servants. She has crossed Mathura. All the
> nobles are taking good care of her and sending her onwards with escorts
> and gifts.[17]

In October 1735, Radha bai reached Kashi. Here her aides began to build
and repair various *ghats* on the Ganga. Donations were made to charities and
individuals.

Although Radha bai was afforded every help on her journey, the Marathas
were dunning the Rajput princes for their annual tribute. Diplomats were
at Udaipur demanding an agreement for annual payment of a tax from the
Rana. His ministers tried to send an emissary to Pune to discuss this. The
Maratha envoy Sadashiv Ballal wrote to Baji rao,

> Here, just hearing the swami's name is enough for people to lose all courage.
> If the *patta* is not paid I will go in Malharji's camp and you should instruct
> him to accept my advice about use of his army to make them pay.[18]

From Kashi, Radha bai's entourage went to Gaya before heading back for
the Deccan with the help of passports sent by Emperor Muhammad Shah, and
was back in Pune in May 1736. Baji rao held his hand during the pilgrimage,
and asked his chiefs not to raid Bangash's territory around Allahabad. The

---

a.  Chhatrasal was not living at this time.

long journey by the elderly lady, treated with honours and hosted in palaces, presented with jewels and money, and escorted to all the places she wished to go, was a diplomatic triumph for Baji rao. Discussions the Maratha agents had with Sawai Jaisingh and his confabulations with Khan Dauran at Delhi, led to the formation of a group in the Emperor's court that favoured the Peshwa. The grandees against conceding any ground to Baji rao were Sadat Khan, Bangash and Qamruddin Khan.

The Peshwa set out soon after to settle these issues unequivocally.

ॐकॐ

# Book Four

## High Noon

I will now head for Gwalior, Bhadawar and collect our arrears, and if the Mughal chases me I will harass him, tire him out to the point where he pants for breath, bring him under pressure, then confront him, and with the Rajashri swami and our revered father's blessings, sink him..... I have already ravaged the territory around Delhi. Sonpat and Panipat remain; I will plunder that too and cut off food to the Mughal..... If the Mughal stays in Delhi, I will go to Agra, enter the antarvedi and plunder the entire region.

- Baji rao's letter to Chimaji Appa, 5 April 1737.

It is said Tahmasp Quli Khan will come to the Deccan. He has no other enemy (except Marathas). He is my adversary and I am his enemy. If he does not go away, I intend to collect the entire Maratha army and cross the river Chambal and not let him come south of the river.

- Baji rao's letter to Brahmendra swami, March 1739.

The Firangis fought with valour and did not lack in soldiering. Our men fought according to the tenets of Bharati war and there have been many battles earlier, but none can compare to this one.

The Lord's *sudarshan* hit the head of the fanatics who harbour religious ill will, and they were cast down. Else Vasai would not have come. The Firangi was a statue of fire.

- Chimaji Appa's letter to Brahmendra swami, 13 May 1739.

# Rewa Uvach

Baji rao had made demands on the Emperor that may appear to be ambitious. The Emperor conciliated the Peshwa until he moved back to Pune, as he knew he would, and then rejecting his demands, tilted towards the Turani group headed by Qamruddin Khan, Bangash and Sadat Khan. Essentially, Muhammad Shah called Baji rao's bluff. The Peshwa and Chimaji must have suffered a few moments of disquiet. However, it did not take them long to formulate a response.

Muhammad Shah's rejection to co-opt Baji rao as one of the protectors of the Mughals pushed him towards confrontation. Baji rao's vaulting ambition led him on to bigger battles and greater risks. On the one hand his mounting debt meant he had to raise funds from new conquests and this led to further more expenses. It was then necessary to be successful in the campaign and the test of success was the amount of tribute obtained. A debt trap was closing in. Yet, the path ahead only led to another campaign.

The festival of *Dassera* in Pune had far greater symbolism that year, the customary *seemollanghan,* or crossing of one's borders, had far greater fervour; and the phalanx of fifty thousand horsemen that came to the bank of the Rewa had a strange glint in their eye. It reflected their resolve and their confidence, their ambition and their invincible spirit. They understood that this was more than an ordinary campaign.

The Mughals also mobilised large armies with their best artillery. The *Wazir,* the *Mir Bakshi* Khan Dauran, Burhan-ul-mulk Sadat Khan and Muhammad Khan Bangash decided to unitedly face the Maratha threat. Perhaps such large armies had not marched north of the Chambal and the Yamuna in many many years.

The Maratha army was smaller, lighter and faster. And its spearhead was Baji rao.

Many millennia ago, on the eve of the Mahabharat war, the great archer Arjun and the Kaurav prince Duryodhan reached Lord Krishna's court to beg him to join their forces. Duryodhan arrived first and sat by a couch near the sleeping Krishna's head while Arjun stood by his feet, and, both waited for Krishna to awaken and catch his eye first. However, when Krishna opened his eyes, he first looked towards the foot of the bed and saw Arjun. Smiling, he asked, *'What brings you here?'* Duryodhan and Arjun then both sought his help. Krishna said, *'I will help you both. One of you will get my strong army of a hundred million, the other will have me on his side. However, I will be unarmed.'* Arjun was given the first choice as Krishna saw him first and he was younger than Duryodhan.

The Mahabharat tells us that Arjun chose Krishna, and an overjoyed Duryodhan returned home with Krishna's huge army. Krishna asked Arjun, *'why did you choose me instead of my fine army?'* Arjun replied, *'I wish to be famous like you. It was always my desire that you be my charioteer'.*[1]

In the subsequent Mahabharat war Krishna held the reins of the horses while Arjun fought the war. It led to the extermination of the entire Kaurav army.

*Chhatrapati* Shahu must have been aware of this epic story. He often said, *'If I were offered the choice between one lakh of troops on the one hand and Baji rao alone on the other, I should prefer Baji rao'.*[2]

It was time to test Shahu's aphorism.

The surge was over. The zenith was in sight. It was high noon.

ॐ☙ॐ☙ॐ

# 24. Baji rao Visits Udaipur and Jaipur

The Rana of Udaipur was greater and was equal to the Raja of Satara, as he never accepted the Mughal as a master; the king of Jaipur was a servant of the *yavana*, and was always at his house owing to his covetousness. Hence, count me as your superior. However, today I will accord you an equal status. We will therefore sit on two cushions of equal stature. I will be to the right and you will be on my left.

- Baji rao to Sawai Jaisingh, as quoted in the *'Vansh Bhaskar'.*[1]

The deliberations of 1735 at Jaipur were aimed at having the Emperor meet Baji rao, concede some of his demands and secure his services for the Mughal Empire. Jaisingh had convinced Khan Dauran that the Marathas had to be brought into the imperial fold by giving them a part of the Empire and then using them to serve the Emperor. He advocated that Baji rao would be satisfied if he were made a deputy *subedar* of Malwa. However, the Mughal court began to talk of two Hindu rulers coming together against the Mughal Emperor and Jaisingh's motives became suspect. Khan Dauran argued vigorously in favour of the Peshwa, showing his mother's tour of holy places as proof of Baji rao's desire to serve the Emperor. He accused Sadat Khan of collaborating with the Nizam to dethrone Muhammad Shah. Jaisingh felt that diplomacy at Delhi would not succeed unless the Peshwa himself came to the north with a sizeable army.

Times were difficult for the Mughal court. Ill omens seemed to come even from the sky. In Delhi and Agra, rain fell for thirty hours at a stretch. Most houses in the capital collapsed and the roads were streams almost five feet deep.[2] All attempts to foil Maratha aggression had failed. Opposing camps in his *durbar* added to the Emperor's confusion. The massive mobilization of his troops and the two-pronged attack of 1734-5 did not staunch the vigour of Maratha invasions. And now came dreadful news that the Peshwa himself was heading for the north.

Jaisingh felt a solution could be found in face-to-face talks with the Peshwa. A grand gesture was the need of the hour. Towards this he extended

an invitation to the Peshwa, with the prospect of a direct meeting with
Muhammad Shah. The Peshwa accepted and decided to go north, leaving
Pune on 8 October 1735, accompanied by his son Nanasaheb.[3] Malharji
Holkar, Ranoji Scindia, Anand rao Pawar, Baji Bhivrao and Pilaji's son Satvaji
Jadhav accompanied him.

Before leaving the Deccan, the Peshwa had been in touch with Chandrasen
Jadhav and a letter from him tells Baji rao not to worry, and he will do what is
needed in the south.[4] The letter supports the idea that there was an agreement
with the Nizam at Rui Rameshwar to have peace between them. This truce
alone allowed the Peshwa to leave the Deccan and campaign for long periods
in the north.

In Satara during the Peshwa's absence, Shahu often deferred taking decisions.
In January 1736 when the Peshwa was on his way to meet Jaisingh, a letter
from the Nizam awaited a reply. However, Shahu said a reply will be sent
after the Peshwa returns. *'Who knows?'* Shahu said, *'Baji rao might meet
the Sovereign*[a]. *They may discuss some things. Hence let us first hear from the
Peshwa'.*[5]

However, in his absence, domestic disputes were often blamed on the
Peshwa. Chimaji, Mahadji Purandare, Pilaji Jadhav rao and others had to
keep Shahu contented with appropriate measures and explanations. Shahu
waited news from Baji rao during his campaigns; often this news reached
him quite late. On the other hand, a string of complaints about the Peshwa
reached his ears. When Sambhaji of Kolhapur attacked Ichalkaranji, Vyankat
rao Ghorpade's base, that noble was away campaigning with the Peshwa.
Chimaji therefore sent Ramchandra Hari Patwardhan to recapture it.
Sambhaji angrily wrote a complaint to Shahu that the Peshwa's army was
ravaging his territory. On hearing this, Shahu in open *durbar* exclaimed,
*'Where do the Prime Minister's mischiefs end? One, he left for the north without
asking me, now he will meet the sovereign and make plans. Earlier, he protected
the Habshi at Janjira. He created a divide in the Angre family. Now he sends an
army to fight my brother! Then he will not be deterred from fighting with me.'*

---

a.   Muhammad Shah

Reporting this, Pilaji Jadhav rao advised Chimaji to recall Ramchandra Hari and keep the king happy and contented.[6]

Starting from Pune, Baji rao headed west, while Satvaji and Baji Bhivrao headed for Bundelkhand. A wide swathe of northern India from Marwar to Bundelkhand was occupied by large Maratha armies. In January 1736 in a letter from near Orchha, Baji Bhivrao informed the Peshwa of developments in Delhi and advocated patience,

> News from Delhi is that Khan Dauran, Jaisingh and the *mukhya* (Emperor) are on one side. Unless the combine of Sadat Khan and Qamruddin Khan is broken, the plan will not be successful. The Mughals are faithless and untrustworthy. The swami must carry forward his plans with patience. Beyond Chameli (river Chambal) up to Delhi there is no money to be had. Whatever money the swami has to get will have to be from Jaisingh. It is better to send one's *vakil* to the capital. Having a large army alone should not be sufficient reason to go and meet the Emperor. It is best not to thirst for more and be satisfied with what is possible. The capital has eminent men and life itself may be in danger. You are wise, a son's advice should not annoy you....[7]

Sawai Jaisingh asked Baji rao to visit Udaipur first and meet the Maharana. Passing through the town of Nandurbar in Khandesh, Baji rao crossed the river Tapi towards the end of January 1736.[8] At about the same time his mother Radha bai reached Kashi from Mathura. The Peshwa was keen that she returned to Maratha-ruled regions before he embarked on his visit to Rajputana. He wrote to his mother on 25 January 1736,

> I am without news about your whereabouts and whether you have returned to Bundelkhand. Complete the pilgrimage soon and return to Bundelkhand. I am waiting for your return even as I go past Lanwada and Dongarpur to Mewar. Days of campaigning are getting over. A major negotiation is on with Delhi. Nijabat Ali Khan from Khan Dauran and Ayamal from Jaisingh are coming, and paying for expenses. After they come and a decision is made, I will convey it to you. The main thing is that the *prithvipati*[a] is keen on a cordial relationship.[9]

The Peshwa travelled to Mewar via Songad, Dabhoi, Banswada and Dongarpur and reached Udaipur in early February 1736. Maharana Jagat

---

a.   Lord of the earth. A term used to refer to the Mughal Emperor.

Sinh II of Udaipur, belonging to the Sisodia clan from which *Chhatrapati* Shahu traced his ancestry, came forth to receive the Peshwa. Udaipur had never allied with the Mughals, and was considered pre-eminent among Rajput princes.

While the Peshwa was still to reach Udaipur, his *vakil* Mahadeo Bhat Nashik-kar (Hingne) came to Jaipur from Delhi and spoke to Ayamal, Jaisingh's minister. The Peshwa's terms for the meeting were payment of five lakh rupees including jewellery, robes, horses, and an elephant. The Emperor on meeting him would have to undertake to give Baji rao twenty lakh rupees in cash and a *jagir* yielding an income of forty lakh annually.[10] Besides, the Peshwa would get a tribute from Dost Muhammad Khan of Bhopal.

Before reaching Udaipur, the Peshwa separated Holkar, Scindia, Anand rao Pawar and Kadam Bande from his own army and asked them to punish Abhay Singh of Jodhpur for helping the Mughals.[11] They entered Marwar and took the fort of Merta.[12] Meanwhile, Baji rao's brother-in-law Baburao Malhar reached Delhi to meet the Emperor. Another agent, Dhondo Mahadev gave the Peshwa's list of demands to the Emperor,

    i.    A *vatan* in Hindustan to be given. The demand was agreed to by the Emperor.

    ii.    A *jagir* to be given to the Peshwa's nobles.

    iii.    The office *sardeshpandya* of the Deccan should be granted to the Peshwa at five per cent of the total revenue for which the Peshwa would make a payment of six lakhs to the Emperor.

    iv.    The Emperor should give the Peshwa a hearing in two or three meetings.

    v.    War against his armies should be stopped.

    vi.    Expenses for the war should be given; which was agreed to.[13]

A historical text named *Vansh Bhaskar* relates the Peshwa's visit to Udaipur.

The Maharana's noble Takht Singh ceremoniously received the Peshwa. Coming forward ten *kos* from Udaipur, the Maharana saluted the Peshwa since he was the elder, and took Baji rao's blessings.

The Peshwa camped at the Champa Bag and the Rana presented him five thousand rupees, robes of honour, an elephant, and horses. The next day, the *Shrimant* was invited to the royal court. The Rana came and received him at the inner door. He placed two cushions for them to sit. The Peshwa however, sat on the floor, keeping the cushion aside. The Rana remained on the cushion and the Peshwa rose and held the flywhisk over his head. The Rana protested saying the Peshwa was worthy of respect, but the Brahmin (Peshwa) said, '*I count you alone as king, because you have sixteen umrao under you'.* The pleasantries over, Baji rao demanded the *chauth* due to him. He said, one and a half lakh rupees per year were due to be paid to the Deccan. The Rana conceded the district of Banhada (Banera) to the Peshwa in exchange.

The Peshwa then was promised a visit the famous Jag-mandir palace built in the middle of Pichola Lake on the morrow. An advisor at that time whispered to Baji rao that there was a plot to kill him in the palace. He[a] flew into a rage and said to the Rana, '*I will not be killed by deceit. I will bring my army. Who will pacify me now?'* Hearing this, the Rana lamented and folded his hands to the *dwij* and said, '*I will pay my respects, do not be carried away by anger. Which fool said there was such a plot? I have been mistakenly blamed.'* The *Shrimant* was not satisfied and demanded a fine of seven lakh rupees. The Rana paid three lakh in gold. Baji rao thereafter visited the palace.[1]

A slightly different description of the visit to Udaipur is found in a nineteenth-century text named *Vir Vinod*.[b] It says,

The Peshwa visited Udaipur by invitation and camped at Champa bag. About the meeting with the Maharana, he was told, 'you are a servant of Satara, and even Satara's king cannot sit on the throne of Udaipur. You should therefore be treated on par with the *Pradhan.'* The Peshwa then said, 'I am a Brahmin, so I have to be accorded greater respect and a higher status'. The Maharana agreed and placed two cushions in front of his throne; on the first he seated Baji rao Peshwa, on the second he seated his *purohit.* Since that day, the priest of Udaipur sits in front of the throne. The Peshwa bid farewell to Udaipur and left for Jaipur.'[14]

The Peshwa with his wife Kashi bai also visited the temples at Nathdwara near Udaipur. Then, he left for Jaipur.

Sawai Jaisingh was the most active Rajput prince in the first half of the eighteenth century with a long career of nearly four decades from the reign

---

a.  The Vansh Bhaskar uses the term *'moorkh'* or 'the fool'.

b.  Vir Vinod has not been able to corroborate the story of the Jag mandir visit.

of Aurangzeb. He was a powerful voice in Muhammad Shah's counsel. His earlier policy of using the Marathas to grasp the entire territory between the Narmada and the Chambal had failed as Baji rao was determined to have it all for himself. The Jodhpur raja Abhay Singh's desire to rule Gujarat also fell through with the Peshwa's own aggression. After three terms as *subedar* of Malwa, the last few years had seen Jaisingh's position to be somewhat diminished in relation to the Peshwa; and from being his patron, he had become a supporter and more of an equal. In the military field, Jaisingh had faced defeat at the hands of the Marathas more than once, and his present posture of an accommodating politician was the result of experience gained in diplomacy and on the battlefield. Jaisingh now looked forward to meeting the Peshwa to conciliate him while persuading the Emperor to concede Maratha demands. It was to be a stern test of diplomacy.

Before the Peshwa reached Jaipur, in March 1736, Maratha armies had locked up Bangash in a ravine in the wedge between the Chambal and Kunwari rivers. Baji Bhivrao, who had enforced the siege, wrote to Baji rao, *'It is clear that Bangash is a coward'.*[15] Bhivrao had completed all the tasks in the region and collected dues. With negotiations on at Jaipur, Baji rao wrote to Baji Bhivrao to stop the fighting. Baji Bhivrao replied on 5 April 1736, acknowledging the Peshwa's instructions,

> To sum up, you have said, *'what is the point in fighting for trivial gains when a major undertaking is underway?'* I may therefore not cross the Yamuna. You are meeting Sawai *ji* shortly and Khan Dauran is expected to come from Delhi. You should recall your armies from Marwar and keep them near you.[16]

Baji rao's meeting with Sawai Jaisingh was altogether different from the one at Udaipur. Baji rao did not accord Jaisingh precedence in rank as he had at Udaipur. Some newsletters of the eighteenth and nineteenth centuries give us a graphic account of the many meetings between the two rulers that give us an insight in the ceremonial meetings of the age.

The *Vansh Bhaskar* gives an account of the Peshwa's meeting with Sawai Jaisingh,

> As the Peshwa approached Bhambolav, a place east of Kishangarh, Jaisingh set out to meet him. Jaisingh demanded the same status at the meeting as the

Rana of Udaipur. However, Baji rao refused, saying, 'the Rana of Udaipur was greater, and was equal to the Raja of Satara as he never accepted the Mughal as a master, while the king of Jaipur was a servant of the *yavana* (Mughal), and was always at their house owing to his covetousness. Hence, count me as your superior. However, today I will accord you an equal status. We will therefore sit on two cushions of equal stature. I will be to the right and you will be on my left.' Hearing this voice of the strong, Jaisingh agreed to sit on the same cushion.

At the meeting place, both armies came face to face. A tent was erected in the middle. Both Baji rao and Jaisingh alighted from their elephant[a] and sat knee to knee on the same cushion. The Brahmin (Peshwa) asked for the hookah and began blowing smoke. The smoke annoyed Jaisingh, but he kept quiet. The ministers from the Deccan were then summoned, save Malharji Holkar, as he had fought with Jaisingh over Bundi, and Baji rao pledged not to insist on reinstating Budh Singh at this meeting. The meeting then ended with Jaisingh asking Baji rao to come back with a well-prepared army from the Deccan to attain his objectives.[1]

The Dastur Komwar papers are another authoritative source of what transpired in the three-month period Baji rao spent in the north,

On 25 February 1736 Jaisingh advanced about a mile from his camp at Jhadli in *pargana* Malpura to receive the Peshwa. As they came nearer they dismounted from their horses. Baji rao saluted with a *mujra*, Jaisingh touched his forehead with his hand, and then they embraced each other. The Peshwa was attended by Ramchandra (Shenvi) and six other officers. After exchanging a few formal words, Jaisingh and the Peshwa retired to their respective camps.

The next day, Baji rao, attended by Raja Ayamal and Ramchandra, visited Jaisingh's camp. Jaisingh received the Peshwa at the threshold of his tent. They embraced, saluted, then sat down on a *masnad*. After a while, they retired to the inner Council chamber and remained closeted for about three hours. When Baji rao took his leave, Jaisingh came up to the outer *Diwankhana* and saw him off.

On Tuesday, 2 March, Jaisingh held court in the evening. Presently Baji rao arrived. Jaisingh took him to his private chamber, offered him betel leaves, scent and a large number of presents. After staying for more than three hours, the Peshwa departed for his camp. The presents offered to the Peshwa

---

a. A horse is mentioned elsewhere.

included crests, pearls, pearl necklaces, costly cloth of hundreds of varieties, and an elephant. The next day wine cups of gold and silver were sent to him; on 4 March, Jaisingh visited Baji rao's camp and returned after nightfall. Three days later, when Baji rao came to Jaisingh's camp, two sedan chairs, one of which was especially equipped for ladies, were sent to his camp. On 14 March, we find Jaisingh camped at Morla village, from where he went to meet Baji rao. On 16 March, Baji rao again paid a visit to Jaisingh who presented him an ivory chess set and a few decorative pieces of sandalwood. On 30 April, we find Jaisingh encamped at Gehalpur to pay the return visit. After the meeting the Peshwa left for Sitagarh. Two months later, at the Peshwa's request, Jaisingh sent him a costly tent house with all its paraphernalia.[17]

In this manner, for over two months and many meetings the Peshwa and Jaisingh deliberated on the future course of action.

In the midst of these meetings, hard-headed negotiations were conducted with the Emperor's representatives in Jaipur and the Peshwa's *vakil* in the court at Delhi.

The Emperor sent Yadgar Beg Khan, Nijabat Ali and Kripa Ram to Jaipur to discuss the terms. Yadgar Khan had authority to offer thirteen lakh rupees from the revenue of Malwa. A second stamped secret proposal was also sent with Yadgar Beg Khan offering a sum of ten lakhs from Rajput territories to Baji rao. It was hoped this would drive a wedge between the Marathas and the Rajputs. The Maratha *vakil* learnt of these documents, and Baji rao was not slow in assessing Yadgar Khan's motives.[18] Finding the Emperor on the defensive, he exponentially raised his demands.[19] The Peshwa's second list demanded:

i.     The *subedari* of Malwa with all its states be awarded to the Peshwa.

ii.    The chiefs of Malwa to pay the Marathas for their expenses.

iii.   Pilaji Jadhav rao to be paid four lakh rupees, on harvest of the *kharif* crop five lakh, and on harvest of the *rabi* crop four lakh; totalling thirteen lakh rupees.

The Emperor accepted these demands. However, Baji rao had not quite finished. A third list was then drawn up and presented by Baburao Malhar to the Emperor:

i.     Chimaji Appa had been a loyal servant and a sum of two lakh be paid to him.

ii.  Pilaji Jadhav rao should be paid one lakh on his coming to meet the
     Emperor, and one lakh later.

These clauses were also accepted by the Emperor. At this stage Baji rao
unveiled the complete extent of his demands, pushing the Mughals as far as
they would go. This last list sent to the Emperor entailed conceding almost
the entire region from Bengal to Marwar to the Marathas.

i.   A Mughal prince to be Viceroy of the Deccan[a] and fifty lakh worth of
     *jagir* for the Peshwa to be granted in the Deccan. Half of the money in
     the Treasury earned by my (Peshwa's) efforts should be given to me.

ii.  The kingdom of Thanjavur and the fort of Shivneri[b] should be given
     to *Chhatrapati* Shahu.

iii. The *jagirdari* and *subedari* of the entire province of Malwa, (already
     granted).

iv.  The estate of Yar Muhammad Khan and Izzat Khan's territory be given
     to the Peshwa.

v.   Forts Mandu, Dhar and Raisen be handed over to keep the Peshwa's
     family. The Emperor agreed to give one fort.

vi.  The entire region south of river Chambal should be given to the
     Peshwa. If the smaller rulers there pay their dues on time, they will not
     be harassed.

vii. The Peshwa has many debts. Therefore, fifty lakh from the tribute of
     Bengal should be paid to the Peshwa.

viii. The Hindu places of pilgrimage: Prayag, Kashi, Gaya and Mathura,
     should be ceded to the Peshwa.

ix.  The Emperor should come to Agra for the meeting to be held with the
     mediation of Jaisingh and Amir Khan. The Peshwa would not go to his
     *durbar* and the meeting would be held during the journey.

x.   The *Sardeshpandya* of the south be given to the Peshwa.

xi.  Many *vatans* in the Deccan should be awarded to the Peshwa.[13]

In exchange, Baji rao agreed to send an army to serve the Emperor and
ensure peace in the region.

---

a.  Effectively replacing the Nizam-ul-mulk.
b.  Birthplace of *Chhatrapati* Shivaji.

The scope and breadth of the demands took the Mughal court's breath away. Considering the Peshwa's proximity and consequent threat to Delhi, the Emperor quickly agreed to Baji rao's demands. However, with the monsoon approaching, the campaign 'season' was soon ending. The Emperor's quick acquiescence eventually proved to be a gambit to tide over the danger of Baji rao's invasion.

Once all the demands reached the Emperor, the Peshwa retired to Malwa. He hoped for an early reply from the Emperor. As days went by, a personal meeting did not appear possible. Khan Dauran assured the Peshwa of an early reply but when there was no answer by the end of May 1736, Baji rao wrote to Hingane, *you left with an assurance that a reply from Khan Dauran would come in twenty days. It is nearly two months now.*[20] It was not possible to keep a large cavalry of fifty to sixty thousand unemployed at Malwa for so long. Baji rao asked Holkar and Scindia to canton in Malwa in the monsoons with ten to fifteen thousand troops and returned to Pune. This then was the first time that the Maratha chiefs stayed back in Malwa in the monsoon season.

Baji rao outlined his plan to Hingane. He wrote,

> Before the end of *Chaturmas*[a], the five lakh rupees, *sanad* of the *subah* (Malwa), *sanad*s of the Rohilla (Bhopal), robes and jewellery must reach me. I will then come after *Dassera*. There will be no delay in my coming there. Immediately the treaty is acted upon, I will be there. I have returned here, but have left an army behind. Once the treaty is acted on, you can assure the Nawab (Khan Dauran) that we have affection for him.[20]

Ranoji Scindia wrote to Hingane far more vehemently,

> Tell the Nawab that we are helping him, and not to trust fabricated news. Our God has given us enough. We get worried when a peace is agreed to and a treaty is signed. When there is no treaty we are happier.[21]

The visit to Rajputana in 1736 did not achieve the aim of obtaining large concessions from the Mughals at one stroke in exchange for an offer of peace. In the month of May, the Emperor appointed the Peshwa as the deputy Governor at Malwa under Jaisingh. However, this did not satisfy the Peshwa.

---

a.   The four monsoon months.

Casting his net wide, Baji rao showed his willingness to push his demands and take advantage of an enfeebled Mughal court. His ambition to be master of the Deccan and Hindustan is mirrored in his petitions to the Emperor. Before he stepped to the negotiating table, he had built a strong military presence, and spread his armies from Kalpi on the Yamuna to Marwar in the west.

Baji rao returned to Pune in June 1736. Chimaji had completed the campaign in the Konkan against Siddi Sat two months earlier. Both brothers waited to hear from the Emperor through the monsoon months. It was only in October 1736 that the reply finally came.

The Emperor granted Baji rao a *mansab* of seven thousand, a *jagir*, a *jhigga* and a *sarpech*. Chimaji was awarded a further *mansab* of five thousand. Baji rao was told to present himself at Delhi where he would be paid fifteen lakh rupees.

There was no mention of Malwa, however.

꒰ೀ꒱ೀ꒰

## 25. The Peshwa Heads North

> 'However, you know the Mughal way of doing business. They do little; boast a lot. What the Emperor thought was true, has to be shown as false. There are two thoughts towards achieving this: one, sink Sadat Khan, or the second, go to Delhi and burn its suburbs.'
>
> - Baji rao's letter to Chimaji Appa.[1]

The choice before Baji rao was either to accept the paltry concessions of Muhammad Shah or obtain them by force. He chose the latter. Immediately the contents of Muhammad Shah's *firman* were known, the Peshwa began planning a fresh campaign to the north.

With a large mounted army of fifty thousand men,[a] Baji rao began from Pune on 12 November 1736. In December, he reached Bhopal, ruled by the Rohilla chief Yar Muhammad. The Peshwa forced him to pay five lakh rupees before moving to Bhilsa[b] on 5 January 1737 where he met Malharji Holkar and Ranoji Scindia. The Bhilsa fort was taken on 13 January after a short siege. He next crossed into Bundelkhand and was at Orchha in February 1737. Pilaji Jadhav rao reported that the tribute from Orchha, Narwar and Datia was collected.[3] Chimaji Appa, writing to Brahmendra swami gave a hint of Baji rao's plans,

> *Rajashri Rau* crossed the Narmada. He will be in Orchha by now and have met Malharji Holkar and Ranoji Scindia. After finishing the tasks in Orchha, it is planned to pass Agra, and once, to go near Delhi. Alternatively the plan is to cross the Yamuna and enter the *antarvedi*.[c] With the swami's blessings, all desires will be fulfilled.[4]

Malwa and Bundelkhand were entirely subjugated. The small state of Bhadawar just south of the confluence of the Yamuna, Kunwari, and Chambal

---

a. Surendra nath Sen says 'In the Peshwa period, the Marathas were no longer compelled to defend their hearth and home. Secure in their native territories, they were now in a position to carry war into enemy country, and in these distant expeditions, designed mainly for plunder, a cavalry force was far more useful than infantry.'[2] This seems to have been true from Baji rao's times.

b. Now called Vidisha.

c. *Doab* of Ganga and Yamuna rivers.

rivers was strategically located. Gopal Singh, the king of the state, controlled vital fords to cross the Yamuna and enter the *doab*. The king and his son Aniruddha, resisted Maratha demands.

Raja Gopal Singh was an old ally of Awadh's *subedar* Burhan-ul-mulk Sadat Khan. In 1729, he had joined Sadat Khan against Hindu Singh, a Chandel leader in the western part of Awadh.[5] Not only did he help Sadat Khan, but he gave Hindu Singh his solemn word that if he submits to Sadat Khan, he could keep his fort and preserve his honour. The besieged Hindu Singh submitted but the strong fort of Chanchendi was occupied by Sadat Khan and never returned.[6]

Ater and Bhadawar were under the protection of Sadat Khan, and Gopal Singh therefore decided to resist the Marathas and mustered an army of seven thousand men, a large cavalry, and forty-five elephants to oppose the Marathas. In the meanwhile, Aniruddha Singh's brother joined the Marathas and suggested to them a way to win the battle. Half the Maratha force was left to face Aniruddha, while the remaining half attacked Ater. The *raja* had to retreat to the protection of Ater fort. From here, he sent appeals to Sadat Khan to rush to his aid. Sadat Khan replied, *'Be sure not to be dismayed, and be sure not to give them a kauri; for look, I will be with you instantly'.*[7]

Baji Bhivrao was entrusted with the task of crossing the Yamuna, and he took the help of Chhatrasal's son Hirde Sa.[8] Eventually they captured the fords and the boats which prevented Sadat Khan from crossing the river. Raja Gopal Singh, in extremis, came out of the fort and met Baji rao.[9] Baji rao levied a heavy indemnity of twenty lakh rupees, of which fifteen lakh were paid in cash, and took hostages in lieu of the balance. Ater's capture on 18 February 1737 finally shook the Mughal court out of their reverie and mighty preparations to oppose the Marathas began.

The *Tarikh–i-Hindi*, written in the years 1741–2 by Rustam Ali, a chronicler of Muhammad Shah's rule, gives the Mughal perspective of the Maratha attack on Bhadawar,

> The Mahratta armies entered the territory of Bhadawar, the chief of which, Amrat Singh, collected an army, advanced from the town of Ater with the utmost intrepidity, and gave battle at the distance of a *kos* from that town. It is commonly reported that the army of the Raja consisted of seven

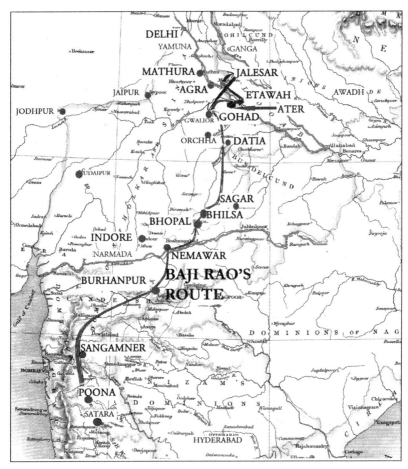

Baji rao: *from* Pune to Ater

## Route from Pune to Ater[10]

Pune – 12 November 1736.

Pabal – 13 to15 November 1736.

Ashvi (near Sangamner) – 25 November 1736.

Chalisgaon – 1 December 1736.

Burhanpur – 8 to 10 December 1736.

Nemawar – 19 December 1736.

Took tribute from Bhopal.

River Betwa – 6 January 1737.

Bhilsa (Vidisha) – 6 to 14 January 1737.

Dhamoni (Saidpur/Madanpur) – 19 to 20 January 1737.

Around Orchha – 24 to 28 January 1737.

Gohad – 7 February 1737.

Ater – 17 February to 5 March 1737.

North of Chambal – 6 March 1737.

South bank Yamuna at Vikrampur ghat – 9 to 11 March 1737.

thousand horse, twenty thousand foot, and forty-five elephants; while that of the invaders amounted to near one hundred thousand horse. The war continued for one month; and although the territory of Bhadawar lay close to the capital (Delhi), yet that Emperor, the *'asylum of negligence'*, took no measures for the expulsion of the foe. It is said that one of the brothers of the Raja, who had long cherished hatred against him in his own bosom, joined with the enemy ….. The Raja was obliged to retreat, fighting all the way with the enemy, and got safe into the fort. Although the enemy had plundered much treasure and property, yet he took besides a contribution of twenty lacs of rupees in cash and ten elephants.[11]

Towards the end of February 1737, Khan Dauran erected his tents outside Delhi and the next day he began marching towards Ater to chastise the Marathas. Two weeks later, *Wazir* Qamruddin Khan started from Delhi by camping at Char *bagh* near the Yamuna. He did not progress far, however, and was 'loitering' forty *kos* from Delhi.[12] By that time, Khan Dauran was in Agra with his forty thousand strong army. Qamruddin stopped on the borders of the province of Ajmer and was joined there by Muhammad Khan Bangash who came from his seat at Farrukhabad. Sadat Khan, coming from Awadh, was in the *doab* when Ater fell to the Marathas. Abhay Singh was at Jodhpur, where he kept himself intoxicated '*by the use of opium. He slept the whole day and spent the whole night in asking what was to be done*'.[13] However, not long after, he started from Jodhpur at the head of his army. The Nizam, to whom Qamruddin Khan looked with hope, came to Burhanpur and moved slowly north. Khan Dauran and the Emperor kept their communications open, and when the Emperor heard that Ater had fallen, he asked Khan Dauran to begin peace talks with Baji rao.[14]

Just then, came news of a Maratha defeat and new life was injected in the dying Mughal campaign.

At Ater, Baji rao was barely thirty *kos* south of Agra. Two large Mughal armies led by Khan Dauran and Qamruddin Khan converging on Agra seemed to block the straight road towards Delhi. Sadat Khan's army from the *doab* was attempting to cross the Yamuna to join them. The Peshwa therefore planned a diversionary raid into the *doab,* perhaps to divide the Mughal armies.

On 1 March 1737, Malharji Holkar, Satvaji Jadhav and Baji Bhivrao with a lightly equipped ten thousand strong army comprising entirely of the cavalry, crossed the Yamuna at Rapri, about thirty *kos* northwest of Etawah, and began looting the cities in the *doab*. First, Holkar came to Etawah and then moved to Shukohabad, Firozabad and Itimadpur, plundering the region. Lalji Khatri, the chief at Shukohabad, gave a lakh and a half rupees and an elephant to Holkar and saved his city. At Itimadpur, Holkar had come within a dozen miles of Agra across the Yamuna. Holkar then turned east and went deeper into the *doab,* attacking Jalesar.

At this time, Sadat Khan was at Etawah. By forced marches, he turned east to find Holkar's army. On 12 March 1737 at sunrise, Holkar came across Sadat Khan's son-in-law Abul Mansur Khan, the later Safdar Jung, leading Sadat Khan's vanguard with twelve thousand horse. Holkar began an encircling manoeuvre around this army. Mansur Khan, however, fell back with the Marathas chasing him, until Holkar found himself face to face with the main army of fifty thousand men led by Burhan-ul-mulk Sadat Khan. Seeing himself unequal to the task of facing an army six times larger, Holkar turned back. The Mughal army gave chase and killed nearly one thousand five hundred Marathas including some of the Maratha chiefs. During the pursuit, the Marathas missed the ford on the Yamuna and entered the river at the wrong place. Many drowned. The remaining army reached Baji rao at Kotila near Gwalior.[15]

The *Siyar-ul-Mutaqherin* describes the action,

> Malrao (Malhar rao), one of greatest Generals in Baji rao's army, having found means to cross the Jamuna, had fallen at once upon the province of Etawah, and was actually burning and sacking everything from the gates of that city to the seat of Moty *bagh*, which is close to Akbarabad (Agra). Wherever he passed, he left nothing but slaughter, desolation and ashes. From there, he turned towards the towns of Saadabad and Jalesar when Sadat Khan suddenly appeared on the Marathas' rear, like a storm that threatens destruction from afar. Finding the freebooters dispersed, he fell so vigorously upon them, that he never ceased killing and slaughtering until he had chased them beyond Itimadabad, which was at a distance of four *kos* from the field of battle. Heaps of dead were to be seen everywhere, and the road, for eight miles together was strewn with corpses. Three Generals of

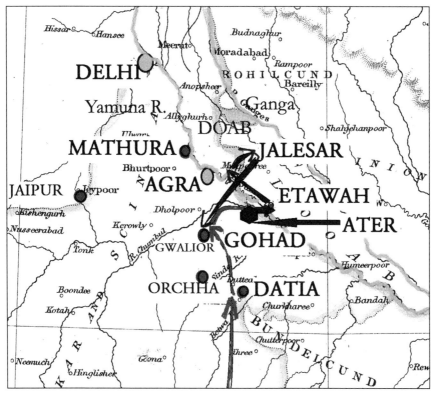

Malharji Holkar In The *Doab*

character were taken prisoner and Malrao himself being severely wounded, thought himself happy to make his escape with a few followers. The main of the runaways, having thrown away their booty, fled towards the Jamuna, and having in their hurry and consternation, mistaken one place for the other, they plunged into a part of the river that had no ford, where disappearing in the eddies of annihilation, they perished in shoals. Malrao with the few that kept pace with him, found with infinite pains his way to Baji rao's camp, to whom he presented himself in the most dismal condition..[7.]

Rustam Ali in the *Tarikh-i-Hindi* describes Holkar's embarrassment in the *doab*,

> The Muhammadan army pursued them, made heaps of the slain, and kept the battle raging for the distance of thirty-five *kos*. A body of the invaders were overtaken near the tank of Itimadpur, and three chiefs with about a

thousand men were taken prisoners. Those who escaped the sword crossed the river Jumna. Many of them missed the ford, and were drowned in the river of eternity, but most of them escaped and joined their countrymen. When the prisoners were brought before Burhanu-1-Mulk[a], he gave each man a rupee for his expenses, and set them all at liberty; but he kept the three chiefs loaded with chains. After this, he returned towards Shah-Jahanabad, from which place Amiru-l-Umara Khan-Dauran was advancing with a body of twenty-five thousand horse, some guns, and many elephants, accompanied by Muhammad Khan Bangash Ghazanfar Jang, at the head of twelve thousand horse. The army, which in the beginning of Zi-1 ka'da had been ordered by His Majesty to proceed against the enemy, met Burhanu-1 Mulk near the city of Mathura, in the beginning of the month of Zi-1 hijja.[16]

Sadat Khan crossed the Yamuna and reached Agra. Before abandoning chase, the *Siyar-ul-Mutaqherin* says Sadat Khan reached the north bank of the Chambal intending to chase away Baji rao's main army, but *'not one man of that accursed race was to be discovered'*. Sadat Khan then retired to Agra. Sadat Khan wrote to the Nizam that he had defeated the Marathas: the *'ganims were too proud. I have punished them'*. Similar letters from Sadat Khan went to the Emperor saying he had defeated the Marathas and chased them south of the Chambal. The Emperor honoured him with expensive gifts.

Sadat Khan's success in the *doab* gave hope to Khan Dauran, and instead of offering terms to the Marathas and turning back for the capital, he decided to move ahead and join Sadat Khan in his proposed chase across the Chambal. At Agra, after two days' rest, Sadat Khan told his men that they should *'be ready to march with four days' provisions and water, and if anyone should be found in his tent after the hour of departure, his horse would be hamstrung, and himself carried in derision around the camp.'* Preparing to carry the food and water in leather bags and vessels, he also loaded his elephants and camels with light artillery and swivels. He then *'published that he was resolved to pursue the enemy beyond the Chambal, and that he would be the first at the head of his troops to throw himself into the water.'*[17]

Just then, Sadat Khan received a letter from Khan Dauran that he was *'setting out to join him, and recommended his waiting a little until he might*

---

a.  The proper way to break the word is as given here. However, for easy pronunciation, it is
    often written as Burhan-ul-mulk.

*proceed with him on the destruction of those freebooters'.* Sadat Khan had just *'mounted a horse, and was at a loss how to act'.* However, he eventually stopped his march, and moved west to join Khan Dauran near Mathura three days later. Qamruddin Khan and Bangash were still about thirty *kos* from Delhi on the way to Ajmer, awaiting the Marathas in that quarter. On Khan Dauran's arrival in Agra, *'six or seven days were spent in visits and entertainment'.*[18] Khan Dauran had twenty-five thousand horsemen, many cannons and elephants. Muhammad Khan Bangash soon joined them with another twelve thousand men.[19] In this manner, there were nearly ninety thousand men around Agra while *Wazir* Qamruddin Khan, somewhat nearer Delhi, was barely a day's march to the west of them.

At Kotila near Gwalior, Baji rao took stock of the situation. The safest option was to turn back to the Deccan in the face of three overwhelmingly large Mughal armies blocking his way to Delhi. The next option of staying at Ater or Gwalior in the ravines of the Chambal for long, was not safe. The last option was to move on and attack Delhi.

In his letter to Chimaji Appa written on 5 April 1737, Baji rao assessed his situation,

> I am presently camped near Jainagar. I sent my heavy luggage and camp followers to Bundelkhand with Raja Jagatraj and became lightly equipped. I sent the information about the arrival of the *sardars* after their fight with Sadat Khan with messengers, which you will have received. Sadat Khan crossed the Yamuna and came to Agra. There I would have faced him, but he had taken shelter in Agra. To go and fight there, it was not certain whether he would be broken in his sheltered place. Staying at the confluence of the rivers Gambhir and Yamuna; the place had too many ravines. Khan Dauran and Muhammad Khan Bangash were coming to Agra and once they joined Sadat Khan, the matter would have been difficult to deal with, and staying at the *sangam* of the rivers would not be wise.
>
> Secondly, Sadat Khan had written to the Emperor, Khan Dauran and Qamruddin Khan that *'the Maratha army came across the Yamuna and I sank them. I killed two thousand, drowned two thousand in the river. Malharji Holkar and Vithoji Bule were killed. Baji rao raided us, this is what happened to him. There is no strength left in his army. I will cross the Yamuna and push*

*the Marathas beyond the Chambal.'* He wrote many things that were mere gossip. He received the Emperor's approbation and rewards in the form of robes, a pearl necklace, an elephant, and a turban. His *vakil* was also rewarded with a turban. Sadat Khan had made his position strong. He wrote contemptuously to many *amirs*. I got this information from Dhondo Govind from time to time. In conclusion, *'my army has no strength left, it is lifeless, it has been sunk and demolished'*, is what he wrote. He showed it as a game of 'hide and seek'.

However, you know the Mughal way of doing business. They do little; boast a lot. What the Emperor thought was true, has to be proven false. There are two thoughts towards achieving this: one, sink Sadat Khan, or the second, go to Delhi and burn its suburbs. Then the falsehood will be exposed. When I found Sadat Khan would not leave Agra, I decided to go to Delhi. Burn the city's suburbs and show the Emperor that the Marathas are still here....[1]

Baji rao, watching developments from across the Chambal, had found the opening he needed to execute his third and most hazardous option.

ॐक्रॐक्र

# 26. The Dash to Delhi

'I have already ravaged the territory around Delhi. Sonpat and Panipat are left, I will plunder that too and cut off food to the Mughal...If the Mughal stays in Delhi, I will go to Agra, enter the *antarvedi* and plunder the entire region.'

- Baji rao's letter to Chimaji Appa, 5 April 1737.[1]

For several centuries, the capital city of Delhi had never seen an invader. This statistic was to soon change. There were revolutions and coups in the city, but an enemy had never forced his way into the city. This gave a sense of security to its residents who, even in those days, considered themselves somewhat privileged. The Marathas under Baji rao had, in a matter of a decade, leapfrogged from the 'barren lands' of the Deccan to the imposing Mughal capital, demanding the cession of entire *subahs* along with large sums of money as *khandani*.

From distant Satara, Shahu was worried about the entire northern enterprise. He wrote a letter of enquiry and advice to his Peshwa,

> Where are you and what are you thinking? Upto where are you planning to go? What cooperation are the chief amirs offering? You must be near Agra. I have heard you plan to meet the Emperor. If so, it's the Mughals you are dealing with, they will give their word but see what is in their interest. You should not trust them. Therefore, if you plan to go inside the city and meet, you should, at any rate, not do so. From a distance, you should obtain your aims through the person you are dealing with. You are an intelligent and successful servant. We are confident you will not make a mistake in your tactics. Yet, you should devote much thought to this so that you return successful. The amirs there are favourable to you and the Nizam-ul-mulk is restlessly coming towards that province. I cannot decipher his intentions, so you should be careful. It is not as if you are unfamiliar with the Mughal way of thinking! Keep your wits and complete the tasks.[2]

The Nizam, Bangash, Jaisingh, Khan Dauran and Qamruddin Khan had all failed to defend the Empire. The arrival of the Marathas just a few

---

a. Should be Badan Singh Jat, the father of Suraj Mal.

miles from Agra had filled the capital with dread. The minor victory in the *doab* made it seem as though the danger had passed. Sadat Khan, swollen with pride after the honours and robes the Emperor sent, Khan Dauran, keen to share the glory, and Muhammad Khan Bangash, the eager Nawab of Farrukhabad, gathered at Agra, secure in the thought of having pushed the Marathas beyond the Chambal. Sadat Khan ridiculed Khan Dauran for allowing Baji rao's agent Dhondo Govind to stay in his camp.

Baji rao wrote to Chimaji in his letter of 5 April,

> On 26 *Dhu al qida* (17 March 1737), I marched leaving the *Paatshah's* road, covering long distances before every halt, through the country of Daman Singh Chudaman Jat[a] along the border of Nevatiya (Mewati) country skirting the hills. Khan Dauran and Bangash went to Agra. They met Sadat Khan on 2 *Zulhijjah* (23 March 1737). Dhondo *pant* was with Khan Dauran. Sadat Khan asked Khan Dauran, *'I have broken Baji rao's army. The camp attendants (bunagas) ran away. The khasa[b] also crossed the Chambal and went away. You are still entertaining him. You have still kept his vakil. For what purpose? Send him away!'* Therefore, Dhondo *pant* was given leave to depart. Khan Dauran need not have listened to Sadat Khan. However, he sent him away as did not think or suspect what he was told was wrong. He (Dhondo *pant*) came back to me. Qamruddin Khan and Azimulla Khan came towards Agra. I did not confront them. Leaving them seven *kos* to my right I passed them and riding twenty *kos* a day, in just two stages, on 7 *Zulhijjah* (29 March 1737), keeping Barapula and Kalika temple to my right, I stayed at Kushbandi[c] near the city (Delhi).[1]

Baji rao in a matter of just four days and nights, from in between the camps of the *Wazir* and Sadat Khan, avoiding several Mughal armies to the south of the capital, rode nearly two hundred kilometres to reach the gates of Delhi. Sadat Khan, Khan Dauran and Bangash were at Radha kund near Mathura on Tuesday 23 March, still one hundred and forty kilometres away, when Baji rao was on his way to Delhi. It was the day of *Ram navami*, the day when the Hindu king Lord Ram was born.

---

a.  Should be Badan Singh Jat, the father of Suraj Mal.
b.  Chief. Here it refers to Baji rao himself.
c.  Could be Kushak Mahal, a 14th-century hunting lodge of Firoz Tughlaq on the grounds of the Teen Murti Bhavan today. But a Persian source says he stayed near the Qutb Minar.

In a celebratory mood, Khan Dauran Samsam-ud-daulah had invited Sadat Khan to a banquet in his tent. In the midst of the feast they learnt that Baji rao had reached Delhi. In the utmost alarm the imperialists broke up camp and began a hasty return to the capital *'placing the finger of vexation upon the teeth of shame'*.[3]

Rustam Ali describes the embarrassment the Mughal Generals endured near Mathura,

> One day, the Amiru-1-Umrao (Khan Dauran) invited Burhanu-1 Mulk (Sadat Khan) to his tents, and prepared a feast for his reception. In the midst of the banquet it was suddenly reported that the enemy's army, having marched through the town of Fathpur, and leaving Dig, the native land of Badan Jat, on the right, had arrived at Dehli. Burhanu-l-Mulk, on hearing this, hit the finger of sorrow with the teeth of distraction, and, mounting an elephant, hastened towards that city. It is commonly said that Itimadu-d-daula Qamru-d-din Khan, who, with the intention of expelling the enemy, was then encamped near Kaman Pahari, also returned to Dehli. In the mean time, Raja Jai Singh, having marched from Jaipur with an army of fifty thousand Rajput horse and above seventy elephants, advanced as far as the town of Nimranu but when he heard the news of Burhanu-1 Mulk's march towards the capital, he returned to Jaipur.[4]

In Delhi, Baji rao made his presence felt at the *Ram Navami* fair being held at the Kalika temple near the Khizrabad grove, where a large number of people had come on the occasion of the festival. He sent his men to plunder some wares, elephants and camels. Baji rao's sudden appearance at Delhi was like a whirlwind on a quiet day. The *Siyar-ul-Mutaqherin* describes the first impact at the many fairs that dotted the environs of Tughlaqabad to the south of the walled city of Delhi,

> On the eighth day of *Zil Hijj*, (30 March 1737) they were at Tughlaqpur. As that town was filled with an immense multitude of Mussulmen and Hindoos from the city, who had flocked thither both on a principle of devotion, and on parties of pleasure, they were all leisurely plundered. An immense booty was made here, and the Marhattas having passed the night near Khwaja Qutubuddin's monument, the next day, which was Arafat day, they plundered the street inhabited with jewellers, and sacked and burned all the shops of that town. About noon they proceeded farther, and sacked the town of Palam, from whence the shoals of runaways and wounded

flying into the city, filled it with dreadful accounts of what they had seen and felt; and the citizens, without further enquiry, lost both their courage and their senses, filled the city with uproar, and the whole soon became one continuous scene of dismay and confusion...[5]

Continuing his long letter of 5 April to Chimaji, the Peshwa writes about his thoughts and deeds on the first day in Delhi,

> I contemplated burning the suburbs of Delhi. However, in that, Delhi is a great city, and there was no use ruining the *Paatshah*. Secondly, the *Paatshah* and Khan Dauran in their mind wish to have a treaty. However, the Mughals do not let them do so. And, an insult breaks the cord of diplomacy and politics. For these reasons, I cancelled the idea of burning, and sent letters to the *Paatshah* and Raja Bakht Mal. Two elephants and horses and camels came from the city, which I appropriated. The people from the cantonment had come for the *yatra* at the Bhavani temple, I roughed up some of them. Next day, on the Emperor's orders Raja Bakht Mal sent me a reply, asking me to send Dhondo *pant*. So we came close to the city. That caused a commotion in Delhi. Therefore I did not send him. I sent a reply, '*Send an able escort and horseman and I will send the vakil. Our staying near the city will create a disturbance there. Therefore we are moving to the jheel.*'[a] And so we marched away. However, when we were passing the city, the Emperor sent out Nawab Mir Hasan Koka - *Daroga Khas Chowki*, Nawab Amir Khan, Khoja Roz Afzul Khan, Raja Shiv Singh, Jamatdar Risale Amir and Muzaffar Khan Naib Bakhsi-giri Ahadi and Nawab Muzaffar Khan – the brother of Khan Dauran – to Rakabganj outside the city with a seven or eight thousand strong army.[1]

Earlier the fleeing citizens had brought their tales of woe and the Mughal court went through a range of emotions. The first to bring the news to the city were the pilgrims who were roughed up and looted. In a state of sheer terror they raised a big clamour at the city-gates and when asked for the reason reported that Baji rao was in Delhi. The matter was reported to the Emperor and his courtiers, who laughed at the news. Ashob, a contemporary chronicler, narrates the scene,

> What could Baji rao have to do at Kalka devi? It was some small raid of Mewati thieves and nothing more. Why had the traders been so careless and overconfident as to take their goods into a waste place? But doubts still

---

a.  Also means lake. Baji rao could have meant the Najafgarh lake or a lake that might have existed at Tal Katora.

lingered in the minds of the courtiers; and in the afternoon a man disguised as a mendicant was sent to Kalka Malcha, and Tal Katora to find out how things stood. The messenger returned before midnight. Appearing before the Emperor he took out of his beggar's wallet a handful of grain, mostly dry unground gram, a few scraps of raw half-baked bread devoid of salt and some pods of red pepper.[a] These were the alms he had received in the Mahratta camp. He told them that in the morning by breakfast time there would be an attack on the city.[6]

There was pandemonium all night in the city and at the Emperor's court. It was inexplicable that the Marathas had reached Delhi when two large armies were to the south of the capital. Doubts were raised whether these had been defeated, which would leave the Emperor no choice but to submit. Sad-ud-din Khan, an artillery man with some experience under the Nizam felt it was beneath the Emperor to take the field against *low fellows, mere ploughmen like the Marathas*, and to cower behind the fort walls was even worse. The residual force of ten to twelve thousand horse and twenty thousand foot soldiers in the city could be sent against the Marathas. The choice for leading the troops fell on Amir Khan, the current favourite of the Emperor.[7]

Leaving a reserve force in the fort to guard the Emperor and tying up the boats on the Yamuna behind the fort for an escape *'lest the women be dishonoured'*, the army gathered under the command of Amir Khan at night near the *phatak* of Misri Khan in the Paharganj area. Some more Mughal officers joined him. They formed an entrenchment from the city to Tal Katora with guns and intervals. Soon it was dawn, but the Marathas were not attacking.

Then the young Mir Hasan Koka Khan, keen to earn some glory from the situation, injected himself into the situation. He called the Emperor 'a coward' for hiding and marched out to join Amir Khan. Amir Khan advised restraint and did not encourage a rash outing to face the Marathas. However, the young hotheads gathered seven to eight thousand men, called Amir Khan names, and began for Rakabganj, where they were seen by the alert Baji rao.

Satvaji Jadhav led Mir Hasan Koka and his raw levies on, drawing them nearly two miles away from Amir Khan. At that point Baji rao received a

---

a.  Red pepper was first crushed by the Marathas with a stone and then eaten with *bhakar*, the bread baked by the Maratha soldier from flour.

message from Satvaji Jadhav and he unleashed the full complement of his army on the Mughal force destroying most of it.

Baji rao's letter of 5 April tells us of his response,

> Satvaji Jadhav went ahead and faced the Mughal force. Some skirmishing took place. He sent a message according to which I sent up Malharji Holkar, Ranoji Scindia, Tukaji Pawar, Jiwaji and Yashwant rao Pawar, Manaji Paigude and Govind Hari. The Mughal was broken. Raja Shiv Singh and ten to twelve courtiers were killed. Nawab Mir Hasan Khan Koka was injured. At the Digarbad (?) *chowk* another two hundred and fifty to three hundred were killed. Four hundred were wounded. Roz Afzul Khan and Amir Khan and Muzaffar Khan ran away to the city. We captured two thousand horses. Five to six thousand ran away. Indraji Kadam, who was with Ranoji Scindia, had two fingers of his hand blown off due to a bullet injury. No other known person was killed or injured. Some men and horses were injured. Then we camped at the *jheel*. There was still four *ghatika* light left in the day.[1]

About Mir Hasan Koka, a Mughal chronicler says,

> He fled in the utmost perturbation. Before he could reach a place of safety he was overtaken and with one prod of a lance point unseated; his horse was seized, his fine clothes and weapons taken, and he was left bleeding on the ground. If any wounded follower came up and appealed to him by his titles, he threw dust on his head and made humble obeisance saying *'For God's sake, be quiet! If you use titles to me the enemy will recognize me and I shall have to pay an enormous ransom.'* Koka Khan was killed outright. Rajah Shiu Singh when he saw the disgrace that his sons and relatives had brought on themselves rode out from the earthworks to their aid. The beaten horsemen could not be rallied and Shiu Singh was left alone. The Mahrattas surrounded him and though he defended himself, as a brave man should do, he was in the end cut down and killed.[8]

The rest were deprived of all their belongings and ran back naked and on foot to Amir Khan. The dead were carried on cots bought from Paharganj and carried to their dwellings. There was terror and preparation for flight to a safer place. The Marathas, now on a hill at Malcha[a] about six *kos* from Chandani chowk, viewed the panic. They could have *'walked in unopposed'*.

---

a.   It is east of the present day Diplomatic Enclave.

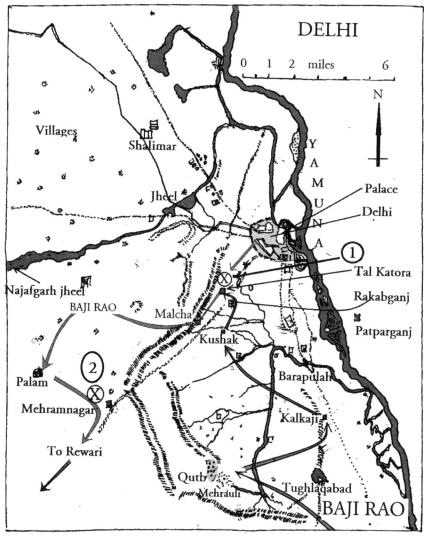

*Baji rao in Delhi*

1. Baji rao's battle at Tal Katora with Mir Hasan Koka.

2. Baji rao's battle with *Wazir* Qammruddin Khan.

The author of the *Siyar* commends Maratha horsemanship, to which he attributes the reverse at Delhi,

> As the people of Hindustan have not that skill in the art of fighting on horseback which characterizes the Marathas, most of them were slain…'.[9,a]

Rustam Ali tells the story from the Mughal perspective,

> Early in the morning, according to the Emperor's orders, Mir Hasan Khan, the commandant of the Emperor's bodyguard, came out to oppose him (Baji rao) with a body of one thousand *mansabdari* horse. Immediately behind him, Amir Khan, and other nobles, with a large army and artillery, came out of the city, and stood before the enemy; but as they had not been ordered to fight, they did not commence the battle. Mir Hasan Khan and Raja Sheo Singh, however, advanced and fought valiantly. During the fight the enemy retreated, and pitched their tents near Tal Katora. The next morning, on hearing the news of Burhanu-1-Mulk's arrival, Baji Rao, the chief of the Mahrattas, rode like a jackal running away at the roar of a tiger, and fled from the place. Qamru-d-din Khan, who had advanced with three hundred men, engaged in a severe skirmish, and retired after killing some of his opponents.[3]

At the *jheel*, Baji rao heard the news that Qamruddin Khan's army was approaching. Qamruddin was the closest from Delhi at a distance of barely a hundred kilometres at Kaman Pahari.[b] After a brief halt at Malcha, he had moved to Mehramnagar to the west of Delhi, near the present-day airport. From here he went to the *sarai* of Alla Vardi in Gurgaon.

---

a.   A strange footnote by the Englishman who translated the *Siyar-ul-Mutaqherin* discusses this. He writes, 'Whether Indians are less skilled than other nations in fighting on horseback is very much to be doubted; for they have been fitted by nature, for a good horseman, and in fact they prove always so, having much longer shanks (portion from knee to the ankle) and longer legs in proportion than Europeans and Moguls. They have also in general no more than nine to eleven ribs, where those nations have them from ten to twelve or fourteen. Hence the navel with an European is at the middle of his body, whereas with an Indian it is four inches higher: hence there is no groom in Hindustan, who will not jump readily upon his master's horse without any stirrup or help: hence the generality of the Indians are light-footed, that they make nothing of following and preceding Englishmen on a full gallop, whether the latter be in a coach or on a horse. Common servants have been seen who would run down a hare.

b.   Kaman Pahari : 27° 39'58" N, 77°12'25" E

The Emperor sat in his court after midnight, waiting for couriers to verify that the enemy had left. The couriers also brought news that the *Wazir* with his cousin Azimullah in the van and the Nizam's eldest son Ghaziuddin in the rear, were approaching the capital. There was immense relief in Delhi on hearing this.

In his letter of 5 April 1737 to Chimaji Appa, Baji rao continues,

> We heard the *Wazir* Qamruddin Khan had come to Badshahpur. We immediately got ready and marched. We gave him battle. Yashwant rao Pawar took an elephant. Some horses and camels also came into our army. Just then, the sun set. Taking rest at night, we thought we will surround the Mughal and sink him. But the *jheel* lake was sixteen *kos* long. On the right was Qamruddin Khan, the city was in front of us. Secondly, Khan Dauran, Sadat Khan and Muhammad Khan Bangash, hearing we had reached Delhi on Tuesday 29 March, who were at Radha kund (Mathura), shed their heavy baggage and marched thirty-two *kos* with twenty-five to thirty thousand men and stayed at Badela. The next day, they camped a further twenty-five *kos* (on the way to Delhi) at the Alla Vardi canal. On Thursday morning (1 April), Khan Dauran and Sadat Khan and Bangash and Qamruddin Khan's forces will unite. Once they unite, it will not be bearable and the city is close. Hence I left the Mughal and camped four *kos* away. Firangoji Patankar from our army had sustained a bullet injury, he died. Another five or ten were killed and ten to twenty injured. On Thursday, Sadat Khan, Khan Dauran and Bangash joined Qamruddin Khan. From Alla Vardi to the *jheel* they have set up camp. I was wondering whether I should take the Mughal on my back, bring him under pressure and destroy him. With this thought I went towards Rewari, Kot Putli and Manohar pur. But the Mughals are still camped at the *jheel* and Alla Vardi canal. We heard Mir Hasan Koka, who was injured in the first battle has died.[1]

At Badshahpur, the *Wazir* did not want a fight in the waning light of the day after a long march with only half his men with him and not in battle order. It was the last day of March 1737. However, his cousin Azimullah was keen to fight. Ashob, whose *Tarikh–i-shahadat- i-Farrukhsiyar* narrates the story says,

> He (Azimullah) drove his elephant on, taking with him his flying artillery and some other troops, and moving a little ahead of the *Wazir*, managed bit by bit to get away from him altogether. He sent back a message that being quite close and in touch with the enemy he intended to attack, and asked

the *Wazir* to follow in support with his whole force. Then after breathing a prayer he drove his elephant forward with the shout "God is great". On the other side the Mahrattas marched out to meet him.[a] Champions on both sides issued from the ranks with weapons ready and fell upon each other. The General ordered his big kettledrums to play and brought his artillery and matchlockmen into action. Baji Rao replied with the roll of his drums and the blare of his trumpets. He then came on and with his vanguard attacked repeatedly the advancing Muhammedans.[11]

As darkness fell, the *Wazir*'s main body soon caught up with his vanguard, and facing increasing numbers of the enemy, the Marathas disengaged. At nightfall, they moved away to Rajputana, travelling all night till they reached Rewari and Kot Putli.

Khan Dauran heard of Baji rao's attack when he was at Gau *ghat* in Agra. He marched for three days with short breaks and reached the *Wazir*'s army on the day after his battle with Baji rao. Sadat Khan reached two days later. By then Baji rao had was in Kotputli. The four Mughal chiefs felt that the best way was to go to the court and wish the Emperor on the occasion of the festival of Id. Sadat Khan earned the Emperor's displeasure. He had asked the Emperor to be granted four *subahs* of Agra, Malwa, Gujarat and Ajmer and promised he would not allow the Marathas to come north. The Emperor gave a general reply but did not give him an audience and brusquely ordered him back to Awadh and Bangash to guard Agra. The *Wazir* and Khan Dauran were asked to go to their homes.

The *Siyar* says,

> The result of all those troubles and movements was, that the Emperor observing that so many Generals and Lords, not one but Sadat Khan had thought of attacking the Marathas or of pursuing them, and they all had availed themselves of some excuse to remain where they were without moving a foot; he fell into a state of despondence, and concluded with his whole council that it would be expedient to put an end to all his anxiety by paying them a *chauth* or tribute.[12]

---

a.  Two brothers of Ashob were scouts who marched ahead of the army. Along with another they rode ahead and found Baji rao and Mastani seated on 'one saddle cover, drinking and singing while they rested'. The presence of these scouts was detected and was the first intimation the Mahrattas received of the arrival of the Mughals. This is probably the only reference that says Mastani accompanied Baji rao to Delhi.[10]

Baji rao's attack on Delhi was designed to show the Emperor that the Marathas were capable of marching up to Delhi if their demands were not met. At every stage, the Peshwa was fully aware of his sovereign *Chhatrapati* Shahu's desire not to harm the Mughal Emperor. The Marathas raided Delhi despite these injunctions, lack of any artillery and the chronic shortage of funds. In Delhi, the presence of the experienced Dhondo Govind in his camp was an asset. Having achieved his aim of showing his army to the Emperor at his capital, he rapidly retreated to Kotputli in the territory of Jaipur, where he knew Jaisingh would not attack him. However, he was still prepared to lead the Mughals on another chase until they were worn out and then pounce on them at an opportune time.

In his long letter to Chimaji Appa written from near Jaipur, Baji rao completes his narrative of the attack on Delhi,

> Khan Dauran wrote many letters to Sawai Jaisingh. Thence he came out with a fifteen or sixteen thousand strong army and some artillery till Baswa, and proceeded to meet Khan Dauran. I am getting affectionately worded letters from Jaisingh to spare his territory. Vyankaji Ram, our man, is with him. He asks him to write. I am not attacking his territory. He has said he will give us food on the way too. Abhay Singh is in Jodhpur. I will now head for Gwalior, Bhadawar and collect our arrears, and if the Mughal chases me I will harass him, tire him out to the point where he *pant*s for breath, bring him under pressure, then confront him, and with the *Rajashri* swami and our revered father's blessings, sink him. Don't worry about me. The main thing is that the Emperor and Khan Dauran want a truce and a treaty. The Mughal has held his courage. The chief among them (who oppose a treaty) is Sadat Khan. His pride will, by the grace of God, be subdued and all will be fine. If the treaty is as per our wishes, we will do it. If not, we will not come to an agreement. I have already ravaged the territory around Delhi. Sonpat and Panipat remain; I will plunder that too and cut off food to the Mughal. I will write again about what transpired. If the Mughal stays in Delhi, I will go to Agra, enter the *antarvedi* and plunder the entire region. If the Nawab Nizam-ul-mulk creates any turmoil, or crosses the Narmada, you should threaten him from the rear. Do as I have written. Plunder him. Do not entertain any doubts about affairs here. Destroy him there itself. It is best to keep the Nizam fettered.....[1]

The Nizam-ul-mulk looked at Baji rao's second expedition north to meet the Emperor with concern. Not only was he still in the bad books of the Emperor since his victory over Mubariz Khan at Sakharkherda in 1724, he had not visited Delhi for close to thirteen long years. Baji rao coming to an agreement with the Emperor could have consequences in the Deccan. The Peshwa had already proposed that a Mughal prince be appointed as a Viceroy in the Deccan, directly affecting the Nizam. Moving north the Nizam ensconced himself at Burhanpur after leaving his son Nasir Jung and Aivaz Khan's son Sayyid Jamal Khan as his lieutenants at Aurangabad.

When Baji rao began his return journey through Jaisingh's territory and onward to Malwa, he crossed the Nizam who was summoned by Muhammad Shah to Delhi. Baji rao was camped at Dhamoni in Bundelkhand. Telling Shahu it was a courtesy visit to Delhi, the Nizam camped at Sironj. Here, Baji rao sent Pilaji Jadhav rao to meet him on 20 May 1737 to gauge his intentions. Pilaji wrote to Baji rao,

> I met the Nawab yesterday and gave him the robes of honour you had sent. The Nizam gave me a turban ornament and some horses today morning. My son Appa accompanied the Nawab one stage to the north. He requested that the Rohilla Nawab (of Bhopal) should not be disturbed.[13]

In this peaceful manner the two crossed each other barely fifty *kos* from each other. Both preserved the peace agreed at Rui Rameshwar five years earlier. By the middle of July Baji rao was back in Pune. Shahu welcomed the Peshwa's triumph.

On 21 April 1737, Vyankaji Ram wrote to Baji rao from Delhi,

> The Nizam is at Burhanpur and has begun moving north. He is coming to Delhi. Once before, the swami (Baji rao) took away his success. He comes here so that his death will be at the hands of the swami. I do not see anybody in Hindustan who can stand before the swami.[14]

On 2 July 1737, the Nizam reached Delhi. The Emperor had decided to use his last gambit. The two-year-long Mughal war was not yet over. Meanwhile Chimaji Appa was in the midst of a campaign to oust the two-hundred-year-old Portuguese power from the Konkan. It was to be a fight to the finish.

# 27. Sashti: War with the Firangi

'The *Firangi*s took Thane and Konkan and held evil intentions. They took the *vatan*s away and converted village after village to Christianity; in the sixty-six villages and in Vasai, people were caught and converted. With the father's dead body still lying in the house, they would take away the children and convert them.'

-Sashti *Bakhar.*[1]

In 1736, the Marathas had completed the three-year war against the Siddi, and with Chimaji's victory over Siddi Sat, they were able to turn their attention to the Portuguese, the second power in the region that was known for its policy of religious persecution. It would surprise many today to find out how difficult it was to dislodge a western power from the coastal region north of eighteenth century Bombay. A two-hundred-year-old rule, a string of well-defended forts, good artillery, a strong navy, and disciplined foot soldiers ensured the Portuguese defended long and well.

The island of Sashti was captured by the Portuguese in 1534, who then attacked small potentates holding places like Vasai, Bandra, Thana and Tarapur – all in the vicinity of Mumbai. The province of Gujarat was ruled by a sultan named Bahadur Shah, and he could not defend Vasai against a strong and determined adversary. Thick jungles, hilly terrain, poor communications, lack of firepower and hardly any navy with Indian rulers of the time, made the Portuguese masters of the north Konkan in short order. The entire sixteenth century was a period of Portuguese growth and they spread their wings from Diu towards the north to Daman, Vasai, Sashti, Bombay, Chaul and Goa. The Mughals came to Delhi around the same time the Portuguese began their acquisitions in the south. Akbar made an effort to dent Portuguese power in 1583 but did not succeed.

The seventeenth century saw two more powers appear from Europe – the English and the Dutch. The Portuguese had by then become a part of a Spanish confederacy. The English defeated a Portuguese naval flotilla off Surat in 1612 and earned the approbation of the Mughals. The Dutch harassed

Portuguese ships as Portugal was at war with the Netherlands. Among Indian powers, the Portuguese fought wars with Bahmani chiefs in the Deccan like Malik Ambar. The rise of the Marathas under *Chhatrapati* Shivaji led to wars between the two from 1660 to 1689. All along, the Portuguese proselytising zeal alienated large portions of the local population.

The English had injected themselves into Mumbai just south of Portuguese-governed Sashti. The island of Sashti is about forty kilometres long and fifteen kilometres wide and, as a fertile place, it served as an immediate source of provisions to Mumbai. The English always claimed it was part of Mumbai and that it ought to have come to them with Catherine's dowry, and Grose, who travelled to India in the late eighteenth century remarks, *'In lieu of accomplishing which, in breach of all the rules of good faith, they put us off with a place* (Bombay) *that had no merit in it, but the bare harbour.'*[2]

In *Chhatrapati* Sambhaji's time, the Maratha king had attacked Goa with such ferocity that the Portuguese Viceroy appealed to St. Xavier, and even laid the staff of his office in the hand of his corpse; divine intervention in the form of a Mughal force rescued Goa from the Marathas and this became a ritual in the years to come when a new Viceroy joined.

There was no peace for the residents of the *Firangan*, however. The Inquisition meant immense coercion and cruelty in the name of religion and the local Hindus had to either submit to conversion or suffer without respite.

The Sashti *bakhar* or Chronicle opens with,

> The *Firangi*s took Thane and Konkan and held evil intentions. They took the *vatan*s away and converted village after village to Christianity; in the sixty-six villages and Vasai, people were caught and converted. With the father's dead body still lying in the house, they would take away the children and convert them. Such a nuisance they began in Maharashtra. Some ran away to the south, all rituals ended, the prayer of God was finished, temples were destroyed, and in their place the *Firangi*s built their own temples. The religion of the *Firangi*s was supreme. No Brahmin was allowed to stay in the land. If anybody did any religious ritual at home, he and his neighbours – who attended it – were all caught, detained and allowed to rot in prisons. Such a disaster happened.[1]

Nearly sixty thousand people from Sashti are said to have been converted at this time, of which six thousand were said to be in the single village of Bandra. People lived in a state of fear. The Inquisition years saw punishments of the more inhuman kind involving torture and burning at the stake. The Inquisition courts in Goa ended in 1774, were resurrected five years later and finally ended in 1812. These atrocities on the people created a strong antipathy for the Portuguese, and explain why, of all the western powers, the Portuguese were singled out for vigorous action by the Marathas.

The strong line of fortifications backed by a good army and navy made the Portuguese position impregnable. The stories of their persecution of Hindus and Muslims in the areas governed by them were the reason the Maratha power was at war with them from 1660 onwards. In the period from 1689 to 1720, there were many other challenges the Marathas faced, and it was only after 1720, when Ramchandra Mahadeo Chaskar was the *subedar* at Kalyan, that the Portuguese question began to appear before the Peshwa more often. Between the years 1720 and 1734, the Marathas and the Portuguese had many engagements and a few treaties. In 1730, Pilaji Jadhav rao led Maratha forces and captured Kambe near Bhiwandi. The attack on Sashti that year did not come about as the Portuguese were alert. All through this time, the Peshwa was biding his time and waiting for the day when he could spare the time and the troops to remove Portuguese rule from the Konkan.

Sometime in 1732, the Viceroy appointed General Dom Louis Botelho to Sashti and asked him to beef up the defences of the island. An engineer named Andre Reberro Coutinho was appointed to plan the forts. At the north-eastern end of Sashti was a narrow creek, and the most vulnerable point was Thane, so it was decided a new fort would be built at this point. This work began in 1734. The construction needed money, heavy taxes, and forced labour from the inhabitants, which further alienated them from the Portuguese.

Meanwhile, the Portuguese plunged into the dispute between the two brothers Manaji and Sambhaji Angre. They first helped Manaji to attack Colaba, and when he did not give them the promised territory, they went over and helped Sambhaji against him. The quarrel between the two Angre brothers made the Maratha navy largely dysfunctional and could not be called upon for the mission in *Firangan*. Sambhaji Angre had his hands full fighting the Portuguese, the Dutch and the English during different periods at this time.

Construction of the fort at Thane began on a grand scale with three huge bastions on the land side. Later, they had to reduce the size of the bastions towards the creek due to lack of workers, money and time. The fort was nearing completion in 1737; all the while watched by the Marathas from across the shallow water channel. A strong fort at Thane would make it difficult to attack Sashti. The attack therefore could no longer be postponed and the Portuguese-Maratha war in the '*Firangan*' finally went live in March 1737.

There is an interesting narrative that says the battle began from a personal slight. Antonio Carneiro de Alcancova, the Administrative General of Revenue in Goa (and not friendly to General Botelho) says, Baji rao had asked the Portuguese for a place near Vasai to set up a warehouse for traders from Kalyan and Bhiwandi. Baji rao sent his representatives to Vasai to discuss it. Botelho, far from doing so, insulted Baji rao by referring to him as a 'negro'. The two words that the Portuguese used to refer to the natives were 'gentio' (idolator) or 'negro', referring to their dark complexion.[3] The Marathas also understood the word to mean 'slave', as they had heard it being used for the slaves of Mozambique. To call the fair Peshwa by a name reserved for slaves was too much for the Marathas to bear, and the attack on Sashti was brought on when Botelho was appointed to that place.[4]

The geography of the north Konkan is worth looking at before one can understand the way the campaign at *Firangan* unfolded. The strongly fortified fort of Vasai stands at the centre of the region from Daman to Colaba. In the south, opposite Alibag, we see this stronghold of Manaji Angre, and by the two islands of Khanderi and Underi, under Angre and Siddi of Janjira's rule. Entering the mouth of the Mumbai harbour, we have the four islands of Karanja, Elephanta, Butcher's isle and Turumbe or Trombay. The island of Mumbai was controlled by the English and immediately north is the isle of Sashti, its narrowest separation from the Indian mainland being near Thane at the village of Kalwa. Sashti had fortified ports on the sea coast at Bandra and Versova besides an isle fort at Dharavi[a] at its northern end.

---

a.   Also called Dongri in Portuguese records.

North of Sashti, on the opposite side of the creek is the fort of Vasai. The fort is inaccessible from the south, the west and the east due to the sea. There is a narrow access from the north. The creek at Vasai has the mouth of the river Ulhas going north east towards Kalyan, which was under the Marathas. Many forts like Asheri, Tarapur, Mahim, and warehouses and places of worship like Manor, Versova and Bandra formed a defensive ring around the *Firangan*. Once the Thane fort was complete, it would have become even more difficult to enter Sashti.

The English traveller Grose, strongly critical of the Portuguese for not giving the island to the English, also blames them for their poor defence of Sashti. Writing later in the eighteenth century, he appears particularly anguished because the Marathas had then become the immediate neighbour to their tiny island of Mumbai. He says the Portuguese

> Took no sort of care to defend it (Sashti) against their constant and natural enemies the Morattoes[a], yet nothing was easier than to secure it. Those people (Marathas) had not then the least maritime force, and the island could only be attacked by land at one very narrow pass, fordable at ebb only, which was called the pass of Tannah. Here they had only a miserable redoubt, of no awe, or strength. At length, however, on the appearance of an approaching rupture with the Morattoes, they began to see the expediency of fortifying this important post; and with an absurdity hardly to be believed, they began the construction of a fort, that would have indeed effectually answered the design, *if the Morattoes could be supposed such idiots as to suffer them to finish it*, when they had not provided even the shadow of a force to cover the building, or repel any interruption of it. Accordingly the Morattoes very quietly let them go on with the fortification, of which themselves were sure of reaping the benefit. For before it was finished, and well-nigh finished it was, they poured their troops into the island, and easily took a fort, the walls of which were in some places open, and the batteries yet unmounted with cannon, after which they had not the least opposition worth mentioning to encounter on the rest of this island...[5]

On 26 March 1737, the Marathas began gathering their forces for an attack on Portuguese possessions. It was the same day that Baji rao was on his way

---

a.  Marathas.

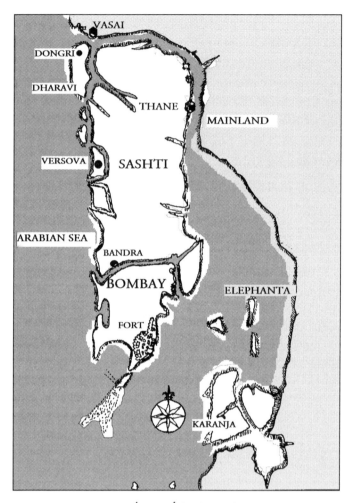

*Bombay, Sashti and Vasai*

to Delhi between two large Mughal armies. The Marathas formed one army aiming for Thane and another for Vasai. Ramchandra Hari Patwardhan had gone to the Konkan earlier. The army for Thane gathered under Khandoji Mankar and Honaji Balkavade near fort Rajmachi, while the men going towards Vasai gathered under Shankaraji Keshav Phadke and Gangaji Naik Anjurkar. At Kalyan a *gondhal*[a] was arranged so the Portuguese would not

---

a.   A call to the goddess Bhavani, usually on occasions like weddings, where many people are
     invited.

look askance at the sudden gathering of people. Here, selected men were told about the campaign and their role.

The cost, it eventually emerged, to win the fort would amount to five rupees.

On 24 March 1737 fell the Hindu festival of *Padwa*, or the start of the new almanac. Chimaji left Pune that day and reached Badlapur near Kalyan two days later. The same day, Maratha forces with the help of the *koli* had managed to get guards on the St Jeronimo water tower of Thane fort inebriated with a copious supply of intoxicants worth 'five rupees'.[6] A small party of Marathas crossed the narrow water channel and reached the foot of the tower, placed ladders against its walls and a hundred men climbed up. Six guards and a Portuguese Captain were killed in a short skirmish. Two cannons were then fired as a signal to other Maratha troops to enter the still incomplete fort. Chimaji Appa at Badlapur heard the shots as the signal that the attack was in progress. Prizes and gifts in gold were given for bravery and Tuknak Parwari is named as having been awarded a gold bracelet worth one hundred and thirty-two rupees.

On 25 March the English in Mumbai reported to their Board that they had received a letter from Botelho that *'he has advice of the Marathas' designs to invade his territories, but does not seem under any concern thereat, as he says he had prepared for their reception so far as in reason he ought or could do.'* Just two days later the English received another letter from Botelho saying *'he was then under arms, and that the enemy were come over the river of Thana, which he supposed would be sufficient to induce him (the President) immediately to send him what succours he could spare, consistent with the friendship and alliance between the two Nations',* whereto the President at Mumbai wriggled out of the situation by replying that he was very sorry for the unhappy situation of their affairs, and the more so since it was not in his power to give them assistance, for besides the application coming too late (the enemy having passed the river) *'all our spare force is absent from the island on board our fleet and at Tellicherry'.*[7]

Louis Botelho, later accused of not doing enough, on hearing the two cannon shots, sent a Sergeant Major with ten men to the water bastion, but the Marathas caught and imprisoned them all. Overjoyed at the easy capture of the fort, the victors began playing loud music and going round the fort '*like ghosts*'.[8] A neighbouring convent was burnt to the ground. Hearing the commotion and expecting an attack at any moment, Botelho panicked and ordered a general retreat from the town, later sailing away to the island of Karanja, south of Mumbai.

Travelling all night, Chimaji with his entire force entered Sashti on 27 March and sent detachments to take over the two ports of Bandra and Versova. Sashti's defences had been breached in just two days. Many armaments and guns left behind were captured. The Marathas completed the construction of the Thane fort and got the island's defence properly organised to prevent the Portuguese from returning. The attacks on Bandra and Versova however, did not yield results. Honaji Balkavade with his men attempted to take Versova by escalade. However, the fire from the Portuguese guns was too severe and nearly fifty men were killed and many injured. Honaji was despondent, as a letter to Chimaji at the time says, '*Please send a letter consoling Honaji who is disheartened and sad at the loss of men in the attack*'.[9] The Portuguese continued to reinforce the forts by sea and withstood Maratha attempts to take them for a long time.

The second army led by Shankraji Keshav Phadke, Gangaji Naik and others headed towards Vasai. They approached from the northern side of the fort and began to move towards its walls. They assured the people living there that they would not be hurt. The Portuguese were alert, however, and with an open ground north of the fort walls it was difficult to approach it unobserved. A bridge over the creek was heavily guarded. A hundred and twenty-five men led by Bajirao Belose crossed the Sopara creek in a boat and captured the post at Gokhivare. By the time more men began to cross the narrow creek from the east, the tide came in and the water began to fill up. Shankraji decided on giving spot awards for all the bravehearts who swim the water channel to go across. On 1 April 1737 he wrote to Chimaji,

> The creek filled with the incoming tide. Then what could be done? I had kept some swimmers ready. I gave gold bracelets of one *seer* each to all who would swim across. Some lost their swords. They found a boat. Then I gave

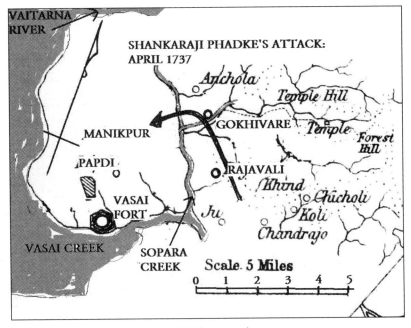

*Shankaraji Phadke's Attack on Vasai*

Satwaji Salokhe and Ramji Tugkar gold bracelets and got sent more people across to Rajavali.[10]

In this manner they reached Manikpur, north of the fort of Vasai. They stayed in the temple there. Chimnaji Bhivrao also came here. Shankaraji says, *'the walled village of Bahadurpura was taken.'* This must have been very close to the fort, however no trace of it is found now.

The fort of Vasai was too strong to be stormed. The sandy soil was not appropriate to lay mines. The Marathas then turned towards the island of Arnala just north of Vasai. Obtaining boats from a local village carpenter, they managed to embark four hundred men who reached the island. The people staying there had already been informed and were in favour of the Marathas. Arnala was taken without any loss of life on 28 March 1737, and soon fresh fortifications were erected around it. Since Vasai itself was difficult to take with a small contingent of just over two thousand men, other smaller forts like Marol, Parsik, Jivdhan, Belapur and Dharavi were taken in April and May 1737. Manaji Angre took the fort of Revdanda south of Mumbai from the Portuguese in April 1737. This phase of the Maratha attack met with success and save a few pockets of resistance in Sashti, the island was captured. North of Vasai, many of the smaller forts were also quickly taken.

At Karanja, Botelho, disheartened, had sent a letter to the Viceroy at Goa informing him of the debacle at Sashti. The Viceroy wrote back on 12 April 1737,

> I received your letter of 8 April and received the unexpected news. It is natural you will be disturbed at the tragedy. It is not a time to lament but to put all our energies together. I am equipping two warships here. The winds are blowing in the opposite direction, so we are equipping the ships accordingly. You have said Goa, Bardes and Sashti[a] may be attacked. Similar fears are expressed at Chaul. I am sending them gunpowder on a warship. There is a shortage of gunpowder here, which is not due to my negligence. We may need to ask for it from the English. We need help of other nations. We have to look to the skies for assistance. It is in the interest of the English to help us, so they should. There are rumours that Versova and Bandra have fallen. Looking at the map it seems we must protect Dongri.[11]

For the Portuguese, the Dharavi fort was important and launching a determined attack, they took it back in the middle of May. Dharavi was a small island right opposite Vasai at the mouth of the creek and therefore of immense strategic value. Any ships coming to Vasai could be attacked if a battery was placed at Dharavi. Once the Marathas occupied it, they could threaten *Firangi* vessels headed towards Vasai from Goa.

The Marathas then launched their first attack on Vasai itself. This attack of 30 May, by escalade, did not succeed. The Portuguese *'captured thirty two ladders while thirty men were captured and many Marathas killed.'*[12] A month later, the Marathas launched a second attack on Vasai in pouring rain. Four thousand men participated. However, the attack failed. The Portuguese found 33 dead bodies, the rest having been taken away by the retreating Marathas.

With the monsoon rains raging in the Konkan, Chimaji Appa returned to Pune on 2 July 1737 to meet Baji rao who was then returning from his

---

a.  A village in Goa bearing the same name.

attack on Delhi. With almost all of Sashti captured and Vasai isolated from the land side, the monsoon months were not a season to wage a war on the western coast. However, Maratha attacks continued in between the wet spells.

On 4 September 1737, a third attempt was made to take the fort of Vasai. Baji rao's trusted lieutenant Baji Bhivrao was sent to lead the attack with a force of nearly six thousand foot and four thousand horse. However, the Portuguese at Vasai were alert and incessant heavy fire from the fort claimed two thousand Maratha lives. Baji Bhivrao sustained injuries to his right shoulder. The Marathas once again had to withdraw with heavy losses.

The fall of Sashti had alarmed the English at Mumbai in no small measure. At a meeting on 3 October 1737, they raised many pertinent issues and discussed how the security of Mumbai could be safeguarded from the ambition of Baji rao and Chimaji Appa.[13]

First, there was a mention of the Peshwa being his own master in military matters,

> ..Without mentioning other of Sow (Shahu) rajah's great officers any further than as they relate to our affair, it will be sufficient to observe to your honours, that two brothers, Badjerow (Baji rao) and Chimnajee, are jointly considered as one Head of a very large district bordering on the Portuguese dominions, in right of which they have command of numerous forces which they dispose of absolutely preserving little more than the bare formality of acknowledging the Sow rajah for their sovereign, whom they keep satisfied so as not to be interrupted by him in their designs by an annual present or species of tribute.

The English then discussed the aim of attacking Sashti. They found the Peshwa and his brother had a two-fold purpose, of which obtaining a port was the more dangerous as it would make them far more powerful on the seas than the combined Angre fleet;

> …their apparent chief aim has for a long time been getting a sea fort for themselves, the attainment of which would certainly in a very short time prove very dangerous to the navigation of this coast, than the naval force of both the Angrias, in proportion to their much greater power, strength and wealth.

The complaint of religious persecution by the Portuguese was taken note of:

> …and this view of acquiring a port and settlement on the sea coast must be considered as the *principal motive that hath determined the Marattas* in their invasion, though perhaps it may have been hastened by the well-grounded complaints of their Gentoo[a] brethren under the Portuguese govt who have been *made frequent examples of the cruelty of their Inquisition* which hath been exercised upon those unhappy subjects with great severity, ignorance, and superstition. A proceeding more impolitick, as they (the Portuguese) were destitute of real strength to protect themselves in the exercise of it.

Coming to the specific attack on Sashti, the minute of the meeting said,

> In the month of March (1737) then, when Badjerow himself had gone up with a great body of troops to levy contributions in the Mogul's territories, which he executed even within sight of the gates of Delhi and put the Mogul court into great consternation, his brother Chimnajee who had concerted and prepared all his measure began his expedition against the Portuguese territories.

The English had begun to look beyond the war when the Marathas will be masters of Sashti and their immediate neighbours, separated by just a thin sliver of water. The English stated,

> On the other hand if the Marathas continue masters of the island Salcette, they will indubitably attempt the setting on foot a sea force, which as before observed will be far superior to that of even both the Angrias joined together, *whose jealousy we have endeavoured to raise and foment against this new encroaching power, but they are so much inferior in strength that they dare not oppose them*, on the contrary Maneckjee (Manaji) has even sent some troops to assist these Marathas who have already begun to build and set out vessels, which consideration joined to that of the easy access to this island by our passes and fords will lay your Honours under the necessity of raising several new works to defend the whole circle of islands.

The meeting ended with a recommendation that the English consider taking over Sashti. However, that was not to happen, not for a few decades to come.

While the English at Bombay contemplated attacking Sashti for themselves, the Marathas then did not harbour any ill will towards the English. The

---

a.   Hindu.

invasion of Mumbai at this time was never contemplated although the English feared they could not match a huge army that could simply march towards their castle with its eleven-feet-high walls. The English were not considered 'enemies', although their occasional mischief in helping the Siddi or the Portuguese was known. The benefits of trade with the English and through them with the world had caught Maratha attention, and the market it provided to goods produced in the Maratha-ruled areas was still considered beneficial. They were, at the time, also considered a 'principled' race, and one that kept its word.

A London newspaper named *'The Daily Gazetteer'* found news about the fall of Sashti newsworthy. On 13 January 1738, it wrote,

> On Tuesday arrived a packet overland at the East India House, giving an account of the people called *Morattoes*, belonging to the Souroger[a] or King of that country, having taken the island of Salset from the Portuguese. There were 60 pieces of cannon and 80 people in the island, who fled on the first appearance of the *Morattoes*. This island produced the Portuguese the value of 25,000 l. per annum.[14]

In this first year of war, the Portuguese lost most of the island of Sashti, and a few places around Vasai. However, Vasai, the nerve centre of Portuguese power in the *Firangan* remained in Portuguese hands. For the present, Chimaji had to leave this campaign to return to Pune. Another trial of strength with an old adversary loomed large.

ॐॐॐॐॐ

---

a. Shahu raja.

# 28. Nizam-ul-Mulk: The Emperor's Last Gambit

'The Nizam was an intelligent man; in his old age he has adopted a wrong line. If he comes out, we are waiting. He is facing the same fate as Bangash.'

'The day before yesterday, the *pathans* finally ate the gun bullocks. The Rajputs began to starve.'

- Baji rao's letters to Chimaji Appa.[1,2]

Ever since the Nizam disobeyed Muhammad Shah, came to the Deccan in 1724, defeated Mubariz Khan and established his own rule in the Deccan, the epithet 'rebel' and a cloud of imperial displeasure hung over his head. The Nizam, of course, was punctilious in calling himself a servant of the Emperor. However, for all practical purposes, he was independent. His many letters to the Emperor suggesting ways to bring the Marathas to obedience, his plots against Shahu, and his battles in person and through surrogates–had all failed to obtain the Emperor's approbation and forgiveness. The old man of sixty-eight still hoped for an imperial summons that would mean the expunction of all his misdemeanours.

The Nizam was camped at Burhanpur when Muhammad Shah tired of his querulous nobles and failed Generals, and finally remembered the Nizam. In February 1737 the Nizam was given a *firman* from the Emperor asking him to come to Delhi. The Nizam then arranged his affairs in the Deccan, wrote a letter to Shahu saying he is going to Delhi to seek the Emperor's forgiveness, and appointed Nasir Jung and Sayyid Jamal Khan as his deputies in the Deccan.

On 7 April 1737, the Nizam left Burhanpur, met Pilaji Jadhav rao at Sironj and passing Gwalior and Agra, reached Hodal about one hundred kilometres from Delhi. Here, *Wazir* Qamruddin Khan came with his troops and his harem to ceremonially receive the Nizam. The Nizam's eldest son Ghaziuddin had been left behind in Delhi in 1724, and, who was now the son-in-law of the *Wazir,* met his father after thirteen years. The procession marched towards Delhi where huge crowds gathered to watch and greet the Nizam. The Emperor as a special gesture asked the Nizam to beat his drums even when approaching the palace. The entire morning was spent before the Nizam could reach the fort.

Approaching the Emperor, the Nizam offered a present and was given a robe of honour along with the '*charqab*' worn only by the imperial Chagatai family. The Nizam-ul-mulk was honoured with the highest title of Asaf Jah.[a] His rank was elevated to eight thousand *swar* and *zat*, he was housed in the best mansion and served food from the Emperor's kitchen.[3]

Emboldened by the Nizam's arrival in Delhi, in early August 1737, the *subahs* of Malwa and Agra were taken away from Baji rao and Jaisingh, and were awarded to the Nizam's son Ghaziuddin. The *subahs* were given on condition that the Nizam will personally march to Malwa and take over the province.

In Delhi, the Nizam gathered an army of thirty thousand and the best Mughal artillery he could find. Many rulers were summoned to join the Mughal army. The Bundela rajas joined the Nizam, swelling his army to nearly seventy thousand men. Leaving Delhi, the Nizam decided to avoid the ravines on the road to Gwalior, crossed the Yamuna at Agra to enter the *doab,* and then re-crossed the Yamuna at Kalpi to enter Bundelkhand. Fully aware that his march into Bundelkhand and Malwa will not go unchallenged, the Nizam wrote to his son Nasir Jung to prevent the Peshwa from coming north, and if he does, to march from Aurangabad and catch him between the two armies.

Chimaji Appa returned from the *Firangan* campaign in July 1737 when the Nizam reached Delhi. Baji rao, having left the armies of Scindia and Holkar in Malwa, had returned to Pune in June. The news of Malwa's *subedari* having been awarded to the Nizam came in the following months. On 8 October 1737, Baji rao and Chimaji left Pune for Malwa accompanied by a large army. The Nizam was already at Sironj. Baji rao therefore took the straight route through Khargone, then headed north east and crossed the Narmada north of Punasa, east of Omkareshwar. He asked Chimaji to stay at Varangaon, less than sixty kilometres from Burhanpur, south of the river Tapi, aiming to stop Nasir Jung from proceeding north to help his father.

---

a.   He who sits instead of Asaf, the minister to Suleiman.

Chimaji received a stream of letters giving details about Nasir Jung's preparation. An informer wrote to him on 3 December that Janoba and Sultanji Nimbalkar, Dhiraji Pawar, Fateh Sinh Deshmukh, Subhanji Thorat and his own unnamed master have pledged to join Nasir Jung when summoned. The news at Aurangabad was that the Nizam was unlikely to break the peace with Baji rao.[4] Another letter of 15 December informed Chimaji that an army of ten to twelve thousand had gathered at Aurangabad along with some Maratha chiefs. *'There was a possibility of Chandrasen Jadhav also coming.'*[5]

Chimaji wrote to Brahmendra swami,

> On 11 December 1737, I am at Varangaon on the banks of the Tapi. *Teerthrup Rau*[a] has gone via Khargone and Punasa across the Narmada. Avji Kavade with eighty thousand horse is with him. Nizam-ul-mulk is near Sironj. His son Ghaziuddin, Orrchha and Datia's rulers, Jaisingh's son, Ahirs and Rohillas have joined him to make a force of fifty thousand. Sadat Khan's nephew and the raja of Kotah (Durjan Sal) will bring another twenty thousand men. *Raya* and their force will soon meet. They have come after promising the *Paatshah* that they will not allow *Rau* to enter Malwa...[6]

Finally, the news on 17 December from Mahipat Anandrao Sumant said that letters had gone out to sixty chiefs to assemble with their armies supporting Nasir Jung. Sayyid Jamal had sent his advance tents. *'The situation is strange'*, the letter writer says. In Malwa a Mughal chief named Mir Mannu Khan attacked and killed a Maratha revenue official. Scindia and Holkar who were there attacked and killed Mir Mannu Khan. The city of Aurangabad had been fortified with cannons on the bastions and an army of twenty thousand had gathered. *'All the preparation for war is complete. All that remains is for a breakout leading to a battle. Seventy thousand men accompany the Nizam with one hundred twenty-five 'hatnala' and 'jejala', and rockets*[b] *are mounted on three thousand camels.'*[78]

Chimaji stayed at Varangaon, poised to block Nasir Jung or attack Aurangabad if the city remained undefended. Nasir Jung was waiting to move north with his army. The Nizam was near Doraha on 10 December.

---

a.   *Teerthrup* = for one's elder or father, Rau is for Baji rao.
b.   The rocket was a simple primitive weapon, but should it strike the enemy's magazine, it caused the greatest damage.

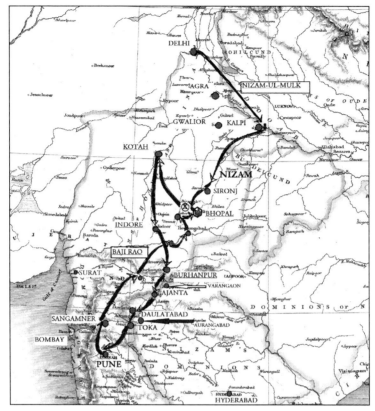

## The Bhopal Campaign

Baji rao's campaign to Bhopal and back.

Pune – 8 October 1737.

Bhamburde -11to 12 October 1737.

Khed – 17 to 19 October 1737.

Junnar – 21 to 22 October 1737.

Near Sangamner – 25 October 1737.

Crossed river Godavari – 26 to 29 Oct. 1737.

Near Yeola – 30 October 1737.

Ambare – 11 November 1737.

Chimaji Appa goes towards Varangaon.

Nagalwadi *buzurg*, Khargon – 13 to 15 November 1737.

Kothda, Handia – 24 November 1737.

Ashte – 1 December 1737.

Bhopal – 4 December 1737.

Siege of Bhopal – 20 December to 2 January 1738.

Piplod – 9 to 13 January 1738.

Sarola, Kotah – 14 to 19 January 1738.

Around Kotah – till 5 February 1738.

Indore – 15 to 16 February 1738.

Malwa – till 6 June 1738.

Handia, south of Narmada – 7 June 1738.

Burhanpur – 16 to 18 June 1738.

Ajanta – 22 June 1738.

Daulatabad - 26 Jun 1738.

Toka, south of Godavari – 27 June 1738.

2 July 1738 – Shikrapur.

3 July 1738 – Pune, at the *sangam*.

The distance between the Peshwa and the Nizam was now about thirty or thirty-five *kos* on that day.[9] At Aurangabad, Nasir Jung was concerned that Raghuji Bhonsle and perhaps Damaji Gaekwad might join Chimaji Appa, in which case it would be difficult to move out of the Deccan. He therefore sent Shujayat Khan, the Nawab of Elichpur, to attack Raghuji. However, in early December Raghuji completely defeated and looted his camp. After this, Nasir Jung began weighing his options about moving out of Aurangabad, although his father asked him to move north immediately.

Baji rao approached Bhopal in mid-December and so did the Nizam. The Nizam wanted to avoid a fight until Nasir Jung came with reinforcements from the Deccan. In the interim, he decided therefore to take a defensive position in the walled city of Bhopal with a lake at his back.

This was a mistake.

Seeing that the Nizam was not attacking him, Baji rao went on the offensive. Baji rao's letters describing the campaign give a complete picture of his strategy, the battle and the final denouement. He wrote to Chimaji Appa on 19 December 1737,

> I came to Malwa to confront the Nizam-ul-mulk. When there was a distance of eight or nine *kos* between our armies, the Nawab's army was overawed and took shelter in the fort of Bhopal. With the lake behind them and a canal in the front they stayed there. I attacked him on 15 December. The Nawab sent Jaisingh's son, Bundele Jat and Rajwadiya's forces at a place suitable for a battle with his artillery. He stood at the back. Our armies were led by Ranoji Scindia and Pilaji Jadhav rao and Sayaji Gujar and others. Absorbing all the fire they crashed into them; one hundred fifty Rajputs were killed, while we lost sixty men. Had there been no canal in front of the Rajputs, we would have beaten them. We are now sitting at a range of twice the rocket range from the Nawab.

Criticising the Nizam's strategy, Baji rao wrote,

> The Nawab sits on his elephant all day. He is in a difficult situation. He pretends he is coming out to war. Food has become scarce. In four days one rupee-worth flour has gone up four times in his camp. There is no forage for elephants and horses. One day they fed the animals the bark of trees and plants in the lake. The Rajputs and Bundele do not trust the Nawab and he

does not trust them. With the camp followers in town, they cannot escape. To come out and fight, they do not trust each other. We have surrounded them from all sides. We keep up a fire all night so they remain alert and awake. One, there is no fodder for their horses, two, they have to be alert all the time. We have inflicted such an excess. The Nizam was an intelligent man; in his old age he has adopted a wrong line. If he comes out, we are waiting. He is facing the same fate as Bangash. The Nawab is a great *amir*, but with thirty to forty thousand-strong army, artillery, and various types of guns, to go to a shelter is not praiseworthy.

According to the Peshwa, the Nizam lost his nerve or erred in his strategy. Taking refuge at Bhopal revealed his weakness. Baji rao discusses the options available for the Nizam and his own counter-measures:

> The only reason to do so (take shelter at Bhopal), is to await armies from Delhi or the Deccan. The *paatshah* ordered Khan Dauran and Qamruddin Khan to come only when he himself sets out. So they are not coming. Now his (the Nizam's) big hope is the army from the Deccan. He sends five to seven emissaries every day. Now Appa, if you stop that army, I can defeat this army with what I have. Dabhade and Bande may not come to me, but you can try and see if they come to help you. Through Mahadoba (Purandare) request the king to send Fateh Sinh baba and Shambhu Sinh Jadhav rao and *Sarlashkar*. Collect whatever armies you can. Once the Nawab is defeated here, all of the south will become free. So everybody should put in his best now. I have no source other than the Nawab to retire my debts. Malharba and Ranoji defeated the Mughal from Shahjehanpur and killed him. Try to get Ranoji Bhonsle to help you. If he does not come, what is the use of having a *saranjam*? Do what you can to stop the Deccani army.[1]

Neither Bande or Dabhade or Fateh Sinh or Ranoji Bhonsle or any of the other chiefs came with their armies. The matter was handled by Baji rao alone.

The siege at Bhopal dragged on. The Nizam's army faced severe shortages. Hunger became a constant companion for man and beast, and between 20 and 28 December 1737 the Nizam was brought to his knees. In his letter of 28 December 1737, Baji rao describes what had happened since his previous letter,

> I was pleased to receive your letters. Here, the Nizam has taken shelter in Bhopal. On 15 December we fought a battle. Since, I have placed *chowkis* all round Bhopal. Food has become scarce. Forage is not available to them.

The Nawab therefore wished to talk and sent Anand rao Sumant. I told him our interest and sent Babu rao Malhar with him; he told the Nawab our terms. The Nawab ordered that Pilaji Jadhav rao and more eminent people be sent the next morning. Then Babu rao Malhar returned to me. On 26 December, Abdul Sher Khan and Sayyid Lashkar Khan and Anwar Khan and Sumant came to a small hillock before us. We sent Pilaji Jadhav rao and Baji Bhiv rao and Babu rao Malhar. They talked. These three told our interest to those three. They said we will tell the Nawab and he will listen to you, but *it is important that the Nawab's honour and reputation be protected.* The Nawab will leave in the morning; you should go back one and a half *kos.* So on 27 December we moved a *kos* away. The Nawab then emerged and stayed in the camp. Once again we had discussions with Abdul Sher Khan and Anwar Khan and they went to the Nawab to appraise him. However, the next morning, suddenly the Nawab went back inside Bhopal.

As the Rajputs and Bundelas were not fully committed to battle, the Nizam decided to be on the defensive and keep the Marathas at bay by his efficient artillery. However, his prolonged stay at Bhopal and the siege led to famine for his army and he was compelled to beg terms. Baji rao continues in his letter to Chimaji,

> Avaji Kavade and Yashwant rao Pawar attacked them. The Jats came to fight. The Nawab was caught in an awkward place. He used the same strategy as Muhammad Khan Bangash. The Nawab is great. *But he should have come to an agreement with me and gone to the Deccan. Or he should have come out and fought. But since he did neither, he is in trouble. He acted inappropriately. What honour is left in this for the Nawab now?* So be it. I have now stopped all passage of food and fodder. The Nawab is standing inside. Our army is at a distance equal to the range of a bullet and we are beating them. The Nawab and his army have become devoid of any life. We have obtained two guns. With the blessings of our king, I will drown the Nizam-ul-mulk here. He was hopeful an army will come from the Deccan, but you are there (to stop the army). You should recruit troops and stop them. Send a letter and a person to Raghuji Bhonsle and see if he comes. We are all fine here. We lost about thirty or thirty-five horse yesterday but nobody of note.[10]

The Rajputs and Bundelas could neither leave, nor withstand the rockets fired by the Marathas. The precarious situation, with starvation and his allies wishing to return to their homes, forced the Nizam to emerge from the fort and begin moving out with his entire army in a Square formation. The Marathas continued to surround him and harass the army. Food became very expensive at *'a rupee per seer'*. Three weeks after the first skirmish, on 8 January 1738, Baji rao describes the misery in the Nizam's camp,

> The day before yesterday on 6 January, the *pathans* finally ate the gun bullocks. The Rajputs began to starve. Seeing this, the Nawab began asking for a treaty and a truce with some urgency. Along with Abdul Sher Khan, Anwar Khan and Sayyid Lashkar Khan, (Raja) Ayamal was also sent to talk. They discussed, and it was decided that the whole of Malwa should be given (to Baji rao). The *paatshah's sanad* should be obtained on reaching Delhi. We will claim all revenue from the kings between the Narmada and the Chambal. The Nawab should send this message to them and go to Delhi. Yesterday such a treaty was signed and the Nawab signed all of Malwa to be given to us. He also promised he would obtain funds from the *paatshah* for us. I sent Pilaji Jadhav rao and Babu rao Malhar to obtain the signed document from the Nawab. The Nawab will now return.
>
> To sum up, in his difficulty, to (be able to) force the Nawab to complete submission one has to consider his artillery and other arrangements. Rohilla, Bundele, Jaisingh's army, Khechi and Narwar's army and the Nawab himself with thirty-five thousand men, and his artillery, which you are familiar with (is a tough proposition). If he walks within the army with the artillery behind him, no man need emerge from the Square. But he began losing horses and men. Fighting further would have taken four days, but would the Mughal retreat? Thinking of all these things and your letter, I felt it was better to come to an agreement.

The Nizam suffered his biggest defeat yet. His glorious march from Delhi with a large army to push back the Marathas, the award of Malwa and Agra to his son, the exalted titles and respect he was given at Delhi, all came to naught as he signed away Malwa and agreed to Baji rao's conditions. Baji rao was struck by the enormity of his triumph. He wrote to Chimaji,

> ...the Nawab who would not utter the words *chauthai* and *sardeshmukhi* had to sign Malwa to us and also had to utter the words. What had never been achieved before has been achieved. It is difficult to get the Nawab to agree. He gave the *subedari* of Malwa which he had obtained for his son. The Nawab in his mind was left staring at '*kalpaant'.*[a] But what could he do? Seeing the calamity he faced, he had to give it. In the *paatshahi* today, there is none other like the Nawab. His submission is most important. The Nawab will now go to Delhi and do what he promised.[2]

---

a.  The end of Time.

The Nizam limped with his force to the town of Durai Sarai[a] about thirty five kilometres from Bhopal where he signed the convention and returned to Delhi. Besides Malwa, he also agreed to try and get fifty lakh rupees for Baji rao from the Emperor; a promise never fulfilled. The Emperor created Baji rao as an imperial officer with the rank of seven thousand *swar* and Chimaji was granted the rank of five thousand *swar*.[11] Ishwari Singh, Jaisingh's son, met Baji rao on 23 January and gave costly presents to him and his chief officers.

Despite the Nizam's defeat, personally he lost nothing. The territories he promised Baji rao were actually part of the Emperor's territory. His own fief in the Deccan remained intact. The *Cambridge History of India* says,

> He (the Nizam) was obliged to sign a convention undertaking to obtain for Baji Rao the whole of Malwa, with sovereignty in the territory between the Narbada and the Chambal and a subsidy of five million rupees. These terms were sufficiently disgraceful. They included nothing that was the Nizam's, and the cession of sovereignty in the tract between the two rivers may have covered a design to protect his dominions in the south by establishing an independent state between them and the territories of the Emperor.[12]

Baji rao's victory over the Nizam brought forth euphoric commendation from Brahmendra swami, who 'extolled him beyond measure' and compared him to the founder of the Maratha state,

> 'The Lord has granted three great achievements to you! First, the defeat of the Siddi, second, Delhi and yesterday you defeated the Mughal.'[13]

There remained the small matter of Durjan Sal of Kotah who had come forth to help the Nizam against Baji rao. Completing the task in Durai Sarai, the Peshwa came to Kotah and plundered the city. Holkar, Scindia and Pawar were with him. Yashwant rao Pawar wrote to Chimaji,

> We have come with the Prime Minister to Kotah. The entire province was looted and devastated. The Kote-kar Maharao had run away to Gadgangaruni. He sent *Vedamurti*[b] Veniram Bhat. It was decided they would pay an indemnity of ten lakh rupees. It will take four days to get the money. Then we will go to Orchha and Datia.[14]

a. Duraha.
b. One who is well versed in the Vedas.

The victorious Peshwa returned to Pune by early July 1738 to help his brother in the Vasai campaign. The Emperor granted Malwa to the Peshwa, although a formal *sanad* was issued a few years later. The Nizam went to Delhi and did not return to the Deccan for another two years by which time the scene in the Deccan had vastly changed.

Soon after the battle of Bhopal, in January 1738 itself, Chimaji Appa returned to the Konkan to complete the unfinished task against the Portuguese.

Suspicions in the Mughal court about the Nizam prevailed before and after Baji rao's invasion of Delhi and the battle of Bhopal. The Emperor always felt that the Nizam had a cosy deal with the Marathas by which they would go north and leave his own territories in the Deccan alone. Since 1732, after the Nizam's efforts to undermine Baji rao at Palkhed and Dabhoi had failed, the Peshwa and the Nizam had bound themselves by an unwritten agreement not to violate each other's territory. At Bhopal, the Nizam was defeated, and Baji rao was finally granted the *subedari* of Malwa which in his son Nanasaheb's time was formally conceded by Muhammad Shah. Mughal authorities, as well as contemporary western historians therefore write with some contempt about the Nizam's efforts to defeat the Marathas.

Blaming Baji rao's attack on Delhi on the Nizam, Hanway, who was in Persia in 1750, wrote,

> In the mean time, Muhommed Shah was not ignorant that Nizam al Muluck was the real author of these disorders; which it would hardly be possible to prevent, unless he returned to court. The Emperor therefore sent him an invitation under the strongest assurances, not only of security to his person, but also that nothing should be wanting to give him pleasure...[15]

Muhammad Shah offered the Nizam the post of *Wazir*, but he declined and said he was a *dervish* and therefore would not accept the appointment. His longstanding enmity with Khan Dauran persisted. The Nizam did try to win Qamruddin Khan over to his faction. However, the *Wazir* refused to join the Nizam in a plot against Khan Dauran. Then the Nizam, isolated, humiliated and ridiculed, is said to have thought of ways to teach his detractors a lesson. He looked beyond India's borders towards Persia. Hanway writes of the Nizam's cold fury which led to a plan to bring a foreign invader to India

and secure his ends,

> Rather than not gratify his private resentment, he resolved to use the arm
> of a foreign enemy. He knew that Saadit Khan, Governor of Awadh, was
> become a malecontent as well as himself; he therefore entered into a secret
> correspondence with him, and it is said they both joined to inform Nadir
> Shah of the state of affairs at the Moghol's court.[16]

In Persia, Tahmasp Quli Khan, better known as Nadir Shah, had
conquered many lands and people, and since 1736 had planned to invade
India. However, he did not commit himself to the undertaking until he had
subdued his many enemies. When news of Baji rao's invasion of Delhi and
the Nizam's defeat at Bhopal reached Persia, it served to further underline the
decrepit state of the Mughals.

A new calamity was poised to strike Delhi in the very near future.

# 29. The Nadir of Muhammad Shah

'The Emperor signed a treaty with the Hindus. Baji rao comes every year and imposes his will around Delhi. The *paatshahi* has sunk'; in this situation the Amirs and Musalmans thought, 'let us talk to the king of Iran, bring his army and act against Shahu raja.'

- Shahu's *charitra*[1]

'You will be astonished to read this. That is why I am sending the letter by a special messenger. The Chaghtai's *paatshahi* is over! It is Irani now!'

- Babu rao Malhar's letter. [2]

The son of a shepherd born in 1688 in the nomadic Afshar tribe of Khurasan in north-eastern Persia was destined to be the hand that destroyed the residual prestige of the Mughal Empire. Nadir Quli, as he was called, was a Turkoman, and spoke the same language as the Mughals since he hailed from the same regions of Central Asia. Where the Mughals increasingly became a settled and milder people on coming to India, the Turkoman retained many of the original hardy features of the race. In a region perpetually facing war between Persian, Uzbeks, Afghan and Russians, Nadir Quli had a hard childhood and spent years cooped up in a prison before indulging in a brief career in robbery in the lawless eastern regions of Qandahar. Nadir Quli then grabbed his patrimony, the fort of Kalat, which had been usurped by his uncle. From this base, he won the city of Nayshabur in Khurasan from the Afghans. The Persian king of the time, Shah Tahmasp, welcomed the liberator into the national army.

However, soon Nadir Quli was at the forefront of Persian liberation from a cruel Afghan rule. The king gave him half his kingdom towards the east. However, Shah Tahmasp's relative inefficiency in the western half led to a general clamour to bring Nadir to power. He deposed Shah Tahmasp in 1732 and Nadir assumed full regality as *Shahanshah* Nadir Shah in 1736.

After spending a year settling affairs with the Turks and Russians and taking the island of Bahrain from the Arabs, Nadir Shah embarked on the conquest of Qandahar. Qandahar, once part of the Mughal Empire, was lost by Shah Jehan to the Persian king Shah Abbas I. The Persians lost it to the Afghans around 1709, and on his accession as monarch, Nadir Shah was determined to win Qandahar back.

In 1737, leading an army of eighty thousand, Nadir attacked Qandahar and after a siege of a full year, captured it in March 1738. North of Qandahar was the Mughal province of Kabul. The Afghans fled Qandahar to the Mughal territories of Kabul and Peshawar and found safe refuge here. Once again, Persia became a neighbour to the Mughals. The difference lay in that there ruled an effete monarch at Delhi and a robust conqueror in Qandahar.

An 'odd' letter from Petersburgh reached *The London Evening Post*, which reported on 7 January 1738 about Nadir Shah's interest in the famed riches of the Mughals. The letter said,

> The last summer Thamas Kuli Kan, or as he now is titled Schach Nadir, being at the siege of Candahar, an Ambassador arrived in his Camp from the Great Mogul, with magnificent presents. The Ambassador met with a favourable reception, but at his departure, Kuli Kan asked him to declare to the Great Mogul, that about 200 years ago, Schach Tahmas the First sent the Mogul Majan a succor of 12000 men whom contrary to agreement, he retained in India without ever suffering them to return. That nevertheless Persia demanded all the descendants of the said 12,000 men to be immediately sent home, and that the Great Mogul do reimburse all the arrears due to the said 12,000 men for 200 years past, in default of which, Persian will endeavour to do herself justice. But this demand being thought a little too exorbitant, he has since dispatched an Ambassador to the Great Mogul, to mitigate his conditions a little, which are now, if the Mogul will pay him 120,000 Persian Rubles a Year for 20 years, he will renounce all other pretensions upon his head. The Indian monarch's answer to these proposals is expected with impatience; if he does not fully comply with them, Kuli Kan is resolved to turn his conquering Arms on that side, to which end he has already ordered magazines to be formed upon the road. From Candahar to Cabul, the first frontier town of the Mogul territories, is ten days march, and from thence to the residence of the Great Mogul, 40 days more.[3]

This extraordinary demand in a contemporary report originating in the Russian city of Petersburg becomes the backdrop for events that were to unfold in the coming years. The wolf was at the door of the Mughal Empire.

Burhan-ul-mulk Sadat Khan

Kushk mahal or Kushk –i- Feroz

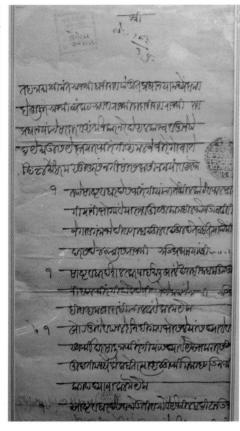

Treaty between the Marathas and the
Portuguese

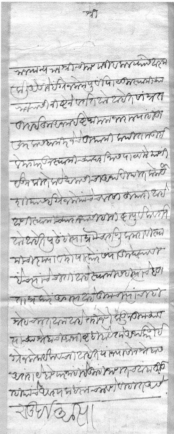

Chhatrapati Shahu's letter to
Chimaji Appa, 1739

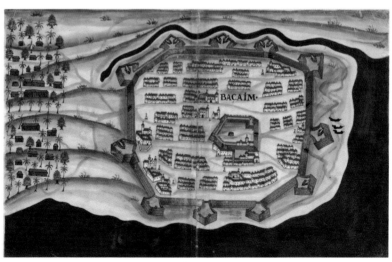

Map of Vasai fort

Nadir Shah's association with India began soon after his accession. Besides the new king's own avarice, he had invitations to invade India from eminent chiefs of the Mughal court. Fraser, author of a biography of Nadir Shah published in 1742, wrote,

> While Nadir Shah was busy securing and fortifying Qandahar, letters came from Nizam-ul-mulk and Sadat Khan, inviting him to march towards Hindustan.[4]

Shahu's *bakhar* written a few decades later says,

> The Emperor signed a treaty with the Hindus. Baji rao comes every year and imposes his will around Delhi. The paatshahi has sunk'; in this situation the Amirs and Musalmans thought, 'let us talk to the king of Iran, bring his army and act against Shahu raja.[1]

Jonas Hanway, who spent long years in Persia with Nadir Shah, wrote in 1752,

> 'During the tedious siege (of Qandahar), some discontented lords belonging to the Mughal's court, are said to have held a treasonable correspondence with him; among these were Nizam al muluck and Saadit Khan. Nadir, who was a master of intrigue and negotiation, being informed of the state of the Moghol's court, and the feeble condition of that prince's army, flattered the passions of those who were disposed to revolt, or secretly to favour his designs; and amused them with promises of his protection and other private advantage, which would accrue to them in consequence of the success of his enterprise.'[5]

Three different authors of the time seem to agree on one historical point– Nadir Shah was invited to India by Mughal nobles, chief of which were the Nizam-ul-mulk and Burhan-ul-mulk Sadat Khan.

Factions in the Mughal court between the *Turani* and Irani nobles strived to get the ear of the Emperor Muhammad Shah. So keen was the rivalry between these factions that they pursued their individual interests to the very end. A few years earlier, in his first stint as the *Wazir,* the proud Nizam had been called a 'baboon' in the Mughal court. The insult still rankled. Tilak Das, attributing the Nizam's invitation to Nadir Shah as an outcome of these insults, wrote,

> When he heard this speech from the lips of the king,
> A flame of fire leapt up within his breast.
> He went to his house, this Nizamu-l mulk;
> Anger beat in his mind, it hurt like a wound.

Then spoke lie aloud these words,
The king's commands are truth,
If I live a little longer
Of this fire I will cleanse my breast.

> When on all the battlements of the fort
> The monkeys leap hither and thither,
> Then will my life reach its fruition,
> When the monkeys bound into the fort.

Then entering his dwelling, with his own hand he prepared a letter:
'You are Shah Nadir, the all-powerful, you have a formidable army,
This throne of Dihli is vacant, this greatness has been recorded as yours,
I am your humble servant, you are my lord, come and take possession.'

> A long letter was written by the noble Nizamu-l-mulk,
> Having by reason of one word become untrue to his salt,
> The post runner took the letter, went to Nadir Shah,
> From noble Nizamu-l-mulk, the servant of the Shah.[6]

Irrespective of whether an invitation was sent by the Nizam, Sadat Khan or anybody else, an invasion of Hindustan seems to have been imminent. After examining contemporary authorities like Fraser and Hanway, Irwine concludes,

> Nadir Shah could not look on himself as the world-conqueror that he wished to be, a veritable equal of Changez and Taimur, without an invasion of Hindustan, and, as I hold, such an invasion was inevitable, invitation or no invitation.[7]

When he was busy with the siege of Qandahar, Nadir Shah sent an emissary to Delhi to ask the Emperor to order the Governor of Kabul to stop the fleeing Afghans entering Mughal territory. Muhammad Shah replied that he would do so. However, it was not done. A second messenger reached Delhi with similar results. In April 1737, Nadir Shah sent his third envoy but this time, ordered him to return after a stay of only forty days. The Mughals once again did not give any reply to the envoy.

In April 1738 Nadir Shah began preparations to attack India. In a later letter to his son he wrote,

> In this situation.... as we considered the neglect and contempt with which Muhammad Shah had behaved, and his conduct to our ambassador irreconcilable with friendship, we marched towards Shahjehanabad.[8]

Nadir Shah had an easy passage to India. On the capture of Kabul, the accumulated treasure from the time of Babar in the fort fell into his hands. The mountain passes between Kabul and Peshawar had always been guarded by Afghan tribesmen, who received a regular pay from the Mughals for this task. The negligent Mughals had allowed their pay to fall into arrears and these men abandoned their posts. On 19 July 1738, Nadir Shah marched to Jalalabad. Leaving on 6 November, he crossed the unguarded Khyber Pass and on 18 November Peshawar was taken without any resistance. An advance party was sent to Attock to build a bridge across the Indus. The rivers Chenab, Jhelum and Ravi were dry and the army crossed them without any difficulty. Lahore was the next objective and Nadir Shah wrote to its Governor Zakaria Khan to surrender and avoid bloodshed. Realising he could not oppose the Persians on his own, Zakaria Khan submitted. An amount of twenty lakh rupees was taken from Lahore. Many suburbs were looted. Spending sixteen days at Lahore, Nadir Shah ensured that all the fords on the rivers he had crossed were well guarded.

The Persian king had marched a distance of eight hundred kilometres from Kabul to Lahore without encountering any resistance. Then, he started for Delhi.

In Delhi, Muhammad Shah and his courtiers continued to live in a paradise all their own. The Emperor did not imagine the Indus would be forded. As message after message came to an Emperor immersed in pleasures of the flesh, he simply waved them away in stuporous neglect. Attributed to him is the memorable phrase of fourteenth-century saint Nizam-ud-din Auliya; albeit with consequences quite to the contrary,

> *'Hanooz Birau, Hanooz Dilli door ast'.*
> 'Go away for now, Delhi is yet far away.'

The fall of Kabul and Peshawar finally forced a response. On 2 December 1738, *Wazir* Qamruddin Khan, the Nizam-ul-mulk and Khan Dauran began with their armies but spent a month at the Shalimar *Bagh* on the outskirts of Delhi. It was first decided that Sadat Khan would be called. However, barely had he crossed the river Ganga when he was sent back. Letters seeking help were sent to many kings and nobles. Jaisingh was called, but he demurred. Baji rao was written to, and the Peshwa decided to gather his armies scattered over Vasai, Malwa and go north to help Muhammad Shah.[9]

When the Mughals heard that the invader had crossed Attock, they began their march from the Shalimar *Bagh* and reached the town of Panipat on 18 January 1739. Muhammad Shah also left Delhi and joined the army at Panipat on 27 January. Karnal, further north, was decided as the place to camp due to its abundant water supply from Ali Mardan's canal and because it afforded a flat plain that could accommodate the large army with its servants. Here the Mughal army awaited the invader.

However, the Mughal army did not know exactly where Nadir Shah had reached. Some 'grasscutters' went foraging some *kos* from the camp and encountered the Persians. Nadir Shah's fifty-five thousand strong horsemen with another one hundred thousand men including six thousand women were camped between Ali Mardan's canal and the river Yamuna. Varying figures are given for the Mughal army, but a plausible figure is seventy-five thousand fighting men with perhaps ten times the number of non-combatants.

Sadat Khan had finally been summoned from Awadh and it was expected he would join the army at Karnal with thirty thousand men. The army therefore decided to await his arrival and entrenched themselves behind a mud wall placing guns on them with soldiers sitting in trenches. By now, the Mughals had taken positions, with the Nizam in the vanguard facing north, the Emperor in the centre, Khan Dauran to the right on the eastern side and *Wazir* to the left or the west.

Just before Sadat Khan reached Panipat, Nadir Shah sent a party to intercept him but Sadat Khan joined the Mughal camp safely midnight of 12 February after a month's rapid marching from Awadh. Khan Dauran went forward to receive him. The next morning came news that some of Sadat Khan's baggage had been taken by Nadir Shah's army. Sadat Khan flew into a rage and decided to start immediately to 'help his men'. Khan Dauran went to the Emperor who passed this message to the Nizam.

The Nizam said, *'it is already three in the afternoon, by which time Sadat Khan's men must be spent by their march, and that it was unreasonable therefore, to fight that day'.* Khan Dauran, suspecting the Nizam of some ulterior motive, replied, *'Sadat Khan was already far off and must undoubtedly be engaged with the enemy. Let others do as they please, for my part I must go and support Sadat Khan.'* The two worthies thus rushed off to battle Nadir Shah in a fit of petulance.[10]

In this hasty and precipitate manner, late in the afternoon of 13 February, two of the four Mughal grandees set off with only the troops they could call and muster in a hurry to face the battle-hardened soldiers of Nadir Shah.

On 11 February Nadir Shah had reached Karnal, on 12 February he personally advanced with a small number, reconnoitred the Mughal camp and returned. On hearing of the Mughal foray, Nadir Shah sent out his Qizalbashes[a] against the Mughals with such fury that in a couple of hours the Mughals were in complete disarray. The Persian Emperor could scarcely believe his good fortune. He wrote later,

> We, whose only wishes were for such a day, after appointing guards for our camp and invoking the support of a bountiful creator, mounted and advanced to give battle. For two complete hours the battle raged with violence, and a heavy fire from cannon and musquetry was kept up. After that, by the aid of the Almighty, our lion-hunting heroes broke the enemy's line, and chased them from the field of action, dispersing them in every direction. [8]

It was a battle between Mughal arrows and Persian guns. Khan Dauran's brother Muzaffar Khan, eldest son Ali Hamid Khan and many Mughal warriors fell. Khan Dauran himself was severely wounded with two bullet wounds and carried away from the battleground. On hearing of his defeat, his men completely looted his own camp and a small tent had to be borrowed to shelter the unconscious *Mir Bakshi.*

Soon the *Wazir* and the Nizam came there to visit him. In his death throes, Khan Dauran spoke of what must be done in the few lucid moments he had before he lapsed into unconsciousness. Pleading with the Nizam and

---

a. 'Crimson headed' from their head gear. These were Shias.

the *Wazir,* he said,

> As to me, my business is done. Indeed, we have done it ourselves. Now take care of your own concerns. Let me tell you in only a few words: beware of letting the Emperor go to visit Nadir Shah, and beware of Nadir Shah proceeding to the city. Better to avert that calamity from hence, and make him go back. Procure this by every means in your power.[10]

Sadat Khan, meanwhile, was still fighting and his remaining men had formed a ring around him. The Qizalbashes charged from all sides, and Sadat Khan, already wounded in the leg was firing arrows from his elephant. Just then, a young Qizalbash from Sadat Khan's town of Nayshabur came close to him and shouted by the name he was known by in his native place; *'Against whom art thou fighting? On what soldiers dost thou reckon? Art thou mad?'* Saying this, using his spear he climbed onto the elephant and held a thin dagger to Sadat Khan's throat. Sadat Khan submitted, was imprisoned and taken to Nadir Shah.[10] The battle was over. As *'The Cambridge History of India'* describes it, *'the melee was rather a massacre than a battle'.*

Nadir Shah received Sadat Khan with kind words and acquainted him with Khan Dauran's death. The Shah opened the negotiation and said, *'you are from my country. Advise me how I can get a ransom from your Emperor and go home to fight the Sultan of Turkey'.* Sadat Khan said it was his rival the Nizam who held the key to the Empire, and he should be summoned for talks. Nadir Shah then wrote a message, and sent a copy of the Quran as a symbol of good faith, to ask the Nizam to come and meet him. The next day the Nizam-ul-mulk went to meet Nadir Shah. Before departing, he advised the Emperor that if any treachery took place, he should go to a strong fort like Mandu. As the tallest noble of the realm, the *Wakil-i-mutlaq,* and the only one from the era of Aurangzeb, the Nizam-ul-mulk had to make the best of a bad situation. What remained was to arrange the terms of a humiliating surrender.

On meeting the Nizam, Nadir Shah said, *'it is surprising that while there are nobles like you on the Emperor's side, the naked Mahrattas can march up to the walls of Delhi and take ransom from him!'* The Nizam replied, *'since many new nobles rose to influence, His Majesty did whatever he liked. Therefore, in helplessness I left him and retired to the Deccan'.*[11] Nadir Shah demanded a huge ransom and an amount of fifty lakhs agreed as the amount to be paid in instalments, and the Shah would begin his return journey to Persia. The Nizam then returned to the Mughal camp with an invitation for Muhammad Shah to have a meal with Nadir Shah the next evening.

On 15 February 1739, the Emperor with his nobles went to the Shah's camp. Nadir Shah gave him a royal reception. The courtesies over, Nadir Shah took the Emperor to task for his lack of diplomatic niceties. He then castigated the military arrangements made at Karnal, telling him it was a sure way to starve to death. He also addressed his administrative laxity, once again scolding him,

> Your predecessors were wont to take the *Jeziah* from the infidels, and you in your reign have given it to them, having in these twenty years, suffered the Empire to be overrun by them. But as hitherto the race of Taimur have not injured or misbehaved with the Safavi family or the people of Persia, I shall not take the Empire from you, only as your indolence and pride have obliged me to march so far, and that I have been put to an extraordinary expense, and my men, on account of the long marches are much fatigued, and in want of necessaries, I must go to Delhi..[12]

Muhammad Shah returned, and when news about Nadir Shah's insistence on visiting Delhi was known, it left a gloom in the Mughal camp. Khan Dauran died the same evening without regaining consciousness and the office of *Amir-ul-Umara* fell vacant. The Nizam promptly requested the Emperor to appoint his eldest son Ghaziuddin Firuz Jang in his place. When Sadat Khan, who coveted Khan Dauran's position heard of the Nizam's appointment, he sought a meeting with Nadir Shah. Foolishly, he told him that the amount of fifty lakh rupees demanded was a mere pittance, and if Nadir went to Delhi he would easily get twenty crore! '*The Nizam*', said Sadat Khan, '*is a cheat and a philosopher. If you entrap him, all will be as His Majesty's wishes*'.[13]

On the Nizam's second visit of 23 February he was peremptorily detained in the Persian camp. Nadir Shah sent him a message demanding twenty crore rupees. The Nizam was shocked at the sudden turnaround. '*Twenty crore rupees has never been seen by anybody in the Mughal dynasty*', he exclaimed; '*Shah Jehan accumulated sixteen crores but the whole of it was spent by Aurangzeb in his long wars in the Deccan. There are barely fifty lakh left in the treasury!*'[14] Nadir Shah said, '*Point out where the money is. You cannot leave this place.*' Muhammad Shah was summoned once again to the Persian camp.

So, on 24 February, the Emperor once again began for Nadir Shah's camp. On his arrival, Muhammad Shah was practically imprisoned in a tent and a thousand Qizalbash guards placed around him. In the evening, Nadir Shah summoned Muhammad Shah and after a three-hour meeting sent him back to his tent. The *Wazir* Qamruddin Khan was also brought into the camp and made prisoner.

Most of the Mughal army had never come to grips with Nadir Shah. The guns remained where they were. The small armies led by Khan Dauran and Sadat Khan defeated, the Persians enforced a siege and the camp began to starve due to the sheer number of people present there. The leaderless Mughal army did not know which way to turn and wandered away to Delhi.

Babu rao Malhar, the Peshwa's *vakil* was in the Mughal camp, and reported to Baji rao on 21 *Jilkad* (20 February 1739),

> The Qizalbash and Khan Dauran fought. Sadat Khan was captured alive from the battlefield. Khan Dauran had two severe wounds, he died in the camp. Many other eminent nobles were killed. Seven to eight thousand were killed in battle. The battle went badly; there is no prestige left in this army. Qamruddin Khan and Nizam-ul-mulk went to Tahmasp Quli's tent. They planned a meeting with Muhammad Shah. On 21 *Jilkad* the Emperor went with three hundred guards. They met and had a meal. To me it looks like the creation of a new world. I cannot find an antidote.[15]

On 25 February 1739, Babu rao Malhar too left the camp at Karnal and made his way to Jaipur. He wrote a detailed description of his travails to Shamji *pant*, probably his uncle,

> The Emperor and the Nizam went and dined with Tahmasp Quli and returned after agreeing on his terms. Then for five or ten days, there was no food. Six to seven rupees were charged for a *seer*. There was no fodder. Five days people fasted. Then Asaf Jah was summoned by Tahmasp. He went (with some others) but did not return for two days. The third day the Emperor was called. He went and stayed near the army. Nobody came to receive him! At night Asaf Jah and Sadat Khan came near him. The Emperor was placed under guard. Asaf and Ghaziuddin and other nobles were imprisoned. Early next day a prince came and took the artillery and Qamruddin Khan. Until then, on the Sunday, fourteenth day of the new moon, we were in the camp. Seeing this with our own eyes, making a fort of our chest, with elephants, horses and people, we got on the road. Abandoning the road, we entered

the forest and stayed there one night. Next day we marched forty *kos* on the road to Delhi. Sadat Khan came to Delhi with an army of Qizalbashes. We followed him to Delhi the third day. The same day we left and stayed at Muhammad Khan's *serai*. Fourth day we were at Palwal. Fifth day we met Suraj mal Jat. Then we reached Jaipur and met Dhondo *pant*. Camels and elephants came from Rewari and will reach in a day or two. God has been kind. You will be astonished to read this. That is why I am sending this letter by a special messenger. The Chaghtai's *paatshahi* is over! It is Irani now![16]

On 28 February, Sadat Khan escorted by four thousand of Nadir Shah's cavalry reached Delhi and took possession of the city. Letters from Muhammad Shah and Nadir Shah were given to the governor of Delhi. He was ordered to hand over the keys to palaces, treasure houses and stores to Nadir Shah's commander named Tahmash Khan Jalair.

The imperial city of Shah Jehan and Aurangzeb waited for the Persian conqueror to enter the Mughal capital.

# 30. A Desperate Struggle in the *Firangan*

'The anguish due to Dharavi is so intense, only God knows how much! But what is to be done? For now, I don't see a way.'

- Chimaji Appa to Nanasaheb.[1]

'The Marathas have lost twelve thousand men so far. But due to their superior numbers, nobody holds it to account.'

– Cardin, Portuguese General in the North *Firangan*.[2]

Withdrawal of a section of Maratha troops and Chimaji Appa's departure in July 1737 from the Konkan for the campaign against the Nizam weakened their position in the *Firangan*. Sensing an opportunity to recoup, the Portuguese began pouring men and material into the territory from Goa and Daman. Portugal sent reinforcements that reached India in September 1737, and in the next two months, one and a half thousand men, of which five hundred were Portuguese, reached Vasai by sea. They also brought provisions, food, and gun powder with them.

The Marathas could not succeed at Vasai unless its blockade was complete and supply routes were closed, so they diverted their attack to Daman. Shankaraji Phadke's brother Mahadji went north and attacked Mahim. Mahadji decided to force the issue at Mahim and the Peshwa sent Ramachandra Hari Patwardhan to help him. Another force went towards Shirgaon.

While the Marathas began their attack to win Vasai, the Portuguese planned to recover their losses. The withdrawal of the Marathas was an opportunity for them to do so. The loss of Thane was the beginning of the loss of Sashti, and for the Portuguese recovering the fort at Thane was of paramount importance. However, seeing the threat to Mahim, they sent three relief parties by sea in December, the last of which were led by an intrepid General named Pedro De Mello *Maestro de campo*. This Portuguese detachment attacked the Marathas on 23 December. The Maratha batteries were destroyed and Mahadji Phadke's ambitious attack failed. Trapped in a forward position with no shelter, he was killed in the attack. Shankaraji described the battle in a letter to Chimaji on 26 December 1737,

> Seventeen *Firangi* ships with one and a half thousand men came, some went
> to Mahim. We sent three hundred men to Mahim. On 23 December, the
> *firangis* emerged from Mahim and attacked us. Three batteries, one manned
> by *dada* (Mahadji), one by Karnaji Shinde and a third manned by Khandoba
> were at the centre of the fight. About two and a half to three thousand men
> attacked the battery manned by *dada*. Ramchandra *pant* charged with
> his cavalry and pushed them back but was shot in his arm. As the cavalry
> withdrew, the *Firangis* attacked the battery. There were some Arabs from
> Surat who changed sides and began killing our own people. In the melee,
> *dada*..... fell. A hundred to one hundred fifty men were also killed. We then
> went to Shirgaon. Although *dada* is killed, I will do my utmost and not be
> found lacking in my duty. If they follow us we will fight them...[3]

De Mello followed up his success and chased the Marathas out of
both Mahim and Shirgaon up to the hill fort of Asheri, then besieged by
the Marathas. The demoralized Marathas abandoned the siege at Asheri
without a fight and a triumphant De Mello returned to Vasai towards the
end of January 1738. Cardin, the General in charge of Vasai, followed up
with an attack on the island fort of Dharavi. Portuguese ships pretended to
head up the creek towards Thana and doubled back to attack Dharavi on 17
February 1738. They also landed men from the rear and managed to stop
the reinforcements coming from Thana. Cardin claimed he had won the fort
with barely two hundred soldiers, while four hundred Maratha horse and a
thousand foot had to watch the loss from a distance. The losses at Mahim,
Asheri and Dharavi pushed the Marathas onto the back foot.

Even as they launched a counterattack to recover lost forts, the Portuguese
were looking for intermediaries who could bring an amicable end to the war.
The arrival of the Nizam in Malwa was the first hope that the Marathas
would withdraw from the Konkan. In December 1737, the Viceroy at Goa
proposed sending a message to Sawai Jaisingh, who had asked for Portuguese
experts for building his astronomical observatories, to broker a peace with
Baji rao. However, the disturbed conditions prevented the dispatch of the
*padre*. The Viceroy then sent a gift to Jaisingh through Surat, with a letter.[4]
However, nothing came of it.

Maratha weakness at sea was a key factor that prevented an effective
blockade of Vasai. Manaji and Sambhaji Angre remained caught up in

their domestic dispute. On 13 January 1737, Manaji wrote to Chimaji Appa, *'Sambhaji Angre Sarkhel took some trading vessels to Suvarnadurg. He is expected to come there from Vijaydurg shortly'*.[5] In December 1737, Krishnaji Naik wrote to his kinsman, *'Sambhaji Angre's fleet is at sea. It took away some trading vessels of the Siddi and the Portuguese. Firangi vessels coming here would have been challenged if Sambhaji Angre was on friendly terms.'*[6] To take a sea-facing fort purely by the use of land forces was difficult and one fraught with the risk of high casualties. In March 1738, Shankaraji Keshav complained to Chimaji that Manaji was not honouring his permits to trading vessels.[7] These letters show the divide between not just the Angre brothers but also divisions between the Peshwa's chiefs and Manaji, who was an ally.

On completion of the battle of Bhopal, Chimaji left Khandesh and ordered the replenishment of various items in the Konkan. After visiting the Ganesh temple at Ranjangaon on 18 January 1738, he reached the Konkan by the end of that month and began directing operations.[8] The Marathas had recruited Arabs and Canarese men in their armies. However, these were found wanting in loyalty as well as performance in battle. They were therefore replaced by residents of Konkan and tested Maratha veterans now free from their engagement in Malwa. Instead of a frontal attack, the Marathas once again began to attack Portuguese territories that sent supplies to Vasai.

De Mello had taken the fort of Dharavi in February 1738. A Maratha attempt to retake the fort of Dharavi in March 1738 failed. Chimaji wrote to Nanasaheb, *'The anguish due to Dharavi is so intense, only God knows how much! But what is to be done? For now, I don't see a way'*.[1] Cardin on the other hand wrote, *'the Marathas have lost twelve thousand men so far. But due to their superior numbers, nobody holds it to account'*.[2] The Marathas could bring thousands of men to the battlefield. The *Firangis*, on the other hand faced shortages on all fronts.

The intense war between the two powers, and the higher casualties that an attacking force normally sustains, turned this fairly local war into a battle of will and attrition. Chimaji was determined to oust the Portuguese and despite his own failing health, personally directed the campaign on the ground. The Portuguese General Cardin, despite his apparent success, got hardly any help from Goa. He therefore resigned his post in April 1738 and De Mello was appointed in his place.

The situation within the fort at Vasai was not favourable for the Portuguese. They had no money and Goa could not spare any men to defend Vasai. As on 18 September 1738, there were four hundred and eleven at Dharavi and some more at Mahim and other places. Vasai had eight hundred and ninety-seven soldiers, of which five hundred and twenty-one were Portuguese. In addition, a further nine hundred were defending the fort from without and one hundred and ninety were stationed on the beach. It was only in October 1738 that Goa managed to send a further four hundred and eighty men to Vasai. As against this, the Marathas had three thousand men at Thane and Pilaji Jadhav rao was in the region with seven thousand foot and seven hundred horse.

The monsoon months did not witness much fighting. Chimaji returned to Pune by the end of May 1738 to recoup his health. The final act in this war began after October 1738.

After the monsoon months of 1738, at a time when Nadir Shah was still in Kabul, Chimaji threw all his resources into the battle in the Konkan. In Pedro De Mello, the Portuguese too had a brave Captain. His ambition to retake the fort of Thane was his undoing; that eventually led to a turn in the fortunes of the Marathas.

On 24 November 1738, De Mello sailed from Vasai with about one thousand freshly arrived troops from Portugal. Sailing south past Bombay, they turned into the creek towards Thane. The water at Thane was shallow. De Mello's artillery could not be brought close to the fort as the water did not permit his larger ships to approach the Thane fort. He therefore had to use them from a distance and they would not serve any purpose. De Mello therefore decided to get closer to the fort with some of his men. Khandoji Mankar was commanding Thane fort and he replied to the Portuguese fire with some of his own. As De Mello edged closer to Thane, he was hit by a Maratha shell and killed. The defeated Portuguese withdrew to Vasai. The English watched the Portuguese defeat, which they had foretold; the force was inadequate, they had said, and the Marathas had an overwhelming superiority in numbers.

Men and material were poured into the Konkan from November onwards. Troops and guns to the Konkan were sent by the Peshwa from

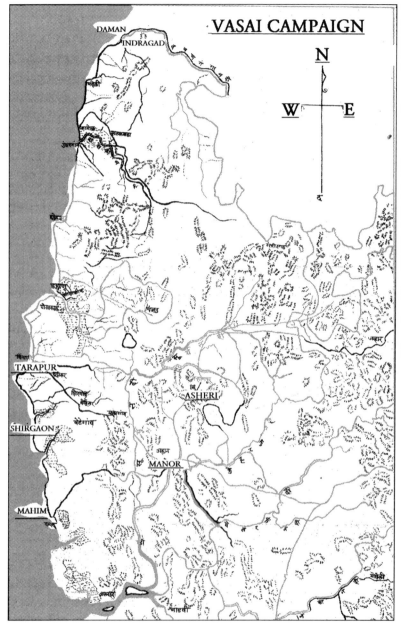

(Maps adapted from YN Kelkar's 'Vasai cha Mahasangram, Courtesy Shri VY Kelkar.)

*Vasai Campaign — Map showing the upper half of the Firangan*

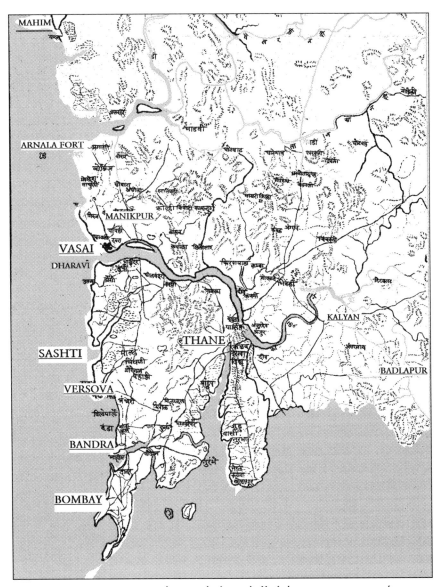

*Vasai Campaign — Map showing the lower half of the Firangan and Bombay.*

his base in Pune. All principal Maratha chiefs fought the battle and were present in the *Firangan* at this time. Many guns were brought from various foundries in Kalyan, Junnar and Pune.[9] Baji rao sent eight thousand horse and ten thousand foot soldiers under Shankaraji Phadke in November 1738. Portuguese supplies to Vasai were coming from Goa to the south and Daman in the north. Ranoji Scindia therefore attacked Daman, while Vyankat rao Ghorpade attacked Goa itself.

Goa had not enough men to withstand Vyankat rao's attack. In January Madgaon was taken, and the fort of Phonda was won by the Raja of Soundha, who was a Maratha ally. The Bardez district of Goa also fell. The Viceroy wrote to General Martinho de Silveira de Menezes, who was defending Vasai,

> Here we find ourselves in a state of consternation created by crossing of the Maratha forces on 23rd instant (12 January by the old calendar) captained by Venkata rao, into Salcette,….this consternation makes it impossible for me to help the fort of Bassain (Vasai) and other forts of that province with men but, on the other hand, puts me in need of utilizing the troops of Bassain to defend this island of Goa.[10]

With Goa itself threatened, the war entered its last phase. However, Goa was saved as the Viceroy managed to secure the good offices of Dadaji Bhave Nargundkar with a well-placed bribe, and the Portuguese fort of Raitur that he was to attack, was saved. Dadaji was in charge of a large tract between the Tungabhadra and Malprabha rivers in the Carnatic on behalf of Sambhaji of Kolhapur. Through the good offices of Dadaji, envoys and rich merchants were sent to the Marathas to contract a peace. The first meeting began at the Maratha camp where the *Firangi* envoy was told by Dadaji that should the Portuguese choose to leave India and sail away in ships owned by them or the English or their own, the Marathas would allow them to go unmolested![11] This opening gambit did not find favour and when the meeting did not appear to be reaching a conclusion, there were new proposals put up from the Maratha side that asked for *khandani* and full religious freedom in Goa. Vasai, Daman and Karanja were to be handed over to the Marathas. These proposals were not accepted by the Portuguese.

Eventually Vyankat rao summoned them again and it was conveyed to them that Baji rao will not return any of the areas won and will even take

Goa. However, should the *Firangis* wish to hold Goa, they should give Baji rao the arrears of tribute of sixty years at the rate of three *khandi*[a] gold per year. He also demanded that Goa should allow Hindu temples to be built and they should be allowed to practice their religion.[12,13] Abolition of the 'shendi' tax was another demand.[b]

The Portuguese then obtained a letter from Shahu to Vyankat rao, asking him to make peace. However, this was not accepted by him. The negotiations dragged on. Bribes were offered. Two lakh rupees were paid as a tribute. However, Madgaon remained in Maratha hands. A treaty was finally agreed on 22 April 1739, however with Maratha allies like the Sawant of Wadi and Dadaji looking after their own interests, the complete removal of the Portuguese power at Goa was not insisted upon. Further negotiations continued in Pune and Captain Inchbird met Baji rao at Paithan in January 1740 to come to an agreement on behalf of the *Firangis*. The treaty was eventually signed after further negotiations in December 1740.

After early 1739, help from Goa to Vasai came to a halt. Chimaji Appa with Shankaraji Phadke, who was now a veteran in the war, began their final thrust by attacking Mahim to the north of Vasai. The Marathas had eight thousand horse, twelve cannons and fourteen elephants and were led by Chimaji, Pilaji Jadhav rao and Shankaraji. On 9 January, Mahim surrendered in short order along with two other forts of Shirgaon and Kelwe. Shankaraji was content that he had avenged the death of his brother Mahadji a year earlier.

The fall of Mahim was noted by the English in Bombay on 11 January, with a hint of what was to follow:

> Received advice that Kelve Mahim, a fort to the northward of Bassein belonging to the Portuguese, was taken by storm by the Marathas, who were hereby masters of the countries of Shirgaon, Dahanu and Kelve quite up to Tarapur, to which they have actually laid siege: another inconvenience from the loss of this place is that it commands in a great measure the communication with Asheri, an important inland fortress belonging to the Portuguese.[14]

---

a. *Khandi* is a measure of weight that equals roughly two hundred and thirty-six kilograms.

b. *Shendi* : a lock of hair on their head, preserved by Hindus.

The battle for Tarapur fort was one of the fiercest. The strong stone walls were supported by valiant Portuguese defenders who would repair any damage done at day during the night. Chimaji and Holkar, who had injured his foot, co-ordinated the entire attack from a platform erected behind the frontline. Many mines were laid under the fort walls and blown up on 24 January 1739. The breaches were attacked by the Marathas who also set up ladders against the walls. Ranoji Scindia, Malharji Holkar, Govind Hari, Ramachandra Hari, Ranoji Bhonsle, Tukoji Pawar and many other Maratha stalwarts led the attack.[15]

In fighting close to the fort walls, Maratha troops were led by the Peshwa's trusted lieutenant Baji Bhivrao Rethrekar. In the intense fighting, he was hit and killed by an enemy bullet. The death of his close friend and confidante caused the Peshwa considerable anguish. The Rethrekar family was close to the Peshwa, and Bhivrao Rethrekar had even named his two sons after Baji rao and Chimaji.

Two days later the Peshwa wrote a memorable letter to Baji Bhivrao's mother, telling her that *'he was now her Baji rao'*,

> Two days back, during the attack on Tarapur, Baji Bhivrao was shot on his face and died. God has done the inappropriate. You have suffered much grief. For me, I have lost a brother. You are older and wise, so you may adjust to your sorrow. To sum up, please consider me as your Baji rao. Keep your benevolent eye on me.[16]

Chimaji Appa wrote to Baji Bhiv rao's younger brother Chimaji,

> Baji rao has gone, with a good reputation. We are pained that one side of me has left us. Mother Venubai *kaki*[a] in her old age has to suffer this. His sons Bapuji and Gangoba are safe with me.[17]

In Tarapur, many *Firangi* women were taken captive and returned to the Portuguese with the utmost respect.[18] The Portuguese chief of the fort was killed, and an apocryphal story says his wife was captured and brought before Chimaji Appa. Reassuring her, Chimaji told her that he was her brother and gave her gifts before sending her back to her people. The lady requested Chimaji that her wish that her husband get a proper burial be granted. Once

---

a.   Baji Bhivrao's mother.

again, Chimaji allowed the Portuguese to bury their captain with all the rites associated with the funeral.[19] These anecdotes reflect on the prevailing Maratha ethos in no small measure.

The capture of Tarapur was followed by the fall of the inland fort of Asheri. Asheri was a difficult fort to capture as it was surrounded by thick forests. However, the flood of victories and overwhelming force made the task easier. Versova, on the island of Sashti was the next to fall on 9 February. Fearing its capture and use by the Marathas, the fortified port of Bandra was demolished on the advice of the English, probably because it faced the island of Bombay. The final fort to be taken back was Dharavi which had changed hands twice in the past twelve months. Its position to the south of Vasai at the mouth of the creek endangered all ships approaching the fort from the south. Manaji Angre sent some men to assist in the attack on Dharavi.[20] On 10 March 1739, Manaji took the port of Uran, close to his base at Colaba. With Mahim and Arnala already in Maratha possession, Vasai was encircled by land and sea.

What remained was a final blow to Vasai, the nerve centre of Portuguese power in the north.

॥ॐॐॐॐ॥

# 31. Vasai!

'The *Firangis* fought with valour and did not lack in soldiering. Our men fought according to the tenets of *Bharati* war and there have been many battles earlier, but none can compare to this one.'

'The Lord's *sudarshan*[a] hit the head of the fanatics who harbour religious ill will, and they were cast down. Else Vasai would not have come. The *Firangi* was a statue of fire.'

- Chimaji Appa's letter to Brahmendra swami, 13 May 1739.[1]

The chief centre of Portuguese power outside Goa was Vasai. The fort itself was considered one of the strongest of its age with walls nearly forty feet high, five feet thick and a perimeter of about three kilometres. Its projecting four-sided bastions made it difficult to take the fort by escalade or firing of the artillery shells available with the Marathas at that time. Mines were difficult to deploy due to the loose sandy soil close to the sea. While the western face of the fort looked at the sea, to its south was a wide creek and to its east there was marshy land. Opposite the creek stood the fort of Dharavi, which had recently been taken back from the Portuguese. The northern face of Vasai alone stood exposed to Maratha attacks. However, a clear open space in front of the fort made it difficult to launch an attack in the face of accurate fire from the fort's three northern bastions.

For the Portuguese, the situation in Vasai was desperate. The entire northern kingdom, a possession of two hundred years, now appeared to be slipping from their hands. Of late, they had concentrated their forces in Vasai, abandoning outposts that could not be defended. The besieged Portuguese General pinned his hopes on help from the English, their neighbour and only other European power in the region. He therefore tried to interest the English, and linked the defence of Bombay with that of Vasai. His plaintive appeals for help were treated with an English instinct for self-preservation.

In April 1739, the Dutch[2] and the English were busy engaging Sambhaji Angre outside his base in Vijaydurg, which they called Gheria, without any

---

a. A weapon of Lord Vishnu.

result. [3] That was one reason Sambhaji could not render any help at Vasai. The English considered the Marathas and Angre as separate powers and did not consider an attack on Vijaydurg as an attack on the main Maratha power. However, any help rendered to the Portuguese at Vasai would have turned the Marathas against them.

John Pereira Pinto, Commandant of Vasai, wrote to the English at Bombay,

> I am likewise, from a regard to our common interest, to tell you that the Marathas have more at heart the conquest of your island than they had that of ours ....and I hold it for indubitable that the gentlemen belonging to the Government of your island cannot but be sensible *that you must be ruined with us if the Marathas gain an establishment on the island of Salsette,*[a] and that they only keep peace with you for a present conveniency, not to have at the same time two enemies on their back. [3]

However, the English were unmoved by this plea for help.

Not much later, in March 1739, Pinto was killed by a musket shot to his throat as he stood surveying the Maratha attack from a north-facing bastion of Vasai fort. The Marathas could see people moving *'behind the walls through loopholes'* and Pinto was shot using an indigenous gun when he was observed standing there.[4] Pinto's successor at Vasai, Caetano De Souza, once again wrote to Bombay,

> The Marathas have carried on mines, covered ways and other approaches to the very foundation of the wall, their batteries being very near the town; that they throw large stones into the place from mortars.

As Maratha attacks intensified, appeals from Vasai became more fervent. The English firstly refused help and then, even for supply of food, only gave help against hard cash. To get money, church plate from Vasai was mortgaged with the English, and brass cannons were offered as security.[3]

Chimaji Appa came before Vasai fort on 7 February 1739. He had with him twenty-five thousand horse, forty thousand foot soldiers, four thousand sappers, five thousand camels, fifty elephants and innumerable *pindaris*.[6] Some sources hint at a much larger force. From then on, all Maratha efforts

---

a.  Sashti.

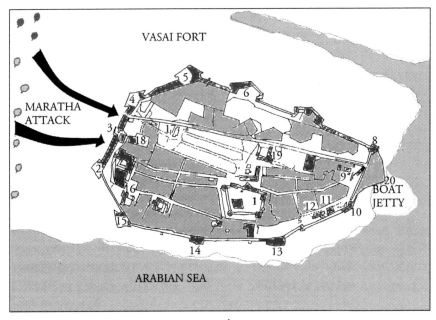

*Vasai fort*

1.  Citadel

2.  St. Sebastian bastion.

3.  Land gate and Cavalier bastion.

4.  Our Lady of Remedies bastion.

5.  Three Kings bastion.

6.  St. James bastion.

7.  St. Goncalo bastion.

8.  Mother of God bastion.

9.  Customs House.

10. St. John bastion.

11. Factory/store house.

12. Church of St. Joseph.

13. Elephant or St. Francis Xavier bastion.

14. St. Peter bastion.

15. St. Paul bastion.

16. Augustinian convent.

17. Jesuit College.

18. Franciscan convent.

19. Palace of the General of the North.

20. Boat jetty.

were focused on this one point. Chimaji in particular set his heart on the capture of Vasai and would not be distracted from this objective. Anguished over his own chronic ill health, he told his men that if he dies before the conquest of Vasai, they should stuff his corpse inside the barrel of a cannon and blow it inside the fort.[7]

The Portuguese garrison had no supplies, no allies and hardly any contact with the outside. The northern wall of the fort was stacked with the best guns they had, for that was where the attack came from. A large area in front of the walls had no vegetation, and therefore no shelter, and any Maratha soldier found in these parts was greeted with blistering fire from the fort. Chimaji found a mansion belonging to Martinho de Silveira about sixteen hundred 'hands'[a] away from the walls of the fort. He fortified it and began using it as a base to attack the fort.[8] Mines were laid from long distances in the face of such fire. Mines would not work as efficiently because *the ground being loose sand near the sea side where the water would not permit mine of any depth, no mine could be carried deep enough to endanger the walls.*[9] Portuguese gunners fired by night and day and the Marathas replied with their one hundred and thirty-four cannons and sixty mortars firing into the fort.[10] The three-month-long attack may have rained over forty-five thousand shells into the fort.[11]

The resilient Portuguese still would not surrender and submit, and the battle wore on with heavy casualties on the Maratha side. In April 1739, the English gave some aid to the defenders and some money.[1] This did not alter the course of the war. General de Silveira, who had succeeded De Mello, was killed during Maratha shelling. The Marathas, enthused by Chimaji's presence through the war, at great risk to their lives, laid mines under the fort walls.

On 2 May 1739, the first mines succeeded in creating a breach. Thirteen mines were set off simultaneously early in the morning to the beating of drums.[12] Two towers named San Sebastian and Remedios were blown up. Another breach was made in the tower named Carvalho. In their hurry to occupy the breach, the Marathas rushed in before all the mines had exploded and many were killed when these mines blew up. The Portuguese kept up a

---

a. A rough measure of a yard.

steady fire at the breach killing several hundred of the attackers. On 3 May, a mine laid by Malharji Holkar exploded and another breach was created. The Portuguese defenders rushed to defend the breach and a desperate hand-to-hand fight began. By then, eight hundred Portuguese officers and men were dead. General Silveiro Menezes was killed during the shelling. With the fort's perimeter punctured at several places, the Marathas could enter in large numbers, forcing the Portuguese to unfurl the white flag of surrender early on 4 May 1739. Vasai had fallen.

Chimaji also wrote to his favourite nephew Nanasaheb on the day Vasai was captured, giving details of the final military moves of the day,

> We laid Vasai under siege and raised platforms to fire our guns. We mined the walls from the north. Ranoji Scindia placed five mines to the tower on the left. Yashwant rao Pawar and Ranoji Bhonsle laid mines under the wall of the fort. On the right, Santaji Wagh under Malharji Holkar had placed his mines. Vasai has very strong walls. It is not a place where mines would work. Yet, our men worked hard to place the mines. On 2 May, we lit the fuses to the mines. Four of Ran*ba's* mines blew up. His men rushed in the breach. Just then, the fifth mine blew up. Heavy stones from the wall came down on the men, who were buried.

The victory at Vasai was an achievement that was treasured more than any Maratha battle before this. Chimaji ended his letter with a sense of achievement and wonder,

> The Maratha army never had a war like this one. It was the extreme limit; it is difficult to expand on it any further. To win this fort was God's grace and *Raya's* saintly deeds.[13]

The Marathas entered the fort on 12 May 1739 and Chimaji wrote a graphic account of the battle for Vasai to Brahmendra swami the next day. He warmly complimented the *Firangi*s for their valour,[1]

> The *Firangi*s fought like true soldiers. Our men fought in accordance with the tenets of the *Bharati* [a] war. There have been many battles before this, but none can be compared to this battle. It is all due to the *swami's* blessing. Our people would not leave the towers. Finally, the fanatic *Firangi*s lost courage and on the day of *ashtami* they sought a truce and

---

a.  A battle fought based on certain moral principles such as treatment of the unarmed, towards women and those who have surrendered.

surrendered. In eight days they agreed to leave the fort with their families. I stopped the firing.[a]

Chimaji's victory was hailed by Sultanji Nimbalkar, who was once Shahu's *sarlashkar* but had gone over to the Nizam. He wrote to Chimaji congratulating him for his fine victory,

> Vasai is a difficult place, you placed it under siege, took the army near the walls, blew up the walls with mines and you won the fort. Hearing this pleasing news is very satisfying. Your efforts so far have been rewarded by God.'[14]

The English at Bombay received the news about the fall of Vasai on 7 May 1739 and described the final battle,

> The President acquaints the Board that yesterday he received the melancholy news of the capitulations being signed the 5/16[b] instant for the surrender of the city of Bassein to Chimnaji, the Maratha General, in the term of one week,—that is to say, on the 12th instant,—occasioned, as the President is well informed from different parts, by the success of the mines which the Marathas sprung on the cortines and bastions to the number of twelve or thirteen. It is observable that the place is so situated and surrounded with water that only three out of the eleven bastions were subject to be attacked, and the mines made such breaches in two of them as rendered the storming very practicable, which the Marathas attempted with the utmost fury and resolution, being repulsed several times and as often returned to the attack, and at length gained lodgments on the bastions. The Portuguese being tired and harassed with so warm an action, which first and last held two days, having several of their officers and many people killed and their ammunition nearly exhausted, and observing the place was no longer tenable against such numbers, hoisted a white flag, and sent one of their officers to treat of a surrender with Chimnaji, who allowed them the space of a week to evacuate the town on most honourable conditions.[12]

The saffron flag, the *zaripatka*, was unfurled on the citadel of Vasai. An elaborate ceremony to propitiate the gods was held. The accounts of the day show that the ritual prayer cost nearly twenty-eight rupees. Fifteen goats were bought for rupees fifteen, flour worth seven and three quarters of a rupee and

---

a. Appendix 6 for Chimaji's complete letter.
b. Old and New Style calendars, based on Julian and Gregorian dates which are eleven days apart.

miscellaneous items like coconuts and *shendur*[a], *abeer* and *bukka*[b] powders were bought for about five rupees.[15]

A striking feature after the surrender, and indeed during the entire period of Maratha expansion, was their magnanimity towards a defeated enemy. Vasai was no exception. In line with the battles with the Nizam and Bangash, the surrendered Portuguese men and their families at Vasai were treated humanely. A war that took the lives of twenty-two thousand Marathas did not end with a massacre of prisoners, and their families were not molested. Chimaji was a man with a generous heart, and to an enemy who fought with so much valour, he allowed seven days to leave the fort. Pilaji Jadhav rao, who was present at Vasai, in his letter to Radha bai urged her to use her influence with Chimaji to release most of the prisoners, retaining only a few as hostages until the Maratha prisoners at Goa were released. Among those released were the women captured at the fort of Tarapur.[16]

The *Firangi*s marched out to ships with their band playing taking with them all their belongings. Chimaji had organized a hundred ships to transport the *Firangi*s and paid the rentals for them.[17] Chimaji also granted full religious freedom to those who remained and three churches were preserved in the region.[18,c]

The Marathas had paid a huge price in men. The Portuguese acquitted themselves well. Chimaji wrote to Shahu,

> The *Firangi*s fought with courage as expected. This is called soldiering. For one and a half *prahar* the *Firangi*s rained fire on us. Absorbing all this fire, the Maratha armies held their positions. This never happened before. It was the limit.[19]

Peace was declared. The Portuguese lost their entire northern possessions except Diu, and Daman. The fall of Vasai and the peace treaty saved Goa, where the Portuguese were able to rule for another two hundred and twenty-two years. Chaul Revdanda came into Maratha possession in 1740. With the acquisition of *Habshan* earlier, and *Firangan* in this war, the island of Bombay was sandwiched between two long coastal stretches ruled by the Marathas. It

---

a.   Minium or red lead.          b.   Fragrant powders.          c.   Appendix 7.

was not surprising that they were extremely anxious about what lay in store for them in the days to come.

On 10 May 1739, the President of Bombay summoned a meeting of his officials. They agreed that their small island would not be able to withstand an attack by the Marathas. The short castle walls with an unprotected city meant there was hardly any defence. The merchants of Mumbai volunteered to raise thirty thousand rupees for augmenting the defence by building a ditch around the town wall thereby safeguarding the business and families of those living therein. The President of the Board at Bombay also felt it was time to send gifts along with a letter to Shahu, taking care not to antagonize the Peshwa by this gesture. A small gift of red and green velvet and white cloth was sent to Chimaji as a compliment for his victory. However, Chimaji asked them to send an envoy to discuss matters. Within days of the fall of Vasai, Captain Inchbird was therefore sent to meet Chimaji while Captain Gordon made his way to Satara.[20]

The fall of Vasai came not a day too soon. Delhi lay prostrate before the Persian king and quailed before his avarice and cruelty. Shahu had ordered Baji rao to support the Mughal monarchy, and he was at Burhanpur for nearly two months waiting for Chimaji to end his campaign in the Konkan and prepare to face the new challenge.

ॐॐॐ

# 32. Nadir Shah Mauls Delhi

'Qamruddin Khan, the *Wazir*, was treated with greater severity. He endeavoured to elude payment of the large contribution demanded of him; Nadir therefore caused him to be exposed openly to the sun, which is reckoned a punishment contumelious as well as painful, and in that country (India) dangerous to health. At length, he extorted from him a whole crore of rupees besides a great value in precious stones and elephants.'

- Jonas Hanway.[1]

One thousand four hundred kilometres from Delhi, in the month of February 1739, Chimaji Appa with a seventy-five thousand Maratha army and innumerable *pindaris,* was at the final stage of the two-year war at Vasai. This massive mobilization of men and material in the Konkan coincided with the invasion of Nadir Shah. A fragment of a letter written by Shahu giving instructions to Baji rao in early 1739 tells us more about the king's policy,

> The king has written that the swami (Peshwa) should move (north) by stages. The messenger has been asked to reach the Peshwa's camp in eight days and hand over this message. Govind rao (Chitnis) has also been told to ask the swami to move ahead. The king had given a promise to the late Emperor Aurangzeb, (and he holds himself by it) that should any foreign power happens to come on you (the Mughals), he will send help. So, all possible help should be provided.[2]

Pilaji Jadhav rao wrote to his brother Sambhaji Jadhav in January 1739,

> Yesterday I received letters from *Raya* (Baji rao) that he is proceeding to Hindustan. Iran's Tahmas Quli has overcome Muhammad Shah. To help him, the armies of Malwa, Malharji Holkar, Ranoji Scindia and Pawar be sent. It will be to the credit of this state to help the Emperor now. We will be taking the armies in Gujarat and Vasai and sending them to Malwa.[3]

Baji rao began gathering an army. He asked Pilaji Jadhav rao and the chiefs of Malwa who were at Vasai to join him. Moving north through Khandesh and Aurangabad he finally stopped near Burhanpur, awaiting reinforcements. Chimaji Appa could not leave the Vasai campaign at this final stage of the battle or spare any troops to go to the north. A similar break in the Vasai campaign in 1738 before the battle of Bhopal had led to a setback and loss of many forts. Baji rao therefore had to wait.

At a time such as this, regional satraps asserted their rights and raided unprotected neighbouring territories. Raghuji Bhonsle of Varhad raided areas of Malwa. Baji rao's officer Avaji Kavade was defeated by Raghuji, but the defeat was temporized by Baji rao in these difficult times. The king seemed to be in favour of Raghuji. Baji rao wrote to Chimaji, '*Avaji Kavade's defeat made the king (Shahu) happy*'.[4] Relations between the Peshwa and the king appear to have cooled. Baji rao wrote a letter of remonstrance to Shahu in this regard. In April 1739, in order to pacify the Peshwa in these critical times, we find Tara bai replying, virtually giving a *carte blanche* to the Peshwa,

> I received your letter. You have said the king, on mature consideration, issue orders to you. The desire here is for you to come here and to convey to you to do what is good for the kingdom. But it will be some time before you come and we cannot bear to wait till then. Instead, it is appropriate that *you should take over and run the administration of the kingdom*.[5]

Baji rao expressed his anguish to Brahmendra swami in his letter in March 1739,

> There is a major crisis that has developed. I am buried in debt and no money is to be had from any quarter. I am facing a problem in fulfilling my own expenses (to fill my stomach) and a major calamity has come forth. Vasai has not yet been taken. Avaji Kavade (Baji rao's chief) has been defeated by Raghuji Bhonsle. In this manner I am surrounded by problems. These domestic squabbles are compounded by the crisis before us, and we have no money.[6]

Four days later Baji rao wrote another letter expressing his impatience due to the delay in completing the Vasai campaign,

> It is said Tahmas Quli Khan will come to the Deccan. He has no other enemy (except Marathas). He is my adversary and I am his enemy. If he does not go away, I intend to collect the entire Maratha army and cross the river Chambal and not let him come south of the river. This is a major crisis, and the job at Vasai is not yet done.[7]

In another letter to Chimaji in March 1739, Baji rao wrote,

> ...to sum up, the *paatshah* and his nobles have landed in a mess due to their lack of courage. The position of Nizam-ul-mulk is the lowest of all. It is

not proposed that the Deccan should be ruled by the *mlechhas* (Mughals) hereafter. We have to capture all their forts. If you send a wise man leading a few thousand troops, this can be done. I will settle affairs of Khandesh from Burhanpur. You should complete the affair at Vasai soon and come up the *ghats*. We have to take charge of the entire *Mughalai*. If you sit with a strong force near Aurangabad, this will be done and we will earn some *taka*. One chief will be sent to Malwa. Send men and chiefs as and when they can be freed from the tasks there. For now Tahmas Quli Khan has won. But if all the Hindus gather their courage and all our forces go north, a *paatshahi* of the Hindus will materialize. The situation looks ripe for such a situation.[8]

Watching events in the north, Baji rao remained at Burhanpur waiting for the campaign at Vasai to end.[a]

The ides of March appear to be generally unfavourable to Emperors and Caesars of each age.

Sadat Khan accompanied by Nadir Shah's escort reached the city of Delhi to find its residents closing the doors of the city in his face. A letter from Surat dated 31 March 1739 says,

> The traitor Saadul Cawn was sent with an army of 20,000 men to Dilly, where they shut the gates against him; but he with his usual perfidy, telling them that the Mogul Mahmud Shaw had beaten Nadir Shaw, and was in pursuit of him, he gain'd admittance, but was no sooner enter'd than he proclaimed Nadir Shaw king.[9]

Leaving Karnal with Muhammad Shah in tow, Nadir Shah reached Delhi on 7 March 1739 and camped at the Shalimar *Bagh*. Muhammad Shah went into the city and prepared to welcome the Persian king. On 9 March, Nadir Shah entered the city and occupied Shah Jehan's palace chamber while Muhammad Shah moved elsewhere in the fort. The Emperor hosted a dinner for Nadir, who was attended to by Sadat Khan at all times.

The same night Sadat Khan was called before Nadir Shah and questioned about the promised ransom of twenty crores, and threatened with dire consequences if he failed. The Nawab of Awadh, Burhan-ul-mulk Sadat Khan

---

a.   The occupation of Delhi and the events in those months have been written by many writers in Persian, Marathi and English. With the help of these a unified narrative is created.

was so terrified that he went home and committed suicide by taking poison. On 10 March was the festival of Id, and Nadir Shah was proclaimed the new Emperor of Delhi. A Persian narrative tells us that Nadir Shah called on Muhammad Shah and assured him of his life and his throne, as he belonged to the Turkoman race. Muhammad Shah *'bowed low in gratitude'* and brought before Nadir Shah all the treasures he could as a gift.

The city had been quiet so far. However, stray disturbances began that morning as the locals began to quarrel with the Persian soldiers. In the afternoon of 10 March, a rumour that Nadir Shah had been assassinated took root.[a] Small groups of Persian soldiery were accosted by armed gatherings and killed. The Persian soldiers, believing the rumour, could hardly resist. The night passed in this manner. When Nadir Shah heard the news, he refused to believe it. He sent a man to find out, but he was killed at the fort's gate. Another was sent, who was also killed. Nadir Shah then sent a thousand Qizalbash to clear the crowds but even they did not succeed in quelling the disturbances.

The next day, 11 March, was the festival of Holi. Nadir Shah, fully armed in his armour rode his horse to Chandni chowk and reached the *Sunehri* masjid or the Golden mosque. Here, he met with a shower of stones from the neighbourhood. Somebody fired at him and although he was unhurt, a Persian officer next to him was killed. These petty attacks led to the infamous massacre and sack of Delhi.

At the sight of his dead soldiers, the conqueror's rage was fully inflamed and he ordered a general massacre of the residents of Delhi.[11] Symbolically, he unsheathed his sword. This was taken as a signal by the Qizalbash to begin a massacre of the residents in the suburbs where these attacks had taken place. Some people fought back, but largely it was a massacre of innocents dragged from their houses with their women, and their wealth looted.

The massacre began from nine in the morning and continued for some five hours. Muhammad Shah, the Nizam and Qamruddin Khan then went to

---

a. This rumour travelled far and wide. A letter from Aurangabad three weeks later spread the 'news' as far as Pune. Nadir Shah's assassination was attributed to *pathan* guards that he had recruited from the frontier regions.[10]

Nadir Shah at the *Sunehri* masjid and begged pardon on behalf of the citizens of Delhi. The Shah relented, sheathed his sword, and sent out orders to stop the massacre. By then the estimates of those killed ranged from eight to fifty thousand men and women.

The dead were left in the streets for a few days when the stench became so overpowering that the bodies were grouped together and burnt. Many households had killed their own womenfolk to prevent them from falling in the hands of the Qizalbash. The entire area from Thanesar, north of Karnal, to thirty or forty miles around Delhi was laid waste by the Persian soldiery. In Delhi, it was as if the festival of Holi was played with blood.

On the day after Holi, Baji rao wrote to Antaji Narayan Bhanu,

> I am near Burhanpur. The plan to go to the north has been stayed. Babu rao Malhar has written to me that Nadir Shah sat on the throne. Muhammad Shah, Nizam and all other nobles are in prison. Nadir Shah has taken the Emperor and nobles' treasures. He has dug all over the city for treasure. Their property was confiscated. Nizam-ul-mulk and Qamruddin Khan's property was confiscated. Their women, leaving a few, were taken away and the rest were given to the Qizalbashes. There is pandemonium in the city. The Qizalbash killed fifty thousand people. Entry and egress from Delhi is not possible. Actions we never ever heard of, have been committed in Delhi by the Qizalbash. It is said Nadir Shah will head for Ajmer next, to the *Pir*. Hearing this, Sawai ji and others have sent their families to the hills of Udaipur. Only when a strong force from the Deccan goes north will Nadir Shah face any opposition.[12]

The Indian rulers, divided and fearful, did not know which way Nadir Shah would turn next. Sawai Jaisingh sent him a congratulatory letter. Baji rao's envoy wrote to him that he was pleased that Muhammad Shah had been removed. At the same time, he was exploring ways to face the calamity. Dhondo Govind wrote to Baji rao from Jaipur, *'It is a new creation. The Nizam's pusillanimity led to the success of Tahmasp Quli'.* He added that Jaisingh was trying to come to an agreement with Nadir Shah. On matters of policy he suggested,

> They are calling the swami here. The swami's strength is known to all. The swami should come to Malwa, which is the first target. To come there, is one policy. *Not to come, is also policy.* But if one comes, it should be with a strong army. Tahmasp Quli is not god, who will slaughter the earth. He is

Vasai fort

Chimaji Appa's statue in Vasai fort

Emperor Muhammad Shah and Nadir Shah

Shrimant Baji rao Peshwa's Samadhi

also clever. If he encounters strong resistance, he will come to an agreement. First, there should be a show of strength, then a treaty will follow. The job will be done by creating a world of illusions. If all the Rajputs and swami come together, this can be done.[13]

On 21 March 1729, Nadir Shah ordered that the Nizam and Qamruddin Khan were prohibited from riding the palanquin or an elephant.[14] The Peshwa's envoy wrote from Jaipur,

> Sawai Jaisingh arrested the Nizam's servants and killed them. Many had their nose and ear cut off. It appears that all this is the Nizam's doing. He is a defector. Nadir Shah will then not return but attack the Hindu kingdoms. He (Nizam) brought Nadir Shah to kill Khan Dauran. Immediately he was killed, the Emperor was taken to meet Nadir Shah. Sadat Khan came to Delhi to impose Nadir Shah's rule but was killed soon after. The Nizam was saved but his state is worse than that. He has to come to the court astride a mule. His rule in the Deccan has gone. In this manner, he has lost out in the affair.

The Rajputs began thinking of a way ahead. The envoy writes to Baji rao,

> Guman Singh (?) came. He said *Raya* (Baji rao) wishes that Ranaji (of Udaipur) should be seated on the throne of Delhi. Even though *Raya* is greater, the smaller kings will not bow before him, and Ranaji and *Rajashri* (Shahu) are not different. A man has gone to Abhay Singh also. However, the main thing hinges on the arrival of the swami. If in the next few days, you come with an army of even twenty-five thousand to the Narmada, it will have an impact of a one hundred thousand strong army. I tell Ranaji that *Rau* is coming north daily. But I have been saying this for two months and all the kings here have been waiting that long. With the swami's backing, the Jat and other forces will come and Sawai *ji* (Jaisingh) will go to Delhi. This is the plan. But until the swami comes to the bank of the Narmada, nothing can happen. And unless all arrangements in the Deccan are complete, the swami cannot come. That is the problem.[13]

Then, the Maratha envoy changed his advice and wrote to Baji rao,

> Tahmas the schemer's show has come to town. The Emperor's brain is not in its place. The swami should now *not* come here. In a hundred thousand ways, stay in Malwa. Even there, stay safe. Here, everybody's behaviour is strange. I will request accordingly. *Do not, do not* – come here. It is not wise. I am looking after myself. After this, on oath, I beseech you not, repeat not, to come here. A new universe has been created. There is turmoil here. [13]

In the end, Baji rao could not think of moving to the river Narmada until the Vasai campaign was over and he had enough money to fund a long campaign with a large army. He remained at Burhanpur. Vasudeo Dixit wrote to Chimaji Appa on 12 April 1739,

> *Rau* is at Burhanpur. The *yavana* from the west is sitting in Indraprasth (Delhi). He has massacred many in the city. An evil man, he is one who hates Hindus.[15]

The attack in Delhi also afforded some hope for the English in Bombay. Discussing the attack on Vasai at a meeting on 17 April 1739, they hoped *'to gain time till the rains set in when the enemy will not be able to continue in their trenches before town (Vasai), and possibly a favourable crisis may ensue, and the Marathas be either called off by the approach of Shah Nadir's troops, or on the success of an embassy sent from Goa to the Shahu raja'.*[16] These expectations were belied, as Vasai surrendered to Chimaji in early May 1739 and Nadir Shah did not come south, as was for a while expected.

In Meerut an army sent by Nadir Shah was beaten back by a local mob of forty thousand men. Then he ordered a division of fifteen thousand men to go there, punish the residents and loot the city.[13] He kept hearing rumours of the Marathas and Rajputs combining and coming to Delhi. Vigorous extortion measures were begun. The Persian king's appetite for wealth made him extort all the rich men of Delhi and gather wealth from all the city's inhabitants. Fraser describes the method used for extorting the *Wazir's* wealth,

> Qamruddin Khan, the *Wazir*, was treated with greater severity. He endeavoured to elude payment of the large contribution demanded of him; Nadir therefore caused him to be exposed openly to the sun, which is reckoned a punishment contumelious as well as painful, and in that country (India) dangerous to health. At length, he extorted from him a whole crore of rupees besides a great value in precious stones and elephants. His secretary (Majlis Rai), who was also a man of fortune, was taxed in a large sum, and delivered to Sarbuland Khan, in order to be tortured if he did not pay it; however, he prevented the persecution by a dose of poison.[1]

The lay people did not escape either. Paharganj, which had many grain merchants, and the Jama Masjid area, were the worst affected. However, the day's extortion was relieved by fireworks, animal fights and song and dance in the evenings.[a]

As the Indian summer approached, Nadir Shah began preparations to leave. He *'drew from the seraglio a virgin princess from amongst the descendants of the Emperor Shah Jehan, and married her to his younger son Mirza Nasrullah'.*[17] He obtained from the Mughals the entire territory west of the river Indus and entire provinces of Sind and Kabul besides part of Punjab. Nadir Shah looted a total treasure with an estimated value of between fifteen and seventy crore rupees. The break-up is given as thirty crores of gold and silver plate and cash, twenty-five crores of jewels, the Peacock throne and nine other thrones and weapons studded with precious stones worth nine crores, rich manufactures worth two crores, and cannon, furniture and so on worth four crores.[18] Taking the largest diamond in Mughal possession, Nadir Shah held it up and called it *'Koh-i-noor'* or the 'Mountain of Light', giving it the name it is recognized by until present time.[19] Besides these, he took one thousand elephants, ten thousand camels, seven thousand horses and masons, carpenters, stone-cutters, smiths, eunuchs and writers to build a city 'like Delhi' in Persia.

Tilak Das, who composed a poem describing those turbulent days, gives an interesting episode before the departure of the Persians. Taking Muhammad Shah along, Nadir Shah rode into town and there, he encountered a *faqir;*

> One *Almast*[b] lived in a house. Seeing his body, Nadir Shah enquired, 'You are an ascetic and holy man, show me your miracles.'
>
> Then the faqir looked and said, 'Nadir Shah, first display your own.'
>
> Then Nadir Shah said, 'Shut your eyes, behold whatever you like.'
>
> Shutting his eyes, the *faqir* saw a fine army with Nadir Shah. From Delhi to Attock was that army of Nadir. Standing fully armed, a splendid array.
>
> Opening his eyes then said the *faqir*, 'Behold, I will now show wonders,
>
> Shut your eyes and look!' Then when the Shah had closed them, he saw,
>
> The soldiers the *faqir* had seen arrayed, all lying headless. Then said the Shah, 'Holy man! Look favourably on me.'
>
> Then spoke the faqir, 'If you wish to be preserved,
>
> Delay not one moment, at once set out for Kabul.'
>
> Then Nadir Shah sent for his men, and ordered them to march.[20]

---

a. Infatuated with Nur bai, one of the dancing girls of Delhi, Nadir Shah wished to take her back to Persia. It was with some difficulty that she extricated herself from this honour.

b. A mystic.

On 1 May 1739, Nadir Shah held a special farewell *durbar*, and honoured Muhammad Shah with all his nobles with robes and gifts of jewelled swords and horses. They were all told to obey Muhammad Shah. With his own hands, Nadir Shah placed the crown on Muhammad Shah's head and tied a sword to his waist. Muhammad Shah bowed and thanked him and formally announced the award of Kabul and Sind to the Persian king. Nadir Shah sent four *firmans* to Indian rulers to obey Muhammad Shah.[a]

On 5 May, with the treasure already on its way, after a brief halt at the Shalimar *Bagh*, Nadir Shah began his march back to his country. The India summer was upon the invaders. He therefore chose a more northward route hugging the foot of the Himalayas. By the last week of May, he was on the Chenab at the town of Akhnoor. Here, as he was crossing, the bridge of boats on the river swollen with water from the melting ice of the mountains was swept away. The inhabitants had fled to the mountains and when Nadir Shah's boats were ready to cross the Chenab, they cut and thre large trees into the river. These came at great speed from the mountains and crashed *'with such violence against the boats, as broke the chains asunder, and a great number of people perished'*.[21] In the rapid currents two thousand Persians were killed. Boats were lost. He had to wait here for forty days until a fresh bridge was built and he crossed the Chenab only in early July 1739. From here, he sent back many Indians taken as slaves at the request of Zakaria Khan. Thereafter he passed through the Khyber and reached Kabul.

An English newspaper of 1740 reported news from India that year,

> Letters from Surat say, that the Scha Nadir had married one of the princesses of the Empire, and his son another, and had replaced the Great Mogul on his throne; but on his return he found the bridges of the river Attock broken down, by which he lost a great part of his treasure.[22]

The people in Persia enjoyed the fruits of the treasure as he remitted all taxes for three years. His soldiers received a sumptuous bonus for their labours. Behind him he left the Mughal Empire in complete disarray. The Marathas did not take advantage of their misery. Shahu was beholden to Aurangzeb and had no desire to supplant the Mughals. In a letter sent by his

---

a.   See Appendix 7.

secretary to Baji rao, he laid a clear document of policy that he wanted the Peshwa to follow:

> Muhammad Shah had lost his *paatshahi*, but God has maintained it. You should remain as the *Amir ul Umara* and behave accordingly. For the maintenance of armies, we will generate the money and give the excess for the *Paatshah*'s treasury. Ask for *jagir*s, and rearrange the affairs of the Empire. There is credit in such behaviour. If you ask me how, it is like repairing an old temple than building a new one. Arranging Muhammad Shah's affairs has merit, to break it, has no merit. Thousands of thieves will take away pieces of the Empire and we will be blamed for destroying it. Secondly, the *Chhatrapati* swami also does not desire the *paatshahi*. He will be happy if you resurrect it. Babu rao Malhar has written thus. He has also written that Ghaziuddin Khan can be called to arrange affairs in the Deccan. By this measure, there will be no obstacle in the south. After Nadir Shah's departure it is not meritorious to have small disputes all over.[23]

The Nizam stayed back in Delhi as the Emperor would not let him return to the Deccan.

Twenty years of continuous campaigning had led to the accrual of Malwa, Gujarat and Bundelkhand to the Marathas. Konkan was captured from the Portuguese. The Nizam had been humbled. It appeared all tasks had been completed, and the monsoon months of 1739 were spent by the entire Peshwa family together in Pune after many years.

In the circumstances, they did not pass as peacefully as expected.

၁၈၆၃၈၆

# 33. An Olive Branch from Mumbai

> 'The conquests of the brother of Bajirav first turned the attention of the President and Council at Bombay towards the Marathas. The marauding savages, as they called them, had descended from their mountains on the rich fields of the Konkan, and had begun to attack with success fortresses manned by the countrymen of the great Albuquerque.'[1]

The English in Mumbai, a group of tiny islands on India's west coast, wielded far greater power than the area they controlled. Their weapons were superior although it was their trade that dictated their actions. There was, of course, the rivalry with other European powers for preferential trading rights in India. Still, they were sorry to see their neighbours, the Portuguese, evicted by the Marathas. The Portuguese were far more entrenched than the English and militarily had a long line of forts. However, the Marathas led by a determined Chimaji Appa had won the entire northern *Firangan* after a war that claimed twenty-two thousand Maratha lives. Moreover, he had given them generous terms, and let them sail away unmolested. The fort of Bandra however, had extensive fortifications and overlooked Mumbai; the English therefore ensured it was destroyed before the Portuguese capitulated.[2]

The Mumbai board now sat and discussed how to appease their new neighbours, and within days of the Vasai victory, an embassy led by Captain Inchbird and Gordon was given instructions and sent to meet Chimaji Appa and *Chhatrapati* Shahu. They were given detailed instructions on what answers they ought to give and how they should refuse any demand for ammunition or a loan of money. The professions of friendship were to be accompanied by the refrain that they were only traders and merely sought access to markets without having to pay high levies.

When Inchbird reached Vasai, Chimaji did not actively participate in the talks, as he was indisposed. Chimaji had been unwell for a few years. A letter he wrote to Shahu around that time speaks of his illness,

> I have received the Maharaj's summons from Ramchandra Mirdhe. I have been ordered to come immediately. What can be more than the order of

the Maharaj for this servant? On return from a campaign, it is only right that I first see the feet of the Maharaj. That the servant delays, is due to the extreme illness he is suffering from. I have no strength to even go out of the house. Ramchandra Mirdhe saw my state. The body has become very weak. There is no strength to come out of the house and sit in the palanquin. Once I am better, I will come without any further orders from the Maharaj.[3]

Inchbird therefore spoke to many of Chimaji's subordinates who then reported to him. Speaking to Khandoji Mankar who insisted on a loan, Inchbird declared, *'the Company would sooner see the island of Bombay sunk under water than they could or would comply with such a request'*. Inchbird was questioned closely about the help the English offered the Siddi in the past and the ammunition they gave the Portuguese, which cost the Marathas so many lives, and Inchbird answered as diplomatically as he could. However, the decision to send an envoy to Shahu without consulting Chimaji or the Peshwa was deeply resented. Inchbird reports,

> They greatly resent your not consulting them in it first; and though I have been at much pains to persuade them to the contrary, yet they still persist, as they were our neighbours we ought first of all to have made our application to them, when they would not only have given us a safe conduct, but, also, sent a proper person along with us to introduce us to the Shahu Raja. They harp so much upon this step, that in case Captain Gordon has any instructions to create a jealousy in Shahu Raja of Bajirav's greatness, you may depend upon it they have it.[4]

William Gordon, the second English envoy, made his way up the Danda Rajpuri river. The Siddi's men escorted him and then the *Pratinidhi's* representative took over. The English discovered later that they had erred in taking the help of the *Pratinidhi* as it offended Baji rao, but had done so on the Siddi's recommendation. Gordon was stopped at many checkpoints as he did not have a pass from the Peshwa or Chimaji, but showing his papers, he was given an escort to Satara where he reached on 23 May 1739, less than two weeks after Vasai was captured.

Shahu was away from Satara. He had gone to attack the Mughal fort of Miraj, and Gordon went there to meet him. He passed through Rahimatpur and Amrapur before first meeting the *Pratinidhi* on 2 June 1739. On 7 June

Gordon visited Shahu, taken to him by Mahadji Purandare, who told the king that the English had come to solicit his friendship. He answered, *'they are a good sort of people, and if I give them protection, will Baji rao molest them?'* Mahadji answered in the negative, and Shahu said keeping good terms with the English would be a greater gain.

Shahu was pleased by the gift of birds that Gordon brought with him. Gordon learnt that Baji rao was then at Burhanpur and had asked for a large army and stores to be sent to him. There was a possibility of Nadir Shah coming to the Deccan. Shahu, according to Gordon, heard this and plucking vehemently at his turban, said, *'Will Vasai and all our new acquisitions make amends for twenty-two thousand brave men lost there?'*

Gordon first met the principal officers of Shahu's court. He next called on the seventeen-year-old Nanasaheb. Gordon reported that Nanasaheb was *'very inquisitive to know the motives of our coming. He seemed to disregard us, and we are informed he entertained a high jealousy of us.'* On 10 June came news that Nadir Shah had departed. Vyankat rao Ghorpade returned from his victorious campaign at Goa on 19 June. According to Gordon, Shahu *'advanced a small distance to meet him; but the other declined it, alleging he owed no sort of subjection to the Raja, on which the latter turned aside to hunt; but Baji rao's son (Nanasaheb) on hearing of it, prevailed on the General to wait on the Raja afterwards, excusing the late error, which the Raja seemed pleased with.'*

On 25 June, Gordon left, and Shahu requested him to *'send eight Guinea hens, two pairs of turkeys, some Basra pigeons, a little mummy and any kinds of curious birds'.* On 26 June, Gordon met Nanasaheb once again, who treated him 'civilly', and gave a trifling present for the Governor, excusing himself for not being able to give anything better.

Shahu's interactions with the English appear quite startling for the ruler of so large an Empire. A strange belief prevailed at Satara that the envoy had left behind a gold cow and calf below the *ghats* as he could not carry it up. On 27 June, Shahu sent a man to enquire about it. Gordon denied the rumour and said they were mere traders and a peaceable people. Shahu then enquired why they *'meddle with my servants, the Angres?'* On Gordon's professions of peace and desire for commerce, Shahu said, *'that will be of small utility to me, as I have assigned the whole to Baji rao'.*

On 30 June 1739 Gordon left Satara for Pune, as he was returning by a different route. Of Pune he remarked,

> That place seems well built, and abounds with people, and is the chief residence of Bajirav, who has a great extent of country, to appearance more fertile and valuable than any other I had passed through. I visited the foundry, where I saw many coehorns[a] and bomb shells said to have been cast there, and a form of a thirteen-inch mortar. I was told they make such with great ease, and have learned the art of running iron for making shot. Bajirav is said to give great encouragement to weavers for fabricing such things as are useful to the natives, and whereof great quantities are imported to Bombay and other parts. His territories are well peopled, and the poorer sort, in the farming way, are rendered easy in their rents, which causes his extent of dominion to be in a very flourishing condition, more so than any other in the possession of the Marathas.

Gordon did not get a chance to meet Baji rao. He passed through Thana on his way back and reached Mumbai on 14 July 1739, where he gave his report to Stephen Law, the Governor. The confidential impressions of this emissary give us an insight into the working of the Maratha power at the time. Concluding his report he wrote,

> By the best intelligence I could obtain, the Shahu Raja had approved of the seizing of Thana and the island of Salsette; *but the attack on Bassein was undertaken without his consent*, not being desirous of the total expulsion of the Portuguese. But as Bajirav's power is uncontrolled by whomsoever, the Raja is compelled to an exercise of an outward civility to him.

> I was not able to come at the real views or intentions of Bajirav, though it was the general voice he had no design of molesting Bombay, as it is esteemed useful for advancing the prosperity of his new acquisitions. The Jogis mentioned under the 23rd June (who seem to be well acquainted with the state of the whole) assured me there was no present design on foot in prejudice of us; and certain they were the Raja had a good opinion of us, as had all others, and this I found confirmed by the several discourses I had with the principal men.

> The sentiments of most are that Bajirav has in view to throw off his allegiance to the Raja, after making his efforts in levying a large sum from the Mogal's dominions, which he intended to execute speedily, and then set heartily about equipping a considerable force.[5]

---

a. A kind of a mortar.

Many of Gordon's assumptions of Baji rao's future course of action were of course based on what he heard from others. Despite never having met the Peshwa he sketched a picture of an all-powerful minister who had overawed the king with full control over his armies:

> Bajirav had forty thousand soldiers; but what number were gone towards Goa I could not perfectly learn, nor how many were this way. It is certain they can raise large armies with much facility. He is very secret in his purposes, insomuch that the forces which attend him are often ignorant where he intends to lead them. They follow him with an implicit obedience.

> I have throughout the foregoing hinted at the power of Bajirav, who will always be capable of rendering abortive any application made to the Shahu Raja, and probably show his resentment thereat; so that although a civil correspondence with the said Raja may not be amiss, care must be taken that he is not solicited for what interferes with Bajirav, whose authority at court is even such, that in the absence of the Raja, and contrary to the advice of the seven principal Counsellors, he can enforce a complete obedience to his sole mandates.

In this manner in the nineteenth year of Baji rao's reign as Peshwa, Gordon found him in complete command; and along with his brother Chimaji, the arbitrar of fortunes of the Maratha state. However, his instructions to his subordinates, as well as Nanasaheb's advice to Vyankat rao Ghorpade to pay his respects to Shahu, are examples of their probity and regard for the king. That their lieutenants, often carried away by the success of the two brothers, might omit the courtesy due to the king, was guarded against and corrected when the need arose. Moreover, Baji rao himself followed all the courtesies due to his king as can be seen by his letter of 21 April 1739 to Mahadji Purandare, advising him on observing all the courtesies due to the king:

> God has given us a big success. You are part of this success and you will be attending the king's court. Let me know what you say and what discussions take place there. On your part, there should absolutely be no severity or unrestrained behaviour.[6]

After Gordon's meeting with Shahu, the king sent a letter to Chimaji and Baji rao about having good relations with the English, *'who are honest and sincere'*. The Marathi letter to Chimaji Appa says,

> The English from the past have been behaving with sincerity towards this kingdom. At present, from Mumbai General Stephen Law's emissary at *qasba* Miraj, Captain Wilem Gardan (William Gordon) came to meet the swami. He came and spoke of many honest and sincere things. It therefore appears, the English way is that of merchants and they have behaved with honesty and fidelity towards the swami's kingdom. In future too, they will behave in the same manner. To secure the pleasure and blessings of the swami is in their mind. The swami also welcomes this in many ways. You have a good relation with them. You should behave in a manner that increases the affection between them and yourself. The English are true to their word. They will not move away from their profession of affection for us, and you know this. Therefore you should do the needful to take this forward. Let it be known. *You are prudent.* [7, a]

Keeping in mind Shahu's wishes to have good relations with the English, Baji rao replied to Stephen Law's letter on 26 June 1739,

> I have received your Excellency's letter and observed the contents, by which I likewise am advised that your Excellency has entered upon the Government of the island of Bombay, and that you desire a correspondence of friendship with the Most Serene Raja, and it is fitting that your Excellency should desire the continuance thereof.
>
> The contentment which the victorious success actually obtained by my arms has given Your Excellency and which you congratulate upon, was just. Your Excellency writes me that your island subsists by trade to the great benefit and advantage of the neighbouring countries, and that in regard to the interest of the subject and the improvement of the good of the country I should concur with the favour of my assistance thereto. And my desire is that the subjects should be advantaged, the trade be continued, and that our State have its interest and profits, and your Excellency will, I hope, with the continuance of your friendship contribute to the above ends more and more every day. [8]

Maratha-English relations remained stable and peaceful then. Baji rao had no reason to move against Mumbai. The embassy of Inchbird and Gordon

---

a.  The last three words are in the king's own hand. The original letter is now in London and the author has a copy. The same letter is translated a little differently by GW Forrest, Selections, Vol. 1, pg 83-4. see plate 8.

ensured their security. The Marathas even appeared to look upon the English with bemusement. The traders, by sticking to business and staying away from interference in the religious affairs of the Indians, did not antagonise the people and the rulers.

The island of Mumbai, secure from Maratha invasions, continued its trade and prospered.

৯৫৩৯৫

# Book Five

## The Eclipse

*Rajashri* Shahu's wish is that it should not be that what *Rau* likes should be kept away, detained or put under guard; and if *Rau* is unhappy on that count, and one still does so, is not good. What he likes should be given to him. Keep him happy. Bad habits are not due to the thing he desires. Only when he regrets it will he stop indulging in it. In view of the above, do not stop the thing (that he loves) and hurt a dear one, is the king's wish.

- Govindrao Chitnis to Nanasaheb, 21 January 1740.


If the Maharaj asks, please inform him. If he sends all the armies now, the time is ripe to liberate all six *subahs* of the Deccan.

- Baji rao to Mahadji Purandare, 7 February 1740.


Whatever Baji rao decides to do, he does. The Peshwa is in full control of his destiny.

- *Chhatrapati* Shahu.

# Rewa Uvach

The Mughal Empire had met its death blow. The second power to face the same calamity in the same year was that of the Firangi Portuguese. Coincidentally these two Empires began at almost the same time and although the European power did not spread into the hinterland, they formed an extremely well entrenched fanatical state.

There the similarities end. The reduction of Vasai and the brutal sack of Delhi in the same months of the year were a study in contrast. In Delhi, the Persian conqueror came to loot, won a military victory and then proceeded to humiliate the Mughal nobility before stripping them of all their wealth and vanity. Women were taken away in thousands by the invader and his men, from the ordinary householder to the palace; men were slaughtered, houses dug up for wealth, nobles tortured, and the most ignominious defeat that could be was inflicted on the people of Delhi. Muhammad Shah, sunk under decades of pleasure and vice, could do nothing more than bow his head, which to his good fortune still stayed on his body. The pompous nobles of the realm met a worse fate. Khan Dauran died in battle, Sadat Khan committed suicide, Qamruddin Khan was stripped and 'exposed' to the sun, and the Nizam's property and harem raided while he was forced to abandon his palanquin for a mule.

In Vasai, the victorious Chimaji Appa was a picture of restraint and moderation. The battle had been hard and the enemy valiant. The loss in men was colossal for the Marathas. The citadel of Vasai lay open to abuse and to loot. The pindaries in the Maratha army could have rampaged through the remains of Portuguese possessions and burnt them to the ground. Yet, Chimaji and Pilaji Jadhav rao gave their enemy the privilege to be treated like 'a king'. They went out with their heads high, in uniforms, playing their band to sail away on ships requisitioned and paid for by the victor. Their women and families were not just respected but protected, honoured and returned to their families. The contrast in the two victors could not have been starker or the tenets of the 'Bharati' war better defined.

The decimation of the two powers meant the Marathas stepped into the space of being India's paramount power despite Shahu's pretensions of being the amir ul umara of the Mughal Emperor. Baji rao's letter to Chimaji clearly laid out his objectives of taking over the Mughalai – all Mughal assets in the north and the south – and for a while there was even talk of the Rana of Udaipur being placed on the throne of Delhi. This did not happen when Nadir Shah placed Muhammad Shah on the throne before his departure. Even if it had, the Rana would have been a ruler without power and beholden to the Maratha Peshwa.

The year 1739 thus marked a climactic change in the Indian political milieu; it was actually the shell of the Mughal Empire that lingered on, often miserably, for the next hundred odd years. The Portuguese restricted themselves to Goa from then on until the present Indian state evicted them in 1961.

It was time to grasp the prize and pronounce the Marathas to be guardians of India's destiny. However, this did not happen and destiny had something else in store over the next year or so. Even then, the Marathas had to tread the path towards supremacy in India and this was to lead to another climactic year two decades later in the fields of Panipat north of Delhi.

There was time on hand for the Marathas. Their enemies had vanished. The long campaigns were done. It was time to consolidate. That was when domestic turbulence reared its head and the rumbling began, this time, nearer home. Looking back, it was perhaps long overdue and inevitable.

Stormy days lay ahead, and the finale had to be played out on the bank of the Rewa. That is the reason I saw it all.

꒰ꙅꙅꙅ꒱

# 34. Family Affairs: Mastani

'...the Peshwa chased away Bangash and reinstated Chhatrasal to the throne. At that time, he divided the kingdom in three parts and gave one part to the Peshwa. And from his palace, the woman named Mastani, who had a beautiful face, the king gave to the Peshwa.'

A document from Banda.[1]

Baji rao, named as Visaji at birth after his grandfather, was born 18 August 1700 at Dubare, near Nashik. His younger brother was named Antaji, later better known as ChimajiAppa. His exact date of birth is not known but was about five or six years younger than Baji rao. Baji rao married Kashi bai of the Barve family around 1710. Baji rao's son Balaji, better known as Nanasaheb, was born in 1721, followed by another son named Ramachandra in 1723, who died when he was barely ten.

Baji rao had a strong constitution unlike Chimaji, who suffered from a chest ailment; either asthma or that medieval scourge Tuberculosis. Chimaji was married to Rakhma bai, sister of Trimbakrao Pethe, the latter day Maratha General, in 1716. Chimaji's son was Sadashiv rao Bhau, who was born in August 1730. Rakhma bai died within a month of his birth and Chimaji married Annapurna bai in December that year.

That Baji rao was an attractive man has been recorded in many *bakhars*. The Peshwa *bakhar* describes a scene where the women of Aurangabad wished to see him. In another meeting with the Nizam the *bakhar* describes how the womenfolk saw him in the Nizam's tent and showered him with pearls.[2] An anecdote, possibly of the 1730s, describes Emperor Muhammad Shah as curious to learn what the bold Peshwa looked like. He sent an artist to draw a sketch for his benefit.

Catching a glimpse of the Peshwa in a candid moment, the artist made a sketch and described him to his master. A later poet put it in verse,

तुरंगमावरी मूर्ती शोभे एक रिकिबीत पाय
दुजा आडवा घोड्यावरती, घोडा ठुमकत जाय

मानेवरती ठेऊनि दिधली अनीन घोड्याची ती
स्कंधी भाला हसत मुखावरी शोभे अनुपम कांती
मंदिल मस्तकी रुभरि आंगी अंगरखा तो साजे
पचंग कटीला वस्त्र नेसले ब्राह्मणघाटीचे जें
स्वताच हाती कणसे चोळुनी दाणे टाकी वदनी
लाल ठेविल्या मिरच्या त्यातुनी खाई मधुनी मधुनी.[3]

Translated, it means,

'Atop a horse, with one foot in the stirrup,
and the second across, the horse trots along...

The reins thrown over the neck,
a spear on his shoulder, a smile beatifies a face of indescribable lustre;

A *zari* turban on his head, a befitting robe on the body,
the garment around the waist tied in Brahminical style,

He rubs the ear of corn with his own hands,
and throws the grain in his mouth,

And the red chillies he carries, he chews - now and then'.

Hearing this, the Emperor exclaimed, '*this is but the Devil'!*[4]

Children were married at a young age in the eighteenth century and the Peshwa family was no exception. There were no brides to be had beyond the age of nine! Nanasaheb was married to Gopika bai, daughter of the Raste family of moneylenders based in Wai, on 11 January 1730. A day earlier, the foundation stone of the great palace of the Peshwas, the *Shaniwar wada*, was laid at Pune. A large enclosure within the old *kot* of Pune was erected for the ceremony. The famous danseuse Mastani had come to Pune after Baji rao's campaign in Bundelkhand. Her first documented performance was on this occasion when she was paid paid a hundred rupees for her dance at Nanasaheb's wedding,[5] and it appears that from that time the Peshwa and the danseuse began to be drawn towards each other. After staying in Pune, Baji rao and Mastani were enamoured of each other and a separate place was built by Baji rao for Mastani to live within the *Shaniwar wada* complex.

When Mastani came to Pune in 1729 she was nearly fifteen years old, well past the age when girls were usually married in the eighteenth century. Mastani is generally accepted to be a daughter of Chhatrasal and his Muslim mistress. However, there are other stories. An intriguing letter written to the Peshwa says,

> We are pleased that *Saheb* has returned home after a major triumph. Again, we are pleased that Mastani is with *Saheb*. If you feel anything is wrong, we take an oath at the feet of *Saheb*. We have not been properly looked after. *Saheb* is almighty. It is not as if we need to make a request. But the people think our daughter has been taken from us; so do not do this. Send her for two months, and then we will send her back. We will come when summoned. *Saheb* is aware of our welfare…[6]

The letter lends itself to a different interpretation that Chhatrasal obtained Mastani from a person who trained girls from a young age in music and dance before sending them to rich patrons.[7]

The *Tarikh-i-Muhammadshahi* says,

> She was a *kaanchani* (dancing girl) possessing fine horsemanship and skill in handling the sword and the spear. She always accompanied Baji rao in his campaigns and rode stirrup to stirrup with him.[7]

Another unsubstantiated account of Mastani's origin is given in the Peshwa *bakhar*. It says Mastani was in the entourage of a Mughal officer named Shahajat Khan who had come south to attack the Nizam. Baji rao being away in Bundelkhand, Chimaji was sent to help the Nizam. Chimaji approached Shahajat Khan instead, and offered him help in subduing the Nizam. Then a few days later, Chimaji suddenly attacked the Khan and completely defeated him. There, in the dead Khan's tent, Chimaji found a beautiful woman preparing to consume poison. The *bakhar* describes her as one so fair that while swallowing a *'paan',*[a] its red juice could be seen even as she swallowed it. Chimaji asked her the reason for wanting to take her own life, and she said, *'there is none who will have me and who can look after me. Will you'?* Chimaji said he had an elder brother who was away, and it would be in fitness of things if he presented her to him. Mastani then came with Chimaji, who presented her to Baji rao. Baji rao was infatuated with her.

---

a.  Betel leaf with many condiments in it that is chewed commonly in India.

*Mastani*
(See 'Notes to Illustrations')

Seeing this, Mastani took a pledge from Baji rao that he would give a share of his kingdom to any son she would have of him. To this, Baji rao agreed.[8]

Borrowing from the *Peshwa bakhar*, the *Bhatt Vansha-kavya* composed in 1893 gives a description of Mastani in Shahajat Khan's camp,

'अन्य नरा दृष्टिस ही अगम्या

मस्तानि नामे भुवनैक रम्या

स्वस्त्रीसही किंबहुना सुनम्या

वेश्या असे शाजत खान गम्या'

'Who no other man could see,

Mastani, the beauty of the world,

The one to who even the *apsaras* would bow to,

Was the mistress of Shahajat Khan.'[9]

Unfortunately, this last account is wholly unsubstantiated by any *contemporary* letter or document of the period. The romance of Baji rao and

Mastani, a Hindu Brahmin Peshwa and his Muslim mistress, eventually led to a marriage of a kind that is not described in any of the documents of the era.

Baji rao, born a Brahmin, had adopted the life of a *Kshatriya* – the warrior class in the Hindu caste system – and spent most of the year with his men. A healthy camaraderie prevailed between the Peshwa and his men, barriers of caste along with injunctions of the era dropped by the wayside as the Peshwa campaigned in the north, saw the life of the nobles and the kings and bit by bit became a man with a more 'worldly' view. His family, comprising his mother Radha bai, his wife Kashi bai and his brother Chimaji, remained more conservative and traditional. The rules of caste were very strong in the eighteenth century, as indeed they still are in some pockets of India, and Baji rao's consumption of meat or spirits was frowned upon in the conservative setup of Pune and Maharashtra. How much of Baji rao's indulgence of spirits and meat was due to Mastani and how much was due to his own outdoor campaigning with his soldiers is difficult to say. That it did not materially affect his military exploits is clear. However, a belief grew over the days that the association with Mastani was to blame for such errant behaviour by the Brahmin Prime Minister.

In 1734 and 1735, Baji rao had two more children by Kashi bai, named Raghunath – the later Raghoba *dada* – and Janardan. Janardan did not live beyond his early teens but a few of his letters survive him. Shamsher Bahadur was born to Mastani around 1734 and later became an important part of the Peshwa family, and the army, is well documented. By itself this was not unusual in the royalty of that age and children were often born to women out of wedlock or in the harem. Mastani, of course, as the beloved of the Peshwa, was much more than that. Instances of children born of women who were not married to the nobles and the royals are well known, and some even featured in history. Mastani's son Shamsher Bahadur too was raised in the manner of any other son of the Peshwa.

An old document from the archives of the future Nawabs of Banda gives us this story '...*the Peshwa chased away Bangash and reinstated Chhatrasal to the throne. At that time, he divided the kingdom in three parts and gave one part to the Peshwa. And from his palace, the woman named Mastani who had a beautiful face, the king gave to the Peshwa*'.[1] An old Marathi *bakhar* says, '*In Saka 1658 (1736 CE), the work of the wada (Shaniwar palace) was completed.*

*Mastani the courtesan was kept there. A place was given to her in the palace.*[10] Later this part of the palace was called Mastani mahal. A door of the *Shaniwar wada* near her dwelling came to be known as the Mastani *darwaza*.

There was therefore a tacit acceptance of Mastani's special place in Baji rao's life. Mastani was supposed to be skilled not just in horse-riding but in the use of the common weapons of the day. It is said she rode stirrup to stirrup with the Peshwa on a tall horse. Baji rao, whose life was spent in campaigning across the length and breadth of the country most of the year, found her company stimulating and enjoyable. In addition to Shamsher Bahadur, she gave birth to two daughters who did not survive infancy. Through the decade from 1730 when she first appeared at Pune, Mastani and Baji rao's wife Kashi bai lived in the same house without any apparent animosity. Their sons grew up together.

Baji rao and Chimaji were occupied with the many campaigns in different parts of the country over many years. On Nadir Shah's return to Persia, Baji rao came to Pune on 27 July 1739. Chimaji returned to Pune from Vasai on 3 September, when Baji rao went forth to receive him at Aundh near Pune. Nanasaheb, who was with Shahu in his campaign to capture the fort of Miraj, also came to Pune.

The first rumblings that all was not well began at this time. Baji rao, living among his family after a long time, was not his usual self. His attachment to Mastani was strong, but his life outdoors had led to some fondness for drink, and a taste for meat. These habits were not unusual in the northern nobility and it was not out of place that a soldier-General who campaigned seven or eight months a year over nearly two decades would remain true to the Brahminical upbringing and culture of a conservative household. In the eighteenth century, these habits were attributed to his association with Mastani. It is difficult to deny the influence of the lady in Baji rao's life and it is possible that she did not discourage these familiar practices. Any neglect of administrative responsibilities was blamed on the Peshwa's habits. The people of Pune began to hear of these and a whisper campaign began against him. Baji rao's conduct was openly frowned upon. Men from his community at Pune openly advocated a social boycott of the Peshwa.

An anecdote in the Peshwa *bakhar* illustrates the quandary not just before Baji rao's family, but even what Shahu faced at the time,

> On a visit to Satara accompanied by Mastani, Baji rao during his entire stay of two to four months, would hardly attend the king's court but would stay at home with the courtesan. He would not utter his wife's name. Shahu Maharaj heard of this. Shahu summoned two moneylenders named Joshi and Angal who were close to Baji rao and asked them to meet the Peshwa and tell him, 'in your stay here, you have hardly come to meet me twice. You are spending eight *prahar* of a day with a *kanchani*. This will not do. If you do not come to your senses, you will be removed from your appointment.' The two spoke to the Peshwa and passed on Shahu's message. Then Baji rao told the duo, 'I will behave as before. But I don't think I can leave her.' The Maharaj assented. Then Baji rao stayed there for a week or two and attended court regularly.[11]

This anecdote is supported by a letter written by Nanasaheb in January 1740 where he says Baji rao *'has lost the king's pleasure'*.[12]

Within the Peshwa's household, Baji rao and Chimaji revered their mother Radha bai. To her, it appeared that her elder son's 'habit' came in the way of his administration and public conduct, and was owed to his association with Mastani. Many letters of the time give us but an incomplete picture of the stormy events in those four months till April 1740. Mention about the Peshwa is guarded and often couched allegorically.

The Peshwa's wife Kashi bai, known as *'Tai'* in the household, was a lady who peaceably lived through all the trials and tribulations her husband faced. On occasion she accompanied him on his campaigns. References are available of her visit to Rajputana with Baji rao. There are also letters from Malwa in the year 1737, when both Kashi bai and Mastani accompanied the Peshwa. Kashi bai was often unwell in the 1730s and there are references of many kinds of medicines and treatments, including 'bathing in the sea' that were tried out.[13] She seemed to be afflicted by some form of trouble in her legs.[14] Later, one finds she travelled to Kashi in 1746, and lived until 1758.

Radhabai, as the head of the household, asked Chimaji to speak to Baji rao and bring him round to acceptable social mores by using some 'intelligent means'.[15] Chimaji spoke to Baji rao and the Peshwa gave assurances; however, these were not followed. Chimaji, who had to leave on a campaign, then sought his nephew and Baji rao's son Nanasaheb's help to separate Mastani and Baji rao, and eliminate his habit. To gain her confidence, Chimaji advised Nanasaheb to become Mastani's friend and influence her relation with the Peshwa.[16]

Nanasaheb began befriending Mastani around the middle of 1739. This process of gaining Mastani's confidence lasted about four months. However, when Mastani learnt that Nanasaheb's pretended friendship was to separate her from Baji rao, she summoned a clerk named Baburao Ganesh in August 1739. Baburao conveyed to Nanasaheb what she had to say,

> I have been sincere in my friendly conduct with Nana for four to six months. However, for the last few months there is not even a chit from him. My name was stigmatised with Nana and even Chimaji. On the birthday of Lord Krishna, I performed a dance. Then *Tai* came and said she received Nana's letter. Seeing this, Mastani felt, '*Tai* gets a letter every eight days or so. What wrong have I done? This is not in keeping with friendship.'[17]

In the process, after two or three escorted meetings, Mastani was one day invited to come without an escort. A few weeks later Kashi bai returned from her visit to the river Bhima, and spoke to Nanasaheb about his father Baji rao and about Mastani. Nanasaheb reported the conversation to Chimaji,

> I spoke to the revered mother *Tai* once or twice. (*Tai* said) 'He has promised *that he will not take again*.[a] In the past, on one or two occasions he took after promising, so I asked him about it. Then he said I will not come to you and sent a message with Subrao *Jethi*.' This confounded her. This is what has transpired so far. Yesterday, *Tai* called Krishna bhat and said that while she was away to the river Bhima for the eclipse, 'there is growing friendship between her (Mastani) and Nana. Two *prahar* into the night she visited Nana here today. People outside are talking that Nana and Mastani have become friends.' Tai will write this to swami, hence I am conveying this to you. I will do as you command. Mastani is here, I have to go to *Rajashri* swami in eight or ten days.[17]

Nanasaheb sought to clear himself of any blame and unworthy conduct in this letter to Chimaji, and in a later letter, expresses relief to find Mastani has left Pune. The seventeen-year-old Nanasaheb was following his uncle

---

a.   A reference to Baji rao where he says he will not take alcohol again.

Chimaji's advice, but found it difficult to walk the tightrope between securing Mastani's confidence and obtaining the objective of keeping her away from the Peshwa. To Nanasaheb's letter Chimaji replied that he will have to continue his efforts.[16]

In September 1739 Nanasaheb wrote to Mahadji Purandare, referring to Baji rao, '*Not much of work is being done administratively. When Ramachandra baba*[a] *calls him, he comes.*'[18] The Peshwa who efficiently disposed off his enemies in battle could not find a way to resist public opinion and his family's insistence that he stay away from his lady love. On 1 November 1739, he left Pune to campaign against Nasir Jung. Mastani was at Pune at the time. On his departure, she was restrained from leaving the palace and going to Baji rao. Another letter written in 1739 speaks of some restraint on the Peshwa due to Chimaji's presence in court. Mastani is reported to be scared and worried.[19]

On 14 November 1739, when Baji rao was at the town of Patas, Mastani fled from Pune and joined him. The Purandare diary mentions,

> On *Margesh war (Margashirsh?) shuddha 5, Mandwari*[b], Mastani, *Raya's* dancing girl, left her mansion and went to the *Raya* at Patas. Her association with *Raya* was extremely close hence *Raya* became fond of amorous pleasures. Therefore Appa and the revered mother told *Raya* to stay away from her for four days and kept her in the mansion. So that she does not go out to *Raya*, guard posts were placed. Angrily *Raya* left for Kurkumbh ….and then went and stayed at Patas. She could not stay without him and nor could he, so she intelligently escaped and made her way to Patas.[20]

Nanasaheb was somewhat relieved when Mastani left Pune and reached Patas. He wrote to Chimaji, '*Mastani has gone from here. A big doubt about me has been resolved.*'[21]

On 1 December 1739 Mahadji Purandare went to Patas and spoke 'words of wisdom' to the Peshwa, and Mastani was sent back to Pune. A letter says, '*let us hope the matter is resolved without loss of face or prestige and harm to the state.*'[17]

In December 1739, there were plans for Sadashiv rao's wedding and Raghunath rao's thread ceremony in Pune to be held in the month of February

---

a.  A diplomat of the times.
b.  Saturday, 14 November 1739.

the following year. It was expected that Shahu would attend the events. At this time, Chimaji wrote to Radhabai that he had spoken to *Rau* and advised him. He added, '*He is better, and is having his meals regularly*'.[22]

In the background of conservative eighteenth-century societal norms, Chimaji Appa's letter of 6 January 1740 to Nanasaheb, throws light on the Peshwa's public conduct,

> Rau was going on his horse. He was not so alert when a village headman came to meet him. So he carelessly told the headman that it is his desire to have some chicken and he should get it for him. He does not realize what he says. These thoughts have arisen from Mastani. When that nuisance goes, one will earn merit. You have written to post guards around the camp. However, it is not possible to do so hence it was not done. It will be detrimental to our reputation. If Mastani complains about events at your end, it will help me to deny them.[23]

Chimaji was coaxing Baji rao to give up alcohol. The Peshwa was also willing to do so. In his letter of 12 January to Nanasaheb, Chimaji makes this clear,

> He (Baji rao) has thought he will use the water of Ganga brought from Garhmukteshwar. He said he should bathe with that water and then I should also do the same. Then he will place the water on my palm and promise that if Mastani is brought to him, he will stop drinking in a month or two. In fact, he will stop from that very day. He first asked Baloba to give me this message. Then again, he asked him not to tell me. He cannot control himself and once I leave, and Mastani is near him, he will indulge in it even more.[24]

On 13 January, a perplexed Nanasaheb wrote to Chimaji that Mastani has not had food and it '*may be worth coaxing her to have food once, although it looks a kind of dissimulation*'.[25] Meanwhile, Chimaji sought Shahu's opinion about Mastani's association with Baji rao. A letter from Govindrao Chitnis to Nanasaheb dated 21 January 1740 says,

> *Rajashri* Shahu's wish is that it should not be that what Rau likes should be kept away, detained or put under guard; and if Rau is unhappy on that count, and one still does so, is not good. What he likes should be given to him. Keep him happy. Bad habits are not due to the thing he desires. Only when he regrets it will he stop indulging in it. In view of the above, do not stop the thing (that he loves) and hurt a dear one, is the king's wish.[26]

---

a.   These forts were often used as prisons.

By the end of January 1740, Mastani was placed under guard so that she could not visit Baji rao, who was busy campaigning near Aurangabad. On 26 January 1740, Nanasaheb wrote to Chimaji,

> I am at the garden on Parvati. Today Saturday evening 7 *Jilkad*, I summoned Mastani here and imprisoned her. Nobody drew a weapon. I will escort her home at night. At home, would you want me to keep her under guard, or with ten people secretly send her to an out of the way fort like Ghangad or Kothala?[a] The swami should preserve the *Raya's* life. The campaign against Nasir Jung was sunk due to this affair. The king's trust was lost. On your orders and with my determination I have taken this step today. Once I take her home, I will do what I feel necessary. I will not kill her. I will keep her home or send her under guard to a fort. You should place posts around the *Raya*. Nasir Jung's campaign does not look like succeeding. What lies in our fate, will happen.[27]

Eventually, Mastani was taken home and placed under a strict guard in the palace. Protesting that she was innocent and did not intend to run away, she wrote to Nanasaheb,

> *Saheb* has placed guard posts around the palace, thinking that I will run away. However, I will not leave without asking *Saheb*. If *Saheb* suspects that Raosaheb will come and take her away, or at night or day she will be taken by some other means, if there is danger of any such event, then if so ordered, I will sleep where ten or twelve ladies in the palace are sleeping. *Saheb* is the Lord. Whatever is ordered will be done.[28]

The period from November 1739 onwards was rather difficult for the Peshwa. On the one hand, he was forced to stay away from his beloved. On the other he was leading a campaign against Nasir Jung, the son of the Nizam. In the midst of these events, the wedding and the thread ceremony of the children of Chimaji and the Peshwa were planned. Both children underwent the rituals between 4 and 7 February 1740 in Pune. Baji rao and Chimaji were away in the midst of a campaign to claim territories promised but not handed over to the Peshwa from as long back as the battle of Palkhed.

Nobody could have imagined then, that this would prove to be the last campaign of the Peshwa.

๛

# 35. A Whirlwind Campaign

'If the Maharaj asks, please inform him. If he sends all the armies now, the time is ripe to liberate all six *subahs* of the Deccan.'

- Baji rao to Mahadji Purandare, 7 February 1740.[1]

The month of May 1739 was indeed a happy one. Vasai, the last bastion of the Portuguese kingdom of the North had been captured. Nadir Shah had decided to return to his country. A letter from Pune to Chimaji Appa read,

> This year the rain has been good. Farmers are planting their crops. The people and the moneylenders are happy. Vasai has been captured this year. We hear the campaign at Goa has also been successful. Events that would ordinarily not have happened have all taken place this year. The two brothers are indeed incarnations in this Kalyug. These deeds are difficult for mere mortals. *Rajashri Raya*'s efforts removed Tahmasp Quli Khan from Delhi and the swami's victory has done the job at Vasai and Goa. What is difficult to achieve has occurred. As *Vidur* and *Akrur* and *Bhishma* saw the Lord in Krishna, we too see the same in the swami.[2]

The Nizam-ul-mulk was detained by the Emperor at Delhi after the departure of Nadir Shah. Robbed of the riches of several generations, a decrepit monarchy limped back to normalcy. The Mughal impotence was exposed before the world; the Emperor and his highest nobles humiliated for over a month, a massacre that killed several thousands, women carried off to Persia– Delhi had not seen such brutality in several generations. The old guard led by Khan Dauran and Sadat Khan were swept away and the likes of the Nizam survived by pusillanimous treasonable conduct. The *Wazir* Qamruddin Khan, publicly 'exposed' and stripped of his hoards, was but a pale shadow of himself. The Nizam-ul-mulk bided his time till he could quietly abandon the monarchy to its problems and return to his own kingdom, which remained untouched by the savagery of the invading Persians.

With the Nizam was Anant rao Sumant, Shahu's emissary, who had taken a liking for him. Despite several summons, Sumant had not returned to the Maratha capital. The Nizam now entrusted him with a mission to the

Deccan. In the middle of 1739 therefore, Sumant began from Delhi and reached Aurangabad where he met the Nizam's son Nasir Jung.

Nasir Jung had gathered an army to help his father at Bhopal in 1738 and had been prevented from crossing the river Tapi by Chimaji Appa. Then came the invasion of Nadir Shah and Nasir Jung held onto the army in case the Persians decided to come to the Deccan. The Marathas, after the long Vasai campaign, had the strength and the opportunity to gain disputed territory, and as the monsoon months came to a close, these issues came to the fore.

From the days of the battle of Palkhed, the Nizam's many promises of land and *jagirs* to the Peshwa had remained unfulfilled. With all enemies defeated, it became necessary to force the Nizam to hand them over. As the Nizam's son and heir apparent in the Deccan, it was Nasir Jung who was in the line of fire. When the Peshwa was still at Burhanpur, he sent two of his lieutenants, Avaji Kavade and Tubaji Anant to campaign in Nasir Jung's territory. However, not wishing to alarm Nasir Jung at this time, he asked Tubaji to be cautious not to make any move.[3] Baji rao was hoping Nasir Jung would cooperate with him; if not, he would be taught a lesson and all the places captured.

In the Nizam's absense, Nasir Jung had found Raghuji Bhonsle, also taking chunks of his territory. At this time, Anant rao Sumant, arriving from Delhi, brought along messages from the Nizam asking his son to ensure that the Marathas did not gain any advantage in his absence. As early as in May 1739 when the victory at Vasai had just been won and Nadir Shah had quit Delhi, a Maratha envoy named Shamji Govind Takle wrote to Purandare,

> Nasir Jung is at Nanded. He has renewed the *jagirs* (and given cash awards) to Sultanji Nimbalkar and Sayyid Jamaluddin Khan and Chandrasen Jadhav. The fort at Ausa is given to Chandrasen. They have all been asked to collect an army. He is also collecting an army. Sumant has come from Hastinapur (Delhi). He intends to send him to Maharaj (Shahu) to earn his goodwill and then obtain help from Raghuji Bhonsle and then begin a war with the *Shrimant*. The *Shrimant* is at present at Burhanpur. Disturbances are at hand. Let us see which way they go. The swami should henceforth exercise caution...[4]

In all his campaigns, Baji rao used strategies that were tailored to the situation and the opponent. His ability to discern or create opportunities and his timing an attack at the right moment had served him in good stead. His limitations were known to him and his enemies - the lack of an artillery force and an infantry that did not match up to the best of the age. Towards the latter part, he did find some mortars and a few guns to conduct siege operations, but these never became the main strike force of his army. He forced his enemies to submission with a purely mounted force. A group of two or three men carried a spare horse, and the preference was for Turkish horses due to their speed. Flight in the face of a strong enemy was not considered an act of cowardice; it was never the intention of the Maratha troops to give battle in an unfavourable situation. The timing and ground had to be right and the enemy vulnerable before the cavalry charge decimated an unprepared enemy. Siege was a proven method that brought the enemy to his knees without losing one's men. Baji rao's long campaigns from Palkhed onwards were geared to tire his enemy and find the right time and place to strike. Baji rao's success lay in his ability to choose when to fight, where to fight and when not to.

The brisk pace at which Baji rao moved was largely owing to his lightly equipped force with no baggage or dependants. The element of surprise that was injected into his attack by rapid movements ended in the defeat of the enemy. Maratha armies had few men from other communities till the end of the 1730s. Use of other communities like Arabs and Kannada speaking men in the Vasai campaign proved a handicap and these men were dismissed when Maratha chiefs were freed from their commitments elsewhere. Nevertheless, for a nation-wide enterprise of conquest, it was inevitable that men from other communities would be recruited. The trend grew with years and in four or five decades these paid mercenaries became a large part of Maratha armies.

The Maratha cavalry had four categories of horsemen. The *Khas paga,* or the *Huzurat* – the Peshwa's cavalry - was equipped and paid from the state treasury and were the elite. The *Siledar* who brought his horse and weapons with him, was paid some part of his pay in advance as '*nalbandi*'.[a] The *Ekanda* was the single soldier with his own horse who joined the armies. They were paid according to the quality of their horses and were equipped with muskets,

---

a.   *Nalbandi* : literally, money to fix the horse-shoe.

but primarily used the famed Maratha spear and sword. The fourth category was the *Pindaris* who received no pay but accompanied armies and made good their effort by looting or mopping up after a battle. For this license to loot, they paid their chiefs a part of what they plundered. Strangely, this finds support in ancient scriptures.[5] Nor was the practice unique in Maratha armies; the Mughals had their own scavenger troops called the *Bederia*. The *Pindaris* did not accompany *Chhatrapati* Shivaji's armies, but after him, they steadily grew in numbers over the next hundred years.

Baji rao and Chimaji had returned to Pune in the monsoon months of 1739. On 1 November 1739, Baji rao left Pune with his army to subdue the Nizam's defiant son and camped at Bhamburde. In the middle of December 1739 he headed out with Chimaji Appa and together they headed for the Godavari.[6]

Since the fall of Vasai, the Portuguese had been trying to obtain Sashti, Bardez and Madgaon in Goa from the Marathas, while it was accepted that Chaul and Korlai forts could not be defended and would be given to the Marathas. The English volunteered to do this for the *Firangis*. Stephen Law, the President at Bombay, therefore sent Captain Inchbird once again to meet Baji rao. On 14 January 1740, Inchbird met Baji rao at Paithan, near the river Godavari. Here Baji rao gave him a list of demands to be approved by the Portuguese. Of these, one clause is illustrative of the relations between the components of the Maratha Empire; in this case the Angre family and the Peshwa. It says that the *Firangis* should help the Marathas if there is any war with the Angres.[7] Although the treaty was approved later, it clearly demarcated areas that would be governed by the Marathas, their right of navigation and so on. The treaties of 1739 and 1740 repeatedly refer to 'Baji rao's Navy', and it appears that the Peshwa and his brother had plans to form their own navy that would challenge the best in the Indian seas. The apprehensions voiced by the English in 1737 looked like coming to fruit.[8]

Early in February, when the Peshwa's family was assembling at Pune, the moves against Nasir Jung began in earnest. The battle was fought largely to the south and west of Aurangabad and is often called the battle of Aurangabad or the Godavari. The Peshwa was supported by his most reliable aides: Chimaji Appa, Pilaji Jadhav rao, Malharji Holkar and Ranoji Scindia. The Marathas

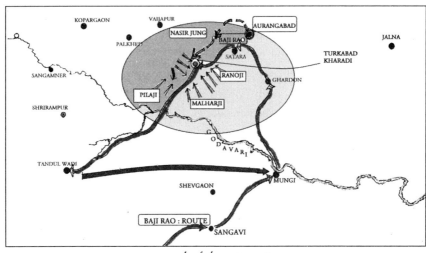

*Battle of the Godavari*

## Baji rao's movements during and after the battle of the Godavari (1739-40)

16 September – 1 November 1739 – Pune.

1 November 1739 – 12 December 1739 – Bhamburde, Pune.

13-14 December 1739 – Yerawada.

16 December 1739 – Lohagaon.

18 December 1739 – Ranjangaon.

19 December 1739 – Hingani, near Shirur.

20-22 December 1739 – Astagaon, near Parner.

21-25 December 1739 – Near Ahmednagar.

26 December 1739 – Shahapur, Ahmednagar

30-31 December 1739 – Sangavi, near Pathardi

1-3 January 1740 – Ranegaon, north-east of Pathardi

13 January 1740 – Mungi, southern bank of Godavari.

14-16 January 1740 – Gharegaon Pimpri, (Ghardon), south east of Aurangabad.

18 – 25 January – 4 February - Satara, south of Aurangabad.

26 January 1740- 5 February 1740 – Aurangabad.

6 February 1740 – Turkabad Kharadi, south west of Aurangabad

8 February 1740 – Tandulwadi Paithan.

9 February 1740 – Krishnapur Paithan.

14 February 1740 – Bodhegaon, east of Shevgaon.

17 February 1740 – Chapadgaon.

19 – 27 March 1740 – around Newasa

28 February 1740 – Galnib, south bank Godavari.

5-6 March 1740- Padali, east of Aurangabad.

7-8 March 1740 – Ektuni, south east of Aurangabad.

Chimaji Appa departs for Pune.

9 March 1740 – Bangaon, east of Aurangabad.

10 March 1740 – Adha, west of Chikhli

11 March 1740 – Deulghat, near Buldana

12 March 1740 – Rohinkhed (fort).

13 March 1740 – Malkapur.

14 March 1740 – Icchapur.

15 – 18 March 1740 – Khandesh

19 – 30 March 1740 – Burhanpur.

5 - 6 April 1740 – Khargone.

8 April 1740 – Multhan, south of Ratlam.

9 April 1740 – Khadki, west of Mandu.

11 – 25 April – Kakriya, near Dhamnod

26 April – Raver, south of the Narmada.

crowded Nasir Jung and attacked him when the ground was right for battle, forcing terms. Baji rao's own letters between 7 and 9 February help trace the course of the campaign.

Baji rao wrote to Mahadji Purandare on 7 February 1740,

> Nasir Jung wanted to go to Shahabad[a] and take Sultanji with him. But it would take seven or eight days to get there. He wants to stay close to the Ganga[b]. He hopes to elicit sympathy from Maharaj. That is not necessary. We are servants of the Maharaj. I have written to Fateh Sinh baba and Raghuji Bhonsle. If the Maharaj orders them to join me it will be well and good. Else, with the Maharaj's goodness I will end the affair as it should end.[9]

The same day in another letter he described Nasir Jung's moves around Aurangabad,

> I was to the north east of the city. Two days back, on Tuesday, Nasir Jung left the city and between the city and the hills, keeping the city to his left, went to Tisgaon[c] via Pahadsinghpur. Then on Wednesday, he left Tisgaon and came to Kharadi[d] near Waluj. We are on his back. Malhar*ba* and Ranoji are on the left, *Subedar* (Pilaji) is in front of him. He has emerged from the city due to shortage of fodder for his horses. I will see if he moves today. It is in our interest that he comes out of the sheltered city, so we have not skirmished with him yesterday. We are close, when we find a gap we will move. At a place where he cannot use his cannons, or near a forest or near canals where he cannot move, we will shove him from all sides. He will not be able to move more than three or four *kos* in a day. He will then come under our power. If the Maharaj asks, please inform him. If he sends all the armies now, the time is ripe to liberate all six *subahs* of the Deccan.[1]

Surrounded by Maratha armies and gradually being squeezed for supplies, Nasir Jung was thus trapped to the south of Aurangabad. There was a battle on 8 February when Chimaji attacked him from the east. Holkar and Scindia led from the front. Nasir Jung was forced to submit. On 9 February 1740, Baji rao wrote to Nanasaheb from Tandulwadi,

> Yesterday, on Friday, we clashed with Nasir Jung. Appa attacked with half the *Huzurat*. They attacked the Mughal and absorbed the fire from his array of

---

a. Eighty kilometres south east of Aurangabad, near Rakshasbhuvan.
b. In the Deccan, river Godavari is often called Ganga.
c. To the west of the city. Tisgaon is seven kilometres to the south west of Aurangabad.
d. Turkabad Kharadi, about twenty-five kilometres south west of Aurangabad.

guns. Two hundred odd men were killed. The Mughal had left his artillery
and moved back. But we lost a couple of hundred horses and fifty men.
His chiefs returned to succour his forces. In the van, Ranba and Malharba
were there and acquitted themselves very well. To his (Nasir Jung's) right,
Phirangoji Pawar was attacked by Pilaji Jadhav rao and Sambhaji Shinde, and
defeated. Many different battles took place. Today with the entire army acting
in cohesion, I will bring the enemy under control. If the Maharaj orders the
entire army to join, the time is right to completely eradicate the Mughal.[10]

The skirmishes continued for a few more days before a treaty was signed
on 27 February 1740 at Mungi Paithan, not far from Baji rao's first triumph
at Palkhed. Nasir Jung had to hand over Khargone and Handia, two key
districts of Malwa on the banks of the Narmada to the Peshwa. These two
districts controlled the communications between Hindustan and the Deccan,
and effectively the passes on the Narmada went into Baji rao's hands.

The narrative is quite different in Mughal sources. The *Khazanah e Amarah*
by Mir Ghulam Ali dismisses the campaign saying, '*When the Nizam-ul-
mulk went to Dehly in the year 1150 (1736-7 CE), he left his excellent son his
viceregent in the Deccan, and in that period, Naser Jung subdued Baji rao, who
till then had been puffed up with intolerable pride*'.[11] In his book on Malwa,
John Malcolm picks up the narrative and writes that Baji rao suffered a signal
reverse near Pune in the battle against Nasir Jung.[12] However, it remains to be
explained how two districts of Malwa were given to Baji rao as a consequence
of the battle.

On 3 March 1740 Nasir Jung met Baji rao. Baji rao with Chimaji then
turned north to take control of Handia and Khargone districts. However,
after a couple of days, Chimaji turned back, leaving Baji rao to go north
on his own. At Aurangabad, Chimaji also met Nasir Jung. On 12 March,
Chimaji wrote the good news to Nanasaheb, quoting Shahu who had said
'*Whatever Baji rao decides to do, he does. The Peshwa is in full control of his
destiny*'.[13]

Chimaji summed up the entire campaign in his letter to Brahmendra
swami on 13 March 1740,

> I am at Aurangabad. On leaving Pune, I joined *Raya* at Ahmednagar. There
> were differences with Nasir Jung, so we are on the banks of the Ganga for

the last two to two and a half months. We managed with *jondhala* that grew in the forests. We had no money, but we persevered and with the swami's blessings, we obtained the *jagirs* from Nasir Jung and agreed on a peace. After deciding that we will jointly manage the region, *Rau* has gone northwards to Hindustan. I was urged to come here, therefore I came. Yesterday went to the palace for four to six *ghatika*s. The Mughal from Bidar had nineteen thousand horse, twenty thousand gunners, one hundred and fifty cannons, three thousand *jejala,* three hundred camels with rockets. However, with the blessings of the swami we prevailed in the battle.[14]

At this time, Raghuji Bhonsle and Fateh Sinh were in the region of Beed and headed towards Hyderabad, plundering Humnabad town on the way.[15] Raghuji was the rising star of the time, and he went further south to reach the southern forts of Arcot and Tiruchirapalli and succour the ruler of Thanjavur. Thus began a new era of fresh Maratha conquest in the south.

Baji rao and Chimaji parted in early March after they had many discussions on the personal issues that had disturbed the tranquillity of the Peshwa household. Chimaji thereafter gave up his efforts to separate Mastani from Baji rao and wrote to Nanasaheb on 29 March 1740,

> *Teerthroop Rajashri Rau* swami left on 19 *Jilhej* (7 March 1740). Since then there is no letter from him. I tried my best, but it is not God's wish. Whatever is his fate, may he be happy. I will be in Pune in two or three days. After that I will send her (Mastani) to him and reduce our role. Whatever fate has in store for him, will happen. That is what I have thought. I have written to *Rau* that I am not well and am therefore going home. I have written to him and asked him to come home. He will do according to what he decides.[16]

Despite recent differences, the two brothers were close to each other. Probably on receipt of Chimaji's letter about his ill health, a concerned Baji rao wrote to their mother Radha bai from Burhanpur,

> I am by the blessing of the elder (Mother), safe at Shahapur near Burhanpur. It was very satisfying to receive a letter with blessings. Please write always and take care of me. The weather is hot; Raghunath and Janardan are with me and both are fine. At present the Konkan air is humid. Let *Chiranjeev* Appa not go out. He may wish to see Vasai, but he should be asked not to go. He should get this work done by the senior chiefs with him. You are with him; you should advise him about it from time to time.[17]

Baji rao's moves from now on appear to show he was moving closer to Jaipur. From Burhanpur he crossed the Narmada at Khargone on 6 April 1740. He began the process of taking charge of his recently acquired districts. He rapidly advanced towards Ratlam, and camped on 10 April at Multhan.[18] From here, two roads lay ahead of him—one to Udaipur and the second through the Mukandara pass to Jaipur.

However, from Multhan, he turned back and passing Khadki to the west of Mandu, camped for nearly two weeks in Kakriya, a few miles north of Narmada near Dhamnod. From here, on 26 April 1740, he reached Raver on the south bank of the Narmada. He was accompanied by his wife Kashi bai and sons Janardan and Raghunath. Both the sons had joined their father after their thread ceremonies. Here the family remained.

While the Peshwa was in touch with his *vakils* in Delhi and Jaipur and planning his own future moves, fate was catching up and had other plans.

❧✿❦✿❧

# Rewa Uvach

To call a fifty-year period in the long history of an ancient nation as the 'Era of Baji rao', needs a little justification. Like many others before him, he was a person who left an impact on the history of a land and created an Empire that stood the test of time. Indeed, the Maratha period of Indian history from the mid-seventeenth century to the early nineteenth century saw a series of great men emerging from the folds of mountains on either side of the western *ghats*, truly a crucible that liberated a large part of the Indian subcontinent from a palpably foreign power. From *Chhatrapati* Shivaji to Nana Phadnis and Mahadji Scindia, this land gave leaders who thought and acted nationally. The concern for India and the quest for freedom, the sustained struggle against oppression and moderation of her leaders marked the Maratha rule as notably different from the rule of Aurangzeb or the invading hordes of Nadir Shah and Ahmed Shah Abdali. In the first half of the eighteenth century, Baji rao was the key person who led the formation of an Empire that emphasized its indigenous roots.

The invasion of Nadir Shah had led to a situation that was startlingly similar to one that occurred two decades later when Ahmed Shah Abdali invaded India. Maratha commitment in the battle at Vasai precluded Baji rao from proceeding north and Nadir Shah, having stripped Delhi, was keen to take it all to his motherland before any challenge from the Deccan came to the north. Eventually in 1760, the Marathas did pick up the challenge from repeated aggression from the north west. As the unequivocally paramount power then, they took a large army north and fought in the plains of Panipat on 14 January 1761 in the cause of India for Indians.

Baji rao had taken the small kingdom centred around Satara and Pune and created an Empire that stretched from the Yamuna to the Tungabhadra and from Gujarat to Varhad. He created a phalanx of able men that served the Maratha state for decades afterwards. His triumphs – coupled with no defeats – mark him as an invincible cavalry leader, and one who operated on a giant stage, from Delhi to Srirangapatnam and Rajputana to Bhaganagar. The sheer number of miles he logged in his twenty-five years of active military service would be difficult to match in the annals of world history.

Kavi Bhushan, a north Indian poet who visited *Chhatrapati* Shivaji and composed many '*chhand*' or couplets in his praise, was an old man when Baji rao strode over the Indian land mass. However, he composed a few lines about Baji rao that bear repetition.

'Baji rao won over some kings by giving awards,
Others by the strength of his sword,
Even courageous rulers made their peace by paying an indemnity
And some learnt their lessons after a thorough foot lashing,
Some strong kings were sent to heaven,
Others were subdued under the point of a spear,
Baji rao, the champion of his religion, rescued Chhatrasal,
And assumed a place higher than the Chaghtai kings.'

'When the Satara king starts with Baji rao and his army
it appears as if the mountains are collapsing or there is a clap of thunder,
Strong rulers like Ravana, leave their forts and their charge and flee to safety,
The Earth itself appears to lose its balance, its guardians appear helpless,
The Shesh nag himself is overturned by the exploits of Baji rao,
Alternately bends forward and rises, tosses and turns restlessly.'[1]

Poets are granted some leeway in expression and hyperbole is a tool of their trade. However, there is little doubt that Baji rao left his mark on eighteenth-century history, founded an Empire and created a new aristocracy that lived on for over a century thereafter. The seeds of freedom and self-governance sown by *Chhatrapati* Shivaji in the seventeenth century bore fruit in the era of Baji rao.

The triumphal march was to end soon. Yet, the story of Baji rao's times will live evermore.

꣠ꕤ꣠ꕤ

# 36. Eclipse on the Narmada

'Became one with *Yama*, on Saka *Raudra Sanvatsar*,
*Vaishakh shukla* thirteenth, Sunday, at night.
The jewel in the Crown, Shahu's Prime Minister,
We see Rao Baji departing to the abode of *Indra*.'

- Purandare *daftar*.[1]

Leaving Aurangabad on 13 March, Chimaji Appa, exhausted by the rigours of war and enfeebled by a chronic chest ailment, had stopped at Parner near Ahmednagar on his way back to Pune. Here he received an urgent message,

> *Sarkhel* Sambhaji Angre has suddenly come to Alibag and taken Hirakot[a], Sagargad (forty-six miles east of Alibag), forts of Chaul and Thal and cut the water supply to the fort of Colaba. Manaji Angre had urged Nanasaheb to protect him.[2]

On receiving this message Nanasaheb sent his chiefs Vithal Shivdeo and Vasudeo Joshi with five hundred soldiers to the Konkan. Chimaji travelled by long marches and after stopping at Ghodnadi, reached Lohgaon on the outskirts of Pune in early April 1740. He first sent a letter of assurance to Manaji, and to the English asking them to succour him. Nanasaheb met Chimaji at Pune, and Chimaji's entire army accompanied Nanasaheb to the fort of Colaba. Nanasaheb reached Colaba on the fifth day. The English took supplies to Colaba and anchored off the coast with their ships. From their ships they fired at Alibag. The English fire forced Sambhaji's men to leave Alibag and move to Hirakot for shelter from the shelling.

Chimaji stopped at Pune for three days to recover, and after meeting his mother left for Colaba, reaching there on 9 April 1740. The same day, the army captured Sambhaji Angre's post at Hirakot, killing about thirty of his men. Tulaji Angre, his brother, was injured and brought prisoner. Nanasaheb went along the creek near Sagargad and encountered some men of Sambhaji whom he killed. Chimaji wrote to Brahmendra swami about

---

a.   Fort on the Alibag beach.

how the two brothers' quarrel and Manaji's ingratitude had been a source
of trouble to him,

> If Sambhaji flees, it will be good. Fearing the English, he has already sent
> away his grabs and big ships to Suvarnadurg. Small boats are here. If he
> stays, we will lay siege and bring him to submission. Sambhaji asked the
> English to give him safe passage, but they refused. Seeing I am away at
> Aurangabad, he attacked here. We had established Manaji's rule here, but he
> has forgotten that and has behaved wrongly with us. He grabbed Uran from
> the *Firangis*. I wrote about money and other affairs to him, but he does not
> take cognizance of it. For the last five years he has not paid any of our dues.
> His eyes need to be opened. Therefore, two of his places that Sambhaji had
> taken – Paal and Mirgad – we have taken and unfurled our flags there. We
> have also taken Uran. Now his eyes have opened. We have saved his life
> from Sambhaji too. I will go to Colaba tomorrow.[2]

On the other hand, Sambhaji wrote to Brahmendra swami on 12 April
giving his list of conquests and the Peshwa's interference in his campaign
against Manaji. He urged the swami to write to Shahu and send orders to
Chimaji to withdraw from the Konkan. However, resolving the matter was
beyond the powers of the swami. The war continued. Chimaji and Nanasaheb
had to stay on in the Konkan.

In late April, with matters yet quite unsettled and skirmishes still in
progress, an unforeseen event in the tiny hamlet of Raver Khedi on the
southern bank of the Narmada, eclipsed every political and military activity
on the Indian subcontinent. What could be heard was the silence, and what
was seen was the darkness, of a total solar eclipse.

While Chimaji and Nanasaheb were fighting Sambhaji Angre's sudden attack
on his brother Manaji in the Konkan, Baji rao was near the Narmada, marking
time and waiting for developments at Delhi. In the middle of April 1740 he
came to the village of Raver on the southern bank of the Narmada. He waited
for word about the many diplomatic initiatives he had set in motion through
his envoys and the ruler of Jaipur. A weakened Emperor without some of his
able supporters like Sadat Khan and Khan Dauran was far more receptive to
the proposals of Sawai Jaisingh. A few letters of the time mention disposal
of administrative matters by the Peshwa. It was expected that he would once
again head north in the near future.

The Emperor was unhappy with Nizam-ul-mulk, and hearing that Baji rao had signed a treaty with Nasir Jung, wished to ascertain where the Peshwa's sympathies lay. To this, the Maratha *vakil* Mahadeo bhat Hingane unequivocally assured the Jaipur ruler and the Emperor that the Peshwa was not with the Nizam.[3]

While these negotiations were still to bear fruit, the first inkling of an illness appeared on 23 April, when the Peshwa became febrile. The entries in the Peshwa diary give an account of donations made every day from then on for the Peshwa's health. On 23 and 24 April, sums of rupees twenty-five and twenty-four were given in alms. On 26 April 1740, a donation of a *mohar* worth twelve rupees is recorded. The Peshwa was blessed by the traditional *aarti* by waving a lighted lamp around him. The fever did not remit and the Peshwa became delirious. On 27 April 1740, the camp by the Narmada reverberated with the *Maha Mrutyunjay* chant. Shiva, the Lord of Death was propitiated, and an idol of one *tola* of gold was made for this purpose. One hundred and sixty rupees were spent in other donations.

The night of Sunday 28 April, after about 8.30 pm the lunar date by the Saka almanac was the thirteenth. A bland entry dated 28 April 1740 says,

> *Tarikh 12 roj Vaishakha shuddha trayodashi*, Monday, at Raver.
> *Rajashri Raya* passed away. A sum of rupee one and anna was spent on gold to be placed in his mouth.[4]

A letter in the Purandare *daftar* says,

> यमरसनृप शाके रौद्र संवत्सरे
> मांधव धवल त्रयोदश्यार्कवारे निशायां ।
> नृपमुकुटमणि श्रीशाहू मुखप्रधानो
> सुरपतिमपिद्रष्टुं प्रस्थितो रावबाजी ॥

Translated it reads,

'Became one with *Yama*,[a] on Saka *Raudra Sanvatsar*,[b]
*Vaishakh shukla*[c] thirteenth, Sunday, at night.[d]

---

a. God of Death
b. There are sixty *sanvatsara* in the Hindu calendar. *Raudra Sanvatsar* occurred only once in the eighteenth century in 1740.
c. The month of *Vaishakh* is also called *Madhav*, *Shukla* is the bright half of a lunar month.
d. *Trayodashi* after 8.30 pm.

The jewel in the Crown, Shahu's Prime Minister,

We see Rao Baji departing to the abode of *Indra*.'[1]

Wife Kashi bai and Janardan, his youngest son, were with Baji rao. The final rites were therefore performed by Janardan. Nanasaheb managed to patch up a peace between the Angre brothers and came to Pune only by 26 May 1740.

Baji rao died as he lived, in a military camp away from home, still actively planning his next moves. While his wife Kashi bai was with him, Mastani was not. There are no available documents today that give us a clue of her whereabouts. Perhaps she was still under guard at Pune, or had been sent to Baji rao when Chimaji returned from Aurangabad and stopped in Pune for three days. Chimaji had already written that he intended to send her to Baji rao on his return.

With the death of Baji rao, Mastani simply disappeared from the pages of history and a grave at her estate in Pabal, where she is said to have died, leaves an incomplete and unsatisfactory account of her last days. There is more than one version of where and how she met her death. It is said she died at the *Shaniwar wada* and her body was then taken to the village of Pabal for burial. There is another that says she was on her way to Baji rao when she heard the news and died on the way. The cause of her death so close after the Peshwa's death lends itself to speculation that it might not have been of natural causes. However, beyond this, the crypts of history are hitherto silent.

Baji rao's death created a sudden void in the power structure of the Maratha Empire. As had happened after Balaji Vishwanath's death, many claimants rushed forward. With Chimaji unwell and Nanasaheb just eighteen years of age, the field was wide open.

Raghuji Bhonsle with Fateh Sinh Bhonsle was at this time in the south. A large Maratha army had been assembled for the express purpose of succouring Shahu's cousin at Thanjavur who was threatened by Nawab Dost Ali of Arcot, his son Safdar Ali and son-in-law Chanda Sahib. The Maratha advance was sudden and rapid. Dost Ali, mustering whatever forces he could, took a stand at the pass of Damalcherry. A short battle on 20 May 1740 ended in the defeat and death of the Nawab, and the Marathas took control of Arcot. Here

Raghuji learnt of the death of the Peshwa. Desirous of influencing Shahu in the selection of the new Peshwa, Raghuji rushed back to Satara. Here, he pleaded the case of Babuji Naik, related to Baji rao and a rich moneylender, for appointment as the new Peshwa.

Baji rao had left a debt of fourteen and a half lakh rupees. The major creditor was Raghunath Patwardhan followed by Brahmendra swami. This debt was inherited by Nanasaheb. A small debt of thirty-six thousand was owed to Babuji Naik and he insisted on its prompt payment. Mahadji Purandare therefore paid him off.

Shahu owed his Empire to Baji rao. Historian Jadunath Sarkar writes,

> By the year 1740, the ambitions of the house of Kolhapur and of the Peshwa's rivals, which the Nizam's Macchiavellian policy used to foster during the first decade of Baji rao's regency, had been extinguished for ever. No Rambhaji Nimbalkar, no Chandrasen Jadhav, no Dabhade, was able to raise his head again and attempt to divide and weaken the Maratha state. The Kolhapur rajahs sank into the position of feudatory princes; Shahu alone stood forth as *Chhatrapati*. And the system, introduced no doubt by Balaji Vishwanath, but given full effect and an India-wide expansion to by Baji rao, completely transformed the political constitution of Shivaji's state and dotted the map of India with numberless centres of Maratha authority and culture. Baji rao was the creator of this 'Greater Maharashtra'. Shahu, in theory at least, was no longer the Rajah of a small, self-contained, one-race, one-language kingdom, as his father and grandfather had been; he was now an Emperor with diverse and far-flung dominions.[5]

Eventually, Shahu did not consider Raghuji or Babuji Naik fit to take over the mantle of the Peshwa. Nanasaheb, staying in Satara for long, and having recently accompanied the king on his campaign to capture Miraj, was a favourite of the king. The young man was thus chosen to take over his father's post. Shahu told Nanasaheb,

> Your father Baji rao and your grandfather Balaji served me most faithfully and in my service did mighty deeds. I sent Baji rao to humble the Persian and restore the Mughal Empire. But he died almost immediately afterwards. His ambition was to guard the Mughal Empire and at the same time to conquer all Hindustan. You are his son; realise your father's ambition. Lead your horsemen beyond the walls of Attock.[6]

Twenty years can change the face of a nation.

In 1720, holding the apron strings of the king-maker Sayyid brothers, Balaji Vishwanath embarked on a bold mission to place Maratha power on the national stage when he led a huge army to Delhi. The submissions of the army of ryots to be awarded recognition of being the custodian of the six *subahs* of the Deccan had two aims. One, it was an affirmation of Shahu as the true Maratha king. The Mughals looked on Shahu as their own, one who grew up in Aurangzeb's *gulal bar* enclosure, looked upon the Emperor with respect, promised never to uproot his Empire and support him. The second was to eke out one's own kingdom from the pieces of the collapsing Mughal Empire. In course of time, the Marathas first became partners and then, under Baji rao, aggressively pursued the cession of Gujarat, Malwa and Bundelkhand from the Mughals. In return, the Peshwa promised to serve the Emperor with his army when needed. The dictum that the Marathas seemed to follow was to rule the land in the name of the Mughals. It was a forerunner to the improved Subsidiary treaties of the English sixty years later.

The period of twenty years afforded Baji rao little time for administrative measures to institute a system of governance, something his son Nanasaheb could do to a large extent. The Maratha administration as it developed was therefore not Baji rao's creation. Chimaji Appa trained the civil servants of the time and Nanasaheb later acknowledged the training in administration he received at the hands of his uncle.

Besides the Mughals, Baji rao's twenty-year association with the Nizam-ul-mulk changed from opposing him at Balapur and helping him at the battle of Sakharkherda in 1724, to defeating him at Palkhed and again foiling him by the pre emptive strike at Dabhoi. The wily Nizam came to an agreement with the Peshwa in 1732, but had to come out and battle him at Bhopal when he was forced to sign a humiliating treaty, promising to obtain the *sanad* of Malwa from Muhammad Shah. The first half of the eighteenth century saw an intense rivalry between these two rulers of the Deccan, the Nizam claiming to rule for the Emperor and Baji rao on behalf of Shahu. In every contest however, one finds the Peshwa getting the better of the Nizam.

Jadunath Sarkar writes,

> Twenty years spent in breathless activity and tireless journeys across the Indian continent, from Delhi to Srirangapatnam and Gujarat to Hyderabad, wore out the most wonderful man of action that the Hindu race has produced since the days of the great Shivaji.[5]

Grant Duff, one of the first historians of the Marathas wrote about Baji rao in 1826,

> Bred a soldier as well as a statesman, Bajee Rao united the enterprise, vigour, and hardihood of a Mahratta chief, with the polished manners, the sagacity, and address which frequently distinguish the Bramins of the Concan.[7]

Duff also adds, *'Baji rao had the head to plan and the hand to execute'*. It sums up the Peshwa's career rather well.

The character of war changed every few decades in those days. The infantry had its day before the cavalry became the predominant fighting arm. To Baji rao's credit, he won all his battles with a near exclusive use of the cavalry. The Peshwa did have some artillery, as can be seen from the English envoy's notes when he saw coehurns being manufactured in foundries in Pune. Mortars were used at the battle of Vasai. However, the era of Baji rao saw the enemy's infantry and the primitive muskets of the day completely overwhelmed by the shock charge of the Maratha cavalry. It was later that the infantry, under de Bussy and de Boigne, made a return with drilled and disciplined battalions that had the confidence in their own weapons and tactics to stand and fire at a cavalry charge of the Maratha *Huzurat*.

Until the mid-seventeen fifties, the Maratha cavalry was unchallenged in India. Then, the Europeans made a beginning when they defeated large Mughal armies in the south and Bussy made the Nizam's artillery one of the best in the Deccan. It was after this that Sadashiv rao Bhau came to depend on the artillery of his Gardi chief at the battle of Panipat in 1761. Once again after this the Marathas reverted to their cavalry and guerrilla tactics, until the veteran war horse Malharji Holkar, now pushing seventy, was beaten by an English force in the Gangetic *doab*...

And so battle tactics changed. And they continue to change. From the trench warfare of the First World War to the panzers of the Second was a huge change. And none of our ancestors could have foreseen the astonishing technical advances in the battles of the twenty-first century.

Yet, Baji rao could not have succeeded without going on the offensive. The difference lay in that he knew how to fight, when to fight as well as where to fight. More important, he knew when not to fight. Mobility was Baji rao's forte, like the wind he could not fight without space for movement.

In victory, Baji rao was magnanimous to his enemy. His letting the Nizam go at Palkhed and Bhopal, his decision 'not to burn the suburbs of Delhi' because 'the thread of diplomatic interaction would break', reveal a mind that is more cultured than many a conqueror. Therefore, he cannot fall into the group of great Generals of the cavalry like Genghiz Khan or Taimur Lane. He never raised mounds of heads opposite his tent.

Twenty years of Baji rao succeeded in winning the entire Konkan from the Siddi and the Portuguese. In both battles it was Chimaji rather than Baji rao who led the final campaigns and secured victory against heavy odds. Chimaji was in many ways Baji rao's shield. Living in Baji rao's shadow, Chimaji's electrifying achievements; in Malwa, against the Siddi, and the Portuguese, are not as well known to the world at large. He was a man no less than his more illustrious brother, and if he did not seek the glory, it was due to his reticence, and his respect for Baji rao. Besides Chimaji, Baji rao had the loyal support of Pilaji Jadhav rao, Malharji Holkar, Ranoji Scindia, Avaji Kavade, Baji Bhivrao Rethrekar, Vyankat rao Ghorpade and so on. Together these men created an Empire.

In the dying months of his life, Chimaji ensured that Nanasaheb was recognised as the Peshwa and would perform the duties of his father as efficiently. Nanasaheb was always closer to Chimaji than to his own father and had learnt the art of governance and war from his uncle. On 16 June 1740, Chimaji wrote another letter to the *vakil* at Jaipur asking him to expedite the process by which the Maratha army could come to the north after the monsoons. '*Nana and I will complete all the tasks of Raya*', wrote Chimaji, and ensured that an army of ten to fifteen thousand men always stayed at Malwa under Scindia and Holkar. That year, he wrote, he had already sent Pilaji Jadhav rao and Vithoji Bule ahead with their armies.

On hearing a Mughal army was coming to Malwa, Ranoji Scindia wrote to Mahadeo Hingane,

> In Delhi people are happy that the *Shrimant's* affairs are disturbed. There is news that Azimullah Khan is coming to Malwa. Earlier also the servants (of the Peshwa) were defeating these enemies. If he comes here, he will find happiness, do not worry.[8]

In the year 1740-41 Nanasaheb led Maratha armies to the north. Holkar and Scindia completely subjugated Malwa and won the fort of Dhar. Avaji Kavade and Govind Hari Patwardhan campaigned all the way to Allahabad. In this manner, there was a vigorous response to Mughal hopes that the Maratha power would be weakened after the death of Baji rao. However, Chimaji's guiding hand was soon to be snatched away. In October 1740 on his way north, Chimaji's health worsened to an extent he had to return from Khandesh to Pune.

Nanasaheb continued northwards. The presence of the Peshwa with a large army so near Agra led to a flurry of activity in Delhi. The Mughals responded by sending Jaisingh to confront the new Peshwa. However, seeing Maratha preparations, Jaisingh called for a meeting at Dholpur with Nanasaheb. At Dholpur, Jaisingh and Nanasaheb agreed to a binding friendship. Securing a promise of the *sanad* for Malwa, Nanasaheb returned to Pune on 7 July 1741.

Before Nanasaheb's return, Chimaji's ailment had worsened and on 17 December 1740 he died at Pune and was cremated near the Omkareshwar temple nearby. The death of Baji rao and Chimaji within months of each other was a setback to the Marathas. However, Nanasaheb energetically pursued his father's goals and was awarded the province of Malwa by an imperial *firman* in 1741. Bundelkhand, Malwa and Gujarat became the northern frontiers of the Maratha Empire. Raghuji Bhonsle's southern campaign was followed by one to the east so that he became the master of Odisha and claimed the *chauth* of Bengal.

In just two years after Baji rao's death therefore, the Marathas had spread from the Yamuna and Chambal in the north to the Kollidam in the south, and from the *subah* of Gujarat in the west to Odisha in the east. What had begun in 1720 with a promise to take the Empire to the north and beyond Attock was finally achieved in 1758, when Maratha armies captured Lahore,

Multan, Attock and Peshawar, extending their sway to the frontiers of the old Mughal Empire.

Baji rao died young and Chimaji Appa died younger. But scarcely did two brothers leave an impact of such magnitude on a land so vast in so short a time.

The era of Baji rao ended a trifle too soon. But the mastery of Hindustan had begun.

ೞಞಀಞಀ

# Appendices

## Appendix 1
### (Chapter 5)

### Letter from Ramchandra *pant amatya* to *Chhatrapati* Rajaram

Letter from Ram Chendra Neelkont Row to Ram Rajah at Ginjee
Inviting him to leave the place when besieged bythe Mogul army.

Into the Presence of the Raja Rama Chatraputty of the Chatree cast who was appointed to the Government in the year of Shalleevahan 1664.

Rama Chandra Neelakonta Aumvata, Pradhan, the faithful observer of the Commanders of his Lord, a Bramarum (or beeble) that enjoys the Treasure of the Lotus Foot of his Sovereign Master, wishes to represent as follows –

That the army of the Droogs & Lower Forts of this Dominion have arrived happily at Punnal ____ Your Highness will be pleased to make me glad & _____ by writing of your Prosperity and Health. The Newswriter having understood your mind has wrote me that when the Maharaja Sumbajee Baubah or uncle & Shawhoo went to Hunt with his followers & hunters that Kabajee Baubah treacherously inviting the Mogul's forces carried them both prisoners to Hasteenapoor: on hearing of which I sent Ballajee Viswanada the head mutsadda of Jaudava Row, in pursuit of them & I myself secured the Fort & drove away the Enemy that they durst not think to approach us; at this time I received a letter from your Majesty Sree Chatraputty Swamy signifying that the Badshah had arrested the Maharajah together with Shahoo, & had made presents to Kabajee Baubah to encourage him to fight against us; having thus encouraged him in various ways he sent for Zoolfacar Khan Bahadur, son of the Vizier Assud Khan &presented him with a Seerapa: & with his own hand tied a Seerapanch on his Turban; he also presented him with a Kulgee-Turah of Precious Stones & Pasha Kabjee dressed him in a Neemastanee (a kind of Robe of honor) &put a string of Pearls about his neck: he also presented him with several other articles & sending for his own Horse he caused him too be mounted upon it &

attached to him his own Guard of Moguls of his own country & 22 _____ & a Buckshee & all the Rajahs of Hindoostan namely Sewajee Jeya Singauje the Ambar Chief – Dhokala Sing, of Joatapoor Bheenacaur Haud Seesoada together with the remaining Jagheerdars & Polligars from Delhi to Rameswar & dispatched him.

He then marched with this army forward & escaping the danger of the Cannon which was fired from the nearest places of Chenjee, he encamped at one Coss distant from the River which was their support: that you & the Mogul begun daily to fight with each other & you also wrote me to take care of that place.

On receiving this news in consequence I now send Suntajee Ghorpuddah, Dhanajee Jaudava, Dhaubauda, Sarnobat with an army; you should keep this army with my father and afterwards take Pralaud Pant, with twenty thousand Horse & come off by Sytan Deedee (the small Gate) & by the cover & support of Vatavalum Wood & by the road of Teeranamulla; then we both should advise and assemble the army & afterwards go against Delhi to take revenge of the Padshah or else our Excellent reputation will be tarnished & the woods in the neighbourhood of Delhi shall remain without Inhabitants.

If we can fix ourselves there then no one can oppose nor delay us but by the countenance of the Maharajah we can possess that place & furnish the Chief thereof; then the Enemy will quit their Investment of Chenjee & go away of themselves _____ therefore you should come to join with me quickly.

(Mackenzie Colin, *Mackenzie collection,* Vol. 13,
India Office records, London.)

Note : The spellings have been reproduced as in the translation.

# Appendix 2

## (Chapter 8)

## Demands of Shahu to Husain Ali

The requests according to the sequel of Rajah Shahoo, the date 24th Shoowal in the 6th Jaloos, (September 19, 1717) written to the ministers and delivered by Ballajee Pundit

> 1st - The old kingdoms, according to the two papers with my signature, be given to me upon the date of Sahnak (?)
>
> 2nd - Let the *Watun* of the *Surdeshmuokee* of the six provinces of the Deccan, according to the sequel, with the tax of ten per cent be given to me. The province of Aurangabad, the province of Khandesh, the province of Varhad with Chandar and Deoghur, the province of Mahummudabad (Bidar), the province of Darool Zufur (Bijapur) with the Carnatic, and the province of Furcundah Buniad (Hyderabad).
>
> 3rd - Let the fourth part of the six provinces of the Deccan, according to the sequel, with 25 per cent be given to me. The names of the provinces are as above and are mentioned in the same order except that 'with the Carnatic' comes not after Bijapur but after both Bijapur and Haiderabad.
>
> 4th - If any of my brothers shall come to you do not keep them near you; and if any of my servants shall come to you for employment, do not employ them in your service.
>
> 5th - Let my mother, my brother, my brother's wife and other persons be brought from the royal presence and delivered over to me.
>
> Three days before this paper was written, yet another was made out by Shahu. It was as follows :—
>
> (Seal of Shahu as before)

I Raja Shahoo am the slave of your Majesty. I have obtained from your royal presence the *Watun* of the *Surdeshmuokee* and the fourth part of the six provinces of the Deccan according to the sequel, *viz.,* the province of Aurangabad, the province of Khandesh, the province of Varhad, the province of Mahummadabad (Bidar), the province of Ferundah Buniad (Hyderabad), and the province of Darool Zufor (Bijapur). My *Baiebunds*[a] are plundering two of these provinces viz Bijapur and Hyderabad, on which account I am making an agreement that under the auspices of your Majesty. In three years I will drive away those plunderers and will make a good *bundobast* of the country. And if in three years I may not be able to drive them out then whatever loss on their account may arise to your Majesty's Kingdom I will recompense your Majesty for it. On this account I write this. 21st *Shoowal* in the 6th *Jaloos* (Sept. 16, 1717)."

Raja Shahoo the Slave of Alumgeer Badshah Gazee

(Proceedings of the Indian History Research Congress XVII, pg 209-10)

---

a.    Relatives

# Appendix 3

## (Chapter 8)

## Distribution Of Chauth and the Areas Allotted

The distribution of income between the King and his chiefs as laid down by Balaji Vishwanath in 1719.

1. *Sardeshmukhi* – the King's private income.

2. *Chauth* – the gross income of the *swarajya*.

   Of this,

   a. 25% to the king as '*Rajbabti*', for political expenses.

   b. 6% *Sahotra* income to be given by the king as he pleases. The king gave it to the *Sachiv*. The income was to be exacted by the person to who it was given.

   c. 3% *Nadgauda* – Amount left with the king for exigencies or to give gifts on special occasions.

   d. 66% to the chiefs as *saranjam* to maintain their armies.

      Clauses :

      i. Every chief is to exact the revenue from the territory given and remit the amounts due to the Government.

      ii. The main army to be with the Peshwa and the *Senapati* and it would be sent wherever needed.

      iii. Every chief to submit accounts of all his campaigns (*mulukhgiri*) to the Government on a regular basis.

      iv. Distribution of regions for collecting revenue:

         Peshwa – Swarajya, Khandesh and Baleghat

         *Senapati* – Baglan and Gujarat

         Kanhoji Bhonsle – Varhad and Gondwana

         *Sarlashkar* – Gangathadi (Godavari basin) and Aurangabad

         Fateh Sinh Bhonsle – Carnatic.

*Pratinidhi* – from river Nira to the river Warana and the district of Bidar.

Angre – Konkan

v.   If so desired, the chiefs could deposit a fixed lump sum every year and not submit detailed accounts. The amount decided was as follows :

Kanhoji Bhonsle – ten lakh rupees.

Fateh Sinh – seven lakh rupees.

Angre – three lakh rupees.

The King's Chitnis, Phadnis and Potnis appointed subordinates to perform the same duties at all the confederate chiefs' provinces.

(Behere NK, *Bajirao Peshwe,* pg 62, 1929.)

# Appendix 4

## (Chapter 19)

Full text of the Nizam-ul-mulk's letter about his campaign with Dabhade against the Peshwa :

> The accursed Baji rao, finding the province of Gujarat unoccupied by defenders, laid siege to Baroda…I reflected that if, God avert it, the rebel got Baroda, it would be a great disgrace and loss, and our work would be ruined while his intrigues would become perpetual in that subah and the ways of the followers of Islam would be completely upset. Therefore, out of the spirit and pride of Islam and fidelity to salt, I decided upon this religious duty, that after crossing the Narmada I should engage at full gallop in rooting this dark-natured wretch out, and thus perform the tasks of holy war (*jihad)* in cutting off the roots of disturbance. Immediately on hearing rumours of the approach of the Islamic army by way of Ali Mohan, the wretch, casting off all at once his plans of dominion, withdrew from the siege and with a view to interposing a long distance between the Islamic army and the rebel horde, in terror of the Muhammedan army, in utter bewilderment, at midnight quickly crossed the Narmada and entered the limits of the Deccan. Through his short sight, seeing that the Muslim army was very distant from him, he began to disturb the pargana of Ankleswar and plundered and burnt the country, dry and irrigated alike.

> Therefore this follower of Mustafa's precepts (Asaf Jah) from the ford of Akbarpur, near the fort of Mandu, sent his baggage and camp with the big guns to Burhanpur, and by favour of the strength and power of God, with great rapidity and in a short time I arrived at Nandurbar; a second time disburdened myself.. and by forced marches reached the environs of Surat in a few days.

> Our army, making many stages in light kit, arrived near the enemy's horde, after performing great exertions, traversing long distances, and enduring hunger and thirst, because for two or three days little food came to hand and we had to traverse waterless deserts and wildernesses, hills and declivities, difficult of passage.

> We surprised the Marathas in their negligence and ignorance of our whereabouts, and they fled away in the utmost disorder. The dead were

countless. Our troops made spoil of their property. The Marathas never turned their faces towards us, but fled. They were plundered by Kolis and Bhils in the jungles and deserts; much booty fell into their hands and the wretches suffered total losses.

The Marathas, when fleeing in terror, had to cross an arm of the sea, when many of them were drowned in the water and some, after abandoning their horses to destruction in the creek, themselves fled away half dead. At the time of their arrival in a dark night on the bank of the creek the strange fate overtook them that their front ranks were slain by the waves and their rear by my soldiers.

Therefore to put it briefly, the Islamic army from the Akbarpur ferry, by forced marches traversing the wildness of Khandesh, Surat and Konkan, owing to the abundance of trees, seldom found any path to take, but just in the nick of time arrived near Surat and drove the Marathas away to the neighbourhood of Daman, which is a Portuguese possession and a city of Konkan or the extreme western limit of the Deccan; and these beasts, like ants and snakes took refuge in narrow places with dense trees and strait paths into which imagination cannot penetrate.

Therefore I turned my reins to the left side of the path of these wretches, intending to fall upon them as soon as they entered Balaghat from *Tal* Konkan and to chastise them at the right time. The subah of Gujarat has been freed from the disturbances created by Baji rao, and the *subah* of Malwa too has remained safe from that wretch's mischief-making, and the holy port (of Surat) which is 'gate to the House of Allah' and the place of embarkation for the pilgrims to the holy cities – has been saved from falling into the clutches of the villain. If my Ghazis (warriors in the cause of Islam) had not made such extreme exertions, the holy port would have fallen into the possession of the rebel and the gate to the House of Allah would have been closed, the Muslims would have been excluded from pilgrimage to the House of Khuda, and total loss would have fallen on the imperial Government. But through the auspiciousness of the efforts of the holy warriors the villains have been crushed, the cities have remained safe, and the cursed one (Baji rao) in the utmost humiliation has fled away.

(Sarkar Jadunath, *Islamic Culture,* Vol. 15, no. 3, pg 342-4, July 1941.)

# Appendix 5
## (Chapter 30)

Chimaji Appa's letter dated 13 May 1739 to Brahmendra swami who had urged the Peshwa to liberate Konkan from the *Firangis,* gives a complete description of the final battle:

With the swami's blessings we besieged Vasai on 7 January 1739. We also erected four or five batteries. Mines were laid. Whatever means we had to capture the place we carried them out. The Firangis fired *garnala*[a] on our mines and batteries; the mines were destroyed. They released water through shafts. They threw fire bombs soaked in oil for days on end. Their musketeers and cannons fired extremely well. But with the swami's blessing, our guns silenced the *Firangi* guns. We destroyed everything except the fort walls. Vasai is a strong place, mines are not much use. But we used mines, using poles on both sides, heaping two to two and a half hand (deep) sand on it, we took ten mines till the wall, two hundred stone cutters were put on the job to split the stones and place them around the mines. On *Vaishakha shuddha panchami* (1 May 1739) having got everything ready, ordering people to their proper places, using trumpets as a signal, once the mines were exploded, all at once we attacked and climbedthe towers using ladders. Then on Wednesday *Vaishakha shuddha shashthi,* (2 May 1739) two *ghatikas* (about three quarters of an hour) before sunrise, we lit the fuses of the mines. On the left some mines blew, some were still to blow. But in their hurry, people charged ahead through the breach. The second mine blew up just then and many were buried or killed. Then the mines on the right blew up. After one or two had exploded, the road to the tower opened up and people began climbing up. More mines exploded. Those who were climbing up were blown away. People then became hesitant, and the attack cooled down. The *Firangis* got the time to fire with their guns and cannons like never before. The army began to lose courage. On the right a big mine laid by men under Malharji Holkar was still to blow up. We searched for it and placed containers with gunpowder in it and selected

---

a. Type of a gun.

men for the job, and decided to attack immediately after it blew up. On
*Vaishakh shuddha saptami* (3 May 1739) Thursday, we exploded the mine
on the right side. Half the tower blew off, and the men climbed on it. From
within the walls, the *Firangis* again readied their guns and fired at us. The
intense fire roasted our men. With the swami's blessings, the men appeared
to have a protective armour like the *Vajra*[a] and without caring about the
fire, they used their weapons in many ways. The Firangis fought like true
soldiers. Our men fought in accordance with the tenets of the *Bharati* war.
There have been many battles before this, but none can be compared to this
battle. It is all due to the swami's blessing. Our people would not leave the
towers. Finally the fanatic *Firangis* lost courage and on the day of *ashtami*
they sought a truce and surrendered. In eight days they agreed to leave the
fort with their families. I stopped the firing. The *Firangi* took their families
to the ships. Yesterday, on *Vaishakha shuddha pournima* (full moon of the
month of *Vaishakha* or 12 May 1739), the *Firangis* all left Vasai. About five
thousand of our men were killed when the mines blew up or by enemy fire.
There were seven to eight hundred dead among the *Firangis* and some more
wounded. The war was fought like the *Bharati* war. Vasai is a strong place.
From the west to the south is the creek. To the east is a marsh. There is no
way to attack from these three sides. The north was the only option, but
even that was sandy. The swami is akin to God. Once you wrote, 'Vasai!
Given, given and given!', thrice, how can the words be false? Vasai otherwise
is not humanly achievable. It was due to the swami's blessing that we won
it. The *Topikar*[b] *Firangi* lost his strength due to a blow from the *Vajra*.
Otherwise we could not have won it. There is no limit to the swami's ability.
Only he knows his own strength. How can we mortals guess it? As ordered
by you I have sent gold figurines and have sent one hundred and twenty five
rupees for a gold crown for Shri Bhuleshwar (a temple near Pune) sent with
Shrinivas Kedar to the swami......

(Parasnis DB, *Brahmendra swami charitra and patravyavahar,*
letter 52, 1900.)

---

a.    A weapon of Indra, king of the gods.
b.    People who wear hats.

# Appendix 6

## (Chapter 31)

### Treaty with the Portuguese after the Capture of Vasai

Translate of the Capitulations on the part of Caetano d'Souza Pereira, Commandant of the city and fort of Bassein, for the surrender of the place to Chimnaji Appa, General-in-Chief of the Shahu Raja's army, now before the town, under the following clauses and conditions :—

1. The said Chimnaji Appa shall permit free passage out of the town to all troops, as well regular as auxiliaries, with their arms in order, drums beating and colours flying, also with four pieces of cannon and two mortars.

2. He shall likewise grant free passage out to all the noble families that are now in the town, with all their moveables and effects, as also to all the Christians, Gentoos and Moors who do not choose to remain in the place, and that with all their goods and effects.

3. He shall permit free and unmolested passage out of the port of this place to all vessels of war now in it, with their artillery, and provided at all points for defence, as well as to all other embarkations, gallivats, &c, whose owners do not choose to remain in the place.

4. He shall furnish all the vessels that may be wanted (charges paid) to convey away to Bombay, Chaul or Daman as well the noble families as the common people, with all in general that choose to leave the place, with their goods and effects, which they shall carry with them; and shall engage that Angria shall not rob or strip them of what they carry, upon the sea, until they have arrived at their destined port.

5. He shall likewise grant free passage to all in religious orders, and to the priests in general (who do not choose to remain in the place), with leave to carry off their goods and effects such as they may not sell beforehand.

6. He shall permit the shipping off and carrying out of the place all victualling stores and munitions of war in the town, belonging to the inhabitants and defenders; and in general all I reassure in gold or silver, with everyone's provisions and moveables, as likewise everything belonging to the churches of whatever sort or value.

7.  That the Christians who remain voluntarily in the place shall enjoy the liberty of worshipping God in the faith they profess, as likewise all over the district belonging to that jurisdiction, without being robbed or stripped of what they have got. The same is to be observed in every respect with the Gentoos and Moors that shall choose to stay behind, each according to his law.

8.  The said Chimnaji shall forthwith release all the prisoners in his power, that they may have the benefit of coming away in my company. And I will restore all that I have got, for him to dispose of as he thinks proper, in return for those of our side.

9.  On the day appointed for the garrison's evacuating the place, which is the 23rd of May (New Style), his army shall retreat to Madrapur (Manikpur?) that I may with my troops go over the walls and embark free of any fear of molestation from his army.

10. Chimnaji Appa himself shall engage not to enter the town with his troops till I am safely embarked with mine and all the people that go with me, and got out of the reach of the artillery of the place.

11. Chimnaji Appa shall purchase whatever provisions, moveables, or effects the inhabitants or others in the place may have and want to sell, by the means of persons of credit or trust, and to that end shall send into the town thirty such persons, or *Banyans*, to agree the price, paying the value to the proprietors, and receiving the things so purchased.

12. That whilst Chimnaji Appa shall be in possession of this city, he shall for ever maintain the privilege of three churches within it—one in the town, one in the district, and one on the island of Salsette—for the Christians that shall remain in the said city or places stipulated for, where they may freely exercise all the acts of their religion, and the said churches shall with their curates be subject to the most Illustrious and Reverend Primate of India, for him to settle their proper jurisdiction for the cultivation of the said Christianity. And whatever images that I may leave behind, of such as I cannot carry with me, shall be suffered to remain in the said churches with the most necessary ornaments for adorning them.

And for the security of the performance of all the above articles of capitulations the said Chimnaji Appa shall sign the same according to his custom, and shall likewise confirm and ratify them with his own seal and that of Bajirav, General of all the troops of the Shahu Raja, which being executed, the said Chimnaji Appa shall send one of his principal commanders, to my satisfaction, to remain as an hostage on board a vessel of war in the channel of the bar of this place, out of the reach of the artillery ; and for the security of such an officer I will send him of mine to stay in his army till these stipulations have been performed, when I will return him his officer in exchange of mine.

And likewise as soon as he has ratified these capitulations he shall order his people to retire from the foot of the walls into their batteries and trenches, to the distance of twenty paces: evacuating also the breaches, leaving in each the number of twenty men. In the interim there shall be no innovation on either side, or any new work be carried on.

(Signed) Caetano D'souza Pereira.

Bassein, 16th May 1739, N.S.

I.   Chimnaji Appa, accept of the above articles of surrender, except the sixth, relating to the munitions of war which I will purchase; and the ninth, which I will not engage for; and for the ratification thereof I set my seal to them in my camp before Bassein, the 16th of May 1739, N.S.

(Forrest GW, *Selections Bombay Sceretariat (Maratha Series),*
Vol. I, part 1, pg 27, 1885.)

# Appendix 7
## (Chapter 32)

### Nadir Shah's Firman Addressed To Baji rao

The firman dated 27 day of Moharram 1152, said,

>I begin with the name of God who is gracious and merciful,
>
>I begin with the name of God,
>
>A precious stone of two religions had gone,
>
>By the help of God he made himself known,
>
>By the name of Nadir, Iran.

Baji rao possessing a charming face and being a man of good luck, a devotee towards Moslem faith, being a candidate for the royal favour, is informed that this time with the help of the Almighty, Delhi is the capital and military place, and is the rising star of the great kingdom: as the great Nawab is, of the Turks. To Emperor Muhammad Shah whose greatness is like that of the heavens, who is the fulfiller of all hopes who is highly respected and noble, whose noble birth is from a Turkish mother, and whose forefathers were of the Gurjanis tribe, the kingdom and crown of India is entrusted, treating him as brother of the same religious profession and as a son; and as you having a sweet face, and being a leader of the brave tribe, who maintains himself, always by the wealth of the state. It is necessary for you to serve the emperor honestly and well, keeping in mind his rights. But up to now it is not reported that you are serving just as you ought, but done is done. As at the present juncture on account of the affection, perfect, noble and hearty friendship between our states having taken place, we understand as if Muhammad Shah's state given by God is connected with ours for putting down the rebels and the invaders of the said state of the Gurjanis, a brave and courageous person is necessary to be appointed. When, therefore, you will be informed of the contents of our noble command. Raja Shahu of great nobility, of good visage, well-experienced and obedient to the Musalman religion, has been appointed to that post, after this you would send news of your good health and safety remembering always that you are to be obedient to the royal order, which order should be received hy Shahu for the performance of the services, heartily and without neglect and fail, he (Shahu) should try his best to act accordingly. By the help of God, every one far or near, if he be obedient to the state would be regarded as worthy of service and deserving of rewards and gifts, but whoever should try to rebel against the state, a victorious friend of religion is ready for war to defeat such an enemy and to suppress him and such a large army will be sent, that by going to the boundaries of the place of rebellion, necessary punishment will be inflicted upon them (rebels). In these matters you must be aware of good warning and act according to your position.

(Kincaid and Parasnis, *A History of the Maratha People,* Vol. 2, pg 236, 1922.)

# Appendix 8

## (Chapter 36)

## Chimaji's letter to Mahadeo Hingane

On 2 June 1740 Chimaji Appa wrote to Mahadeo Hingane what could be the statement about the Peshwa's official position vis a vis the Emperor at that time, and his ambitions. It must be remembered when reading this, that in the new dispensation and in the absence of Baji rao, Chimaji's first objective was to ensure earlier promises about Malwa were honoured by the Mughals and the new Peshwa would not have to begin the campaign all over again. He therefore attributes Baji rao's actions to loyalty for the Emperor and seeks the award of money and necessary *sanads* through Sawai Jaisingh, and instructed his *vakil* accordingly.

> Many of the *Paatshah's* nobles created their own fiefs and disobeyed the orders of the Emperor. To bring them under control, to earn the goodwill of the poor ryots, tend to the lands and obtain revenues for the Emperor's treasury, arrange the affairs of the Emperor and obtain his approbation; is what the late *Rau* has persevered for in the last eight or ten years. With the help of Sawai *ji*, he negotiated many things with the Khan Dauran and hoped to complete the tasks he set out before him. Our expenses and our debts had to be met with money from the *Paatshah*, in the absence of money these things did not happen. There were many obstacles. The *Raya* wished to fulfil his commitments and when Asaf Jah sent Sayyid Lashkar Khan we decided that we will obtain money from elsewhere but complete our commitments. That is why *Raya* sent you to Sawai *ji*. Then the *Raya* entered Malwa. From Aurangabad, we dispatched you to Sawai *ji*. Then immediately he crossed the Rewa (Narmada), he fell ill and on *Vaisakha shuddha trayodashi* he passed away. God's action was most inappropriate, but there is no remedy for it.

> Although it is not in the hands of man, people who can look ahead and plan - and Sawai *ji* is such a person - if you ask me how, I can cite our father Balaji *pant* Nana always had in his mind, body, and word, the welfare of the ryots. He helped the ravaged land recover by exterminating the wicked and obtained the goodwill of his people. On Nana's demise, *Raya* was appointed Peshwa. The king blessed him and with Nana's goodwill and good deeds behind him, *Raya* desired the welfare of God and the Brahmin and wished

to restore the temple at Kashi and other places. He restored many places south of the Rewa, and it was his wish to build a temple to Vishweshwar at Kashi. *Raya* has attained fame ten times that of our father Nana. The *Raya* was a brave and reputed doer and his son Nana has inherited from his father the intelligence to obtain fame and success. Our seniors had the blessings of the ryots and God and the Brahmins and they carried it with them. We wish the welfare of all our people. The late Peshwa's able chiefs are with us.

Nana and I are now going to the *Chhatrapati* and after receiving the robes of the office of Peshwa we will come back to Pune. The chiefs will also be back. It will take two or three months to collect an army of one lakh men. Then, we, or Nana alone will come to that province to complete all the tasks that *Raya* had contemplated. We will satisfy the Sovereign and be worthy of his approbation. You must have told all this to Sawai *ji* and you can ask him to write to the *Paatshah* that all the machinations of the N named (Nizam) will be defeated and what the Sovereign and Sawai *ji* wish will happen. He should be prepared to honour the treaties contracted with the *Raya*, in fact he should do better than that, and of the fifteen lakh to be paid, the five lakh that were ready to be sent should be sent at the earliest. Once the army is ready, one of us will come. You should send Rajamal to receive us and we will meet Ranaji and Sawai *ji* and Abhai Singh. If the Nizam behaves like a short-sighted person, we will, with our chiefs and a lakh-strong army, not hesitate to put him in his place. We are all well acquainted with each other and we are not different from the people who performed when the *Raya* was alive. You should reassure the Sovereign accordingly.

For all the Hindus, *Raya* was the shelter. He was fully equipped in every way. There was none other in the south and in Hindustan. So be it. *Raya* has not taken anything with him. He has left things as they were. We were all with *Raya* and we are determined to enlarge on what he planned to do. We are capable of punishing those who are not loyal to the Sovereign. Once Sawai *ji* and Ranaji and Abhai Singh are with us, what is not possible? To sum up, nothing has changed with the *Raya*'s departure. The only difference is that *Raya* was planning the campaign from Malwa in the monsoons and we are executing it after Dassera. You should convince Sawai *ji* and the Sovereign and in these stringent times you should forward the funds to complete the job in hand.

(Khare GH, *Hingane daftar,* 1.15.)

# Notes to Illustrations

1 Baji rao Peshwa (Cover) – This seated painting of Baji rao Peshwa I of the Maratha school is from a series of paintings made in Satara about the year 1854 from original paintings. This painting is now in the Chhatrapati Shivaji Maharaj Vastu Sangrahalaya (CSMVS) – 'the Museum' in Mumbai.

2 *Chhatrapati* Shahu – is said to have been drawn by Sadashiv Chitari and shows a white haired ascetic king on horseback. There is a hukkah in his right hand and holds the reins of the horse in his left. Originally part of the Menawali collection of DB Parasnis, it is now located at the Dr. Babasaheb Ambedkar Marathwada History Museum at Aurangabad. Reproduced with permission.

3 Shrimant Baji rao Peshwa on horseback – Perhaps the only contemporary painting of Baji rao. Originally with the family of Pilaji Jadhav rao. Presently at the Bharat Itihas Sanshodhak Mandal. The painting is slightly damaged due to moisture. Reproduced with permission.

4 Emperor Aurangzeb on horseback – The painting of 1690 to 1710 is from the time he spent in the Deccan. The original painting is at the Cleveland Museum of Art and reproduced here with permission.

5 Emperor Farrukh Siyar and Sayyid Husain Ali – Reproduced courtesy British Library Board, London. Shelf mark J 18,5.The painting is of of 1715 vintage.

6 Shrimant Baji rao Peshwa – This painting was originally part of the Menawali collection of DB Parasnis, it is now located at the Dr. Babasaheb Ambedkar Marathwada History Museum at Aurangabad. Reproduced with permission.

7 Pilaji Jadhav rao – This painting of Pilaji is at the Bharat Itihas Sanshodhak Mandal, Pune. It was donated to the Mandal by the Jadhav rao family and is probably a contemporary painting of the Maratha *subedar.*

8 Maharana Sangram Singh of Marwar with Sawai Jaisingh of Amber – This water-clour painting dated 1732 by Kriparam is drawn with opaque watercolor, gold and ink onn paper. It is held at the Los Angeles County Museum of Art and is in the public domain.

9 Malharji Holkar – Lithograph of Malharji Holkar was originally drawn at Pune at Chitrashala – a school of art. It is presently a part of the Wellcome Collection and used under Creative Commons license.

10 Nizam-ul-mulk – This painting of the Nizam-ul-mulk is taken from Wiki commons.

11 Khan Dauran, *Wazir* Qamruddin Khan and Muzaffar Khan – This painting reproduced with permission from the Museum of Fine Arts Boston is drawn

with ink and light colour on paper circa 1735. Persian inscriptions identify each figure: Muzaffar Khan (on right), Qamaruddin Khan *Wazir*, and Khan Dauran Khan. Muzaffar Khan was Khan Dauran's brother.

12 Shaniwar wada – This water colour of the Shaniwar wada was done by landscape artist Edward Lear in June 1874. It is presently at the Houghton Library.

13 Brahmendra swami – from the book by DB Parasnis, published in 1900.

14 Janjira fort - a view of the mainland from bastions of the fort. A photograph by the author.

15 Emperor Muhammad Shah – This opaque watercolour, with gold and ink on paper, is with the Los Angeles County Museum of Art. It was created in Delhi between 1725-1750. It shows the Emperor presiding over the Holi celebrations in Delhi. Ironically, it was the same festival when Nadir Shah infamously massacred the residents of the city. The painting is in the public domain.

16 Seals of Baji rao Peshwa and Sripat rao Pratinidhi on a letter in October 1729. The seals side by side show their equal status in Governmental matters, and partly explains their rivalry. The seal of the Peshwa and the *Pratinidhi* appear together on letters written by the *Chhatrapati*. The letter is in the Bharat Itihas Sanshodhak Mandal Museum, Pune.

17 Burhan-ul-mulk Sadat Khan - Sadat Khan was the first Nawab of Awadh. The fish was a symbol of his royal house, which explains why he is shown standing on a fish.

18 Kushk mahal or Kushk –i- Feroz – a 14th century hunting lodge built by Feroz Tughlaq lies within the grounds of the Teen Murti Bhawan at Delhi. It is possible Baji rao camped here. This picture is courtesy Vikramjit Singh Rooprai, a heritage activist from Delhi.

19 Treaty between the Marathas and the Portuguese signed by Vyankat rao Ghorpade and Dadaji rao on behalf of Baji rao Peshwa on 22 April 1739 after the war in Goa. The original letter is available at the Bharat Itihas Sanshodhak Mandal and the entire treaty is published in Purandare *daftar* Volume 3, letter 182.

20 Letter from *Chhatrapati* Shahu's office to Chimaji Appa in 1739 about the English envoy William Gordon. Image acquired from the British Library, London. The letter is translated on page 303.

21 Bacaim or Bassein, now called Vasai. This Portuguese map shows the fort and one can see it surrounded by water on three sides. The map, as was common in maps of the time, has east towards the top.

22 Vasai fort – this picture taken by the author shows the seaward entrance to the fort of Vasai.

23   Chimaji Appa – No original painting of Chimaji has been found so far. His statue has been erected inside the fort of Vasai. Photograph by the author.

24   Emperor Muhammad Shah and Nadir Shah – a painting depicting the meeting between the two in 1739. Public domain from wiki.

25   Shrimant Baji rao Peshwa Samadhi – The Samadhi on the bank of the Narmada was built by the Scindias. It is at Raver khedi, a tiny village in that region. This photograph was taken by the author in April 2008.

26   Mastani – (on page 312) This picture, purportedly of Mastani, was published by noted researcher DB Parasnis a hundred years ago. The original from where the picture was taken is in the possession of the Phadnis family at Menawali. It is not clear whether this is a contemporary painting

27   'Hilt of the Peshwa's sword' (Back cover) – Painting by Robert Mabon in 1792. Water colour at Yale Centre for British Art. Published with permission.

# References

## Book One - Dark Night
### 1. Not a Tranquil Time

1. Rajwade VK, Ed., *Radha Madhav Vilas Champu, Jairam Pindye,*pg 250, 1922.
2. Smith VA, Ed,. *The History of the Late Revolution of the Great Mogul,* Bernier F., pg 168, 1914.
3. Sen Surendranath, *The Military System of the Marathas, pg 18, 1958.*
4. Rajwade VK, *Marathyanchya itihasachi sadhane,* vol 15.276, 1912.
5. London Gazette, number 757, dated 17 to 20 February 1672.
6. Fryer John, *A New Account of East-India and Persia,* pg 81, 1681
7. Hatalkar VG, *Relations between the French and the Marathas,* pg 22, 1958.
8. Sane KN, *Chitnis Malhar Ramrao's Shrimant Chhatrapati Sambhaji maharaj charitra,* pg 12, 1882.
9. Sarkar J, *Anecdotes of Aurangzeb,* pg 74, 1988.
10. Sarkar J, *History of Aurangzeb,* Vol.5, pg 4-5, 1924.

### 2. The Kingdom for a 'Vatan'

1. Sane KN, *Chitnis Malhar Ramrao's Thorale Shahu maharaj yanche charitra,* pg 2 footnote, 1893.
2. Sardesai GS et al, *Sane KN - Kavyetihas sangraha Aitihasik Patre Yadi,* letter 3, 1930.
3. Madras Presidency, *Records of Fort St. George*: Diary and Consultation Books, 1672-78-I.756 (Madras, 85 vols, Record Office, 191043), 14 November 1689, p. 92.
4. Bendre VS Ed., *Keshav Pandit's Rajaram Charitam,* pg10-11, 1931.
5. Ranade MG, *Rise of the Maratha Power,* pg 30, 1900.
6. Niccolao Manucci, *Storia do Mogor, or Mogul India*, 1 653-1 708, translated by W. Irvine, Indian Text Series (London, 4 vols, 1907-08), III, 143.
7. Kulkarni AR, *Maharashtra in the age of Shivaji,* pg. 130,170,240, 1969.
8. Rajwade VK, *Marathyanchya itihasachi sadhane,* Vol. 15.347-8, 1912 and Sardesai GS *Marathi Riyasat* Vol. 2, pg 190, 2012.
9. Sardesai GS *Marathi Riyasat* Vol. 2, pg 188, 2012.
10. Sardesai GS *Marathi Riyasat* Vol. 2, pg 245, 2012.

### 3. The Mughals Lose the Deccan

1. Sane KN, *Chitnis Malhar Ramrao's Shrimant Chhatrapati Sambhaji maharaj va Thorale Rajaram maharaj charitra,* pg 43, 1882.

2.    Sarkar J, *History of Aurangzeb,* Vol. 1, pg 64 footnote, 1912.

3.    Shejwalkar TS, *Nizam Peshwe sambandh, Lecture 1,* pg5, 1963.

4.    Rajwade VK, *Marathyanchya itihasachi sadhane,* Vol. 8.47

5.    Parasnis DB, *Aitihasik goshti, Itihas Sangraha,* 2-17. *Maasir i Alamgiri,* pg 243-4.

6.    Sarkar J, Ed., *Maasir i Alamgiri,* pg 238.

7.    Stewart Gordon, *Modern Asian Studies ii, i* pg 1-40, 1977, pp. I-40.

8.    Sarkar J, *History of Aurangzeb,* Vol.5, pg 235, 1924.

9.    Mortimer Wheeler, *Cambridge History of India: The Indus civilization,* Vol. 4, pg 300, 1937.

10.   Sarkar J, *Anecdotes of Aurangzeb,* pg 37, 1988.

11.   Rajwade VK, *Marathyanchya itihasachi sadhane,* Vol. 2, pg. 8.

## 4. The Prisoner Of Islampuri

1.    Sardesai GS, *Marathi Riyasat* Vol. 2, pg 180, 2012.

2.    Brij Kishore, *Tarabai and her times,* pg 105, 1963.

3.    Sarkar J, *History of Aurangzeb,* Vol.5, pg 203, 1924.

4.    Behere, NK, *Bajirao Peshwe,* pg 20, 1929.

5.    Sane KN, *Chitnis Malhar Ramrao's Thorale Shahu maharaj yanche charitra,* pg 4-5, 1893.

6.    Ibid, pg 5.

7.    Sarkar J, *History of Aurangzeb,* Vol.5, pg 205, 1924.

8.    Sardesai GS, *Marathi Riyasat* Vol. 2, pg 287, 2012.

9.    Sarkar J, *Anecdotes of Aurangzeb,* pg 11chk, 1988.

10.   Malik Zahiruddin, *The Reign of Muhammad Shah,* pg 104, 1977.

11.   Sane KN, *Chitnis Malhar Ramrao's Thorale Shahu maharaj yanche charitra,* pg 10, 1893.

12.   Ibid, pg 12.

13.   Ibid, pg 10.

14.   Khare Vasudeo Vaman, *Ichalkaranji cha itihas,* pg 22, 1913.

15.   Sardesai GS, *Vividh Dnyan Vistar,* pg 106, Feb 1924.

16.   Sane KN, *Chitnis Malhar Ramrao's Thorale Shahu maharaj yanche charitra,* pg 12, 1893.

17.   Behere, NK, *Bajirao Peshwe,* pg 39, 1929.

18.   Rajwade VK, *Marathyanchya itihasachi sadhane,* Vol. 2, pg 10.

## 5. The Rise Of Balaji Vishwanath

1.    Sardesai GS, *Marathi Riyasat* Vol. 3, pg 127, 2012.

2.    Rajwade VK, *Marathyanchya itihasachi sadhane,* Vol. 2, pg 1, *Peshwe Shakavali.*

3.    Ganpat rao Harihar Patwardhan Kurundwad, *Bhatt-Vansha-Kavya,* pg 5, 1893.

4.  Mackenzie Colin, *Mackenzie collection,* Vol. 13, India Office records, London.
5.  *Sanpuri bakhar,* pg 1, 1950.
6.  Sane KN, *Chitnis Malhar Ramrao's Thorale Shahu maharaj yanche charitra,* pg 20-21, 1893.
7.  Behere NK, *Bajirao Peshwe,* pg 32-3, 1929.
8.  Sane KN, *Chitnis Malhar Ramrao's Thorale Shahu maharaj yanche charitra,,* pg 24, 1893.
9.  Sardesai GS, *Selections Peshwa daftar,* Vol. 30.2, 1933.
10. Sane KN, *Chitnis Malhar Ramrao's Thorale Shahu maharaj yanche charitra,* pg 28-9, 1893.

## 6. The Rise and Fall Of Zulfiquar Khan

1.  Irwine W., *Asiatic Society of Bengal,* No. 1, part 1, 1900.
2.  Ghulam Husain Khan, trans Nota Manus, *Siyar-ul-mutaqherin,* Vol. 1, Ch 1, pg 44, 1901.
3.  Irwine W., *Later Mughals,* Vol. 1, pg 220, 1922.
4.  Ibid, pg 251.
5.  Ibid, pg 253.
6.  Ghulam Husain Khan, trans Nota Manus, *Siyar-ul-mutaqherin,* Vol. 1, Ch 1, pg 62, 1901.

## Book Two - First Light

## 7. The Sayyids Become All-Powerful

1.  Earles Joseph, *Letters of the Emperor Aurangzebe,* pg 6, 1788.
2.  Sarkar J, *Anecdotes of Aurangzeb,* pg 32, 1988.
3.  Sen Surendranath, *The Military System of the Marathas,* pg 25-6, 1958.
4.  Ibid, pg 30.
5.  Ibid, pg 33.
6.  Irwine W., *Later Mughals,* Vol. 1, pg 269, 1922.
7.  Ghulam Husain Khan, trans Nota Manus, *Siyar-ul-mutaqherin,* Vol. 1, Ch 1, pg 92, 1901.
8.  Ibid, pg 95-6.
9.  Ibid, pg 97.

## 8. The Marathas go to Delhi

1.  Ghulam Husain Khan, trans. Nota Manus, *Siyar-ul-mutaqherin,* Vol. 1, Ch 1, pg 101, 1901.
2.  Michael Kennedy, *The Criminal Classes Of India,* pg 145, 1985.

3. Rajwade VK, *Marathyanchya itihasachi sadhane*, Vol. 2, pg 1, *Peshwe Shakavali.*
4. Parasnis DB, *Brahmendra swami charitra and patravyavahar,* letter 183, 1900.
5. Rajwade VK, *Marathyanchya itihasachi sadhane*, Vol. 2, pg 31, *Peshwe Shakavali.*
6. Ghulam Husain Khan, trans. Nota Manus, *Siyar-ul-mutaqherin*, Vol. 1, Ch 2, pg 118, 1901.
7. Ibid, pg 130.
8. Ibid, pg 133.
9. Grant Duff, *History of the Marathas,* Vol. 1, pg 320, 1826.
10. Irwine W., *Later Mughals*, Vol. 1, pg 384, 1922.
11. Malik Zahiruddin, *The Reign of Muhammad Shah*, pg 116, 1977.
12. Mortimer Wheeler, *Cambridge History of India: The Indus civilization*, Vol. 4, pg 396, 1937.

## 9. Downfall Of the Sayyids

1. Irwine W., *Later Mughals*, Vol. 2, pg 91, 1922.
2. Satish Chandra, Ed., *Mehta Balmukund, Balmukundnama,* pg 65-6, 1972.
3. Ibid, pg 67-8.
4. Sardesai GS, *Selections Peshwa daftar,* Vol. 30.309, 1933.
5. Irwine W., *Later Mughals*, Vol. 2, pg 46, 1922.
6. Ibid, pg 49.
7. Irwine W., *Indian Antiquary*, Vol. 33, pg 1 and 69, 1904.
8. Pagdi, Setu madhav rao, *Annals of Bhandarkar Oriental Research Institute,* Vol. 51, pg 93-121, 1970.

## 10. Baji rao Pandit Pradhan: Early Days

1. Sane KN, *Chitnis Malhar Ramraos Shrimant Chhatrapati Sambhaji maharaj charitra,* pg 45, 1882.
2. Sardesai GS, Kale YM, Wakaskar VS, *Sane KN's Kavye-tihas Sangraha*, letter 495, 1930.
3. Sardesai GS, (Jadunath Sarkar foreword), *Marathi Riyasat,* Vol. 3, pg 215, 2012.
4. Sardesai GS, *Selections Peshwa daftar,* Vol. 10.4, 1933.
5. Ibid, Vol. 30.24.
6. Ibid, Vol. 30.26.
7. Ibid, Vol. 10.6 &11.
8. *Sahyadri,* pg 434, May 1940.
9. Yusuf Husain, *The First Nizam,* pg 153, 1963.
10. Rajwade VK, *Marathyanchya itihasachi sadhane*, Vol. 2, pg 31, *Peshwe Shakavali.*
11. Thakur VV, *Holkarshahi cha itihas,* pg 20, 1944.
12. Kunte BG, *Modi Illustrative documents,* pg 6, 1978.

## 11. Nizam's Fateḥ at Sakharkherḍa

1. Pagdi Setu madhav rao, *Maharashtra ani Marathe,* pg 107, 1963.
2. Ghulam Husain Khan, trans. Nota Manus, *Siyar-ul-mutaqherin*, Vol. 1, Ch 3, pg 232, 1901.
3. Ibid, pg 237.
4. Sardesai GS, *Selections Peshwa daftar,* Vol. 22.4, 1933.
5. Ghulam Husain Khan, trans Nota Manus, *Siyar-ul-mutaqherin*, Vol. 1, Ch 3, pg 244, 1901.
6. Irwine W., *Later Mughals*, Vol. 2, pg 265, 1922.
7. Ghulam Husain Khan, trans Nota Manus, *Siyar-ul-mutaqherin*, Vol. 1, Ch 3, pg 246footnote, 1922.
8. Irwine W., *'Nadir Shah and Muhammad Shah' a poem by Tilak Das,* 1897.
9. Sardesai GS, *Selections Peshwa daftar,* Vol. 10.16, 1933.
10. Ibid, Vol.10.18.
11. Ibid, Vol.10.19.
12. Ibid, Vol.10.21.
13. Ibid, Vol.10.24.
14. Ibid Vol. 10.1.
15. Ibid, Vol. 30, pg 268.
16. Pagdi Setu madhav rao, *Eighteenth century Deccan*, pg 95, 1963.
17. Rajwade VK, *Marathyanchya itihasachi sadhane*, Vol. 6.16.
18. Irwine W., *Later Mughals*, Vol. 2, pg 149, 1922.
19. Vad GC, *Chhatrapati Shahu Rojnishi*, sl. 12, pg 5, 1908.
20. Sardesai GS, *Selections Peshwa daftar,* Vol. 10.30, 1933.
21. Yusuf Husain, *The First Nizam,* pg 130, 1963.
22. Irwine W., *Later Mughals*, Vol. 2, pg 148, 1922.
23. Kirkpatrick William, *Nizam's letter, Asiatick Miscellany,* Vol. 1, pg 493, 1785.
24. Pagdi Setu madhav rao, *Eighteenth century Deccan*, pg 122, 1963.

## 12. Kanhoji Angre's War in the Konkan

1. Desai WS, *Bombay and the Marathas*, pg 63, 1970.
2. Slight John Paul, Brit Empire and the Hajj, Ch 1, 1865-1956, 2015.
3. Sen Surendranath, *Early career of Kanhoji Angre*, pg 13, 1941.
4. Desai WS, *Bombay and the Marathas*, pg 66, 1970.
5. Sen Surendranath, *Early career of Kanhoji Angre*, pg 14, 1941.
6. Pissurlenkar Pandurang, *Indian Historical Reaserch Commission*, Vol. 19, pg 167, 1942.
7. Danvers Frederick Charles, *Portuguese in India,* Vol. 2, pg 392, 1894.
8. Desai WS, *Bombay and the Marathas*, pg 75, 1970.
9. Ibid, pg 70.

## 13. Rivalry in the Carnatic

1. Pagdi, Setu madhav rao, *Annals of Bhandarkar Oriental Research Institute,* Vol. 51, pg 103-4, 1970.
2. Sarkar Jadunath, *Islamic Culture,* Vol. 15, no. 3, pg 341. July 1941.
3. Vad GC, *Chhatrapati Shahu Rojnishi,* sl. 14, pg 5, 1908/ Sardesai GS, *Selections Peshwa daftar,* Vol. 20.4, 1933./ *Sahyadri,* pg 13, May 1940.
4. Sardesai GS, *Selections Peshwa daftar,* Vol. 30, pg 276, 1933.
5. Ibid, pg 277.
6. Pagdi, Setu madhav rao, *Annals of Bhandarkar Oriental Research Institute,* Vol. 51, pg 99, 1970.
7. Ibid, pg 102-3.
8. Vad GC, *Chhatrapati Shahu Rojnishi,* sl. 25, 1908.

## Book Three - The Rising Sun

## 14. 'A Masterpiece in Strategic Mobility'

1. Yusuf Husain, *The First Nizam,* pg 149, 1963.
2. Joshi PM, *Selections Peshwa daftar, (New Series),* Vol. 1, letter 3, 1957.
3. Sarkar Jadunath, *Islamic Culture,* Vol. 15, no. 3, pg 341. July 1941.
4. Dalvi Gopal Dajiba, *Jadhav Kaifiyat,* Vol. 1, pg 81, 1912.
5. Sardesai GS, *Selections Peshwa daftar,* Vol. 10.41, pg 276, 1933.
6. Ibid, Vol. 10.40.
7. Ibid, Vol. 10.42.
8. Parasnis DB, *Itihas Sangraha, Sanads,* pg 23-5, 1917.
9. Sardesai GS, *Selections Peshwa daftar,* Vol. 10.43, 1933.
10. Sardesai GS, Kale YM, Wakaskar VS, *Sane KN's Kavye-tihas Sangraha,* letter 15, 1930.
11. Vad GC, *Chhatrapati Shahu Rojnishi,* sl. 30, 1908.
12. Sardesai GS, *Selections Peshwa daftar,* Vol. 10.48, 1933.
13. Vad GC, *Chhatrapati Shahu Rojnishi,* sl. 29, 1908.
14. Ibid, sl. 214.
15. Sardesai GS, *Selections Peshwa daftar,* Vol. 30.50, 1933.
16. Parasnis DB, *Itihas Sangraha, Aitihasik Tipane,* 2.35, 1916.
17. Vad GC, *Balaji Bajirao rojnishi,* Vol. 2, pg 228, 1906.
18. Sardesai GS, *Selections Peshwa daftar,* Vol. 30, pg 282, 1933.
19. Ibid, Vol. 10.50.
20. Ibid Vol. 10.52.
21. Ibid, Vol. 30, pg 283.
22. Mortimer Wheeler, *Cambridge History of India: The Indus civilization,* Vol. 4, pg 400, 1937.

23. Grant Duff, *History of the Marathas*, Vol. 1, pg 360-1, 1826.
24. Sardesai GS, *Selections Peshwa daftar*, Vol. 15.86, pg 83, 1933.
25. Joshi PM, *Selections Peshwa daftar*, *(New Series)*, Vol. 1, letter 6, 1957.
26. Sardesai GS, *Selections Peshwa daftar*, Vol. 10.53, 1933.
27. Malik Zahiruddin, *The Reign of Muhammad Shah*, pg 109, 1977.
28. Ibid, pg 111.
29. Sarkar Jadunath, *History of Jaipur*, pg 175, 1984.
30. Montgomery of Alamein, *A Concise History of Warfare*, pg 322, 1972.
31. *Sahyadri*, pg 433, May 1940.
32. Vad GC, *Balaji Bajirao rojnishi*, Vol. 2, pg 228-30, 1906.

## 15. Across the Narmada

1. Sardesai GS, *Selections Peshwa daftar*, Vol. 13.23, 1933.
2. Sardesai GS, *Marathi Riyasat* Vol. 3, pg 329, 2012.
3. Rajwade VK, *Marathyanchya itihasachi sadhane*, Vol. 6.585.
4. Sardesai GS, *Selections Peshwa daftar*, Vol. 10.4, 1933.
5. Ibid, Vol. 10.9.
6. Rajwade VK, *Marathyanchya itihasachi sadhane*, Vol. 6.591.
7. Vad GC, *Chhatrapati Shahu Rojnishi*, sl. 214, 1908.
8. Sardesai GS, *Selections Peshwa daftar*, Vol. 13.10, 1933.
9. Grant Duff, *History of the Marathas*, Vol. 1, pg 379-80, 1826.
10. Sardesai GS, *Selections Peshwa daftar*, Vol. 13.24, 1933.
11. Parasnis DB, *Brahmendra swami charitra and patravyavahar*, pg 16, 1900.
12. Ibid, letter 30.
13. Ibid, letter 31.
14. Ibid, letter 32.
15. Sardesai GS, *Selections Peshwa daftar*, Vol. 17.52, 1933.
16. Ibid, Vol. 30, pg 284, 1933.
17. Raghubir Sinh, *Malwa in Transition*, pg 203-4, 1936.
18. Sardesai GS, *Marathi Riyasat* Vol. 3, pg 310-11, 2012.
19. Sardesai GS, *Selections Peshwa daftar*, Vol. 30.315, 1933.
20. Ibid, Vol. 13.15.
21. Ibid Vol. 13.17.
22. Raghubir Singh, *Studies on Maratha and Rajput History*, pg 124, 1989.
23. Ibid, Vol. 13. 18-19.
24. Vad GC, *Chhatrapati Shahu Rojnishi*, sl. 41, 1908.
25. Sardesai GS, *Selections Peshwa daftar*, Vol. 13.29, 1933.
26. Ibid, Vol. 13.30.
27. Ibid, Vol. 13.33.

## 16. 'Our Realm has Reached the Yamuna'.

1. Sardesai GS, *Selections Peshwa daftar,* Vol. 13.45, 1933.
2. Ghulam Husain Khan, trans Nota Manus, *Siyar-ul-mutaqherin,* Vol. 1, Ch 3, pg 261, 1901.
3. Parasnis DB, *Marathyanche Parakram- Bundelkhand prakaran,* pg 6, 1895.
4. Ibid, pg 57.
5. Ibid, pg 61.
6. Sardesai GS, *Selections Peshwa daftar,* Vol. 13.10, 1933.
7. Parasnis DB, *Marathyanche Parakram- Bundelkhand prakaran,* pg 65, 1895.
8. Sardesai GS, *Selections Peshwa daftar,* Vol. 30.315, 1933.
9. Parasnis DB, *Bundele yanchi kaifiyat,* pg 3, 1897.
10. Rajwade VK, *Marathyanchya itihasachi sadhane,* Vol. 3.14.
11. Irwine W., *Bangash Nawabs, Asiatic Society of Bengal,* pg 298-9.No. 4, 1878.
12. Parasnis DB, *Bundele yanchi kaifiyat,* pg 4-5, 1897.
13. Khare GH, *Sanivara wada.*

## 17. Sawai Jaisingh sends an Envoy

1. Sardesai GS, *Selections Peshwa daftar,* Vol. 10.66.
2. Chandra Satish, *Indian History Congress,* pg 182, 1948.
3. Sarkar Jadunath, *History of Jaipur,* pg 186 (note), 1984.
4. Chandra Satish, *Indian History Congress,* pg 184, 1948
5. Vad GC, *Chhatrapati Shahu Rojnishi,* sl. 198, 1908.
6. Bhatnagar VS, *Life and Times of Sawai Jaisingh,* pg 207, 1974.
7. Ibid, pg 208.
8. *Sahyadri,* pg 379, May 1940, Sardesai GS, *Selections Peshwa daftar,* Vol. 10.66,71,74 and Vol. 30.73.

## 18. The Senapati's Revolt

1. Sardesai GS, *Selections Peshwa daftar,* Vol. 12.42, 1933.
2. Vad GC, *Chhatrapati Shahu Rojnishi,* sl. 214, 1908.
3. Kincaid CA, Tale of the Tulse Plant, pg 41.
4. Parasnis DB, *Itihas Sangraha, Sanads,* pg 15, 1917.
5. Sardesai GS, *Selections Peshwa daftar,* Vol. 30.2, 1933.
6. Ibid, Vol. 30.7.
7. *Sahyadri,* pg 450, May 1940.
8. Sardesai GS, *Selections Peshwa daftar,* Vol. 12.5, 1933.
9. Ibid, Vol. 12.13.
10. Ibid, Vol. 12.41-2.

11. Ibid, Vol. 12.23.
12. Ibid, Vol. 30, pg 297.
13. Kincaid and Parasnis, *A History of the Maratha People,* Vol. 2, pg 190, 1922.
14. Sardesai GS, *Selections Peshwa daftar,* Vol. 12.34, 1933.
15. Sane KN, *Chitnis Malhar Ramrao's Thorale Shahu maharaj yanche charitra,* pg 60, 1893.
16. Malik Zahiruddin, *The Reign of Muhammad Shah,* pg 102, 1977.
17. Sardesai GS, *Selections Peshwa daftar,* Vol. 30, pg 301, 1933.
18. Joshi PM, *Selections Peshwa daftar, (New Series),* Vol. 1, letter 9, 1957.
19. Reu Pt. Bishweshwar Nath, *Indian History Congress,* Calcutta, pg 212, 1939.
20. Sardesai GS, *Selections Peshwa daftar,* Vol. 12.39, 1933.
21. Ibid, Vol. 17.12.
22. Ibid, Vol. 30, pg 299.

## 19. The Battle Of Dabhoi

1. Sane KN, *Chitnis Malhar Ramrao's Thorale Shahu maharaj yanche charitra,* pg 50, 1893.
2. Irwine W., *Bangash Nawabs, Asiatic Society of Bengal,* pg 809, No. 4, Nov.1878.
3. Grant Duff, *History of the Marathas,* Vol. 1, pg 364-65, 1826.
4. Sane KN, *Chitnis Malhar Ramrao's Thorale Shahu maharaj yanche charitra,* pg 49, 1893.
5. Malik Zahiruddin, *The Reign of Muhammad Shah,* pg 109, 1977.
6. Sardesai GS, *Marathi Riyasat* Vol. 3, pg 391, 2012.
7. Parasnis DB, *Brahmendra swami charitra and patravyavahar,* letter 26, 1900.
8. Sardesai GS, *Selections Peshwa daftar,* Vol. 12.46, 1933.
9. Sarkar Jadunath, *Islamic Culture,* Vol. 15, no. 3, pg 342-4, July 1941.
10. Gense JH & Banaji DR, *The Gaekwads of Baroda,*Vol. 1, pg 11, 1936.
11. Rajwade VK, *Marathyanchya itihasachi sadhane,* Vol. 3.166.
12. Sane KN, *Chitnis Malhar Ramrao's Thorale Shahu maharaj yanche charitra,* pg 50, 1893.
13. Sardesai GS et al, *Sane KN - Kavyetihas sangraha Aitihasik Patre Yadi,* letter 496, 1930.
14. Parasnis DB, *Brahmendra swami charitra and patravyavahar,* letter 188, 1900.
15. Grant Duff, *History of the Marathas,* Vol. 1, pg 366-7, 1826.
16. Sardesai GS, *Selections Peshwa daftar,* Vol. 17.30, 1933.
17. Sardesai GS, Kulkarni KP, Kale YM, *Aitihasik Patravyavahar,* letter 436, 1933.

## 20. Entente at Rui Rameshwar

1. Sardesai GS, *Selections Peshwa daftar,* Vol. 30.90, 1933.
2. Parasnis DB, *Bharat varsha, Vol. 1, Holkar kaifiyat,* pg 6, 1898.

3. Sardesai GS, *Selections Peshwa daftar,* Vol. 14.1, 1933.
4. Ibid, Vol. 14.2.
5. Irwine W., *Later Mughals,* Vol. 2, pg 277, 1922.
6. Sardesai GS, *Selections Peshwa daftar,* Vol. 9.7, 1933.
7. Parasnis DB, *Brahmendra swami charitra and patravyavahar,* letter 121, 1900.
8. Sardesai GS, *Marathi Riyasat* Vol. 3, pg 453, 2012.
9. Ibid, pg 471. *Aiti Sankeern sahitya,* 1946 letter 6/6 dated 12-1-1733.
10. Sardesai GS, *Marathi Riyasat* Vol. 3, pg 215, 2012.
11. Sardesai GS, *Selections Peshwa daftar,* Vol. 15, pg 94, 1933.

## 21. The Campaign in Habshan

1. Parasnis DB, *Brahmendra swami charitra and patravyavahar,* pg 20-21, 1900.
2. Purandare KV, *Purandare daftar,* Vol. 1.102, 1929.
3. Banaji DR, *Bombay and the Sidis,* pg xx, 1952.
4. Ibid, pg 6.
5. Sarkar J, *Anecdotes of Aurangzeb,* pg 93-4, 1988.
6. Parasnis DB, *Brahmendra swami charitra and patravyavahar,* pg 43, 1900.
7. Ibid, pg 14.
8. Ibid, pg 18.
9. Ibid, pg 27.
10. Sardesai GS, *Marathi Riyasat* Vol. 3, pg 407, 2012.
11. Rajwade VK, *Marathyanchya itihasachi sadhane,* Vol. 3.244.
12. Parasnis DB, *Brahmendra swami charitra and patravyavahar,* pg 51, 1900.
13. Sardesai GS, *Selections Peshwa daftar,* Vol. 3.2, 1933.
14. Sardesai GS et al, *Sane KN - Kavyetihas sangraha Aitihasik Patre Yadi,* letter 26, 1930.
15. Purandare KV, *Purandare daftar,* Vol. 1.103, 1929.
16. Sardesai GS, *Selections Peshwa daftar,* Vol. 3.4, 1933.
17. Ibid, Vol.3.10.
18. Parasnis DB, *Brahmendra swami charitra and patravyavahar,* pg 47, 1900.
19. Rajwade VK, *Marathyanchya itihasachi sadhane,* Vol. 3.330.
20. *Bombay Quarterly Review,* Vol. 4, pg 73, 1856.
21. Dhabbu DG, *Sarkhel Kulabkar Angre,* pg 29, 1939.
22. Banaji DR, *Bombay and the Sidis,* pg 63, 1952.
23. Sardesai GS, *Selections Peshwa daftar,* Vol. 33.79, 1933.
24. Ibid, Vol. 33.80.
25. Ibid, Vol. 3.72.
26. Forrest GW, *Selections Bombay Sceretariat (Home Series),* Vol. 2, pg 61, 1887 and Dhabbu DG, *Sarkhel Kulabkar Angre,* pg 31-33, 1939.

## 22. The End Of Siddi Sat

1.  Parasnis DB, *Brahmendra swami charitra and patravyavahar,* letter 281, 1900.
2.  Ibid, pg 53.
3.  Sardesai GS, *Selections Peshwa daftar,* Vol. 3.15, 1933.
4.  Ibid, Vol. 3.19.
5.  Ibid, Vol. 30. 65 and 69.
6.  Ibid, Vol. 3.45.
7.  Ibid, Vol. 3.21.
8.  Grant Duff, *History of the Marathas,* Vol. 1, pg 347, 1826.
9.  Pagdi, Setu madhav rao, *Annals of Bhandarkar Oriental Research Institute,* Vol. 51, pg 120-121, 1970.
10. Sardesai GS, *Selections Peshwa daftar,* Vol. 33.152, 1933.
11. Ibid, Vol. 33.170.
12. Ibid, Vol. 33.191.
13. Ibid, Vol. 33.193.
14. Ibid, Vol. 33.221.
15. Ibid, Vol. 33.222.
16. Ibid, Vol. 3.129.
17. Ibid, Vol. 3.128.
18. Ibid, Vol. 3.127.
19. Ibid, Vol. 3.142.
20. Ibid, Vol. 3.160.
21. Ibid, Vol. 3.175.
22. Ibid, Vol. 3.192.
23. Parasnis DB, *Brahmendra swami charitra and patravyavahar,* letter 364, 1900.
24. Rajwade VK, *Marathyanchya itihasachi sadhane,* Vol. 10.378.
25. Sardesai GS, *Selections Peshwa daftar,* Vol. 3.182, 1933.

## 23. Rajput Affairs, Mughal Wars...and a Pilgrimmage

1.  Irwine W., *Later Mughals,* Vol. 2, pg 278, 1922.
2.  Bhatnagar VS, *Life and times of Sawai Jaisingh,* pg 224, 1974.
3.  Pagdi, Setu madhav rao, *Annals of Bhandarkar Oriental Research Institute,* Vol. 51, pg 121, 1970.
4.  Irwine W., *Later Mughals,* Vol. 2, pg 279, 1922.
5.  Ghulam Husain Khan, trans. Nota Manus, *Siyar-ul-mutaqherin,* Vol. 1, Ch 3, pg 267, 1922.
6.  Sardesai GS, *Marathi Riyasat* Vol. 3, pg 464, 2012.
7.  Bhatnagar VS, *Life and times of Sawai Jaisingh,* pg 226, 1974.
8.  Sardesai GS, *Selections Peshwa daftar,* Vol. 14.23, 1933.

9.　Sardesai GS, *Marathi Riyasat* Vol. 3, pg 462, 2012.
10.　Sardesai GS, *Selections Peshwa daftar,* Vol. 14.24, 1933.
11.　Ibid, Vol. 17.46.
12.　Ibid, Vol. 14.21.
13.　Ibid, Vol. 9.12.
14.　Ibid, Vol. 14.47.
15.　Ibid, Vol. 30.131, Bhatnagar VS, *Life and times of Sawai Jaisingh,* pg 231-2, 1974.
16.　Ibid, Vol. 30.134.
17.　Ibid, Vol. 14.39.
18.　Ibid, Vol. 30.142.

## Book Four - High Noon
### Rewa Uvach

1.　Debroy Bibek, Mahabharat, Vol. 4, pg 162, 2011.
2.　Sardesai GS, *Marathi Riyasat* Vol. 3, pg 215, 2012.

## 24. Baji rao Visits Udaipur and Jaipur

1.　*Vansh Bhaskar, Budh Singh Charitra*, Vol. 6, pg 3235-38.
2.　Ghulam Husain Khan, trans. Nota Manus, *Siyar-ul-mutaqherin*, Vol. 1, Ch 3, pg 269, 1922.
3.　Sardesai GS, *Selections Peshwa daftar,* Vol. 22, pg 168, 1933.
4.　Ibid, Vol. 17.59.
5.　Ibid, Vol. 17.56.
6.　Ibid, Vol. 11.20 and 23.
7.　Ibid, Vol. 14.54.
8.　Ibid, Vol. 14.42.
9.　Ibid, Vol. 14.51.
10.　Ibid, Vol. 14.50.
11.　Ibid, Vol.13.49.
12.　Ibid, Vol. 14.14.
13.　Ibid, Vol. 15.86.
14.　Shyamal Das, *Vir Vinod, Maharaja Jagat Sinh* II, Vol. 2, pg1222
15.　Sardesai GS, *Selections Peshwa daftar,* Vol. 14.55, 1933.
16.　Ibid, Vol. 14.56.
17.　Bhatnagar VS, *Life and times of Sawai Jaisingh,* pg 235, 1974.
18.　Irwine W., *Later Mughals*, Vol. 2, pg 285, 1922.
19.　Raghubir Sinh, *Malwa in Transition*, pg 244, 1936.
20.　Khare GH, *Hingane daftar* Vol. 1.6, 1945.
21.　Ibid, Vol. 1.7.

## 25. The Peshwa Heads North

1. Parasnis DB, *Brahmendra swami charitra and patravyavahar,* letter 27, 1900.
2. Sen Surendranath, *The Military System of the Marathas,* pg 64, 1958.
3. Parasnis DB, *Itihas Sangraha, Aitihasik Charitra,* pg 69, 1909.
4. Parasnis DB, *Brahmendra swami charitra and patravyavahar,* letter 46, 1900.
5. Srivastava AL, *The First two nawabs of Oudh,* pg 45, 1933.
6. Ibid, pg 46.
7. Ghulam Husain Khan, trans. Nota Manus, *Siyar-ul-mutaqherin,* Vol. 1, Ch 3, pg 289, 1922.
8. Sardesai GS, *Selections Peshwa daftar,* Vol. 15.16, 1933.
9. Ibid, Vol. 15.47.
10. Khobrekar VG. *Marathyanchya swaryanche mukkam,* pg 166-169.
11. Elliot HM, Dowson J., *The History of India as told by its own historians,* Vol. 8, pg 53, 1877.
12. Ghulam Husain Khan, trans. Nota Manus, *Siyar-ul-mutaqherin,* Vol. 1, Ch 3, pg 286, 1922.
13. Ibid, pg 287.
14. Sardesai GS, *Selections Peshwa daftar,* Vol. 15.19, 1933.
15. Ibid, Vol. 15.17.
16. Elliot HM, Dowson J., *The History of India as told by its own historians,* Vol. 8, pg 55, 1877.
17. Ghulam Husain Khan, trans. Nota Manus, *Siyar-ul-mutaqherin,* Vol. 1, Ch 3, pg 290, 1922.
18. Ibid, pg 291.
19. Irwine W., *Later Mughals,* Vol. 2, pg 288, 1922.

## 26. The Dash to Delhi

1. Parasnis DB, *Brahmendra swami charitra and patravyavahar,* letter 27, 1900.
2. Sardesai GS, *Marathi Riyasat* Vol. 3, pg 497, 2012.
3. Irwine W., *Later Mughals,* Vol. 2, pg 288, 1922 (quoting Rustam Ali, pg 272).
4. Elliot HM, Dowson J., *The History of India as told by its own historians,* Vol. 8, pg 54-5, 1877.
5. Ghulam Husain Khan, trans. Nota Manus, *Siyar-ul-mutaqherin,* Vol. 1, Ch 3, pg 291, 1922.
6. Irwine W., *Later Mughals,* Vol. 2, pg 290, 1922. (quoting Ashob).
7. Ibid, pg 290-1.
8. Ibid, pg 294.
9. Ghulam Husain Khan, trans. Nota Manus, *Siyar-ul-mutaqherin,* Vol. 1, pg 317, 1922.
10. Irwine W., *Later Mughals,* Vol. 2, pg 296-7, 1922.

11. Dighe VG, *Peshwa Baji rao I and Maratha Expansion*, pg 136, 1944.
12. Ghulam Husain Khan, trans. Nota Manus, *Siyar-ul-mutaqherin*, Vol. 1, pg 318-9, 1922.
13. Sardesai GS, *Selections Peshwa daftar*, Vol. 15.42, 1933.
14. Ibid, Vol. 15.29.

## 27. Sashti: War with the Firangi

1. Naik GG, *Sashti bakhar*, pg 1- 4, 1935.
2. Grose, *A Voyage to the East Indies*, Vol. 1, pg 64-5, 1772.
3. Pissurlekar Pandurang, *Portuguese Marathe Sambandh*, pg 153, 1963.
4. Kakodkar PR trans. Pissurlekar Pandurang, *The Portuguese and the Marathas*, pg 184, 1975.
5. Grose, *A Voyage to the East Indies*, Vol. 1, pg 68, 1772.
6. Naik GG, *Sashti bakhar*, pg 39, 1935.
7. Forrest GW, *Selections Bombay Sceretariat (Home Series)*, Vol. 2, pg 68, 1887.
8. Kelkar YN, *Vasai cha mahasangram*, pg 104, 2008.
9. Sardesai GS, *Selections Peshwa daftar*, Vol. 16.50, 1933.
10. Ibid, Vol. 16.42.
11. Braganza Pereira AB, Desai SS trans. *Marathyanchya Itihasachi sadhane, Portuguese khand 3,* pg 404-5, 1968.
12. Kelkar YN, *Vasai cha mahasangram*, pg 136,
13. *India Office Records*, IOR/H/332, pg 509.
14. *Daily Gazetteer, London*, 13 January 1738.

## 28. Nizam-ul-Mulk: The Emperor's Last Gambit

1. Parasnis DB, *Brahmendra swami charitra and patravyavahar*, letter 33, 1900.
2. Ibid, letter 35.
3. Irwine W., *Later Mughals*, Vol. 2, pg 301, 1922.
4. Sardesai GS, *Selections Peshwa daftar*, Vol. 15.56, 1933.
5. Ibid, Vol. 15.57.
6. Parasnis DB, *Brahmendra swami charitra and patravyavahar, Appendix,* letter 134, 1900.
7. Sardesai GS, *Selections Peshwa daftar*, Vol. 15.58, 1933.
8. Sen Surendranath, *The Military System of the Marathas,* pg 71, 1958.
9. Sardesai GS, *Selections Peshwa daftar*, Vol. 15.59, 1933.
10. Parasnis DB, *Brahmendra swami charitra and patravyavahar*, letter 34, 1900.
11. Sardesai GS, *Selections Peshwa daftar*, Vol. 15.67, 1933.
12. Mortimer Wheeler, *Cambridge History of India: The Indus civilization*, Vol. 4, pg 357, 1937.

13. Sardesai GS, *Selections Peshwa daftar,* Vol. 9.22.
14. Sardesai GS, *Selections Peshwa daftar,* Vol. 15.68, 1933.
15. Hanway Jonas, *The Revolutions of Persia,* Vol. 2, pg 350, 1762.
16. Ibid, pg 352.

## 29. The Nadir Of Muhammad Shah

1. Sane KN, *Chitnis Malhar Ramrao's Thorale Shahu maharaj yanche charitra,,* pg 74, 1893.
2. Rajwade VK, *Marathyanchya itihasachi sadhane,* Vol. 6.131.
3. *London Evening Post,* dated 07 January 1738.
4. Fraser James, *History of Nadir Shah,* pg 129, 1742.
5. Hanway Jonas, *The Revolutions of Persia,* Vol. 2, pg 357, 1762.
6. Irwine W., '*Nadir Shah and Muhammad Shah*' a poem by Tilak Das, pg 49, 1897.
7. Ibid, pg 26.
8. *Asiatic Researches,* Vol. 10, pg 539-47, 1811.
9. Rajwade VK, *Marathyanchya itihasachi sadhane,* Vol. 6.130.
10. Ghulam Husain Khan, trans. Nota Manus, *Siyar-ul-mutaqherin,* Vol. 1, Ch. 4, pg 309-11, 1922.
11. Irwine W., *Later Mughals,* Vol. 2, pg 353, 1922.
12. Fraser James, *History of Nadir Shah,* pg 166, 1742.
13. Irwine W., *Later Mughals,* Vol. 2, pg 356, 1922.
14. Ibid, pg 357.
15. Parasnis DB, *Brahmendra swami charitra and patravyavahar,* letter 41, 1900.
16. Rajwade VK, *Marathyanchya itihasachi sadhane,* Vol. 6.131.

## 30. A Desperate Struggle in the Firangan

1. Sardesai GS, *Selections Peshwa daftar,* Vol. 34.92, 1933.
2. Pissurlekar Pandurang, *Portuguese Marathe Sambandh,* pg 158, 1963.
3. Sardesai GS, *Selections Peshwa daftar,* Vol. 16.106, 1933.
4. Braganza Pereira AB, Desai SS trans. *Marathyanchya Itihasachi sadhane, Portuguese khand 3,* pg 479, 1968.
5. Sardesai GS, *Selections Peshwa daftar,* Vol. 34.9, 1933.
6. Ibid, Vol. 34.82.
7. Ibid, Vol. 34.106
8. Ibid, Vol. 16.75.
9. Ibid, Vol. 22.121, Dighe VG, *Peshwa Baji rao I and Maratha Expansion,* pg 185, 1944.
10. Pissurlenkar PS, trans. By Kakodkar PR, *The Portuguese and Marathas,* pg 261, 1975.

11. Kelkar YN, *Vasai cha mahasangram,* pg 231, 2008.
12. Pissurlekar Pandurang, *Portuguese Marathe Sambandh,* pg 188, 1963.
13. Sardesai GS, *Selections Peshwa daftar,* Vol. 16.147, 1933.
14. Forrest GW, *Selections Bombay Sceretariat (Maratha Series),* Vol. I, part 1, pg 27, 1885.
15. Parasnis DB, *Brahmendra swami charitra and patravyavahar,* letter 49, 1900.
16. Rajwade VK, *Marathyanchya itihasachi sadhane,* Vol. 3.167.
17. Ibid, Vol. 3.168.
18. Pissurlekar Pandurang, *Portuguese Marathe Sambandh,* pg 161, 1963.
19. Kelkar YN, *Vasai cha mahasangram,* pg 203, 2008.
20. Purandare BM, *Aitihasik Sankeerna Sahitya,* Vol. 7, letter 4.

## 31. Vasai!

1. Parasnis DB, *Brahmendra swami charitra and patravyavahar,* letter 52, 1900.
2. Sardesai GS, *Selections Peshwa daftar,* Vol. 16.156, 1933.
3. Forrest GW, *Selections Bombay Sceretariat (Home Series),* Vol. 2, pg 74, 1887.
4. Forrest GW, *Selections Bombay Sceretariat (Maratha Series),* Vol. I, part 1, pg iv, 1885.
5. Pissurlenkar PS, trans. By Kakodkar PR, *The Portuguese and Marathas,* pg 318, 1975.
6. Pissurlekar Pandurang, *Portuguese Marathe Sambandh,* pg 162, 1963.
7. Kincaid and Parasnis, *A History of the Maratha People,* Vol. 2, pg 269, 1922.
8. Sardesai GS, *Selections Peshwa daftar,* Vol. 16.152, 1933.
9. Forrest GW, *Selections Bombay Sceretariat (Maratha Series),* Vol. I, part 1, pg 30, 1885.
10. Sardesai GS, *Selections Peshwa daftar,* Vol. 22.121, 1933.
11. Dighe VG, *Peshwa Baji rao I and Maratha Expansion,* pg 189, 1944.
12. Forrest GW, *Selections Bombay Sceretariat (Maratha Series),* Vol. I, part 1, pg 39-40, 1885.
13. Sardesai GS, *Selections Peshwa daftar,* Vol. 16.162, 1933.
14. Ibid, Vol. 34.193.
15. Ibid, Vol. 22, pg 72.
16. Ibid, Vol. 16.165.
17. Kelkar YN, *Vasai cha mahasangram,* pg 258, 2008.
18. Forrest GW, *Selections Bombay Sceretariat (Maratha Series),* Vol. I, part 1, pg 40-41, 1885.
19. Pissurlekar Pandurang, *Portuguese Marathe Sambandh,* pg 164, 1963.
20. Forrest GW, *Selections Bombay Sceretariat (Maratha Series),* Vol. I, part 1, pg v-vi, 1885.

## 32. Nadir Shah Mauls Delhi

1. Hanway Jonas, *The Revolutions of Persia,* Vol. 2, pg 382, 1762.
2. Sardesai GS, *Selections Peshwa daftar,* Vol. 30.222, 1933.
3. Rajwade VK, *Marathyanchya itihasachi sadhane,* Vol. 6.130
4. Sardesai GS, *Marathi Riyasat* Vol. 3, pg 521, 2012.
5. Ibid, Vol. 30.227.
6. Parasnis DB, *Brahmendra swami charitra and patravyavahar,* letter 41, 1900.
7. Ibid, letter 42.
8. Ibid, pg 117-8.
9. *Daily Post London,* dated 23 November 1739.
10. Rajwade VK, *Marathyanchya itihasachi sadhane,* Vol. 6.134.
11. Mortimer Wheeler, *Cambridge History of India: The Indus civilization,* Vol. 4, pg 361, 1937.
12. Rajwade VK, *Marathyanchya itihasachi sadhane,* Vol. 6.133.
13. Parasnis DB, *Itihas Sangraha, Aitihasik Charcha, 4,* pg 13, 1909.
14. Parasnis DB, *Itihas Sangraha, Aitihasik Tipane, 2.6.*
15. Sardesai GS, *Selections Peshwa daftar,* Vol. 30.229, 1933.
16. Forrest GW, *Selections Bombay Sceretariat (Maratha Series),* Vol. I, part 1, pg 36, 1885.
17. Irwine W., *Later Mughals,* Vol. 2, pg 371, 1922.
18. Ghulam Husain Khan, trans. Nota Manus, *Siyar-ul-mutaqherin,* Vol. 1, pg 316, 1922.
19. Fraser James, *History of Nadir Shah,* pg 220-1, 1742.
20. The true history of the Kohinoor, *The London Illustrated Magazine,* pg 91, Apr 1891.
21. Irwine W., *'Nadir Shah and Muhammad Shah' a poem by Tilak Das,* pg 56, 1897.
22. Gladwin Francis trans. *'Memoirs of Khojeh Abdul Kareem',* pg 1-9, 1743.
23. *London and County Journal,* dated 12 June 1740.
24. Satara Historical Society *Aitihask Lekhmala,* Vol. 2, letter 268, 1940.

## 33. An Olive Branch from Bombay

1. Forrest GW, *Selections Bombay Sceretariat (Maratha Series),* Vol. I, part 1, pg ii, 1885.
2. Forrest GW, *Selections Bombay Sceretariat (Maratha Series),* Vol. I, part 1, pg 34, 1885.
3. Sardesai GS, *Selections Peshwa daftar,* Vol. 17.98, 1933.
4. Forrest GW, *Selections Bombay Sceretariat (Maratha Series),* Vol. I, part 1, pg 72, 1885.

5.    Ibid, pg 77-80.

6.    Purandare BM, *Aitihasik Sankeerna Sahitya*, Vol. 7, letter 5.

7.    *India Office Records*, MSS.Mar.G40

8.    Forrest GW, *Selections Bombay Sceretariat (Maratha Series)*, Vol. I, part 1, pg 84, 1885.

# Book Five - The Eclipse

## 34. Family Affairs: Mastani

1.    Parasnis DB, *Bundelkhand – Marathyanche Parakram*, pg 85-6, 1895.

2.    *Peshwa bakhar*, pg 23, 1878.

3.    Bhide Sadashiv Moreshwar, *Sahyadri*, Vol. 11, issue 5, pg 434, May 1940.

3.    *Peshwa bakhar*, pg 26, 1878.

4.    Sardesai GS, *Selections Peshwa daftar*, Vol. 30.363, 1933.

5.    Ibid, Vol.9.36.

6.    Sardesai GS, *Marathi Riyasat* Vol. 3, pg 589, 2012.

7.    *Peshwa bakhar*, pg 29-30, 1878.

8.    Ganpat rao Harihar Patwardhan Kurundwad, *Bhatt-Vansha-Kavya*, pg 31, 1893.

9.    Parasnis DB, *Bundelkhand – Marathyanche Parakram*, pg 84, 1895.

10.   *Peshwa bakhar*, pg 39, 1878.

11.   Parasnis DB, *Itihas Sangraha, Aitihasik Charcha, 3*, 1909.

12.   Sardesai GS, *Selections Peshwa daftar*, Vol. 9.19, 1933.

13.   Ibid, Vol. 9.77.

14.   Ibid, Vol. 9.34.

15.   Satara Historical Society *Aitihask Lekhmala*, Vol. 2, letter 275, 1940.

16.   Parasnis DB, *Itihas Sangraha, Aitihasik Charcha, 3*, letter 3, 1909.

17.   Purandare KV, *Purandare daftar*, Vol. 1.132, 1929.

18.   Sardesai GS, *Selections Peshwa daftar*, Vol. 30.250, 1933.

19.   Parasnis DB, *Itihas Sangraha, Aitihasik Charcha 3, footnote*, 1909.

20.   Purandare KV, *Purandare daftar*, Vol. 1.133, 1929.

21.   Sardesai GS, *Selections Peshwa daftar*, Vol. 9.35, 1933.

22.   Ibid, Vol. 9.30.

23.   Ibid, Vol. 9.31.

24.   Ibid, Vol. 30.334.

25.   Ibid, Vol. 9.32.

26.   Parasnis DB, *Itihas Sangraha, Aitihasik Charcha 3*, letter 4, 1909.

27.   Parasnis DB, *Itihas Sangraha, Aitihasik Tipane*, 2.7.

## 35. A Whirlwind Campaign

1. Purandare KV, *Purandare daftar,* Vol. 1.139, 1929.
2. Sardesai GS, *Selections Peshwa daftar,* Vol. 16.172, 1933.
3. Ibid, Vol. 15.74.
4. Ibid, Vol. 15.79.
5. Sen Surendranath, *The Military System of the Marathas,* pg 73-4, 1958.
6. Khobrekar VG. *Marathyanchya swaryanche mukkam,* pg 181.
7. Pissurlekar Pandurang, *Portuguese Marathe Sambandh,* pg 201, 1963. Sardesai GS, *Marathi Riyasat* Vol. 3, pg 553, 2012.
8. *India Office Records, IOR/H/332,* pg 509.
9. Purandare KV, *Purandare daftar,* Vol. 1.138, 1929.
10. Purandare BM, *Aitihasik Sankeerna Sahitya,* Vol. 7, letter 6.
11. Mir Golam Ali E Azad, *Khazanah e Aamerah, Asiatick Miscellany, A Short Account of Naser Jung,* Vol. 1, pg 499.
12. Malcolm John, *A Memoir of Central India,* Vol. 1, pg 86, 1824.
13. Sardesai GS, *Selections Peshwa daftar,* Vol. 15.84, 1933.
14. Parasnis DB, *Brahmendra swami charitra and patravyavahar,* letter 55, 1900.
15. Sardesai GS, *Selections Peshwa daftar,* Vol. 15.85, 1933.
16. Ibid, Vol. 9.33.
17. Ibid, Vol. 9.37.
18. Khobrekar VG. *Marathyanchya swaryanche mukkam,* pg 184.

## Rewa Uvach

1. Bedekar Ninad, *Shiva Bhushan, 530-1,* pg 168, 2011.

## 36. Eclipse on the Narmada

1. Purandare KV, *Purandare daftar,* Vol. 1.426, 1929.
2. Parasnis DB, *Brahmendra swami charitra and patravyavahar,* letter 56, 1900.
3. Khare GH, *Hingane daftar,* 1.13 and 1.15.
4. Sardesai GS, *Selections Peshwa daftar,* Vol. 22, pg 88-89, 1933.
5. Sardesai GS, *Marathi Riyasat* Vol. 3, pg 215, 2012.
6. Kincaid and Parasnis, *A History of the Maratha People,* Vol. 2, pg 273, 1922.
7. Grant Duff, *History of the Marathas,* Vol. 1, pg 347, 1826.
8. Khare GH, *Hingane daftar,* 1.18.

# Bibliography
## Primary Sources

1. *Aiti Sankeern Sahitya*, 1946.
2. Bendre VS Ed., *Keshav Pandit's Rajaram Charitam*, 1931.
3. Braganza Pereira AB, Desai SS trans. *Marathyanchya Itihasachi sadhane, Portuguese khand 3,* 1968.
4. Chandra Satish, *Indian History Congress*, 1948.
5. Dalvi Gopal Dajiba, *Jadhav Kaifiyat,* Vol. 1, 1912.
6. Danvers Frederick Charles, *Portuguese in India,* Vol. 2, 1894.
7. Earles Joseph, *Letters of the Emperor Aurangzebe,* 1788.
8. Elliot HM, Dowson J., *The History of India as told by its own historians,* Vol. 8, 1877.
9. Forrest GW, *Selections Bombay Sceretariat (Home Series),* 1887.
10. Fraser James, *History of Nadir Shah,* 1742.
11. Fryer John, *A New Account of East-India and Persia,* 1681
12. Ghulam Husain Khan, trans Nota Manus, *Siyar-ul-mutaqherin,* 1901.
13. Hanway Jonas, *The Revolutions of Persia,* Vol. 2, 1762.
14. Hatalkar VG, *Relations between the French and the Marathas,* 1958.
15. *India Office Records,* IOR/H/332,
16. *India Office Records,* MSS.Mar.G40
17. Irwine W., '*Nadir Shah and Muhammad Shah*' a poem by Tilak Das, 1897.
18. Irwine W., *Asiatic Society of Bengal,* No. 1, part 1, 1900.
19. Irwine W., *Bangash Nawabs, Asiatic Society of Bengal,* No. 4, 1878.
20. Irwine W., *Indian Antiquary,* Vol. 33, 1904.
21. Joshi PM, *Selections Peshwa daftar, (New Series),* Vol. 1, 1957.
22. Khare GH, *Hingane daftar* Vol. 1, 1945.
23. Khare GH, *Hingane daftar.*
24. Khobrekar VG. *Marathyanchya swaryanche mukkam.*
25. Kirkpatrick William, *Nizam's letter, Asiatick Miscellany,* Vol. 1, 1785.
26. Kunte BG, *Modi Illustrative documents,* 1978.
27. Mackenzie Colin, *Mackenzie collection,* Vol. 13, 27, 28, India Office records, London.
28. Mir Golam Ali E Azad, *Khazanah e Aamerah, Asiatick Miscellany, A Short Account of Naser Jung,* Vol. 1.
29. Naik GG, *Sashti bakhar,* 1935.
30. Niccolao Manucci, *Storia do Mogor, or Mogul India,* I 653-I 708, translated by W. Irvine, Indian Text Series (London, 4 vols, I907-08).
31. Pagdi, Setu madhav rao, *Annals of Bhandarkar Oriental Research Institute,* Vol. 51, 1970.
32. Parasnis DB, *Bharat varsha, Vol. 1, Holkar kaifiyat,* 1898.
33. Parasnis DB, *Brahmendra swami charitra and patravyavahar,* 1900.
34. Parasnis DB, *Bundele yanchi kaifiyat,* 1897.

35. Parasnis DB, *Itihas Sangraha, Aitihasik Charitra,* 1909.

36. Parasnis DB, *Itihas Sangraha, Aitihasik Tipane,* 1916.

37. Parasnis DB, *Itihas Sangraha, Sanads,* 1917.

38. *Peshwa bakhar,* 1878.

39. Pissurlekar Pandurang, *Portuguese Marathe Sambandh,* 1963.

40. Pissurlenkar Pandurang, *Indian Historical Reaserch Commission,* Vol. 19, 1942.

41. Purandare KV, *Purandare daftar,* Vol. 1, 1929.

42. Rajwade VK, Ed., *Radha Madhav Vilas Champu, Jairam Pindye,* 1922.

43. Rajwade VK, *Marathyanchya itihasachi sadhane,* 1912.

44. Rajwade VK, *Marathyanchya itihasachi sadhane,* Vol. 2, *Peshwe Shakavali.*

45. Reu Pt. Bishweshwar Nath, *Indian History Congress,* Calcutta, 1939.

46. Sane KN, *Chitnis Malhar Ramrao's Shrimant Chhatrapati Sambhaji maharaj charitra,*1882.

47. Sane KN, *Chitnis Malhar Ramrao's Thorale Shahu maharaj yanche charitra,* 1893.

48. *Sanpuri bakhar,* 1950.

49. Sardesai GS et al, *Sane KN - Kavyetihas sangraha Aitihasik Patre Yadi,* 1930.

50. Sardesai GS, *Selections Peshwa daftar,* Vol. 1 to 45, 1933.

51. Sarkar J, *Anecdotes of Aurangzeb,* 1988.

52. Sarkar Jadunath, *Islamic Culture,* Vol. 15, no. 3, July 1941.

53. Satish Chandra, Ed., *Mehta Balmukund, Balmukundnama,* 1972.

54. Shyamal Das, *Vir Vinod, Maharaja Jagat Sinh* II, Vol. 2.

55. Smith VA, Ed,. *The History of the Late Revolution of the Great Mogul,* Bernier F., 1914.

56. Thakur VV, *Holkarshahi cha itihas,,* 1944.

57. Vad GC, *Balaji Bajirao rojnishi,* Vol. 2, 1906.

58. Vad GC, *Chhatrapati Shahu Rojnishi,* 1908.

59. *Vansh Bhaskar, Budh Singh Charitra,* Vol. 6.

## Secondary Sources

1. Banaji DR, *Bombay and the Sidis,* 1952.

2. Behere, NK, *Bajirao Peshwe,* 1929.

3. Bhatnagar VS, *Life and Times of Sawai Jaisingh,* 1974.

4. Bombay Quarterly Review, Vol. 4, 1856.

5. Brij Kishore, *Tarabai and her times,*1963.

6. Debroy Bibek, Mahabharat, Vol. 4, 2011.

7. Desai WS, *Bombay and the Marathas,* 1970.

8. Dhabbu DG, *Sarkhel Kulabkar Angre,* 1939.

9. Dighe VG, *Peshwa Baji rao I and Maratha Expansion,* 1944.

10. Ganpat rao Harihar Patwardhan Kurundwad, *Bhatt-Vansha-Kavya,* 1893.

11. Gense JH & Banaji DR, *The Gaekwads of Baroda,* Vol. 1, 1936.

12. Gladwin Francis trans. *'Memoirs of Khojeh Abdul Kareem',* 1743.

13. Grant Duff, *History of the Marathas,* Vol. 1, 2,3, 1826.

14.   Grose, *A Voyage to the East Indies,* Vol. 1, 1772.

15.   Irwine W., *Later Mughals*, Vol. 1, 1922.

16.   Kakodkar PR trans. Pissurlekar Pandurang, *The Portuguese and the Marathas*, 1975.

17.   Kelkar YN, *Vasai cha mahasangram,* 2008.

18.   Khare GH, *Sanivara wada.*

19.   Khare Vasudeo Vaman, *Ichalkaranji cha itihas,*, 1913.

20.   Kincaid CA, Tale of the Tulse Plant.

21.   Kulkarni AR, *Maharashtra in the age of Shivaji*, 1969.

22.   Malcolm John, *A Memoir of Central India,* Vol. 1, 1824.

23.   Malik Zahiruddin, *The Reign of Muhammad Shah,* 1977.

24.   Michael Kennedy, *The Criminal Classes Of India*, 1985.

25.   Montgomery of Alamein, *A Concise History of Warfare*, 1972.

26.   Mortimer Wheeler, *Cambridge History of India: The Indus civilization*, Vol. 4,  1937.

27.   Ninad Bedekar, *Shiva Bhushan, 530-1,* 2011.

28.   Pagdi Setu madhav rao, *Eighteenth century Deccan*, 1963.

29.   Pagdi Setu madhav rao, *Maharashtra ani Marathe,* 1963.

30.   Palsokar, Col. RD, *Bajirao I - An Outstanding Cavalry General, 1995.*

31.   Parasnis DB, *Aitihasik goshti, Itihas Sangraha,* 2-17.

32.   Raghubir Singh, *Studies on Maratha and Rajput History,* 1989.

33.   Raghubir Sinh, *Malwa in Transition,* 1936.

34.   Ranade MG, *Rise of the Maratha Power,* 1900.

35.   Sahyadri, Baji rao special issue, May 1940.

36.   Sardesai GS *Marathi Riyasat* Vol. 2, 2012.

37.   Sardesai GS, *Vividh Dnyan Vistar,* Feb 1924.

38.   Sarkar J, *History of Aurangzeb, Vol. 1 to 5,* 1924.

39.   Sarkar Jadunath, *History of Jaipur ,*1984.

40.   Satara Historical Society *Aitihask Lekhmala*, Vol. 2, 1940.

41.   Sen Surendranath, *Early career of Kanhoji Angre,* 1941.

42.   Sen Surendranath, *The Military System of the Marathas, 1958.*

43.   Shejwalkar TS, *Nizam Peshwe sambandh, Lecture 1,* 1963.

44.   Slight John Paul, *Brit Empire and the Hajj*, 1865-1956, 2015.

45.   Srivastava AL, *The First two nawabs of Oudh,* 1933.

46.   Stewart Gordon, *Modern Asian Studies ii, I* 1977.

47.   Yusuf Husain, *The First Nizam,* 1963.

৯৩৯৩

# Glossary

- Amatya – Finance Minister
- Amir-Ul-Umara – minister
- Antarvedi – doab of Ganga and Yamuna
- Bagh – Garden
- Bakhar – A narrative
- Bakshi – Head of Administration
- Banjaras – Gypsies who sold goods to armies
- Bekhabar – who does not know
- Bel-Bhandar – an oath
- Bhadrapad – Month in the Hindu calender
- Bhagavata – pertaining to Lord Vishnu
- Bhakar – baked bread.
- Bhang – Cannabis
- Bhat – Can mean a warrior
- Bhatt – A Brahmin surname
- Bhils – A tribe
- Bunaga – support services to an army
- Cartez – Passport
- Chaturmas – four monsoon months
- Chaudhary – Village head
- Chauth – One-fourth revenue to a province
- Chhatrapati – Maratha king
- Chiranjeev – One with a long life
- Chitnis – A writer or secretary
- Chowk – a crossing
- Daftar – Office
- Dakshina – gifts to the learned.
- Daroga – Police officer
- Dassera – The festival celebrates the victory of Ram over Ravana.
- Dastak – Passport
- Deshashtha – Brahmins from the Deccan plateau.
- Dharma – Principles of moral behaviour.
- Dhol – Musical drum
- Dhu al qida – Hijri month
- Diwan – Chief of the administration
- Diwankhana – drawing room
- Doodh-Bhaat – Milk-rice
- Durbar – Count of thinking
- Fateh – Victory
- Faujdar – Head of the police
- Firman – Order
- Gad/Garh – Fort
- Gallivants – Type of warships
- Gamin – Enemy
- Gharis – A measure of time
- Ghat – Path through a hill range
- Ghatika – Twenty four minutes
- Ghats – path through the hills
- Gosavi – wandering Hindu fakir
- Grabb – Type of warships
- Gully – Type of warships
- Habshi – Abyssinian
- Holi – A festival of colours observed by Hindus
- Hon – About two and a half to three and three quarters of a rupee
- Hookah – Smoking pot
- Howdeh – Place to sit on an elephant
- Hukumatpanah – A kind of supreme commander
- Huzurat – The King's army
- Jagir / Vatan – Fief

- Jagirdar – Landlord
- Jama – upper garment
- Jazira – island
- Jethi – wrestler
- Jheel – lake
- Jhigga – a turban ornament
- Jiziya – Tax on infidels
- Jubba – a long sleeved shirt
- Kaaba – the place of worship for Muslims in Mecca.
- Kaifiyat – a narrative or ann apologia
- Karbhari – administrator
- Karkuns – Clerks
- Khand – A piece of land
- Khandani – Indemnity or tribute
- Khanzada – son of the Khan
- Kharif – The summer crop
- Khasa – The chief or the king
- Khaskhel – A rank in the army
- Khijmatdar – Servant
- Killedar – Chief of a fort
- Kinnar khand –Celestial regions, populated by celestial beings.
- Kokanashtha / Chitpawan – Brahmins from Konkan
- Kos – a distance of about three kilometres
- Kowrie – farthing
- Kunwar – Prince
- Mansab – mansab is 'rank', from Arabic.
- Masnad – the throne cushion
- Mokasa – The balance of chauth after the deduction of the king's share
- Moksha – Salvation or death
- Morattoes – Marathas
- Mujumdar – In charge of revenue
- Mukadam – a foreman
- Mulukh-Giri – a campaign
- Mutalik – A deputy minister
- Mutsaddi – A strategist
- Nazar – Gift
- Paatshah – Mughal Emperor
- Paga –Stable
- Pakwan – Delicacy
- Pandit – A learned man
- Pant – A Brahmin of some distinction.
- Pathan – Resident of Afghanistan
- Patil – Village chief
- Patti – Tax.
- Peshkash – A gift
- Peshwa – Prime Minister
- Phadnis – In charge of Administration
- Prabhus – A caste
- Pradhan – Prime Minister
- Prahar – A measure of time
- Pratinidhi – Representative' who stood in for the Maratha king
- Purana – Epic
- Purohit – priest
- Rabi – the winter crop
- Rajadhiraj – king of kings
- Rajashri – The king or an honorific prefix before the name
- Raya – an affectionate name for Baji rao
- Rewa – Narmada
- Rishi – Sage
- Rozmura – daily allowance to troops
- Rudra, ati rudra – Shiva
- Sachiv – Secretary, member of the Maratha Cabinet
- Sanad – Grants of land for revenue
- Sar-Subedar – Head of the region
- Sardeshmukhi – Head revenue collector

- Sarkhel – Admiral
- Sarlashkar – A commander of the army
- Sarpech – ornament for the turban. An honour.
- Sashti – sixty six villages of the island of Sashti north of Mumbai
- Sayyid – Religious teacher
- Senakarte – Collector of armies
- Senapati – Head of the army
- Shaban – Hijri month
- Shahzada – Mughal prince
- Shamal – Signifies a dark complexion. Here it refers to the Siddi
- Shaniwar  – Saturday
- Shaniwar  – Saturday
- Shastrees  – Learned in the scriptures
- Shenvi – a caste from north coastal Karnataka
- Shia – Sect of Islam
- Shravan – Month in the Hindu calender
- Shri – The Lord
- Shrimant – title for the Peshwa
- Siddi – from Abyssinia.
- Silahdars – Cavalry soldiers
- Sovkar, Sawkar – Money lender
- Subah – Province
- Subedar – Head of a province
- Sunni – Sect of Islam
- Swar – one who commands a number of riders
- Swarajya – Swa'=Own; 'Rajya'=Rule
- Taka – Cash
- Tambra / Tamra – Above
- Tamra – Mughal.
- Tawarikh – A Persian narrative
- Tawarikhs – Persian narratives
- Teerthrup – father/elder
- Turani – The Turkish party
- Umrao – A nobleman
- Uvach – Said (in Sanskrit)
- Vakil – Enemy
- Wada – A mansion or palace
- Wadi – A village
- Wazir – Mughal Prime Minister
- Yatra – A pilgrimmage
- Zat – A rank in the mansabdari system
- Zil Hijj/Zul Hijja – Hijri month

ॐॐॐॐ

# Index

# About the Author

Uday S Kulkarni is trained as a Surgeon and an alumni of the Armed Forces Medical College, Pune. After serving in the Armed Forces, he retired in the rank of Surgeon Commander and began practice as a surgeon in Pune. He then obtained a post graduate Bachelors in Communication and Journalism from Pune University with Distinction. He returned to his love for History in 2010 when he wrote a full length non-fiction account of the third battle of Panipat titled 'Solstice at Panipat- 14 January 1761'. In 2013, he discovered long lost documents taken to England by Charles W. Malet and John Briggs in the eighteenth or nineteenth centuries. These documents yielded a complete *bakhar* of Panipat amongst other papers. It was published along with a translation in 2014 with the help of the late Ninad Bedekar. His first book on 'Panipat' was also translated into Marathi in 2015 by Vijay Bapaye. He began working on the book on Baji rao Peshwa in June 2015 and was able to put out the print edition by the end of 2016. Further books are planned and promise several interesting years of research.

Dr Kulkarni stays in Pune with his family and continues the practice of surgery while sparing his free time to the study of History. He lectures about various aspects of Indian history to interested audiences. He is involved in the conservation of hills and open spaces in the city of Pune.

# Mula Mutha Publishers
## Other Publications


## Solstice at Panipat - 14 January 1761 :
An Authentic Account of the Panipat Campaign.
Author - Uday S. Kulkarni.
First Edition : 2011.
Second Edition : 2012.
Reprint : 2015.


## Solstice at Panipat - 14 January 1761 : (Marathi)
An Authentic Account of the Panipat Campaign.
Author - Uday S. Kulkarni, Translation - Vijay Bapaye
First Edition : 2015.


## बखर पानियतची/Bakhar of Panipat
Original Marathi version with English Translation
An eye-witness account of the Panipat Campaign by Raghunath Yadav
Edited & Translated by Uday S. Kulkarni
Transliteration by Ninad Bedekar
First Edition : 2014.
Reprint : 2015.


## अनंताकडून अनंताकडे : (Anantakadun Anantakade)
23 Essays on Philosophy (in Marathi)
Dr. Snehalata S. Kulkarni
First Edition : 2003.
Second Edition : 2010.